Hindiyya al-ʿUjaimi

Embracing

Gender, Culture, and Politics in the Middle East

miriam cooke, Suad Joseph, and Simona Sharoni, *Series Editors*

Embracing the
DIVINE

PASSION AND POLITICS IN THE
CHRISTIAN MIDDLE EAST

AKRAM FOUAD KHATER

SYRACUSE UNIVERSITY PRESS

Copyright © 2011 by Syracuse University Press
Syracuse, New York 13244-5290

All Rights Reserved

First Edition 2011

11 12 13 14 15 16   6 5 4 3 2 1

For a listing of books published and distributed by Syracuse University Press, visit our Web site at SyracuseUniversityPress.syr.edu.

ISBN: 978-0-8156-3261-0

Library of Congress Cataloging-in-Publication Data
Khater, Akram Fouad, 1960–
    Embracing the divine : passion and politics in the Christian Middle East / Akram Fouad Khater. — 1st ed.
        p. cm. — (Gender, culture, and politics in the Middle East)
    Includes bibliographical references and index.
    ISBN 978-0-8156-3261-0 (cloth : alk. paper) 1. al-Ujaimi, Hindiyya, 1720–1798.
I. Title.
    BX4713.595.A48K53 2011
    271'.9302—dc23   2011032377

Manufactured in the United States of America

To my brother Emile,
A purer heart I have not known

(21 November 1954–17 June 2010)

DR. AKRAM KHATER is professor of history at North Carolina State University and director of the Middle East Studies Program and the Khayrallah Program for Lebanese American Studies. A native of Lebanon, he earned a BS degree in electrical engineering from California Polytechnic State University and holds MA and PhD degrees in history from the University of California, Santa Cruz, and the University of California, Berkeley, respectively. Before coming to Raleigh, he taught at Ball State University in Indiana. His books include *Inventing Home: Emigration, Gender and the Making of a Lebanese Middle Class, 1861–1921* and *A History of the Middle East: A Sourcebook for the History of the Middle East and North Africa*. He has published a substantial number of articles and reviews and has made conference presentations throughout the United States and overseas. He has been particularly active in bringing his expertise to audiences at North Carolina colleges, high schools, and churches. Professor Khater has been awarded a number of teaching accolades (Outstanding Teacher and Outstanding Junior Faculty) and grants during his tenure at North Carolina State and has also obtained fellowships from the National Humanities Center, American Philosophical Society, National Endowment for the Humanities, Fulbright Foundation, and Council of American Overseas Research Centers. His professional affiliations include the Middle East Studies Association, American Academy of Religion, American Historical Association, and the chair of the Committee on Middle East Studies at North Carolina State. He also sits on the editorial boards of several journals, including the *International Journal of Middle East Studies,* and book series.

CONTENTS

ILLUSTRATIONS

ACKNOWLEDGMENTS

This book began with a felicitous happenstance. On a late spring afternoon in 1990, I was sitting in the Bibliothèque Nationale in Paris reading manuscripts for my doctoral dissertation. Restless from the tedium of my current reading, I went to flip through the Arabic manuscript card catalogue and came across a book titled *The Strangest Woman in the World*. With such an unabashedly over-the-top title I could not but request the book. This was the beginning of my acquaintance with Hindiyya al-'Ujaimi and her life story, which has always elicited similarly unrestrained superlatives and opprobriums. I knew then that I had to write a book about her.

To do so took a long while, and along the way I incurred a great deal of debt to institutions and colleagues. It was not until the summer of 1995 that I finally made my first sustained effort to research her life and story. Thanks to a Faculty Research and Professional Development grant from North Carolina State University (NCSU), I was able to visit the archives of the Propaganda Fide (the old ones near the Spanish Steps) and spend five blissful weeks going through the multiple volumes and folios dedicated to the Hindiyya affair. The archivists there were most kind in helping me to navigate the archive as well as obtaining all the volumes I needed to begin my work. I thank them for their help.

After that productive stint (nourished as it was with excellent Italian food), I was forced, once again, to put aside Hindiyya and devote myself to two other books. So it was that I was not able to recommence my research in earnest until the summer of 2001, when I was fortunate enough to receive a grant from the Council of American Overseas Research Centers to be a fellow at the American Academy in Rome, a stone's throw away from the archives. During my stay there I was able (when I could drag myself away from the idyllic setting of the academy and its genial staff) to complete my research at the new (and air-conditioned) Archivio Storico of the Propaganda Fide, as well as the Jesuit Archives in the Vatican. As with my previous stay, my second visit was greatly facilitated by the knowledgeable and kind assistance of the archivists at both institutions. A subsequent Fulbright grant in the fall of 2002 allowed me to spend a semester in Lebanon mining the archives of the Maronite Patriarchate in Bkirke. While there, Sami Salameh was most generous with his time in guiding me through the literal maze of the patriarchate's archives. Without him I would not have been able to write half of this book. I would be most remiss not to mention that during my stay in Lebanon I was also greatly assisted in my research by the staff of the Bibliothèque Orientale of the Université de Saint Joseph, particularly Ms. Magda Nammour, as well as the staff of the Archives of the Lebanese Order in Dayr Luwayzé and the Archives of the Melkite Order.

Three years after my return to the United States, the National Humanities Center afforded me the opportunity to finally sit down and begin the process of writing this book by granting me a yearlong residential fellowship. During that year I was able to avail myself of the great knowledge and intellectual depth and breadth of colleagues at the center like Sahar Amer, Kristen Brustad, Madeleine Dobie, Gary Macy, Ruth Nisse, Cara Robertson, and Madeline Zilfi. The library staff at the center, primarily Eliza Robertson and Jean Houston, were unfailingly helpful in obtaining the most scarce of sources within days of each of my unceasing requests. And afterward, when I continued the process of writing back at NCSU, the staff of the D. H. Hill Library took up the onerous task of supplying me with a constant stream of books and articles. Jim Clark, Mimi Riggs, Anne Rothe, Marihelen Stringham, and Gary Wilson were exemplary in their patience and acumen. Finally, I was given the opportunity to conclude my work on this book thanks to a semester-long sabbatical leave provided to me by NCSU and selflessly supported by my colleagues at the History Department, who gave of their time so that I could be free of teaching responsibilities.

Aside from the generous institutional support, I have received an immense amount of intellectual guidance and support from a host of colleagues who are far too many to enumerate and whose help made this book possible. Here, I will have to limit my acknowledgment to those who have helped with parts of the book. Thus, I would like to thank Beth Baron, Edmund Burke III, Julia Clancy-Smith, Ellen Fleischmann, David Gilmartin, Suad Joseph, Aleksandra Majstorac Kobiljski, Anthony LaVopa, Marnia Lazreg, Keith Luria, Ussama Makdisi, Michael Marten, Bruce Masters, Sarah Shields, and Steven Vincent and the anonymous readers from the Syracuse University Press. Each has read a part or all of this manuscript in one form (half-baked) or another (slightly less so). Neil Oatsvall, my graduate assistant, provided outstanding help in cataloging and indexing my research into something approximating order. I am deeply grateful to Mary Selden Evans, the executive editor at Syracuse University Press, for her unfailing support on this project. The meticulous and outstanding editing by Andrew Pachuta and D. J. Whyte went far in making the final draft of this book far better than the manuscript I sent them, and Kay Steinmetz was remarkable in shepherding the manuscript through the labyrinth of production and making my life so much easier throughout the process; I am greatly in their debt.

On a personal note, I would like to thank my extended family in Lebanon, whose hospitality not only afforded me, my wife, and daughters the physical comfort and peace of mind necessary to undertake research but whose generous spirits fed my sagging ones after particularly difficult days. Among them, my brother Emile stood out as a beacon of kindness and brotherly love. His premature departure has left a large hole in our collective heart.

It is difficult to overstate the debt of gratitude I owe to my wife, Jodi Stewart Khater. Her help on the long and circuitous path to this book (including many days spent with me in various archives) has been critical, to say the least. Her wisdom and faith in me propelled me along, even when the road seemed interminable (twenty years is a long time, after all). Her probing questions forced me to clarify the foggiest of my thoughts and to crystallize the purpose of this book. Her knowledge of, and experiences in, the Middle East were instrumental in articulating this narrative of the Christian world there. And she was the best exemplar of intertwining strong faith with deep intellect.

Finally, my beautiful daughters Lauren and Micah sustained me with their love and inspired me with their embrace of learning and discovery.

TIMELINE

1750	Hindiyya establishes the Sacred Heart of Jesus order in the newly dedicated Bkerki convent; future patriarch Yusuf Istifan returns from the Maronite College in Rome to Mount Lebanon
Jan. 1752	Pope Benedict XIV orders the dissolution of Hindiyya's order and the destruction of all books and printed records pertaining to her and her order
June 1752	Maronite bishops and Patriarch 'Awwad reject the decision of Benedict XIV to dissolve Hindiyya's order and disband the nuns; they place her and Katerina in separate convents under strict ecclesiastical supervision
Apr.–Sept. 1753	First inquisition by Fr. Desiderio di Casabasciana
1754	New decision by Pope Benedict XIV, tempering his previous criticism but still recommending banishing Hindiyya to an isolated convent and appointing "devout and wise" confessors for her
1755	Brother Innocenzo's failed mission to discipline and banish Hindiyya
Feb. 1759	Hindiyya's complete physical and spiritual union with Jesus Christ
1768	Patriarch Yusuf Istifan establishes the Sacred Heart of Jesus as an official church holiday
1768	Papal indulgence obtained from Pope Clement XIII for the Sacred Heart of Jesus confraternity
June 1774	The Vatican issues the "Seven Edicts," rebuking Patriarch Yusuf Istifan for refusing to submit himself to the authority of the Vatican, to desist from giving indulgences and permitting the consumption of meat on the holiday of the Sacred Heart, and to accept their resolution for the conflict between him and the bishops
1775	Pietro di Moretta arrives in Bkerki to begin implementing the Vatican's edicts and to conduct an investigation of the events which took place in Bkerki
1775–77	Testimonials are traded between supporters and opponents of Hindiyya; affidavits surface about the "satanic

	fraternity" purportedly headed by Nassimeh and Wardeh Abou Badran, two nuns in the Bkerki convent
June 1777	News of the death of Nassimeh Abou Badran and Wardeh the Aleppan, two nuns in the Bkerki convent, becomes public
Oct. 1777	Hindiyya and her nuns are expelled from the Bkerki convent by Sa'ad al-Khuri, the *muddabir* (secretary) of Emir Bashir, the ruler of Mount Lebanon
1778	Second inquisition by Pietro di Moretta and the final closure of the Bkerki convent and all other convents affiliated with the Sacred Heart of Jesus order
July 1779	Final report by the Propaganda Fide on the Hindiyya affair; the council decrees the extraction of a confession from Hindiyya for her misdeeds, her banishment to an isolated convent, and the destruction of all her writings
Sept. 1795	Patriarch Philippe Jumayyil issues a patriarchal circular threatening anyone who possessed copies of Hindiyya's books with excommunication
Feb. 13, 1798	Hindiyya passes away in the convent of Sayyidat al-Haqli

MAIN CHARACTERS

Bishop Jirmanus Diyab (died 1799). He succeeded Bishop Saqr as the spiritual director of Hindiyya and her Bkerki convent. One of her most ardent supporters in her struggles against Vatican oversight and inquisition.

Bishop Jirmanus Saqr (died September 18, 1768). He oversaw Dayr Mar Hrash, a convent where Hindiyya spent some time between 1748 and 1750. He was the Maronite bishop and first senior cleric to support her in her quest to establish a new religious order. Bishop Saqr also acted as her scribe in writing down *Secret of the Union* and her other works.

Bishop Mikhail Fadel. Educated in the Maronite College in Rome, Bishop Fadel was appointed bishop of Tyre in 1762 and assumed the episcopal chair of Beirut in 1781. Became patriarch of the Maronite Church between 1793 and 1795, when he passed away. He was a strong supporter of Hindiyya during the patriarchate of Sima'an 'Awwad. However, later (during the patriarchate of Yusuf Istifan) he became one of her chief opponents.

Father Antonio Venturi. Jesuit priest and missionary in Aleppo and Mount Lebanon. He was born in Tuscany, Italy, in 1701. He was Hindiyya's last Jesuit confessor, scribe, and supporter. Joined the Jesuit company in 1719, arrived in Damascus as a missionary in 1733, and four years later moved to Aleppo. He became Hindiyya's confessor sometime in 1739. From that point until he was finally recalled to Rome in 1748, he supported Hindiyya, with some reservations about her self-proclaimed vocation.

Fr. Desiderio di Casabasciana. Hindiyya's first inquisitor. He was a friar in the order of the Lesser Friars of the Holy Land, who was an expert in Oriental ecclesiastical affairs.

Fr. Pietro di Moretta. Appointed by the Propaganda Fide to investigate the accusations against Patriarch Istifan, leveled by some dissenting Maronite bishops, of transgressing Catholic norms by permitting the eating of meat on Friday, declaring Hindiyya a living saint, and seeking to centralize ecclesiastical power in himself at the expense of the bishops. In addition, di Moretta was to investigate Hindiyya for heresy. He became her chief opponent and worked to bring about her demise and the dissolution of the Sacred Heart of Jesus order.

Friar Isidorios Mancini. Appointed by Pope Benedict XIV to investigate Hindiyya's writings and reports of her activities. He wrote a scathing critique of Hindiyya and judged her at best a deluded woman.

Halabiyyat. Nuns in Hindiyya's convents who were predominantly from Aleppo and who for the most part were strong supporters of Hindiyya in the 1770s.

Helena Hawwa. Hindiyya's mother

Hindiyya al-'Ujaimi. Maronite visionary woman and nun

Katerina. Hindiyya's longtime companion and assistant in the Sacred Heart of Jesus order. She was accused of (and blamed for) fomenting divisions within the order, for orchestrating Hindiyya's fame through faking miracles and visions, and for being responsible for the deaths of two nuns in the convent.

Jabaliyyat. Nuns in Hindiyya's convents who were predominantly from Mount Lebanon and Beirut and who for the most part came to be ranged against Hindiyya in the 1770s.

Niqula al-'Ujaimi. Hindiyya's brother, who vacillated between supporting and opposing her. He was ordained a Jesuit priest and acted as the confessor of the Bkerki convent in the early 1770s, before the dissolution of the Sacred Heart order.

Patriarch Sima'an 'Awwad (1743–1756). The first Maronite patriarch to support Hindiyya. He, along with Maronite bishops and the Khazin family, defended Hindiyya against the attacks of Jesuit missionaries to the point of rupture with Rome over the matter.

Patriarch Tubiya al-Khazin (r. 1756–1766). Did not become involved with Hindiyya and only emerges as part of the conflict with Bishop Yusuf Istifan (who was to succeed him as patriarch).

Patriarch Yusuf Istifan (r. 1766–1793). Supported Hindiyya wholeheartedly and encouraged the development of the cult of the Sacred Heart of Jesus and its associated confraternity. Almost lost his patriarchal seat because of this support.

Pope Benedict XIV (r. 1740–1758). Pope who commissioned the first inquisition of Hindiyya and who decreed the dissolution of her religious order.

Pope Pius VI (1775–1799). Pope who commissioned the second and final inquisition of Hindiyya and who succeeded in disbanding her religious order and placing her under ecclesiastical arrest in a series of convents ending with Dayr Sayyidat al-Haqli, where she died in 1798.

Shukralla al-ʿUjaimi. Hindiyya's father.

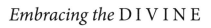

Embracing the D I V I N E

1. Bilad al-Sham.

1

INTRODUCTION

"[Jesus] placed his hands on my hands, his feet on my feet and his lips on my lips, and I gazed upon the whole universe."[1] Hindiyya al-'Ujaimi, a Maronite[2] nun from Aleppo, dictated this evocative and provocative vision of her latest encounter with Christ to her confessor, Bishop Jirmanus Saqr, in 1755 as part of her mystical narrative titled *Sirr al-Ittihad*, or *Secret of the Union*. In pronouncing these words she was nearing the climax of a spiritual journey that culminated in a physical union with the eternal body of Christ and a "boundless" expansion of her knowledge. Yet these words were not the description of a subjective and ineffable mystical experience. Rather, their public pronouncement was a challenge to the patriarchal hierarchies of the Levantine and Roman Catholic Churches. The frenzied events she unleashed—two inquisitions by the Holy See in 1753 and 1778, a concerted campaign on the part of some Latin missionaries to discredit her, and turmoil within the Maronite Church between supporters and detractors—are testimony to the radical nature and perceived magnitude of her transgressions across gender lines. Hindiyya's religious charisma, visions, and popularity (notoriety) placed her at the center of a confluence of Latin missionary, Maronite, and Vatican histories. As such, her tale is more than a life story: it is a historical journey through the politics of gender and religion within the Maronite and Roman Catholic Churches during the eighteenth century. This book tells that story.

The Moral of the Story

In and of itself, Hindiyya's tale is engrossing—a singular woman who against all odds transformed the Maronite Church and its relationship

1

with Rome over the course of the eighteenth century. She was born in Aleppo in 1720 at a time of great commercial and religious effervescence. In the midst of the competing forces of mammon and church, Hindiyya began to have visions of Christ at a very young age. In those almost daily and incessant visions, the living Christ stoked the spiritual and bodily passion of Hindiyya by singling her out for the task of saving the lost souls of the world. She was to accomplish this by establishing a new religious order dedicated to the worship of the Sacred Heart of Jesus—the focal point of his divine love and mercy for humanity and the center of a wildly popular cult in Europe in the late seventeenth century. Beset by self-doubt and skepticism from a string of Jesuit confessors, Hindiyya nonetheless was animated by her love for Christ—and her own ambitions—to reject parental and paternalistic pleas, Vatican restrictions, and societal mores. She left Aleppo at the age of twenty-six and arrived in Mount Lebanon, where she endured four years of rejection and loneliness before she convinced a local Maronite bishop to support her cause. In 1750 Hindiyya finally succeeded in establishing her order, only to be met with stiff and sustained opposition from Latin missionaries who saw her unrestrained visions as a challenge to their control over the project of religious modernization in the Middle East. She also faced Vatican mistrust of feminine spirituality and independent local religious authority. On the other hand, Maronite ecclesiastical authorities saw in Hindiyya an "authentic" symbol and source for the creation of an expansive and energized local church. For the next twenty-five years her religious order and political fortunes rose and dipped between active opposition and benign neglect on the part of Rome and amid a Maronite Church and community split over the authenticity and propriety of her visions and project. Matters came to a tragic halt when two nuns in one of her convents died during exorcisms initiated after scandalous reports of satanic cults and consorting with the devil. The accumulated tragedies and outrage were too much of a burden for even the most ardent supporters of Hindiyya within the Maronite Church. Subsequently, in 1778 the second and final inquisition brought the demise of Hindiyya and her religious order (but not her impact by any means) when she was sentenced to spend the rest of her life imprisoned in a solitary cell in a convent. In

1798 Hindiyya died in such a cell on top of a forbidding mountain, leaving a legacy that shaped the Maronite Church and its relations to Rome for many years to come.

Compelling though it may be in its cinematic scope—resplendent with the requisite villains, mysterious events infused with sinister and sexual tensions, tragedy, and pathos—Hindiyya's story holds within its folds a larger tale about the construction of a new Christianity in Bilad al-Sham.[3] In its constituent parts, this tale has much to tell us about religious minorities in the Middle East, the role women played in the history of religion in the Middle East, early modern cultural encounters between the "West" and the Middle East, and the relationship between gender, modernity, and religion. It is to these broader themes that I now turn.

From the end of the eighteenth century and through the early part of the nineteenth century, two—at times conflictual—projects competed to reform Levantine Christianity and to transform it from a diffuse religious culture to a disciplined and disciplining institutionalized religion. In the words of Wilfred Cantwell Smith, both projects sought to objectify religion by changing its definition from "sect" (a mixture of localized folk traditions and the most rudimentary of scriptural knowledge) to systematic ideas and practices meant to institute and demand an individual recognition of God.[4] Using apostolic approaches, Latin missionaries and a new generation of local Catholic clerics in Bilad al-Sham exhorted and edified the believers and tried to corral them within stricter boundaries of religious belief and practice that were textually based and "scientifically" elucidated. Both groups saw women as key to this process. They were the mothers who would raise Christian children, and they were the conduits for bringing the new religion into the most intimate aspects of society. Perceived as marginal actors in religious public life, Maronite and Melkite women were viewed by Latin missionaries as more inclined to accept their new ideas of Christianity and, perhaps more importantly, their religious authority. While not necessarily of the same mind on the matter of women and religion, Levantine Catholic authorities and hierarchs nonetheless jealously regarded women as central to maintaining local control over the nature and future of Christianity. In their eyes women were repositories of religious honor and authenticity.

The friction between these two competing visions created a space within the religious landscape of the Levant which allowed some (over-whelmingly Aleppan) women to construct and advance their own alternative notions of Christianity. Hindiyya was the most prominent of those women. Her story as well as those of other women we will encounter in this book are tales of their strenuous—and at times tragic—struggles to wrench some element of liberty and independence in a male-dominated society and church. As with the first generation of women's histories in the Middle East, these narratives are engaging in part because Christian women have been conspicuously absent from historical narratives of religion in the Middle East.[5] Their absence is manifest at two levels: as Christians and as women. First, the history of Christianity has been largely elided from the English-language scholarship on the modern Middle East. Most studies of Christians in the Middle East stop somewhere around the early Islamic conquests, with few lingering works taking the narrative toward the end of the 'Abbasid period and the Crusades. After that, the scholarly gaze of Middle Eastern studies becomes transfixed on Islam. The impressive, if numerically limited, body of work of a new crop of scholars studying Western missionaries and, to a lesser extent, Christians in the region represents a growing exception to this mesmerized state of being.[6] Nonetheless, it is an exception that highlights the reality that religious minorities have been relegated to the farthest margins of the scholarly field, inadvertently reinforcing neo-Orientalist imaginings of the Middle East as a monolithic historical and contemporary space.[7]

However, in studying this particular episode, I am not simply aiming to fill a historical gap, important though that may be. Rather, by bringing the history of a religious minority to the foreground I hope to provide a wider perspective on the historical transformations of the Middle East. More specifically, the eighteenth-century encounters between the Vatican and Middle Eastern Christians, detailed in this book, anticipate many of the issues which faced those seeking to create a "modern" Middle East in the nineteenth century. Latin critiques of the oppressed status of Maronite and Melkite women, of the preponderance of ignorance and superstition among lay and religious alike, and of the corrupt moral character of "East-erners" are all echoed by later Orientalist depictions of Muslims in the

Middle East. Similarly, the attitude of intellectual, moral, and religious superiority which infused the words and actions of some Latin Catholic friars and priests and justified (in their minds at least) their missionary activity and zeal were quite similar to those evinced by Protestant missionaries in the nineteenth century toward Christians and Muslims in Bilad al-Sham.[8] From this comparative perspective, Islamic responses and initiatives of the later period appear less peculiarly "Islamic" and more as transformations brought about by interactions with contingent social, cultural, and economic factors that have precedents and parallels among the Christians of Bilad al-Sham.

Equally, the predominant representation of Christianity as a "Western" subject is implicitly questioned by illustrating how Hindiyya, along with other men and women of her generation, Arabized Christianity even as they Christianized Arabic. Their evocative and expansive use of Arabic to publicly describe their profoundly Christian experiences (greatly aided by the establishment of the first Arabic printing press in the early eighteenth century) was one element of this movement. While Arabic had previously been used liturgically and theologically in limited fashion, its use as a religious tool and identity after the onset of the eighteenth century became widespread. This was attained only through direct and circuitous collaborations between Muslim scholars, Maronite and Melkite intellectuals, and Latin missionaries, as well as their confrontations over its meanings and trajectory. On the one hand, this transformation of Arabic into a language of Christian identity paved the way for non-Muslim voices to reenter the public spaces of the Ottoman Levant in later years under the rubric of the nineteenth-century Nahda (Arab Renaissance) and for making Arabic a secular language of reform and modernization during that period. On the other hand, the employ of images drawn from local Ottoman culture to describe universal visions of Christianity perforated the artificial distinctions between a supposed Middle Eastern Islam and Western Christianity. Hindiyya's life, visions, and writings—in addition to the literary, theological, and philosophical works of Maronite intellectuals–recentered Christ and Christianity in a distinctly Maronite "Holy Land," from whence was to emanate once again the salvation of all of humanity. This was not a self-conscious political movement but rather a religiocultural amalgamation that drew on the Arabic language, constructed Maronite history, and the environment of Mount Lebanon to proclaim a manifestly Maronite but universally applicable version of Christianity. In seeking thusly to create a distinct Maronite identity, Hindiyya and her contemporaries conjoined the Ottoman and Roman Catholic worlds into a hybrid and fluid collective sense of self that made mush of the distinctions between all three categories even as it insisted on those delineations.

At another level, the intense and prolonged discussions and arguments which raged between the Vatican and Latin missionaries, on the one hand, and Hindiyya and her Maronite advocates, on the other, transformed both the Maronite and Roman Catholic Churches and their relationship. When, in the 1770s, Patriarch Yusuf Istifan, a graduate of the Maronite College in Rome, defended Hindiyya and the Maronite church against Vatican demands for submission to papal authority, he premised his arguments on the historical independence of the patriarchate of Antioch. When conflict erupted over the overbearing ecclesiastical activities and claims of authority by Latin missionaries in Aleppo and Mount Lebanon, Maronite and Melkite clerics predicated their complaints on their historical rights as ancient Christian communities. When the Khazin *shuyukh*, the Maronite overlords of the Kisrawan district in Mount Lebanon, wrote the king of France complaining of the overreach of the Jesuit missionaries, they spoke of the historical relationship between Catholic France and its Maronite protégés. Regardless of the outcomes of the power struggles—or mutually beneficial spells of cooperation—neither party was left unchanged. The Vatican had to adjust, rethink, and reevaluate its approaches to Middle Eastern Christians in order to maintain access to their communities. The Maronite and Melkite Churches (among others) had to acquiesce to safeguard the patronage of Rome, which was—at least in part—propelling their rise to economic and political prominence in the Ottoman Empire. However, these exchanges carried out over decades were not insularly about a balance of power and authority between Rome and the Maronite and Melkite *ta'ifa*, or sect. Rather, the missives and negotiations over the contours of the relationship between Latin and Levantine Christians represent a strand in the larger history of Christianity. Like other aspects of that history which took place in Canada, Mexico, India, and China, this thread is interwoven into the larger tapestry, rendering it essential for understanding how Christianity was formulated during the eighteenth century. The encounters between Rome (the center of Catholicism) and the peripheries shaped not only local Christianity but also the Vatican's policies and ideologies in palpable ways. In short, this particular history not only makes the notion of Christianity as "Western" untenable but makes the Middle East an important part of the history of Christendom.

In addition to the elision of the history of their community, Christian women are largely absent as women from the historical literature on the Middle East. The little scholarship that has focused on the topic of non-ancient Christianity in the Middle East has largely ignored the role of women.[9] It is critical to begin reclaiming these stories because they highlight the centrality of gender—and, more specifically, gender-based paradoxes—to the history of Christianity and religion in the Middle East. In particular, there are two paradoxes which suffuse the history of Hindiyya as well as other religious women across the eighteenth century. The first is most obviously the paradox of "an ideological system that espouses universal equality (in this case, the spiritual equality of all Christians before God) at the same time that it upholds sexual difference as a natural fact and basis for social (and spiritual) differentiation."[10] The religious revivalism and enthusiasm which characterized Levantine Catholicism in the eighteenth century swept up some men and women into a utopian world of spiritual equality before God. Latin and local proselytizers exhorted all to come equally and as individuals unto Christ as sinners seeking salvation. This spiritual equality and individuation of faith was belied by the social constraints of the secular and religious worlds wherein a clear hierarchy of authority—if not always power—elevated men above women. The dialectical relationship between the two realities became an engine of change within and outside the church. Hindiyya and other religious women shunned the social expectations of their communities in the name of Christ and divine authority. Visions of Christ, religious callings, and salvation of souls (their own as well as others) were posited as far more important and relevant than marriage, housework, and menial labor. Some women shed the restraints on their movements in and out of public space, on their acquisition and production of learning, and on their social demeanor and behavior in the name of a God-given liberty to pursue their religious perfection. The intense personal relationship with Christ—premised in some instances on the eroticized adoration of his body—justified a public renunciation and condemnation of the material world surrounding them and, in a few instances, even of men as a category and authority.

These radical (and other not so transgressive) positions were most apparent in the language employed by Hindiyya, among others. In her conversations with Christ or missives to the Roman Congregation for the Propagation of the Faith (Propaganda Fide), she resorted to the trope of the "weak and meek woman."[11] Yet she and other women of the eighteenth century employed this formulaic self-characterization as a mechanism to raise questions and even opposition to male authorities (and, in the case of Hindiyya, challenge Christ himself) in subtle and direct contradictions of the linguistic turn of phrase. Their very acceptance of the lowly social and intellectual position permitted them to act as conduits for the word and power of Christ, who favored the meek over the mighty, which in turn allowed them far greater social and religious power. In this they echoed Marguerite Porete, a fourteenth-century French mystic, who claimed "I—because I am lowly—am the exemplar of Salvation."[12] Thus, while most social norms stipulated a subservient role for women within and outside the church, Hindiyya used the characteristics of that role, and the visions and bodily experiences of Christ it invited, to propel herself past its boundaries into the most unusual position of a living saint. In other words, Hindiyya's visions were "a socially sanctioned activity that freed a woman from conventional female roles by identifying her as a genuine religious figure"[13] and brought her to the attention of others, giving her a public language she could use to transcend the limitations of "womanhood" within and without the church. Her words thus became a source of power that allowed her to rise above the possibilities that were open to women at that time, and in the process she set a precedent for later religious women.

Hindiyya's spiritual raptures and bodily knowledge attained through a physical and metaphysical union with Christ highlight the second aspect of the gender paradox—namely, the tension between the masculine and feminine means of knowing. In the seventeenth and eighteenth centuries efforts were afoot within Western Catholicism to create an Enlightenment church that could withstand the secularizing onslaught of the *philosophes* of Europe. The Vatican was beset by intellectuals like the *encyclopédistes* Voltaire, Reimarus, and Lessing, who rejected revelation as irrational and promoted reason as the only means to knowing God. By extension, sensory knowledge attained through the body became highly suspect. Descartes' "I think therefore I am" encapsulates this absolute devaluation of the body as a means to knowing the world. John Locke, who in his *Essay on Human Understanding* posited sensation and reflection as the dual source of all ideas, discounted all senses but sight.[14] Catholic thinkers were not immune to this trend. Intellectuals like Nicolas Malebranche were arguing in the early part of the eighteenth century that knowledge can be attained only through ideas, which were immaterial representations of the will of God. Influenced by these two Cartesian philosophical trends, Catholic reformers like Pope Benedict XIV (r. 1740–1758) sought to build an Enlightenment church based on "science" and averse to "superstition." His travails and those of other like-minded Catholics were dedicated to establishing a more Cartesian church, where the masculinized mind and reason were separate from, and predominated, the fallen female body and its suspect senses, which led to unbridled imagination, a sure path away from orthodoxy. This is not to imply that the divorce of the mind from the senses, the natural from the supernatural, and the profane from the sacred was absolute either within the Catholic Church or outside it. David Hume (1711–1776), for example, was skeptical of reason, which he felt was profoundly depressing and cured only by "lively impression of my senses."[15] Clergy at various levels of the Roman Catholic hierarchy still afforded miracles a place in the body of religious knowledge. Yet what is patently clear is that the gap between mind and body had grown considerably by the eighteenth century, with the first elevated as the preeminent source of theological knowing. Within this context, revelation and sensual knowledge were permissible only as subjective (feminine) sources of knowing God, but they had no role to play in discerning objective (masculine) truth. And while acceptable as personal experiences that brought "emotional" unenlightened Christians closer to God, they became in the eyes of the hierarchy of the Roman Catholic Church far inferior to rational thought and textual knowledge.

In contrast, Hindiyya and other Levantine women emphasized their somatic experience of the sacred as central to religious knowledge and truth. Like Medieval female mystics in Europe, these women pursued states of "religious ecstasy through their bodies rather than through the cognitive interpretation of texts."[16] Words and texts were still important but primarily in relation to the wider contexts of carnal knowing. Thus, the words chanted in preparation of the Eucharist were powerful insomuch as they transformed bread and wine into the flesh and blood of Christ. Hindiyya's experience of taking the Host was of the magical incantation of words coupled with the sensation of consuming the body of Christ. Her expansion of knowledge came about through her physical union with the body of Christ. The written rule for her order—her collection of advice, hymns, and theological reflections—was transmitted through her carnal visions of Christ, whereby her body felt the words spill out of the mouth of Christ in a torrent of emotions that left her prostrate and entranced for hours. Whether these were real or contrived moments is irrelevant since in either case bodily and cognitive knowing were conjoined just as she (the feminine body) became perpetually one with Christ (the masculine Word). Most profoundly, Hindiyya and the *Hindawiyyun* (her supporters) posited that this knowledge superseded the Vatican's rationalized and textualized theology specifically because it allowed for knowing Christ as divine and human, rather than a disembodied Logos. Thus, Hindiyya's sensual—and even erotic—private encounters with Christ became public sources for knowing the will of Christ even as Hindiyya's body became the repository of renewed revelation of the divine mysteries.

In this sense, both aspects of the gender paradox generated dynamics of change in the structure and language of Levantine Christianity by inserting a feminine voice into the male-dominated discourse, by questioning the sources of religious authority (divine or human, local or Latin, male or female), and by problematizing religious tradition and authenticity in establishing women as conduits for new divine revelations. The impact of these transformations was not limited to the cloistered world of nuns but was felt beyond their conventual walls, for religion in Bilad al-Sham was not a separate, individuated identity, any more than it was the sole and hegemonic determinant of communal belonging. Rather, it encompassed and was shaped by the realities and struggles of quotidian life. For example, whether people chose to believe in the miracles and visions of Hindiyya or dismissed them (or changed their minds about them over time), her private moments from her childhood in Aleppo to the apogee of her religious influence in Mount Lebanon became part of public discourse and life. Thus, the bold proclamations and assertions of Hindiyya and other religious women of Aleppo and Mount Lebanon sent ripples through the bodies of the Maronite and Melkite communities, igniting debate and arguments about gender and the role of women within church and society. In this manner gender played a key role in shaping the intertwined religious and secular histories of the Catholic communities of Bilad al-Sham and the relationship between Rome and Levantine Christians.

Hindiyya's story is also about the politics of religious modernization. Over the course of the eighteenth century, when the Catholic Church was losing its influence over the "national" churches in Europe and some forty years after its retreat from China, Jesuit missionaries sought greater control over the practices and meanings of Christianity in the Middle East. Hindiyya's story is an integral part of the larger history of the Vatican's project to map the religious world into bipolarities of orthodox and heretical Christianity. In employing polarizing discourses—"natural belief" and "civilized religion," "Latin" and "East," "orthodoxy" and "heresy"— Latin missionaries sought to sunder the religious world of Bilad al-Sham into two irrevocable parts of "modern" and "traditional." Hindiyya represented a counterproject, which localized Christianity, superseded the Vatican's textual religious authority, and sought to replace it with mystical knowledge. Her visions of Christ and the celestial knowledge he imparted to her provided the Maronite Church with a source of religious authority implicitly higher than that of the Vatican. Her emergence as a galvanizing symbol was a central part of the project of reclaiming Maronite control over Middle Eastern Catholicism while equally transforming Christianity through an alternative and localized "modernity." This struggle between local and global forces over defining religious normative practices and language presaged the more secular modernization projects of the nineteenth century. In other words, the relevance of Hindiyya's story is not constrained to shedding light on the interactions between the Vatican and Middle Eastern Christians at a critical phase in that complex and shifting relationship. Rather, it also raises critical questions about the history of "modernity" itself, which has been depicted as a primarily secular phenomenon that commences sometime in the late nineteenth century in the Middle East.

Intrinsically, I am arguing that our focus on the nineteenth century as the modern moment in the Middle East when reform suffused the air is problematic at two levels. On the one hand, it misplaces that "moment," if it ever was so contained a phenomenon, chronologically. By focusing our historical research and narratives on the nineteenth century, we privilege a time when European power and influence in the Middle East was clearly ascendant; and this makes it more difficult to parse modernization (hybridized transformation) from Westernization (wholesale imitation). As the stories in this book will amply illustrate, modernity—or the process of a localized and contingent cultural transformation depicted as a rational emancipation from custom and self-consciously linked to a global phenomenon—predated the nineteenth century.[17] For instance, Aleppan Melkite nuns used their reading and understanding of the theology of François de Sales to demand greater independence than ever accorded to Melkite women in managing their spiritual and worldly affairs. Hindiyya used her visions to establish a new theology and religious order genealogically connected to the European cult of the Sacred Heart of Jesus but superseding it in scope and power. In the nineteenth century the Batishtaniyyat, a group of religious Aleppan women, sought to perpetuate and expand the cult of the Sacred Heart started by Hindiyya by appealing to the need for new revelations that would fit the "modern" world. In all of these earlier manifestations of "modernity," women sought self-emancipation from their existing constraints by adapting new ideas of religious freedom and spirituality to fit their local circumstances. In this they are not that different from nineteenth- and twentieth-century Middle Eastern feminists who employed more secular arguments to attain greater access to education, employment, and the political arena. Presenting this history as an example of earlier modernization is not to simply shift the "starting date" but rather to question the representation of modernization as a historically discrete, rather than a diffused, phenomenon that cannot be simply ascribed to a particular time period and culture.

On the other, and weightier, hand, Hindiyya's tale challenges the dichotomy of religion and history inherent in many studies about modernity in the Middle East.[18] Our focus on the nineteenth century conflates modernity and secularism and exaggerates the tension between reform and religion in the Middle East. Certainly, studies of the nineteenth-century Middle East have elucidated attempts to find a place for religion within the projects of modernity. Studies of Jamal al-Din al-Afghani, Muhammad 'Abduh, and others in the Salafiyya movement come to mind. However, that very construction assumes that religion is, at best, outside modernity, if not marginal and even largely hostile to it. Indeed, one of the defining elements of modernity is the self-referential binary of secularism/religion that is constructed, along with other binaries, to characterize it as a discrete and clearly delineated historical event. As David Shaw argues, this opposition between religion and history is "an artifact of modernity" and one which created an ontological dissonance between historians and the past.[19] Similarly, "Anthropological studies of popular religion have emphasized, almost exclusively, the collective and public aspects of religious expression but have ignored private, individual piety."[20] To overcome this binary, we need to write histories of religion that are not dedicated solely to telling the stories of religious institutions and intellectuals or to describing religion as a social and political force. Rather, and difficult though it may be, we must narrate tales of faith and belief, those intangible yet powerful elements of the human experience. We must allow a role for the supernatural in human history by accepting that it moved individuals and communities in small and great ways— even if it does not move us in a similar manner. To omit the emotional and sensual, that is, the bodily experiences of humanity, obscures the very qualities that made religion such a powerful force in human history. We cannot dismiss religious sentiments as irrational since they in reality provide a rationale for human action and history. Instead, we need to bridge the chasm—opened by modernity's assumption of an attenuated and compartmentalized religion—between the secular and religious, natural and supernatural, faith and reason—and see them as an intertwined whole rather than separate categories. Finally, we need to recognize that individual and private forms of piety influenced the creation of identity and models of behavior. This book is a step toward that rapprochement.

We begin Hindiyya's story and our exploration of its historical meanings in Aleppo, where she was born. Chapter 2 looks at the socioeconomic and religious milieu of Aleppo as a relatively cosmopolitan city in the Ottoman Empire. In particular, this chapter examines the religious revival among the newly formed Maronite Catholic bourgeoisie of Aleppo and the contradictions between their material well-being and religious pretensions. These contradictions were in part the result of the commercial success of the city and its upper classes. In equal part they were the outcome of a successful Latin missionary movement that brought a new concept of Christianity (a stricter religious tradition with more exacting expectations than Eastern Christianity) to the inhabitants of the city. Out of these contradictions emerged a localized Christian renaissance that expressed itself in a literary movement and in the resurgence of monasticism as a desirable vocation. Following the example of ten nuns who preceded her by a decade or so, and at the purported beckoning of Christ through her visions, Hindiyya embarked on a journey of dissociating herself from family, friends, and neighbors and retreating into a solitary, reflective life. Her individual desires—stirred and encouraged by a sometimes impatient and even threatening Christ—thrust her into series of confrontations, first with her social peers and ultimately with her Jesuit confessor. In following these confrontations, the chapter brings into relief the social tensions besetting Aleppo and the nature of competing projects of Christian modernization that pit local Christians against Latin missionaries. The chapter concludes with Hindiyya departing from Aleppo to Mount Lebanon as a final act of divinely inspired rebellion against earthly restraints. Hindiyya's journey to this decision is also occasion to examine the transformation wrought by religious revivalism on gender roles.

Taking up the story from the point of Hindiyya's arrival in Mount Lebanon, chapter 3 focuses on the construction of sanctity. Specifically, it raises the question as to why Hindiyya—as well as her male and female predecessors and successors—came to the mountains of Lebanon to establish their monastic orders and houses. I answer this question by tracing the representation of these mountains as a primitive "Holy Land," a novel concept in many ways. For Latin missionaries this representation gave their mission to a Catholic community a raison d'être. It allowed them to establish a sanctified link to Christ, even as they contended they were bringing religious enlightenment to primitive Christians. For Aleppan nuns and monks (like Hindiyya) the natural spirituality and landscape of Mount Lebanon stood as a religiously authentic counterpart to the fallen nature of Aleppo, which they construed to be a materialistic city with an adulterated ethnic and sectarian urban landscape. This juxtaposition became the seed of the idea of Maronite exceptionalism and difference from the surrounding Muslim and non-Maronite Christian communities. As Hindiyya stood at the confluence of these two narratives, she changed herself from a visionary woman to a prophetess emulating the transformative sojourns of Christ and Moses in the wilderness. This transfiguration brought her to the attention of the hierarchy of the Maronite Church, who finally accepted, and in large measure adopted, her vision and mission, not least of which because she became the beacon of Maronite religious authenticity and superiority. At the same time, it brought her into a far closer relationship with Christ bodily and intellectually. Her intensified intimacy gave her access—through her body—to the universe of knowledge unfolded to her by Christ. She became the channel for an alternative and distinctly feminine source of religious knowledge, truth, and authority, all of which stood in stark juxtaposition with the textually bound Roman Catholic Church. Hers was also a local voice that sought to center Christ's church in the mountains of Lebanon. In this manner, she took the contentions of Latin missionaries to their logical extreme. Their exhortation for personal faith and salvation became for Hindiyya (and her ever widening circle of followers) a personal relationship with Christ that superseded the teachings and authority of the missionaries and even the Vatican. In addition, she accentuated the holiness of Mount Lebanon to the point where it vied with Rome's claim to being the center of the Catholic faith.

Catapulted by circumstance and design into such a prominent position, Hindiyya quickly became the center of a controversy that involved Latin missionaries, the Maronite Church, and the Holy See. Chapter 4 follows the controversy as it unfolded and in turn enfolded more and more people and institutions. What is most striking about it is the gendered nature of the debate that erupted around Hindiyya. Thus, the chapter focuses in particular on a two-part question animating the fiery and protracted discussions and contentions: the first asks about the nature of ecclesiastical hierarchy and religious authority within the Maronite Church and, more importantly, in relation to Rome and the second ponders where women fit within that hierarchy. As the chapter makes clear, these were not novel (or purely Maronite) questions. There was a famous preceding episode that involved ten Melkite nuns from Aleppo, which the chapter discusses along with their endeavor to establish greater religious independence. But Hindiyya raised the same issues far more powerfully since she was armed with the authority of Christ. Emerging in an already tense religious environment—where local clerics and Latin missionaries had been sparring over the right to oversee Middle Eastern Christian communities—she posited that her bodily experience of Christ gave her an authority that superseded that of priests, bishops, and even popes. Most importantly, she argued that this knowledge and authority could be obtained only by a woman—like her—who possessed the feminine qualities of humility and even ignorance. In such a manner, she turned male stereotypes of women on their head, making them a source of spiritual genuineness and power as opposed to male hypocrisy and, hence, departure from the presence of God. The Vatican, in the midst of a Catholic Enlightenment seeking to substantiate religion by reason, dismissed Hindiyya's claims specifically because as a woman she was more emotional and more prone to be deluded by the devil. The chapter charts the arguments as they were traded back and forth and examines their impact on the Maronite Church and community. Ultimately, Hindiyya was subjected to an inquisition that proved inconclusive. The priest dispatched to interrogate and investigate her sent back to the Propaganda Fide a glowing report that embraced her as a truly saintly woman. The cardinal and priest who examined her writings in Rome came to a starkly differing conclusion, branding her as a naïve woman, at best, and potentially a heretic. Equivocation, distance, and other concerns ultimately worked in Hindiyya's favor; and she was more or less left to her own devices for some twenty years.

The time Hindiyya enjoyed in relative freedom from the inquisitorial gaze of the Vatican allowed her to grow and expand her order from one to four convents, from twenty to over one hundred nuns and a large lay membership in an affiliated confraternity, and to enrich her coffers through donations and offerings. More critically, she became well established as a focal point of local Christianity and a preeminent symbol of resurgent spirituality in the Levant. Her writings and news of her miracles circulated widely from Mount Lebanon to Aleppo and beyond to Europe. However, her contradictions and the passions unleashed by the new Christianity came to haunt her and define the last years of her life. Chapter 5 looks at those contradictions, passions, and years by examining three key moments in this period. The first is Hindiyya's physically and spiritually passionate union with Christ. The second centers around the exorcisms performed on two nuns in the Bkerki convent accused—by Hindiyya and her supporters—of belonging to a secret Masonic satanic cult whose purpose was to undermine and even kill Hindiyya and whose practices were scandalously sexual. The final episode is the second inquisition unleashed by the death of the two nuns, which brought the demise of Hindiyya, the dissolution of her order, and the attempt to destroy and ban her writings.

The thread that connected all three episodes was the passion unleashed by a revivalist Christianity focused so intently on the adoration of Christ and self-mortification for sin. What emerges quickly is that the passion was equally intense in two directions. The first was obviously centered on Hindiyya's bodily and spiritual relationship to Christ, one that had its own sexual overtones similar to those of other visionaries. However, the second was exactly the opposite. It was an equally intense fear of a very real hell. Hindiyya's description of the place was nightmarish in the intricate detail of agonies and pains suffered by sinners. To her—and presumably those around her—hell was no longer an abstract concept of punishment but an intensely felt and feared consequence of sin. And the physical manifestations of these feelings were hardly different from those she experienced in her union with Christ. Similarly, her charged regimen of self-mortification and aversion to carnal sin (and men) as well as her strict prescriptions to her nuns to avoid contact with men were equaled by the much sexualized discourse on the satanic cult and the practices of its followers. Thus, within the same convent, nuns were experiencing the struggle between good and evil through passions coursing through their bodies. In this manner, religious discourse became a way to explore female sexuality within a society and church that considered such elements taboo at best. The final episode in this narrative intertwining spirituality and sensuality was the inquisition to which Hindiyya was subjected. Aside from rightfully seeking to assign blame for the death of the two nuns, the inquisition was clearly intended as a way to brand Hindiyya and her bodily ways of knowing as heresy. In other words, the unbridled passions had to be brought under the control of the Vatican, which regarded local religious leaders to be under the spell of Hindiyya. In the age of Catholic Enlightenment, the Vatican declared Hindiyya not so much a witch but a woman who allowed her body to become the conduit of evil. In this manner it attempted to restore the "natural" order and relationship between mind and body, men and women, Rome and the Maronites.

The epilogue (chapter 6) concludes by looking at the enduring legacy of Hindiyya through examining the persistence of a counternarrative that rejected the Propaganda Fide's judgment of the error and heresy of Hindiyya and her movement. While the Vatican successfully dismantled the institutions associated with the Sacred Heart, it had a devil of a time in erasing Hindiyya's influence. Her insistence on her innocence and the failure to confiscate all her writings were two elements that kept the Vatican and its Maronite allies from achieving their goal. The perpetuation of the ideas and visions of Hindiyya under the guise of a new religious association which emerged in Aleppo at the end of the eighteenth century illustrated further the limitations of the power of the Vatican in shaping Christianity in Bilad al-Sham. In looking at these subsequent events, this chapter focuses on the inconclusive struggle to define the gender order among Levantine Christians. While the Vatican worked diligently to impose a gender order that silenced religious women and relegated them to walled convents, the ripples of Hindiyya's life and project—amplified by later women—went on challenging and destabilizing that order well into the nineteenth century.

From her spiritually precocious childhood and after her lonely death in a convent high above the Mediterranean, Hindiyya al-'Ujaimi embodied a new religious fervor and movement that transgressed existing and imported strictures. She, along with other women and men, saw in the intimate and passionate embrace of Christ the means to renounce family and social expectations, to discard ecclesiastical rules, and to herald a new Christian era in Bilad al-Sham. In the midst of a world in flux materially and religiously, her divinely inspired and humanly motivated endeavors transformed the Maronite community, were integral to the religious modernization of Bilad al-Sham, and shaped the relationship between Levantine Catholics and the Vatican. In recounting Hindiyya's story, this book elucidates those changes and their meaning by tracing the intimate link between personal sentiments and political passions, between somatic experiences and abstracted knowledge, and ultimately between history and religion.

2

ALEPPO

The Making of a Visionary (1720–1746)

"On June 6th [1753] Sister Hindiyya, the mother superior of the Sacred Heart of Jesus convent, was summoned and asked about the names of her parents, her place of birth and her age . . . She answered, my father is called Shukralla and my mother Helena [they are] from Aleppo, and I am thirty-three years old which I complete on the Feast of Transfiguration."[1] It was a simple answer to the first question posed by the apostolic inquisitor, Fr. Desiderio di Casabasciana. He was delegated by the Vatican to determine whether Hindiyya was truly a visionary who mystically and physically communed with Christ or a woman deluded by the devil. Over the next ten days, in a stone and sparse room at the convent of Bkerki with three wooden chairs and a table at which sat Desiderio's secretary (Fr. Raymondo) recording the proceedings, Hindiyya answered 116 questions. At times, the scribe noted, she was visibly agitated and reluctant to answer, but for most of her testimony she appeared poised during those morning, afternoon, and evening sessions. The tone of questions and answers was, for the most part, straightforward, especially when contrasted with the emotionally ridden textual rendering of her journey into mystical union with Christ and her second inquisition in 1778. There was almost a routine aspect to Desiderio's questions and Hindiyya's answers, or at least a shared understanding of the boundaries and language of a religious inquisition. Together, her answers delineated a sequence of secular and spiritual events that began with her birth in Aleppo and ultimately brought her to that room on top of a mountain in Lebanon, overlooking the Mediterranean.

But like her first answer, all her responses were abridgements of an expansive and intricate set of events that had earned Hindiyya years of notoriety and fame, support and animosity, and on June 6 the inquisitorial gaze of the Vatican.

On the surface, this inquisition tells an inexorable tale of one young woman's religious devotions, visions, prayers, asceticism, struggles against her sins, and, most critically, visions of, and tangible encounter with, Christ. However, in looking through her answers to the scaffolding beneath, we begin to see a larger story populated by Jesus, patriarchs and priests, merchants and missionaries, family and community. Her hagiography and *Sirr al-Ittihad* (*Secret of the Union*), the autobiographical account of her mystical union with Christ, recount similar teleological narratives, albeit with different emphases and very different language.[2] Certainly, the nature of these documents lends itself to selectivity as they aim to smooth out the wrinkles of a complex life into a saintly linearity. In fact, to varying degrees all of these texts are fraught with a tension that reflected the contradictions which coursed through Hindiyya's life in Aleppo and beyond. On the one hand, we read of a woman who was enthralled with visions of her "beloved" Jesus and who ultimately wanted nothing but to be evermore in his presence. Yet she was deeply uncertain and burdened by a vocation that was at extreme odds with her prescribed role as a young Aleppan woman and that drew the ire and ridicule of family and acquaintances. Publicly she was expected to behave in a manner becoming of the elite status of her family and of the expectations placed upon her as a young woman growing up in such an environment. Privately, she increasingly wanted nothing to do with the secular trappings of wealth or the social life of the comfortable elites as she sought a closer relationship and knowledge of Christ. Hindiyya was thus torn between living as a bourgeois Aleppan and living as a visionary Christian. Her very personal dilemma was born out of two crosscurrents that tugged at her throughout her life in Aleppo: the secular life and materialistic mores of an emergent Christian elite in Aleppo and a religious revivalism stoked by Latin missionaries and local clergy. Caught in the middle, Hindiyya found it increasingly difficult to conceal or sustain her private struggles, and ultimately she had to make a public choice between the two.

Question 1: She Was Asked about Her Parents . . .

We begin where Hindiyya started her story. She was born in Aleppo on July 31, 1720, and baptized on August 6 of that same year. (In her answer she had stated that she was born on August 6. This could have been a lapse in memory, a conscious effort to sanctify her birth by associating it with the Feast of Transfiguration—one of the most important celebrations in the Eastern rites—or perhaps an allusion to what she may have considered her true birth: baptism.) Her given name was *Hindiyya*, literally "Indian woman." Her aunt seems to have been rather unhappy with such a name, especially since when coupled with the family name, 'Ujaimi (or "little Persian"), it became less a name and more a description of a motley origin: the Indian Persian woman. Thus, the aunt insisted that Hindiyya's baptismal name should be *Hanneh* (or *Anne*), a name particularly popular in the Christian West. However, this attempt at occidentalizing her niece did not work as she was known to everyone henceforth as Hindiyya and she herself insisted on using that name exclusively.[3] Why her parents would name her so is not clear (although such foreign location names were not uncommon in Aleppo, a city of traders); but for those who believed in her this appellation became a link to her authentic "Eastern" roots, and for those who derided her it offered another way to implicate her in nefarious behavior as a dark woman with a dark name.[4]

She was one of ten children (only four of whom survived into adulthood) born to her mother, Helena Hawwa, and her father, Shukralla 'Ujaimi, who were both members of the Maronite elite in the city. Like so many other Maronites who migrated to the city in the second half of the seventeenth century, her mother's ancestors had come there from the northern mountains of Lebanon. One Jesuit missionary, Père Boisot, remarked on this migratory movement. Writing in February 1686 to Girardin, the French ambassador to Istanbul, Boisot noted,

> Around fifty years ago, the Maronite Christians did not constitute but a small number [of the population] in Aleppo. For worship services they only needed a small room next to the Armenian Church [the Church of Forty Martyrs] which seated no more than 40 or 50 people. However, that nation has grown a great deal with the arrival of large numbers

2. View of Aleppo, 1703. Courtesy of the National Library of Israel, Eran Laor Cartographic Collection, Shapell Family Digitization Project and The Hebrew University of Jerusalem, Department of Geography, Historic Cities Research Project.

of [Maronites] who come from Mount Lebanon with their families to Aleppo, where they work diligently in various professions and in silk and today they number more than 4,000 souls.[5]

An event which took place in Aleppo in 1695 confirms Boisot's observation. In that year the Maronite community split over who would be the bishop of the city. The two parties were known as "Ehdenis" and "Bsherranis"—the two names referred to rival towns in north Lebanon, an indication of the origin and enduring connection of Aleppo's Maronites.[6]

We do not know for certain why Hindiyya's great-grandparents and their family left Mount Lebanon for Aleppo, but it is very likely that their personal reasons were similar to those of many others from the same area who were escaping overpopulation, hardships, and deprivations and seeking a better life. During the sixteenth and seventeenth centuries the Maronite population of northern Lebanon grew to such an extent as to promote migration out of the area south toward the central parts of Lebanon and east toward Aleppo. In addition to population pressures exerted on an area of limited resources, the political situation in Mount Lebanon in the seventeenth century was rather tumultuous. Reading the chronicle of the Maronite patriarch Istifan Duwayhi, *Tarikh al-Azmina,* one can understand the desire to leave the villages of northern Lebanon. The traditionally Maronite north appears to have been constantly in the grip of one crisis or another during the 1600s. For example, Duwayhi wrote that in 1644 Pasha al-Arnaout was deposed from Tripoli, but the new governor quickly "followed in the footsteps of al-Arnaout, and he took from the subjects [taxes], far beyond the limit and he treated them unjustly, and so they left [the area] because of oppression and maltreatment."[7] Fifteen years later, in 1659 and well into 1660, the pashas of Damascus, Tripoli, Sayda, Beirut (al-Arnaout—a political survivor if ever there was one—had relocated there), Safad, and Jerusalem brought their combined military forces together against the princes and *shuyukh* of Mount Lebanon, leaving a great deal of destruction in the wake of their military campaign. In 1661 an outbreak of plague "killed many and spread despair among the Christians who were afraid of an increase in oppression [from the authorities]."[8] Starting in 1675, the Hamadeh clan, a local Shi'a ruling elite, fell out of favor with the pasha of Tripoli over tax collection because the pasha suspected the Hamadeh family of withholding money from him. In the ensuing confrontation, which lasted over nine years, the Hamadeh clan and their followers fought the pasha's forces across the northern part of Mount Lebanon, destroying crops and homes and killing many of the local Christians in the process.[9] Matters became so desperate for the Maronites of northern Lebanon that even their patriarch, the very same chronicler Istifan Duwayhi, had to leave his patriarchal seat and seek safety farther south. Maronite notables gathered together then and threatened to leave the country if things did not improve. They did not get better for another ten years.[10] If all of this were not enough, Duwayhi peppers his chronicle with a seemingly endless list of disastrous weather, locust, plague, cholera, and other sundry pests and pestilences of biblical proportions. The wonder is not so much why Hindiyya's ancestors left Lebanon but rather why anyone would want to remain there. Of course, such condensed and selective chronicles focus, by sensational necessity, on the calamities of the time. Nonetheless, the reality of periodic hardships made life in the villages economically difficult, if not untenable, at the time.

If it is understandable why the Hawwas would wish to leave northern Lebanon, there remains the question of why they chose Aleppo, a city some two hundred miles north and east of them—a significant distance on foot or donkey. For the Hawwas, as well as for other Christians and Jews who came to and stayed in Aleppo, the city provided an abundance of commercial ventures and a relatively stable and secure government.[11] Trade and caravans from Iran, India, Anatolia, and Europe came together in its caravansaries and khans, and its markets were filled with products from east and west. Pedro Teixeira, a Spanish sojourner, in 1605 described the European trade with Aleppo. He noted that just the hire of camels for the transport of goods between Aleppo and the port city of Alexandretta "comes to eighty thousand sequins, worth about ninety thousand ducats; a sum which I should doubt if I had not made up the account thereof minutely with certain gentlemen there, to make sure of my matter."[12] He further notes that the English factory employed ten merchant families and traded up to 300,000 ducats worth of goods annually, while the French factory had even more merchants and their trade amounted to 800,000 ducats.[13] But by far the Venetians had the largest trade in this early period, exchanging woolen cloth, silk, and brocade for raw silk, indigo, spices, and pistachios produced in Aleppo and points farther east. In total, this trade was worth one and a half million ducats each year.[14] About eighty years later, in 1683, the French consul in Aleppo, Laurant D'Arvieux, estimated that the trade between Aleppo and the British had increased twentyfold and was close to six million livres, while France was importing at the time goods from the city worth one million livres.[15] It was not simply the Europeans who found this trade—even with its ups and downs—a profitable venture. In 1645 Muhammad Nasir, an Indian merchant based in Aleppo, was involved in commercial transactions between India, Aleppo, and Venice that amounted to almost 120,000 *ghurush* and, according to Bruce Masters, "dwarfed anything registered by either European or Iranian merchants in the seventeenth century."[16] In short, Aleppo had become by the middle of the seventeenth century a prominent trading center where fortunes, or at the least a decent living, could be made.

Commercial opportunities in Aleppo were accentuated—and cemented—by privileges newly acquired in the seventeenth century. After 1675 the commercial treaties signed between European powers and the Ottomans allowed for the employ of local Christians as translators (*dragomans*) for the European merchant houses based in the empire.[17] In Aleppo, as elsewhere, this provided local Christian agents with the added legal and economic benefits of extraterritoriality. As European power and influence grew within the Ottoman Empire during the eighteenth century, those associated with French, British, or Italian consuls and ambassadors became more influential politically and economically in their towns and cities. In Aleppo, the dragomans came to constitute their own social class, who wore a "pretentious fur cap" to symbolize their distinct status and who even refused to pay their share of the community's taxes despite threats of ecclesiastical excommunication.[18] Competition for these socially influential and financially lucrative positions became criminal in at least one instance, when Yusuf Dib instigated the arrest of another "Aleppan merchant working as Dragoman for the Levant Company."[19] Coupled with greater and relatively faster access to European markets, these new privileges not only attracted an increasingly larger number of Maronites but also translated into the rise of many wealthy Maronite families across the eighteenth century.[20] It was in this manner that the Hawwa family became one of the wealthy households in the Maronite community of Aleppo by the time Hindiyya was born in 1720. For instance, Hindiyya's maternal cousin was a "turjman [dragoman] . . . [and] one of the elites of the city."[21] Her own social circle included the "wives of notables like the wives of the Pasha, the franj [Europeans] and dragomans."[22] Her father, Shukralla 'Ujaimi, a merchant himself, was obviously successful enough for the Hawwas to allow him to marry Helena.

This sudden—at least relative to the slower-paced life in villages left behind—wealth brought about notable changes in the material culture and social mores of some of the elites, including Hindiyya's own family. Homes of the wealthy merchants of Aleppo became bigger, more ornate, and more

3. Maronite Elite Woman of Aleppo from Alexander Russell, *The Natural History of Aleppo*, vol.1 (London: G. G. and J. Robinson, 1794). Courtesy of the Otrakji family collection at www.mideastimage.com.

lavishly furnished. For instance, the house where Hindiyya grew up sat somewhere in the northwestern suburb of Saliba al-Jdaydeh, a predominantly Christian neighborhood which, along with seven other *mahallat* (or locales), constituted the Christian district of Aleppo.[23] Houses there were bought and sold for thousands of piasters, while dwellings in the poorer neighborhoods were valued at 84, 87, and 132 piasters during the 1750s.[24] The 'Ujaimi house was typical of those occupied by the Christian bourgeoisie, with apartments richly appointed, especially in China and carpets "to rival those of the [Ottoman Pasha's] Seraglio."[25] Clothes became equally luxuriant, displaying in colors, material, and style the newfound wealth and access to the finest products of Iran, India, and Istanbul. The affluence of this relatively cosmopolitan city loosened the bonds of secular and religious traditions among the Christian elites of Aleppo, and women and men began to distinguish themselves through a conspicuous display of material culture. Alexander Russell, a British "physic" living in Aleppo during the 1740s, observed that "Christian ladies are extravagant in the article of dress which only varies in a few circumstances from the Turkish fashion."[26] Here, he was making a reference to the Ottoman local elites, who adorned themselves with furs, elaborate headdresses, silk trousers, necklaces, rings, ankle bracelets, henna for the hands and feet, and kohl for the eyes. Hindiyya's hagiographer—perhaps hyperbolically intending to accentuate the modesty of his charge—spoke equally of gold, pearls, and elegant clothes as some of the fineries enjoyed by Christian women in Aleppo and which Hindiyya rejected.

Some Maronite and Melkite ecclesiastical authorities noted these and, from their perspective, even more troubling trends. For instance, in 1697 the Melkite deacon Jirjis bin Safarshah wrote a long list enumerating the sins of the Aleppans, which included "drunkenness . . . consumption of opium . . . [and] emulation of their non-Christian neighbors." In a letter to the Maronite community in Aleppo dated 1709, Patriarch 'Awad in turn exhorted his "flock" to return to modesty in dress for their women, and he ascribed the "Muslim persecution" of Christians to the scandalous behavior of the women in the community.[27] These clerical chastisements were not overly effective as some Aleppans either ignored them or even ridiculed their puritanical tones. One of the parishioners of the Melkite deacon satirized the long list of sinful behavior by adding to it the following: "He who eats breakfast, lunch and dinner has sinned. He who drinks water if he is thirsty has sinned. If a person feels sleepy and goes to bed, he has sinned. If he sleeps without his shoes he has sinned. If he is asked a question and he answers then he has sinned."[28] Another indication of the uneven impact of these admonitions is the fact that they had to be repeated throughout the eighteenth century and well into the following one.[29] Jirmānūs Hawwa, ordained bishop of Aleppo in 1804 and a cousin of Hindiyya, fulminated in a letter to the "people of our parish" about the "sins of the Christians," which have brought upon them the vengeance of God. Bishop Hawwa dedicated the greater part of the letter to his diktats for the behavior of the women and girls in the Aleppo diocese. Among other things, he stressed that

> girls must not cut their hair into bangs and side-burns at all, not even the very young amongst them, so that the girl can be distinguished from the married woman. . . . The braids should not be more than seven whether it is for the girl or woman. . . . Women and girls must not wear *qanabiz* [plural of *qinbaz,* a long-sleeved garment open in front and fastened by a belt] at all but rather dresses that must not be transparent or unlined, and they must not wear loose open sleeves but rather small and buttoned ones . . . women and girls must not wrap fancy scarves around their necks, and they must not make [and wear] transparent veils.[30]

It would appear from the other matters which he prohibited that few, some, or many women were in the habit of wearing perfume on the street; that they were remarkably loud and visible on the streets of Aleppo during funerals and weddings; and that they made use of every holiday and occasion to break out into public festivities.[31] This rupture of propriety seems also to have occurred in the relations between men and women. Social boundaries keeping the two apart, except within the family, were being actively circumvented or passively ignored. One observer noted, for instance,

> Some [Christians] (particularly of the Maronites) have deviated from this custom, and adopting the use of tables, chairs, and service in the European style, not only make the female part of the family sit down with them at meals, but permit them occasionally to appear before the Europeans, whom they entertain at their houses.[32]

More drastically, "the crime of incontinence is more frequent among the Christian youth . . . than among the Turkish. The sexes, in common life, are not so strictly separated, and caution is lulled by the use of strong liquors, while the passions are inflamed."[33] A poem by the Maronite bishop Jirmanus Farhat (dated 1718) admonishes parents to keep tighter control of their children, who by keeping bad company are led astray and in danger of being corrupted by fornication (zina). One need not accept the exaggerated aspects of these alarmist discourses to allow that the socioeconomic transformation of Aleppo had generated anxieties about the changes in social mores and behavior. Another marker of the growth in material comfort and its impact on Aleppan society is to be found in food. Within the household and at public banquets, tables were larger and spread with a greater variety of food than ever before. Alexander Russell dedicated some thirty pages in total to the topic of food in Aleppo. On one of those pages he described a typical lunch for a merchant in the city. "The dishes are brought up covered, and set down in the middle of the table, one at a time in succession; the whole amounting to twenty to thirty dishes."[34] While the poorer inhabitants of the city lived on a daily fare of some four to five dishes, the wealthy could choose from over 130 different recipes to satisfy their burgeoning desire and girth. Hindiyya certainly had access to this comfortable bourgeois life, replete with material luxuries and social opportunities. At her maternal cousin's wedding she was bedecked "with fine textiles, gold and pearls as was the custom of the country."[35] At the picnic for the wives of the pasha, European residents, and the dragomans "delicious and expensive foods, drinks and perfumes were offered."[36] One anonymous hagiographer wrote that when she was thirteen years of age she donned a necklace made of large squares of gold strung together to upstage her sister, Marie, who wore a smaller necklace.[37] In short then, one gets the impression that some among the Aleppan elites were making use of their good fortunes to carry on a bacchanal existence.

Question 3: She Was Asked If She Had at That Time Knowledge of God . . .

Hindiyya was not one of them. From an early age—we are told by various sources—she began to turn her back on such things of the world, and increasingly she came to focus on matters of the spirit. (She obviously had moments of weakness, as with the necklace episode.) In describing her youth to Fr. Desiderio, Hindiyya said that when she was only three years of age she would "hide in a corner of the house and kneel looking up at the sky" in prayer. She added in answer to a subsequent question, "I remember that I did not have then knowledge of God, but I did these things naturally and because God wanted that."[38] While there may have been an innate—"natural"—desire in her soul to know God at such a tender age, it was also the case that she was kneeling amid a spiritual revivalism that had been going on for a century and that was transforming Aleppo and its Christian communities in profound and intimate ways. In many striking ways, this was the counterpoint to the worldliness so evident in Hindiyya's surroundings. Driving this religious effervescence and upheaval were two main, and at times clashing, factors. One was the arrival of Latin missionaries assiduously (and at time aggressively) seeking to align the Maronite Church more closely with the Vatican and to bring other Aleppan Christian sects into the fold of the Roman Catholic Church. Another was the rise of a vibrant and confident local religious culture that sought to Arabize Christianity even as it Christianized Arabic. This movement was catalyzed by the vigorous example and activities of Latin missionaries, financially supported by the rising fortunes of the Christian community in Aleppo, and peopled with graduates of the Maronite College in Rome as well as intellectuals and literati who studied with local Muslim professors. Hindiyya's fervent supplications to God and her growing devotion to Christ were, at least in part, promoted and shaped by these religiocultural currents.

By the seventeenth century Aleppo had become a proselytizing center for Latin missionaries in the region. The Lesser Friars of the Holy Land came to Aleppo in 1571, followed by the Capuchins and the Jesuits in 1625, and finally the Carmelites in 1627. This sudden increase came about in part because of the rising influence of France within the Ottoman Empire in the wake of the Capitulations, or the series of treaties that provided broader privileges than ever before to the French and their protégés. While the first of these broad treaties was concluded in 1535 during the reign of Süleyman the Magnificent, it underwent several iterations over the years that increasingly gave French consuls and merchants (as well as their British and Austrian counterparts in parallel treaties) more rights. Among

4. Jesuit Missionary, Levant. From the Otrakji family
collection at www.mideastimage.com.

these was the right of Latin missionaries to serve the European communities and to proselytize in the Ottoman Empire. This was a privilege that
was vigorously defended and supported by a succession of French consuls
in Aleppo like Pierre D'Olivier (1630–1631), Ange de Bonin (1639–1642),
François Picquet (1652–1661), Marquis François Baron (1661–1667), and
Laurant d'Arvieux (1681–1689). Each of these consuls played a significant

role in establishing and safeguarding the Latin missions (especially those of the Jesuits) in Aleppo. For instance, when the first two Jesuit missionaries, P. Jean Stella and Gaspar Manillier, arrived in Aleppo in August 1625, the Venetian consuls worked diligently (along with the Greek Orthodox prelates) to expel the missionaries from Aleppo. It appears that their efforts were successful, at least temporarily, as the Jesuit missionaries were forced to leave the city. Two years later, after a sustained campaign initiated by the king of France, Louis XIII, and carried out by the French ambassador to Istanbul and Consul D'Olivier, the Jesuits were able to come back to the city.[39] Twenty-five years later, the French consul to Aleppo, Picquet, continued this tradition of support by promising the Latin missionaries "to protect and help them with all his power."[40]

For the Vatican, the opening of Ottoman lands for missionary work and French political support were together a boon for its goal of bringing the Eastern churches back into the Catholic fold. In the wake of the Council of Trent (1545–1563), whose purpose was the defense of Catholicism from "heretics" and "schismatics," the Vatican redoubled initiatives directed at Eastern Christians. Apostolic delegates were sent to Ethiopia (1551), Egypt (1561, 1582), and Lebanon and Syria (1578). While these early delegations did not result in any unification between the Eastern churches and Rome, they did pave the way for more concerted efforts. These came about with the establishment of the Sacra Congregatio de Propaganda Fide, or Council for the Propagation of the Faith. At its foundation in 1622, Pope Gregory XV declared that

> The Holy Office of the Pope embraces all that could lead to the salvation of souls . . . it is for this that the Holy Church has adopted two means of proceeding, one is judicial for which we have set up the Holy Inquisition, and the other is moral, or more to the point apostolic, where we will continually dispatch Missions of laborers amongst the peoples who have the greatest need.[41]

With the creation of the Propaganda Fide the Vatican inaugurated a more vigorous missionary campaign that was intended, among other things, to bring into the Catholic fold of the Vatican the "heretical" Eastern Christians: Arabic-speaking Greek Orthodox and Jacobites.

These renewed and more systematic efforts bore fruit in Aleppo. Latin Catholic missionaries sent account after account to the Vatican describing a steady stream of men and women who joined the Roman Catholic movement. According to one estimate, three-quarters of the Suryani Christians had become Catholic by the end of the seventeenth century.[42] In a report sent by the Jesuits to the Propaganda Fide, they maintained that between five and six thousand individuals were taking communion from them in Aleppo by 1714.[43] Even though those reports were highly exaggerated, conversions were indeed taking place and sometimes, for the Orthodox prelates, in alarmingly large numbers. Thus, the Orthodox patriarchs of Constantinople, Jerusalem, and Antioch had to admit in a report sent to the Ottoman sultan that the majority of Melkites in Aleppo had become Catholic.[44]

Success was due to a variety of factors, some local and others pertaining to the nature of the new missionary work. The most notable of these—and really the most self-evident—is the fact that the missionaries came to Aleppo to proselytize. One Jesuit missionary, Père Nachhi, explained to the general of the Society of Jesus, "we did not come here [Syria] looking for our comfort" but rather to bring "salvation" to the benighted souls of heretics and schismatics.[45] To accomplish this, the Jesuits and other missionaries undertook a door-to-door campaign of spiritual education and exhortation. Alexander Russell noted, for example, that "the houses of the Maronites, and of the other Christians in union with the Romish church, are open to the Latin missionaries who regularly make their daily rounds in the Jideida [sic]."[46] Missionaries wrote letters to their superiors in Europe telling them how doors to homes in the villages of Mount Lebanon and the city of Aleppo have been opened wide to them. Frère Anselme de l'Annonciation, of the Carmelite order, exulted, "When we enter the homes of the Greeks, Armenians, Syrians and Nestorians . . . they receive us with a welcome that they do not show to their bishops, and not even their patriarchs."[47] Setting aside the triumphalist and self-congratulatory tone and purpose of this and many other similar letters, what emerges is the diligence of Latin missionaries in taking their work outside the confines of churches and into the most intimate quarters of the Christian communities. Moreover, bringing the gospel into the households of Christians in Aleppo reached those who had been until then excluded in large part from the public religious life of the community: women and girls. Latin missionaries considered this exclusion both a malady that "is worse than the plagues of Egypt"[48] as well as an opportunity to spread their version of the Catholic faith. Presaging nineteenth-century arguments that called for the "modernization" of womanhood through education, one Jesuit priest noted in 1652 that "women's lack of devotion and their extreme ignorance, which is notably greater than that of men, with regard to all that pertains to the mysteries of our religion, causes the loss of the youth."[49] Hindiyya and her family were among those who were influenced by this new missionary ethos and approach. She told the inquisitor Fr. Desiderio that three of her confessors were Latin missionaries. While she dismissively described the first as an "old Maronite priest," she recalled that the second confessor of "my father, and sisters and me was" a Franciscan priest, followed by Father John of the Lesser Friars of the Holy Land and, after the age of fifteen, a sequence of Jesuit priests.[50]

In his splendidly encyclopedic book *Les Chrétiens du Proche-Orient*, Bernard Heyberger describes such visits through the account of one missionary, the Carmelite Anselme de l'Annonciation.[51] Following the instructions of St. Ignace, Anselme would begin his visit by asking after the well-being of the family and if the children were praying to God. The children were then brought into the room, and he would have them make the sign of the cross and then teach them the Pater, Ave Maria, and Credo. He instructed them to obey their parents and their masters and admonished them not to steal, swear, talk with Muslims, or keep the company of bad children. Most importantly, he asked them to pray morning and evening. Then, holding the Crucifix, Anselme would proclaim "very briefly but fervently" to the family some fifteen acts which he had composed. Among other things, these included acts of faith, love of God, love of neighbor, hope, and contrition. If the family spoke to him of any difficulties they were facing, Anselme would take the occasion to counsel them and to edify them with examples of Christian faith and perseverance taken from the lives of European saints, which he claimed were very well received.[52] As gifts he would give them pious images and medallions, and he would leave behind pamphlets which he had translated into Arabic and copied by hand and that included exhortations about the mysteries of faith, the beauty of virtue, and the horror of sin.[53] These pamphlets were quite common, and all missionaries in Aleppo distributed them liberally among the faithful. For example, in 1652 Père Chezaud had either composed or translated over fifty of these pamphlets of faith and transcribed them all by hand.[54] It is very likely, since missionaries regularly visited the 'Ujaimi household, that Hindiyya had heard exhortations similar to those delivered by Anselme and sampled the contents of religious pamphlets through her parents or younger brother, Niqula (who himself joined the ranks of the Jesuits).

Schools were another tool of proselytism employed by all Latin missionaries in Aleppo. Practically every group of Latin missionaries set up a school in their residence or in a donated room, or they were able to teach at existing schools. The same and clearly indefatigable Carmelite Père Anselme de l'Annonciation "goes morning and evening into the public schools of the schismatics to teach catechism and Christian doctrine."[55] Equally, Père Queryot, a French Jesuit, was occupied every Saturday with teaching "over 70 students . . . Christian doctrine."[56] It was not only the Latin missionaries who established such schools. In 1682, Père Justinien de Tours, a Capuchin monk, wrote about a group of "around twenty-two or twenty-three Syrian and Armenian girls" who had taken on religious vows as seculars in Aleppo.

> They established a school for children, and taught them to read in Arabic and Armenian . . . but the main goal of these good religious women, in teaching the youth . . . was to teach them prayers, catechism, belief in God, obedience to the Church, and the manner after which they were to confess and take communion.[57]

Hindiyya may have been alluding to this establishment when she spoke about her grandmother walking her every morning to school. Beyond elementary education, selected Maronite and Melkite children from Aleppo (as well as Mount Lebanon) were sent to Rome to continue their education at the Maronite College (established in 1584) and Collegio Urbano (founded in 1627). Among those who attended the Maronite College was Hindiyya's cousin, Touma Hawwa.[58]

Augmenting these missionary approaches was the invigorated literary movement that was taking place in Aleppo between the 1650s and the latter part of the seventeenth century. This included the establishment of printing presses (a short-lived one in Aleppo and a more permanent one in Lebanon), refutations of Muslim and Eastern Christian critiques of Catholicism, and the translation of spiritual guidebooks and the lives of saints into Arabic. Among these was *Le guide du pécheur* by Louis de Grenade, which the Capuchins translated into Arabic around 1635;[59] the life of Teresa de Avila was rendered in Arabic by the Carmelites in 1662 and over twenty other spiritual works were translated by either Latin missionaries or Maronite clergy educated in Rome.[60] For instance, Father Butrus Tulawi, a Maronite cleric educated in Rome, translated into Arabic several spiritual guides and books including *Le miroir de l'âme, La vie monacale,* and *La vie de Ste Thérèse*. Finally, the Jesuits introduced the ideas and practices of the worship of the Sacred Heart of Christ (a concept they were intimately involved in promoting in France) into Aleppo by establishing a brotherhood of the Sacred Heart around 1695 and by translating *Chemin de la dévotion au coeur de Jésus* in Aleppo in 1724.[61] On the other hand, the printing press in Shuwayr (Mount Lebanon) produced a series of printed translations between 1734 and 1744 that were available in much greater circulation than the previous manuscripts.[62]

This overview is further substantiated by the list of publications which appeared in the seventeenth and eighteenth centuries in Arabic. The majority of translated works were meant to establish a narrowly defined normative practice of Christianity along the lines of Latin Catholicism, even as that practice was being spread among wider circles of Eastern Christians. Whether adapted by local authors, translated from European originals, or composed by missionaries, these works helped to establish a distinctive Christian identity. For Hindiyya, the comfortable circumstances of her parents along with the introduction of missionary schools in Aleppo provided the opportunity to learn how to read at least at a rudimentary level (but not write). Invariably, the texts she mentioned reading in her youth and later were religious. Growing up she would ask her brother Niqula to read aloud to her the Passion of Christ. Her companion Katerina noted in her deposition to Fr. Desiderio that she and Hindiyya would take turns reading from the translated tome *The Christian Perfection* by Alfonso Rodriguez (1532–1617).[63] Another formative work that she certainly knew about from her Jesuit confessor and chronicler, Père Antonio Venturi, was the Arabic translation of the biography of Marguerite-Marie Alacoque, a seventeenth-century French visionary who focused her religious energies and life on promoting the worship of the Sacred Heart of Jesus. Père Pierre Fromage, who lived in Aleppo from 1723 until his death in 1740, collaborated with Abdallah Zakher in translating this book into Arabic soon after its publication in France in 1729. These factors opened the mental and spiritual horizons of Hindiyya (and many other Aleppans) to a broader Christian world and experiences.

Beyond the written and spoken word, Hindiyya experienced Christianity visually in ways that were novel in terms of both content and availability. A few hundred yards from her house rested the Armenian Church of Forty Martyrs. Inside, on the north wall of the church, she would have beheld, during one of the various all-Christian processions that passed through there, a large painting (14.5 by 12.5 feet) entitled *The Final Judgment*. This imposing piece of religious art was completed in 1708 by Ne'meh al-Musawwir (Ne'meh the Painter) and his son Hanania. Both, along with the grandfather Yusuf and the grandson Girgis, constituted four generations of Aleppan artists who collectively produced more than one hundred pieces of iconographic art between the 1650s and the end of the eighteenth century. Executed with bright colors interlaced with gold, *The Final Judgment* is arresting in its depiction of a serene and gentle Christ below whom are ranged in two rows the fathers of the church and female saints amid clouds. Beneath these saintly figures is the mass of humanity being guided either by angels into paradise or far more evocative devils into hell.[64] However, visual portrayal of religious themes was not limited to churches as wealthy Christian elites were able to purchase painted icons for their private residences. For instance, Hindiyya recounted being moved to tears by a painting of baby Jesus with St. Anthony of Padua. Antonio Venturi also noted in his hagiography that her father, Shukralla, was particularly fond of a painting of the Virgin Mary holding Christ.[65]

In addition to religious iconography, Christianity was represented to the inhabitants of Aleppo through a theater of sorts. Following the baroque model of public piety prevalent in Europe, some missionaries organized public processions through the streets of Saliba al-Jdaydeh. On Christmas of 1668 the Carmelite Justinien de Neuvy choreographed a procession "led by an acolyte burning incense around the cross carried by a child dressed as an angel [who was] between two other children each carrying a taper. They were followed by images of Christ and the Virgin carried on banners, and then [came] the Armenian chanters accompanied by musical instruments."[66] Religious confraternities also paraded around town in various commemorations. As early as 1638 the confraternity of the Immaculate Conception was established by Maronites in Aleppo and that of the Rosary was founded by the Jesuit Michel Nau in 1679, and both sponsored annual processions. In 1701 one observer noted that every first Sunday of each month the image of the Virgin was carried with throngs of Christians following her around the square, where the four churches of Jdaydeh were located.[67] While we do not know for certain whether Hindiyya had witnessed any of these processions, it would seem quite likely that at some point or another she must have encountered such public demonstrations of piety.

Finally, a local cultural revival was creating a rejuvenated and Arabized model of Christian belief and piety which paralleled—and at times competed with—the Latin missionary movement. The list of individuals who formed this early Nahda includes, among others, Istifan Duwayhi, Butrus Tulawi, Jibrail Hawwa, Abdallah Qara'li, Yusuf al-Sharabati, Jirmanus Farhat, and Abdallah Zakher.[68] Practically all were members of the Maronite or Melkite clergy. Emblematic of the formation, career, and impact of these and other intellectuals is Jirmanus Farhat. He, like Hindiyya, was born in Saliba al-Jdaydeh in 1670 to a wealthy merchant Maronite family; and he spent the rest of the seventeenth century in Aleppo. There, he studied theology, philosophy, and history with Bulus Tulawi in the Maronite *madrasa,* a school established in 1668 by Istifan Duwayhi along the lines of the Maronite College in Rome. As a result of the revival of classical Arabic among the Christian community, Farhat studied with two Arabic teachers, one of whom was Maronite (Yusuf al-Dibsi) and the other Muslim (Shaykh Sulayman the Grammarian). While Farhat did receive some education in Latin and Italian, it is Arabic which captured his imagination and became the vehicle and subject of his literary career. Well educated in Arabic poetry, he composed poems inspired by such luminaries as the Persian philosophers Ibn Sina (known in the West as Avicenna; d. 1037) and al-Suhrawardi (d. 1191), adapting the tradition thematically to treat the baptism of Christ, sin, the human soul, and "the search for redemption through faith and the Virgin Mary."[69] This pattern of using Arabic—hitherto an "Islamic" language—instead of Syriac—long considered the Christian liturgical language—to write religious and secular works continued throughout his long career. Early in his clerical career, Farhat employed Arabic as a tool of translation, transmitting European Christian thought and ideas for local consumption. For instance, he translated Alfonso Rodriguez's *The Christian Perfection,* the book which Hindiyya read with her companion Katerina. Later in his life he took to writing his own works, which included poetry, grammar books, a dictionary, history, and—especially after he became bishop in Aleppo in 1725—religious treatises. Among these latter books we find liturgies (*Liturgy for the Mass in Celebration of the Eucharist*), sermon guidebooks (*Fasl al-Khitab fi Sina'at al-Wa'az*), and Catholic Christian polemics against Eastern Christian and Muslim critics. Farhat's long list of achievements, along with those of other Maronite and Melkite intellectuals, adds up to a prodigious production, which augmented missionary work in promoting a Christian consciousness and discourse. That it did so in Arabic only accentuated its "authenticity" as a counterpoint to the Latinization efforts on the part of missionaries.

It is hard to tell exactly what impact these various religious currents had on Hindiyya. But what we can surmise with a great deal of certainty is that she grew up in an environment thick with religious fervor, discourse, and symbolism, which in turn were focused on a novel representation of Christianity. While in Eastern churches the notion of redemption was focused on Christ's conquest of death through resurrection, the new model of Latinized Christianity focused on the suffering and sacrifice of Christ on the Cross. Unlike Western Catholicism, Eastern churches did not have hymns (like "Stabat Mater") that embodied the agonies of the trek along the Via Dolorosa, nor did they have stations of the Cross, flagellations, or passion plays. In contrast to Eastern Orthodoxy, Latin

Christianity insisted upon and emphasized the humanity of Christ even as it introduced a personal piety centered on spiritual contemplation and aspiration to be Christ-like. What is also patently evident is that this was a Christianity which demanded a great deal of effort and commitment on the part of the penitent. Fasting along with occasional church attendance—the means by which most Eastern Christians proclaimed their faith—were not satisfactory in the eyes of Latin missionaries who worked diligently to redefine Christianity in Aleppo—and beyond—as the perpetual struggle against sin, or the "natural" state of people. Confession, communion, prayer (and a great deal of it), learning the proper faith through books and pamphlets, joining confraternities, abstention from material indulgence—these were spiritual exercises to promote a stronger individual faith and Christian community. Certainly, not all Aleppan Christians listened to or even accepted these pronouncements at face value. As will emerge later, the missionary project was repeatedly contested and reshaped by local interests and counterprojects, and even some missionaries and European observers were rather hesitant about some of its aspects. Other Aleppans simply ignored local and missionary exhortations to be "better Christians."

Yet this rich and heady religious brew did lead to conversions to Catholicism, to a plethora of religious publications, to the establishment of confraternities, to the expansion of churches and increase in their endowments, and to the rise of a vibrant male and female monastic movement. Among those who were apparently moved—to some extent at least—by the new brand of Christianity were close relatives of Hindiyya. First, there was her mother's uncle, Jibrail Hawwa, who left Aleppo at the end of the seventeenth century to return to Mount Lebanon, where he, along with two other Aleppan priests, established the first Lebanese monastic order. Following in his footsteps was his nephew and Helen's cousin, Touma Hawwa, who traveled to Rome and enrolled in the Maronite College in 1729.[70] Closer to home, Hindiyya's brother Niqula ran away from home when he was in his teens, joined the Jesuit order, and became a priest— something that his parents tried to discourage him from doing since he was the only surviving boy.[71] The parents themselves were devout Christians. One of Hindiyya's hagiographers wrote that her father, Shukralla, was "a model for his time and town, and even the priests themselves were chastised by him" (presumably because he behaved more devoutly than they did).[72] Hindiyya also noted that "my mother would call me in the middle of the day and make me say these prayers, and she also made me say them at night at bedtime."[73] Even putting aside the romanticized retrospective of these statements, we are still left with the fact that within the larger material tendencies of Aleppan Christian elites, Hindiyya grew up in a cocoon of religious enthusiasm and practice.

Question 54: She Was Asked Whether She Saw Jesus Christ in This Vision . . .

Thus, while Hindiyya may have had a "natural" longing for God at the age of three (unlikely though that seems), the religious fervor suffusing her life certainly promoted and sustained her journey toward Christ. In this she was part of a religious revivalism, which took many forms and attracted a number of adherents. But what is remarkable about her particular experience is that her spiritual passage took her first beyond the secular and religious norms of her society and then across the ecclesiastical boundaries set by the Vatican and its Latin missionaries. In other words, her transgressions turned her private spiritual yearnings into a public political crisis. And it all began with her kneeling in a corner of the house looking up at the sky and searching for God. In response, she came to see, hear, touch, and converse with Christ—a gift that propelled her from the ranks of the devout into being a visionary.

The object of Hindiyya's attraction to prayer and contemplation came into greater focus when her mother, Helena, began to instruct her in Christian dogma at the age of five. Among the things she explained to her daughter was the dual nature of Christ as a perfect god and man, the Immaculate Conception, and his atonement for humanity—an emphasis that reflected more the perspective of the Western Catholic Church than that of the local Eastern Church. Perhaps more critically, Helena introduced Hindiyya to the idea that sin is what keeps people from the presence of Jesus on this earth and beyond. When Hindiyya was seven years of age, she began to ask her mother to "show me and introduce me to Jesus Christ . . . But my words made my mother laugh . . . and she said to me: Oh, my daughter, I am a sinner and so I cannot see him because those who commit sin cannot see Jesus Christ."[74] Hindiyya took this as a challenge. If, as the missionaries were teaching, Christ has a tangible presence, if he was both human and divine and not just a distant God, then she wanted to draw nearer to him. And if sin was what was keeping him hidden, then she wanted to abandon sin altogether for a glimpse of Jesus. Thus, she later told Fr. Desiderio, "I would see the other young girls playing and they would call me to join them in play and, despite my inclination to join them, I would refrain from that because I would say: this is not respectful of Jesus Christ."[75] The list of things that she construed as offensive to Christ grew longer after subsequent conversations with her mother. Either in that same year or a year later—the sources do not specify—Hindiyya asked her mother what God considers good or sinful behavior. Her mother, a "devout and goodly" parent as she is described in Hindiyya's hagiography, listed obedience and respect of parents and modesty at church and in prayer as matters pleasing in the eye of God. However, "roving eyes" or a first step toward transgression of sexual mores, joking, greed, and lying were among the various things that Helena instructed her daughter to avoid. Whether Helena obtained this list from the missionaries who frequented the house or from her attendance of Maronite church sermons is not clear. Either way, Hindiyya took this counsel to heart.

Hindiyya's early devotion to Christ bore fruit when Jesus appeared to her when she was eight years old.[76] She had in her room a picture of the Virgin Mary with infant Christ, and she would frequently kneel in front of it to pray "free of all restrictions." (Space and private time for contemplation were certainly privileges of wealth in a densely populated society.) During that year and after an especially fervent prayer, she saw Jesus move as if "he is a living human being looking at me with kindness and smiling. And I saw then that he was moving his head, eyes, mouth and hands as if he was really alive."[77] When Hindiyya first had this vision, she got up in fear and ran out of the room. One presumes that such a sight would have been disturbing at any age, yet it was also intriguing enough for her to seek solitude again and again in prayer beneath the same picture. As a result, Christ began to appear to Hindiyya on an almost daily basis for the following ten years. Once she overcame her initial fearful reaction,

Hindiyya was to experience an even more amazing vision. The second time that Jesus appeared to her, he not only moved but also spoke, saying "Hindiyya, do not be afraid, do you not love me?" It is a curious question that combines thesis and antithesis in an economy of words. The first part clearly establishes Christ as a supernatural and divine power who can frighten—among other things—a mere mortal like Hindiyya. Yet it is quickly followed with a question that exudes puzzlement or uncertainty, either of which undermines the magisterial condescension of the first phrase. She answered that she loved him very much and she began to cry.[78] Thus began an intimate relationship between Christ and Hindiyya. It was a tentative start for a long and at times tortuous relationship, in which Hindiyya demurred as much as she acquiesced and Jesus threatened her as much as he comforted her soul. At its foundation was the love that Hindiyya espoused for Christ, who endowed her with this affection by his grace and who, from the tone of his question, appears to be soliciting her love. This circular relationship was evident in the remainder of the interaction described above. After she ceased to cry, Jesus asked her how much she wanted to love him and she answered, "As much as you want me to love you." Christ then responded by saying, "I will give you a great gift with which you can love me with your unlimited merit."[79] Absent from this circle of divine condescension, exchanged love, and human ascension is the rest of humanity—at least for the moment. The intimacy not only excluded family, missionaries, and all others but also gave Hindiyya a unique gift—promise of infinite and god-like love—thus setting her apart in more ways than one.

Extraordinary as the first vision was to Hindiyya, it was only the start of an almost daily visitation with Christ. Fr. Desiderio questioned—with some incredulousness—Hindiyya "about the multitude of these gifts . . . and whether they continued uninterrupted until she was seventeen years of age." Hindiyya responded without any hesitation or doubt—at least in what we can read from the text—that "Jesus Christ . . . would condescend to speak with me three or four time per day. But this was not always like this since some days he only spoke to me once or twice."[80] Appearing as a child five or six years of age, Christ endeavored to teach Hindiyya either through words or with his facial expressions. Their dialogue centered around Hindiyya and whether she was behaving in a manner becoming of one chosen by Jesus—for what was neither evident nor yet revealed to Hindiyya. In *Secret of the Union* Hindiyya wrote more explicitly about these encounters and their purpose. Describing this early part of her relationship with Jesus, she said,

> I would see Him, and He would teach me what to say and I learned from Him . . . and He would make me despise sin and explain to me what is sinful without speaking with me. Rather, it [learning about sin] was only by gazing upon Him as if beholding His body is a means to explain the nature of sin and its ugliness.[81]

This physicality and sensuality of spiritual learning and knowledge became a central trope in their relationship. Still, at other times Jesus addressed the same point orally. During one of the many hours she spent kneeling before another painting of Jesus on her wall (one that depicted Christ "bound and tied" to the Cross), Jesus appeared to her and chastised her for faltering. "He said to me: did I not tell you to avoid doing things which displease Me[?] why did you laugh a great deal today[.] This displeases Me and you should not do it again."[82] Difficult as this was for someone like Hindiyya, who had "a joyous character inclined to laughter," she still sought to exercise greater control to assure herself of Christ's favors.

For that purpose, restraining her behavior was not sufficient for Hindiyya, and she quickly moved on to disciplining her body. The intensification in her devotional practices was brought about by her first confession. Ever since the age of seven (1727) she desperately sought to confess her sins to the local Maronite priest, yet because he thought that she could not tell the difference between good and evil, he would not grant her that wish. When she turned eight, however, she went to confession for the first time, and "I felt inclined to love Jesus Christ even more intensely so I increased my efforts at prayer and I began to taste in it a pleasure I had not tasted before. And I began to take delight in mortification of the flesh."[83] Why confession should bring about such a decision she did not say. However, at the moment when she was first asked to do penance for her sins, Hindiyya apparently concluded that prayers were not sufficient. She started with "secretly" placing stones and pebbles in her bed and delighting in sleeping on them "even if they hurt me."[84] At other times, she would place "a plant with thorns the length of a finger" or a board with nails on her chest all day, drawing blood in the process. From there she moved to far more strenuous practices, which involved, among other things, a belt studded with iron needles that she would tighten around her waist "two or three days per week."[85] All of this was to experience, albeit in a humanly limited manner, the agony of Christ and, at the same time, the humanity of God. As Bynum notes, medieval female mystics "were not rebelling against or torturing their flesh out of guilt over its capabilities so much as using the possibilities of its full sensual and affective range to soar ever closer to God."[86] In this, Hindiyya was following the precepts of Paul, who wrote to the Romans, "Therefore, my friends, I implore you by God's mercies to offer your very selves to him: a living sacrifice dedicated and fit for his acceptance."[87] Hindiyya was also convinced that Christ wanted her to practice asceticism. While he never spoke to her regarding this matter, she "would notice that as I intensified my asceticism . . . Jesus would grow gentler toward me, and I would feel greater solace to know that he greatly approved of my asceticism."[88] More explicitly, she contended that "I would hear in my heart the voice of my master ordering me to practice this ascetism and how I was to carry it out."[89]

After her first confession, Hindiyya also tried to abstain from food on Friday, taking only bread and water. Her mother was distressed with such behavior and beseeched her to refrain from fasting. It was only after a priest intervened and commanded her to eat that Hindiyya obeyed, and then only begrudgingly. Abstaining from food, or at least attempts to do so, became a recurring theme in Hindiyya's early life and in her relationship with her mother. After her first communion at the age of eleven and at each partaking of the host after that, she shunned food because a fire "would be in my belly." This internal conflagration was caused by Hindiyya's belief in Christ's "real" presence in the host. (Transubstantiation was not a commonly held idea among the Eastern churches but rather a concept propagated by the post-Tridentine Catholic Church.) Her mother tried to force her to eat, and her sisters endeavored to make her speak; but "I could not swallow the food and I would spit it out," and I could "utter but few words."[90] She was lost in contemplation, reflecting on how

"Jesus Christ was incarnated and how He gave us, because of His great love for us, His holy body as nourishment for our souls in the secret of the Eucharist."[91] This scene became a recurring theme at the 'Ujaimi dinner table. Her siblings, with a strong hint of derision, would say that she never ate before consulting with Jesus first. When she could not prevail in her desire to abstain from food, Hindiyya took to throwing ash on all her food in order to deprive it of its ability to evoke a sensual response. In this Hindiyya was again quite similar to many European female saints, whose vitae are replete with the common theme of fasting and devotion to the Eucharist. As Grace Jantzen notes, "feasting, particularly eating the body and drinking the blood of Christ in the Eucharist, was central to women's piety."[92] Saints like "Margaret of Cortona, Angela of Foligno, Columa of Rieti, and Catherine of Genoa, for example, craved frequent reception and substituted the Eucharist quite explicitly for the food they denied themselves in long fasts."[93] And, just like Hindiyya, Catherine of Siena and Columba of Rieti lost their appetites for corporeal food after prayer or communion.[94]

Nonetheless, Hindiyya did not display the same intensity evident in these earlier female saints and mystics. Her fasting and rejection of food were neither overly consistent nor as passionately discussed as one finds in the biographies of some European religious women. She certainly did not approach the obsessive rejection of food displayed by Catherine of Siena, who survived on the Eucharist, cold water, and a few bitter herbs and who died emaciated and wracked by stomach pains.[95] Also absent is the imagery (in visions or dreams) of eating and drinking from the wounds of Christ or the "mother" Jesus, which was quite popular in European devotional literature.[96] Her descriptions of matters relating to food have an almost mundane and matter-of-fact quality to them, and they are wholly absent from *Secret of the Union,* while her Arabic hagiography simply mentions her abstention from "delicious foods." In the only surviving picture of her, a painting done by a priest and one-time supporter, we see a woman who is neither anorexic nor emaciated but rather fairly healthy. Thus, her fasting—a practice common enough within Eastern Christian communities—could not have been overly severe, at least not when the painting was rendered and if it was rendered faithfully. This is neither to negate her claims to fasting nor to underestimate its substantial or symbolic role in her life as a pious woman. Rather, it is simply to note that other ascetic practices were more prominent in her vita.

What dedication or passion may have been lacking in her pursuit (or simply the description) of fasting Hindiyya more than invested in blood-letting.[97] Fasting provided a somewhat indirect route to understanding and feeling the agony of Christ, the steps necessary toward communing with him. Bloodletting was far less ambiguous in sensual effect or meaning. For Hindiyya this ritual began when Christ appeared to her with "the Virgin and many angels . . . and he said to me . . . Hindiyya, my daughter, I want you to shed from your head as much blood as I have spilled from my agonies."[98] Three or four days later, while Hindiyya was contemplating "the mystery of the flogging [of Christ]," she was struck with "terrible pains." Angels and Christ appeared and "exhorted me and then Jesus Christ told me to extract in blood the same amount He shed in that mystery and the pains will leave me."[99] When her pains reached their climax and she could no longer sustain them, she asked "the women surrounding" her to bleed her; and after an initial hesitation, they did so, and she lost consciousness. Thereafter, Hindiyya reported bleeding herself or receiving help from others "many more times" than she could count, and every time she felt those "terrible pains." Her greatest concern was that this admonition to bleed her was coming from Satan and not Christ. But her confessor, Jesus, and her guardian angel all assured her that this commandment was divine and not devilish. An equally troublesome concern that she had was with exactitude in fulfilling Christ's wish. In other words, how much blood did Christ shed, how much did Hindiyya shed, and were they the same? In her estimate, she bled the equivalent of fifteen *ratl Halabi,* or slightly over six kilograms of blood, an alarmingly large amount even if the blood was extracted over a period of time. Christ would appear to her when she had extracted the "right" amount of blood and tell her that she had fulfilled his wish for that mystery and could turn her attention to other mysteries. Inherent in this repeated practice was the intimacy it generated between Christ and Hindiyya. In fasting Hindiyya rarely saw Christ, but during her phlebotomies he was ever-present, encouraging and guiding her toward the desired end. Moreover, while fasting was a generalized attempt at experiencing the bodily agony of Christ, bloodletting created a far more perfect symmetry between the experiences of Hindiyya and her beloved. First, the quantity of blood extracted was measured to be the same (or so she believed or said) as that of Christ. Such an emphasis and concern over exactitude was not incidental but rather must be seen as an attempt at the creation of similitude in experience. Moreover, and unlike most medieval European female saints and mystics, Hindiyya was not passively receiving the blood of Christ as nourishment but shedding blood like Christ. While she never claimed to be doing so on behalf of humanity, the process physically took away her "extreme pains." Later in her life, nuns close to Hindiyya would take away the blood and give it to penitents seeking solace and healing. In this manner, a common enough practice became the means through which Hindiyya came closer to Jesus by feeling a modicum of his agonies and experiencing the power of healing that the shedding of blood could bring to her and others.

To perpetuate and deepen this budding intimacy, Hindiyya constantly sought solitude—the most rare of luxuries in the crowded urban life of Aleppo. Yet it was a necessary way to spend more time with Christ and display her indifference to, and even alienation from, the world around her. Throughout her years in Aleppo she worked to escape people's attention and company. As with fasting, this was a process that entailed overcoming internal weaknesses and concomitant external pressures. By her own admission, Hindiyya was "inclined toward vanity," and her hagiographer describes her as "very beautiful."[100] From the perspective of eighteenth-century Catholic doctrine, both features represented obstacles to spiritual elevation because of their inherent sexuality. Thomas Aquinas, for example, whose writings were instrumental in shaping Catholic doctrine, contended that proximity to God could be achieved only through the intellect, a characteristic inherent in men and absent from women. The body, the anchor tying humanity down to earthliness and sin, was depicted as feminine. Thus, for Aquinas, woman "was an occasion for sin to man," causing him to fall into sexual passion and away from the contemplative practices which were the conduit to God.[101] Control of women's bodies became then a safeguard against temptation and sin, and Hindiyya seems to have accepted that notion. She began by shunning fine clothes and jewelry. "I disciplined my body . . . by avoiding beautiful and elegant clothes and by donning modest rough ones."[102] But sometimes she had to mollify her mother by wearing "expensive and elegant" clothes like the ones that her sisters wore. At her cousin's wedding (the dragoman), Helena forced Hindiyya to wear "fine clothes, gold and pearls as was the custom of the country." But despite her inability to refuse her mother's wishes, she managed to find a solitary place to pray, where she tucked the jewelry inside her clothes "out of respect for her bridegroom [Jesus]."[103]

In addition to seeking anonymity through plain clothes and unadorned appearance, Hindiyya tried—with mixed results again—to withdraw from her social milieu. Invariably, her episodes of solitude were undertaken in search of spiritual communion with Christ. As she told her inquisitor, at age three she sought a corner of the house in which to pray away from her family. Later, in her teen years, when the family would get together she would sit by herself speaking to "He whom her spirit loved." She was silent and withdrawn so often that "when she opened her mouth to speak she could barely utter a word."[104] Her silence must have appeared rather odd and inexplicable in a community where conversations were the constant lubricant of daily life. Social events that she was expected to attend became a burden she could hardly withstand. In one such incident,

> The wives of the Pasha, Europeans and dragomans, and others like them . . . prevailed on her mother [Helena] and the girl [Hindiyya] to accompany them to the gardens. So, she obeyed her mother and went along . . . in spite of herself, and as soon as everyone arrived at that happy spot, beloved by everyone as if it is paradise on earth, they began to present delicious foods, enchanting drinks and alluring perfumes. . . . When the virgin Hindiyya saw this, and instead of being uplifted, she felt as if it were a rotten prison and she began to cry and refused to sit down there. No one could change her mind, and her mother was forced to send her home. As soon as she arrived to the solitude [of her house] she found there comfort and happiness.[105]

Her proclivity for solitary reflection and existence only became more accentuated as she came of age and it was expected of her to engage in regular social intercourse. She "ran away from" women, strangers, and relatives alike who approached her. What compelled Hindiyya to journey further and further away from family and stranger alike was what brought her to her knees in the first place: the search for Christ. To her, the companionship of Christ—who "allowed me to kiss his hands and sometimes his feet . . . and who sometimes shook my hand, hugged me and kissed me several times"—seemed far more desirable than the social gatherings at her house.[106] In such company there was protection from sin, balm for the spirit, and a bodily ecstasy that only increased as she drew closer to Jesus.

In seeking to isolate herself from the world, Hindiyya was following a model of extreme piety deriving out of the traditions of Eastern Christianity. Starting with the early history of the church, austere and very secluded monasticism was first practiced in Egypt and Syria; and many of these early monastics were women.[107] More pertinently, Hindiyya had the example of St. Maroun, the founder and patron saint of Maronites. Istifan Duwayhi (who graduated from the Maronite College in Rome in 1655) gives us a glimpse of this example in a sermon he delivered while serving as the bishop of Aleppo in 1663 on the life of St. Maroun. Entitled "On Saint Maroun: He Was a Tower," Duwayhi recounted to his parishioners in the Notre Dame Maronite church of Aleppo how the saint renounced the body and the world in order to attain salvation. By retreating from the temptations of the world and its inhabitants, St. Maroun drew closer to God. Duwayhi concluded his sermon by speaking of three women, "Saint Tomanina the student of Saint Maroun, the pious mother of Marina [who herself was] the mother of Kura, all of whom were Aleppans," who followed St. Maroun's example and retreated from the world to dwell in the "wilderness."[108] It is likely that Hindiyya had come across stories of the early "mothers" of the church as well as a rendition of this sermon—in parts or as a whole—through stories that were passed around in the community. Setting aside plausible conjecture, we know that Hindiyya, on many of her visits to the Notre Dame church in Aleppo, had set eyes upon one of the most famous ascetic saints in Aleppo and beyond: St. Simon the Young, a disciple of St. Simon the Stylite.[109] Her hagiographer wrote how she would spend time gazing at his painting by Yusuf al-Musawwir. The painting depicted St. Simon sitting in a tall tower at the center of the tableau, with Christ appearing to his right from a circle of clouds to bless the saint. Secluded in his tower, he looms larger than any of the other figures at once physically distant from their world and yet linked to them as their benefactor, transmitting the grace of God to those beneath him figuratively and spiritually.[110] More immediate and tangible was the example of Hindiyya's uncle, Jibraīl Hawwa. In 1694 he—along with two other fellow Aleppan Maronites, Abdallah Qara'li and Yusuf al-Batn—left Aleppo and traveled in to the Qadisha valley, high in the mountains of Lebanon, to establish a reclusive monastic order.[111] Hence, the path away from the world was well paved by local predecessors and contemporaries as well as models of European pious women introduced through books and stories told by missionaries.

Question 57: She Was Asked If She Ever Disobeyed Her Mother . . .

If the road was clear, the journey itself was taxing. Fasting, self-mortification, and spiritual exercises were difficult in and of themselves at any age. Then there were the many moments of doubt when Hindiyya (as a child and as a young woman) was not sure whether she was really seeing Christ or simply imagining such encounters. What made matters worse were the responses Hindiyya's behavior elicited from those around her throughout her career as a visionary but quite notably during her life in Aleppo. When she engaged in self-starvation, contemporaries would have seen it as a most painful renunciation—or quite possibly a most foolish act from someone who had no need to go hungry. When she threw ash on perfectly fine food at the dinner table, she was robbing the symbol of its celebrated sensuality. When she turned her back on meals at home or feasts at weddings and picnics, she was standing aloof from a social ritual that was integral to the definition of Aleppo's elites. As Caroline Bynum argues in *Holy Feast and Holy Fast,* the repudiation of food was not looked upon by contemporaries as a sign of anorexia (as some historians have contended) but as the rejection of one of the most central aspects of social life.[112] Hindiyya's choice of plain and "rough" clothes stood out against the backdrop of refined fashions (following the designs of Istanbul). Silence in a loquacious society could be seen as a sign of pious modesty, but it was also construed as odd, rude, and unbecoming of a young woman. Disdaining conversation must have been viewed by some as inherently critical of both subject and participants, particularly as Hindiyya made it clear on repeated occasions that secular conversations led to sin. Collectively, then, Hindiyya's moments of transgression gave rise, intentionally or otherwise, to the paradox of her life in Aleppo (and beyond): in trying to be invisible, she became highly visible. The more she sought to retreat from daily life and her social environs, the more conspicuous she became by her physical absence and her abstinence from food and the material trappings of her family and class. And the closer she drew to Christ, the more she appeared—by intent, interpretation, or both—to be rejecting the norms and mores of her society. Therefore, family and strangers saw in Hindiyya's behavior a rejection of the roles assigned to women, a transgression of gender boundaries, and a criticism of their own lives.[113] The response of some was to try to contain her behavior through pressure to change or through ridicule and dismissal.

Hindiyya's mother was the first to be concerned by these transgressions. (We do not hear much about the father, and the few comments in the sources hint that he was either unconcerned with the affairs of Hindiyya or not the one in charge of the household.) From the perspective of Helena, Hindiyya's behavior was troubling on many levels. Helena certainly wanted to encourage modesty and piety in her children, but Hindiyya was overstepping the boundaries of "normal" religiosity into questionable, if not outright strange, territory. In her role as a mother she was probably very concerned with Hindiyya's abstinence from food and nourishment. On various occasions, after Hindiyya's communion when she would not eat but two or three spoonfuls of soup, Helena "would start crying" in frustration over her daughter's behavior.[114] But there was also the issue of authority and power within the rubric of the family. Hindiyya's search for the approval and love of Christ and insistence on a higher degree of modesty led her to two instances of outright filial disobedience—at least the ones that have been recorded in her hagiography. The first occurred when she was seven years of age, when her mother told her to "go sleep with my father as was the custom with young girls in this country."[115] Hindiyya refused. On a later occasion she would not walk to school with the male servant and insisted on having her grandmother walk her there instead. (The sources do not specify the reason behind her refusal, so we can only speculate that perhaps it was out of modesty in public or lack of trust in the servant.) In both cases, Hindiyya prevailed, but her hagiographer was quick to point out that these were isolated cases in the life of a most obedient child who obeyed "her mother blindly and who would do anything her mother told her without argument."[116] For us, these two incidents highlight the first of many choices that Hindiyya had to make between her earthly and sublime obligations. For a child who "trembled whenever her mother spoke to her" and a mother who "liked to raise her children in an ideal manner, that is she openly scolded her daughter Hindiyya but loved her secretly,"[117] these moments were among the first of many tests of wills. As a strict disciplinarian who made Hindiyya tremble in fear, Helena certainly does not appear as the kind of person to brook opposition from her children. While we do not know the exact details of how Helena reacted to Hindiyya's bouts of disobedience (beyond crying at times), it is clear that she was displeased enough to force her daughter to eat, attend social events, and dress in a certain way. Moreover, the fact that Hindiyya sought to hide her devotions to, and visions of, Christ from her mother "until I was about 20 years of age" indicates that she expected Helena to disapprove and dissuade her from such behavior; and she only felt utterly free in her vocation after her mother passed away. Indeed, the one time Hindiyya mentioned her visions of Christ to her mother, the latter's reaction was rather negative, to say the least. Hindiyya mentioned in *Secret of the Union* that after she had first seen Christ, "I ran away crying. When my mother saw me in this state, frightened, shaking and crying, she asked me 'what happened to you?' I answered her, 'Mother, I saw a person and I love him very much but I am afraid of him when he speaks with me.' So she rebuked me and hit me."[118] Given Helena's stern reaction—to what she clearly perceived to be Hindiyya's encounter with a man—Hindiyya never broached the subject again.

For Helena and the two other daughters in the family (Marie, who was the oldest, and Marguerite, who was the ninth of ten children[119]), it was other people's perception of Hindiyya that must have been equally disturbing. Within the larger city of Aleppo, the 'Ujaimi family lived in a small community of Maronite merchants and dragomans that could not have surpassed a few hundred people. In such a tightly knit community, little could remain private. Hindiyya's devout Christianity, attire, and anti-social behavior quickly brought the family public attention and scrutiny. Her hagiographer wrote that many sought to meet her once they heard of her "saintly" behavior, elites "offered a great deal of money to see her," and one priest boasted of having heard her confession once.[120] In reality, the attraction may have been as much a fascination with the bizarre behavior of Hindiyya as it was a search for an audience with a saintly woman.[121] Regardless of the purpose, the effect was the same, which was to make Hindiyya—and by necessity her family—an object of public curiosity and not always in a positive sense. For instance, we find that proposals for marriage to her (or her sisters) were conspicuously absent from any record of her life. For a "beautiful" woman from a well-to-do family, this must have been rather unusual and is likely due to her aberrant behavior. This could not but make her siblings and parents rather unhappy since she was undermining one of the most central expectations in the social life of the Maronite community.

Her distance from her family only seemed to increase as she moved into her teens and her visions grew more focused on her extraordinary religious vocation. Her belief in a distinct purpose for her life came from a vision she had when she was quite young. Her family also ridiculed her vision of "otherness," as she noted in responding to a question by Fr. Desiderio about graces that Christ bestowed upon her:

> I will tell you another thing that I am not sure is appropriate, and that is at the age of four or five I would feel in my heart a clear voice telling me that I will establish a confraternity of men and women and that I will be its president, that is its founder . . . and I would repeatedly tell that to my mother and sisters. My mother would laugh and my sisters would chastise me and tell me not to repeat such words. . . . My sisters would persecute and hit me sometimes because of that.[122]

In *Secret of the Union,* Hindiyya was more explicit in describing the reaction of her family and acquaintances to her behavior.

> Because of my repeated visions [of Christ] I faced many trials and different persecutions. Some would dissuade me from this behavior which

they found strange because of my avoidance of everyone and my solitude. . . . As for my mother, even though she desired that I shun sin, she did not want me to pursue this abnormal behavior but rather that I should behave in a permissible manner. For these reasons I faced trials at the hands of my own mother and I felt alone and unique in my tribulations without anyone to help me.[123]

Hindiyya's profound sense of loneliness derived quite obviously from her departure from the social and cultural norms of Aleppo. In other words, it was the darker side of the solitude she sought fervently. What may have been, for her family at least, endearing at a very young age and slightly amusing when Hindiyya reached her early teens became positively disturbing when she reached a marriageable age. Her visions and increasingly extreme ascetic behavior could not be contained for long within the confines of the 'Ujaimi household. Saliba al-Jdaydeh's tightly packed houses and narrow alleys as well as talkative servants and family members would have made privacy difficult, if not impossible, to maintain, especially with such dramatic events unfolding. If that were not enough, then her unusual behavior at social gatherings rendered public her private activities and made them fodder for gossip. In so doing, she opened herself and her family to social ridicule and possibly approbation—as well, one must add distinction and pious reputation. All of these tribulations engendered not only tension within the 'Ujaimi household but also doubt in Hindiyya. She repeatedly mentions questioning herself, her actions, and the veracity of her visions of Christ. But it was not only the pressures she experienced within her milieu that troubled her. Rather, her uncertainty was also bred by many moments of doubt when Hindiyya was not sure what Christ wanted with her.

Question 104: She Was Asked If She Knew Something Special . . .

The answer to her doubts and uncertainties finally came in a resplendent vision when she was seventeen years of age (1737). At the prompting of Fr. Desiderio, she related that she saw Christ, "particularly with the eyes of the body" and not in the mind, in a vision unequal in substance or meaning to any she had had before.

While sitting in my room, which was not large, I saw a spacious hall in the midst of which had been erected a beautiful throne where Jesus Christ was sitting. The seraphim with six wings were carrying the throne around which ranged male and female saints bearing in their hands lit lanterns shimmering with brilliance like the sun. . . . The numerous angels were singing hymns . . . and the male and female saints were chanting other things. . . . I noticed that the saints were all crowned some with one crown and some with two and others with three crowns. . . . They would pass by the throne of Jesus Christ in pairs taking the crowns off their heads and prostrating themselves before Him . . . then I heard clearly with the ears of the body Jesus Christ calling me . . . and He said to me: "Hindiyya, I want you to establish first an association for my heart in Kisrawan [Lebanon] which will later become a religious order. Tell this to your confessor." Then he lifted his hands and blessed me. After the blessing Jesus Christ took with the same hand his heart and gave it to me and at that moment the vision ended.[124]

This was not the first time that she had heard this from Christ. When she was four or five years old she heard a "clear voice in the heart" telling her that she will establish an association for men and women. However, that revelation was comparatively vague and easily dismissed as childish fantasy. In fact, and as mentioned earlier, her mother would laugh at her and her sisters would "chastise me . . . and beat me sometimes" because of her repeated declarations. In contrast, the pomp and circumstance of the latter vision gave it a weight that was never present before and that could not be as easily dismissed. The whole heavenly court was in full session, from seraphim to saints, to attend to this momentous event.[125] Their presence promptly elevated Hindiyya to the celestial stature of those ranged around her and Jesus. She was not simply the human child stealing a few moments of meditation or seeing Jesus gesture to her in private. Now she consorted with Christ in his heavenly abode before angels and saints. But there was more to it than that. The contrast between the Christ who spoke to her before she reached this age of "maturity" and the personage who appeared to her here was quite revealing of the transformation that Hindiyya and her vocation were about to undergo. Before this "marvelous" vision, Christ had always appeared as baby Jesus, a young infant or toddler speaking to her. Here, Hindiyya "began to see Jesus Christ . . . as he was in the world when he was thirty [years old]."[126] The nature of the request and the relationship shifted markedly as the two simultaneously came of age. They were no longer children speaking to each other, even if one was a divine personage. Both Hindiyya and Christ were now adults conversing with a seriousness of purpose that was much more difficult to ignore or minimize and a physicality that increasingly came to shape their encounters. What transpires between Christ and Hindiyya during this vision only affirms this shift. After bestowing his graces on Hindiyya by the laying on of hands (something that had not happened to her before), Christ entrusts her with the symbol of his love and sacrifice on behalf of humanity. In other words, he gave Hindiyya the means to human salvation. In direct command and allegorical symbolism, Hindiyya was being told by Christ to leave her private world of visions and asceticism (one already rendered flimsily transparent to strangers' gaze) and step into a public life with lofty purpose and responsibility. Henceforth, Hindiyya was imbued with a sense of mission as she never was before. Concomitantly, her confidence and determination grew. This became readily apparent in her relationships to her family, to the city where she was born, and most notably to her confessor.

Not long after Hindiyya received this vision her mother passed away, another victim of the plague in Aleppo. The year could have been 1737, when the English traveler Pokocke came through Aleppo and reported an outbreak of plague; but it was more likely in 1743, when there was another epidemic, which "killed scores of people."[127] The event, in either case, was mentioned by Antonio Venturi, her last Jesuit confessor, in a letter he wrote to his superiors as well as in her hagiography.[128] The hagiographer simply noted that "her mother died so her father entrusted her with the management of the house."[129] But this was far from a passing event. Helena's departure brought about a significant power shift in the family and seems to have freed Hindiyya from the lingering vestiges of familial boundaries and control. Instead of being the subject of ridicule and persecution by her siblings, she was now free to "advise and teach" her two "wayward" sisters.

Hindiyya even began to "forbid her sisters from that [wearing fine clothes, jewelry and makeup, because] it was not proper."[130] Her father, who rarely made an appearance in her earlier years, emerges only once or twice and then in an enfeebled role. Venturi renders him, in his letter, as sick and incapable of taking care of his family. In fact, Hindiyya has to provide for him and her sisters from her dowry when his fortunes, along with those of many Maronites, dissipated in the mercantile downturn and crisis which characterized the 1730s and 1740s. Ultimately, the last act in this familial transfer of power came years later, when in 1748 and after she had left Aleppo for Mount Lebanon Hindiyya completely turned her back on her family.

> One day her father sent a woman to speak to her [Hindiyya]. When the woman approached to speak to her on behalf of her father, she shunned her not wishing to hear her words. Rather, she said to her, Our Lord Jesus Christ said that whosoever does not leave his father and mother . . . will not deserve my love. And she left without listening to what her father had to say.[131]

Within the community, Hindiyya also came of her own. Stories of her "marvelous" vision and her vocation spread quickly through the Christian quarter of Saliba al-Jdaydeh. The traded tales elicited familiar and unfamiliar reactions. On the one hand, Hindiyya told Fr. Desiderio that she was met with derision on the streets of Aleppo. For example, after Christ appeared to her in all his glory, he continued his almost daily visitations, telling her, among other things, that he wanted her to be his bride. When she finally acquiesced some three years later and placed a ring on her hands, "some people saw me and began to mock me saying that this was the ring which Jesus Christ had given me, and that Jesus Christ had married me through the ring."[132] A couple of years after the ring incident, Hindiyya was deeply troubled because "women were mocking me in their conversations saying that I am a saint."[133] But others used the same appellation in a sincere manner, ascribing to Hindiyya miraculous acts and a saintly demeanor. Her aunt (perhaps the same one who did not like her name) was once cooking some lentils that were proving impossible to soften until

Hindiyya invoked the holy power of Jesus. The aunt exclaimed, "Truly, Hindiyya is a saint."[134] Beyond the magical cooking of lentils,

> She was considered by her city and seen by the people as an impregnable refuge to whom they turned in times of need. . . . Her virtue became well known amongst the nation and the people began to descend upon her . . . asking for her grace and prayers. Some even begged her to take them with her when she went to heaven. . . . Whoever set eyes upon her thought that they have beheld an angel or saint coming from heaven.

Her first recorded miracle helped convince those "elites who offered a great deal of money to . . . have her intercede [with God] on their behalf" that she was indeed a saint. At the behest of one wealthy Maronite woman whose husband was on his deathbed, Hindiyya successfully beseeched Christ to prolong the life of the man for four months "until he could settle his accounts."[135] (An odd miracle, really, yet it seems appropriate in its mercantilist tones for a community whose religious renaissance was funded by commerce.) Embellished though her powers may have been by a sympathetic hagiographer, her reputation as a miracle worker is largely corroborated by her detractors. Father Gabriel de Quintin, the superior of the Capuchins in Aleppo, wrote to the Vatican in 1750 in a dismissive tone that "all the people have come to her from everywhere—Christians, Turks, Druzes—and they say she has cured them all." A poster commissioned by the Jesuits in Aleppo detailed among her purported sins that the ʿawam (commoners) presented her with "votive offerings and gifts."[136] So while some still dismissed Hindiyya and her visions in the 1740s, other Aleppans were flocking to her as never before, for reasons we will explore more fully in chapter 5.

Father Venturi was initially delighted by these events. He had succeeded his fellow Jesuit Giacinto Triva as Hindiyya's confessor sometime in 1739. Born in 1701 in Montepulciano in Tuscany, Venturi joined the Company of Jesus in 1719. After studying at the Roman College in Rome, Venturi joined the ranks of Jesuit missionaries in Syria, traveling to Damascus in 1733. Four years later he arrived in Aleppo, where he impressed Père Fromage, superior of the Jesuit mission and one of the most accomplished and active missionaries in Syria, enough for the latter to write a letter extolling his "courage" in comparison to more timid missionaries. (We may assume that by "courage" Père Fromage meant that Venturi ventured out into the homes and shops of Aleppans more than other missionaries.) Venturi also distinguished himself by learning to read, write, and speak Arabic enough to hear Hindiyya's confessions and write down many of her revelations and visions. For the first three years the relationship of devotee to confessor was guarded. Hindiyya was reluctant to fully apprise Venturi of her visions and spiritual inclinations. Speaking of her ascetic practices, she told Fr. Desiderio that for "a long time" she kept from Venturi the knowledge that she was disciplining her body, and even when she did divulge her practice she still chose to "trick him" into thinking that she only used one "instrument," when in fact she was using several. For the same three years she also kept from Venturi Christ's announcement that he wanted her to be his "bride."[137]

In 1742, at Christ's insistence or because she was feeling more confident in her relationship to Venturi, Hindiyya finally divulged to him Christ's desire. At first, Venturi did not say anything, leaving Hindiyya with uncertainty and even fear that his reaction would be one of dismissal or derision. However, Christ once again appeared to Hindiyya in the evening of that same day and pointedly told her to ask Venturi to procure a ring for her. Despite her trepidations, Hindiyya asked Venturi for the ring, and this time her confessor responded by saying, "I will do what God inspires me to do." Three or four weeks later he gave her a ring and told her to do what Christ had commanded her.[138] Droll though this sounds in the record of her first inquisition, in fact Venturi was thoroughly exuberant to hear of his protégée's vocation. In reports to his superiors as well as in his hagiography of Hindiyya, Venturi left no doubt that he thought of her as a saintly woman whose visions were indeed from Christ and who was capable of performing miracles.[139] To prove his point "rationally," he provided examples of her supernatural acts and then endeavored to prove that they could not have been induced by the devil. He recounted, among other things, how Hindiyya would know ahead of time about the pending arrival of a local woman bent on asking her hand in marriage for a male relative and that she would disappear, not to be found until the woman left. He also told of an incident where one Jesuit monk asked for permission from Venturi to visit Hindiyya, which he granted. However, Hindiyya knew "by the spirit" that he would get lost, so she sent a servant to meet him at a "far away place" where the monk had gone off course.[140] Moreover, Venturi stated that he was not satisfied with Hindiyya's claims at face value but sought to prove for himself that they were divine in nature. Following the methods outlined by Claude de la Colombière in his spiritual direction of Marguerite-Marie Alacoque, Venturi sought to ascertain whether Hindiyya was obedient and humble sufficiently to be virtuous.[141] (Thus, he aligned his career with that of the celebrated Colombière even as he associated Hindiyya with the salutary repute of Alacoque.) He would forbid her from attending mass or taking communion and deprive her of confession for long periods of time, to see whether she would submit her will to him, the representative of the mother church, which in his mind was itself the embodiment of Christ on earth. Moreover, her physical and emotional trials before and after he became her confessor seemed to him valid evidence that her calling was from God and not the devil. His emphatic conclusion was that Hindiyya was indeed a woman touched by grace.

To see others in Aleppo treating Hindiyya with the deference due to a holy woman was gratifying for Venturi because it affirmed his views of her. In many ways, Hindiyya appeared to be the embodiment of all that the Latin missionaries had been striving for in their work in the Middle East. Here was a woman who spurned the material world to dedicate herself systematically, under the direction of a Jesuit confessor, to spiritual growth and development. Her adoption of Roman Catholic ideas about a personal spirituality focused on confession, the Eucharist, and the dual nature of Christ demonstrated the transformation of local religious culture and its greater reorientation toward the centralized authority of the Vatican. Her religious education, begun in a rudimentary fashion by her mother at home and subsequently systematized by various confessors culminating in Venturi, was a vindication of a central missionary approach to proselytizing among the Christian youth. Finally, the fact that Hindiyya belonged to a wealthy Maronite family fit within the missionary rubric, which saw in the conversion of social and political elites a most effective method of broadcasting and amplifying the work of conversion. In other words, Venturi may have also seen Hindiyya's saintliness as a way to "kindle a more living spirit among lethargic and discouraged Christians."[142]

But there is also a personal dimension to the relationship between confessor and penitent. Venturi believed, as did previous confessors of other visionary women, that he was in the presence of a woman who communed with Christ, who could prophesy about him and the future, and who could intercede with God on behalf of humanity. These were not insignificant matters for a missionary like Venturi, whose whole purpose in life was to build God's kingdom on earth. Thus, when he recounted Hindiyya's virtues in his report, he was not simply doing so to justify to his superiors his belief in her saintliness but also to present himself and others with evidence of God's miracles. Equally, his hagiography of Hindiyya was not only a record of her life and her visions but what he believed to be momentous events that would shape Christianity in the Middle East and beyond. To be intimately affiliated with this instrument of God, like Colombière was with Alacoque, was not only an affirmation of Venturi's faith and work but also a source of distinction and power.

However, the balance of power inherent in this relationship and its very nature began to change soon after Hindiyya received her transformative vision. A few days after Jesus had appeared to her and instructed her to establish a religious order dedicated to his sacred heart, Hindiyya approached Venturi to tell him about this vision.

> He did not wish to hear my words but immediately interrupted me saying: "This is impossible." Then he sat and asked me whether I had seen Jesus Christ, so I answered "yes." Then he asked me "what did He [Christ] say to you?" I began to recount the matter to him but he interrupted me again saying "No, no this is from the devil."[143]

Instead, Venturi offered to help her establish a religious association in Aleppo, and he sent her "three or four women from the *rum* [Melkite] sect to talk to me about spiritual matters and about Jesus Christ." That solution proved untenable since Hindiyya could not speak to them, either because Christ deprived her of the power of speech in their presence or because she had nothing to say to them. Speaking to them was also a diversion from her intent to implement the wishes of Christ or her own ambitions. Without a resolution, the tension generated by Hindiyya's recurring vision continued unabated for several years, and the pattern remained the same. Christ would appear to Hindiyya to demand that she fulfill his command, whereupon she would approach Venturi with the renewed request, only to be rebuffed by her confessor, who proclaimed such visions satanic. When Hindiyya began to receive revelations that contained the rule for the new religious order, sometime in the early 1740s, she once again approached Venturi. His response provides one clue for the cause of his steadfast rejection of her pleas. In dismissing this vision he revealed that "the Jesuits cannot establish convents and monasteries in Kisrawan." He added, "You are the daughter of our religious order and you must remain in this order, so do not think at all about these matters for they are trials from the devil."[144] Venturi was afraid of losing his protégée, in whom he had invested years of his life. Moreover, he did not want to lose control over Hindiyya, whom he saw as a most valuable instrument with which to further that work and expand Jesuit influence over the Christian communities of the Middle East.

But Hindiyya was not easily dissuaded. Just when she was beginning to think that she was indeed being deluded by the devil, Christ appeared to her and showed her his wounds as evidence that he was indeed Jesus because "the devil does not have wounds." Reinforced in her belief in her visions and vocation, she sought out Venturi and "insisted" that he should hear her out. She said to him,

> Father, if the visions I have had about the association and the rule that Jesus Christ has been dictating to me word for word are from the devil then all the visions that I have had are from the devil because the person I see now is the same I have seen and heard in all my other visions. Either it is all from the devil or it is all from God.[145]

To this impeccable logic, Venturi stuttered, "No, no it is not like that." When Hindiyya protested that Venturi had seen fit to believe her earlier visions and now he was denying this one, all Venturi could do was to order her to be quiet and obedient, a transparently desperate exercise of patriarchal authority. Its desperation betrayed the first notable shift in power in the relationship between Hindiyya and Venturi.

But the whole exchange was not just about the locus of religious power; its substance also concerned the source of that power. The arguments between the two implicitly raised the question of whether the will of God is known through direct revelation to ordinary people or via the hierarchy of the Catholic Church. In reaching this impasse Hindiyya had taken her religious instruction to its logical conclusion, just as other visionary women had done before. By internalizing Latin missionary efforts to promote a Christianity based on intensely personal relationships between God and individuals, she contended that she had developed an intimacy with Jesus that opened her directly to his instructions and revelations. The result was the series of visions that had until then been deemed by Venturi to be truly divinely inspired. Yet those previous visions had, in their abstraction, left Hindiyya within the norms of religious orthodoxy and control established by the Jesuits. The last vision threatened to take her outside those boundaries, and this was troubling to Venturi.

Venturi's attempt to reestablish his authority, as the representative of the Roman Catholic Church, over Hindiyya was undermined by the obvious hypocrisy of his attitude toward her visions. A subsequent vision dealt a further blow to his authority and that of the Jesuits as a whole. Some weeks after the frustrated interaction between Hindiyya and Venturi, Christ appeared to her and gave her a rather pointed revelation. He said,

> Inform your confessor the personage who I [Hindiyya] see said to me that your religious order will be sorely tried in ways that no other religious order in the world has ever been tried. That which is hidden in the order will be uncovered to humiliate and embarrass them [the Jesuits] because they have chosen to stray spiritually . . . and they want to extinguish the truth and destroy those who would expose falsehoods.

Naturally she was reluctant. But Christ assured her that he was the "light and whosoever follows Me will not stumble in his darkness."[146] Venturi was not pleased to hear these utterances; he fulminated, according to Hindiyya, that this is "the devil, the archon of devils," and he silenced her and left her alone. He did not come back for four weeks, depriving Hindiyya of confession and absolution by way of disciplining her increasingly rebellious spirit. Yet, when he did return to the 'Ujaimi household, he found that Hindiyya had not backed down from her determination to "obey Jesus Christ"—and disobey Venturi and the Jesuits—by pursuing her goal of establishing her religious order in Mount Lebanon. At that point it had become clear that Hindiyya was winning the tug-of-war, and Venturi admitted as much when he dejectedly declared, "The labors of many years have been for naught." Seeking a way to resolve the matter while retaining a modicum of control over Hindiyya and her growing religious stature, Venturi tried to convince her to join the Jesuit-run convent in 'Ayntura, a small village in Mount Lebanon. She turned him down: "I cannot do that because I want to obey Jesus Christ who wants me to establish a confraternity of the Sacred Heart of Jesus." However, she left some room for compromise when she told him that she was willing to join the convent as a layperson. Venturi, seeking to retain some modicum of control over his penitent, agreed to this arrangement and wrote a letter on her behalf to the Jesuit director of 'Ayntura convent.

Question 105: At This Point the Apostolic Delegate Postponed the Question . . .

On October 4, 1746, Hindiyya left Aleppo, traveling with an Armenian widow and a Greek woman in a caravan heading for Tripoli, from whence she was to make the trip to 'Ayntura. After twenty-six years in the city of her birth, Hindiyya left, never to come back again. Her departure was the culmination of a journey that took her from ordinary (if privileged) social circumstances through a rejuvenating and devout Christian culture to the solitary perch of a visionary woman. She consistently portrayed herself as a woman being pulled by the divine will of Christ across the secular and religious landscapes of Aleppo. Christ's love and exhortations, as well as the fear of hell, all compelled her to pray, meditate, and discipline her body in a manner unusually fervent for the Christian inhabitants of Aleppo. Yet she also partook of a dynamic religious culture that swirled around her household and community. Together, religious instruction and revelation provided Hindiyya with the motivation and ability to transgress the social and cultural norms of family and community. At an early age she obeyed her parents almost blindly. When Christ began to speak to her and his commands conflicted with the demands of her family, her filial piety wavered and ultimately dissipated to the point where she barely asked her father for permission to leave Aleppo.

At the same time, Hindiyya (and some of her male and female cohorts) saw in the ostentatious material circumstance of their bourgeois milieu a hypocritical departure from the teachings of Christ. She, among others, could not reconcile her religious fervor with the worldly extravagance of her family and class. Therefore, her visions and behavior were explicit rejections—and implicit criticism—of that hypocrisy. Her private communion with Christ became a public condemnation of the Christian elites of Aleppo. Moreover, Hindiyya's visions made it possible for her to reject the social expectations for women: housework, marriage, birth, etc. Her derision of adornment and her preference to subdue and hide her beauty were denunciations of the gendered images after which women of her class and time were expected to model themselves. Her words were a source of power that allowed her to transcend the gendered social circles and speak with equanimity to men and women as the "bride of Christ." In other words, Christian thought and ideas became the vehicle of emancipation for Hindiyya from the secular and fallen world of Aleppo.

Throughout this process her last Latin confessor, Antonio Venturi, promoted her sense of uniqueness by selectively fitting her vitae within the rubric of European visionary women, such as Marguerite-Marie Alacoque. Although this proved effective in attracting followers to Hindiyya who came to believe in her saintliness, it also affirmed for her beyond any previous doubts that she was indeed selected by Christ. The belief that she was graced by such a distinction made her more diffident in the face of any attempt to dissuade her from absolute obedience to her heavenly beloved. It also gave her a divinely inspired authority that was difficult to contend with, even for Venturi and the Jesuits. Thus, with instructions from Jesus, she began a journey that took her not only away from Aleppo but also outside the theological grasp of her Jesuit mentor and his religious order.

3

MOUNT LEBANON

A Voice in the Wilderness (1746–1750)

On October 12, 1746, Hindiyya arrived in Dayr Ziyarat al-Adhra (Visitation of the Virgin), a Jesuit convent established in 1744 in 'Ayntura, a village in central Mount Lebanon. Her move to the mountains of Lebanon was meant to distance her from encroaching pressures and demands to transform her private communion with Christ into a public intercession for supplicants. In addition, like other Aleppans of her generation who moved to Mount Lebanon for religious purposes, she was escaping the materialism of city life for the imagined purity and spirituality of the "wilderness" of the Lebanese mountains. However, most critically, her voyage to Mount Lebanon was the only way to fulfill the responsibility she believed Christ had placed upon her. Since Ottoman authorities prohibited the construction of convents and monasteries in Aleppo, her move was necessary to establish the new religious order dedicated to the Sacred Heart. Yet the events which unfolded in her first four years in Mount Lebanon diverged greatly from any expectation she may have had in Aleppo. The Jesuit missionaries who had been her main supporters in Aleppo became, with but one exception, her nemeses and detractors. The one Jesuit who continued to believe in Hindiyya and her visions, Father Venturi, was recalled to Rome, leaving her alone without succor. The landscape of Mount Lebanon that appeared "hallowed" from the distance of Aleppo emerged as a place of physically arduous living and filled with human blemishes and imperfections. This cascade of realizations sent her into the depths of despair and doubt about her visions, her calling, and even the ethereal personage who had been her companion since childhood in Aleppo. Yet, like other visionaries before her, these trials were the necessary way for Hindiyya to submit her will to that of Christ in order to be one with him. In other words, this was a crucible of trials, which ultimately elevated her from the ranks of the extraordinarily devout to a living prophet. Her tribulations transformed her from a lonesome woman hesitantly communing with Christ to the founder and leader of a new religious order who drew ever nearer to completing her mystical union with Christ and from one who needed the blessing of male clerics to a religious woman who radiated grace to them and the larger church. Following her journey across this physically and spiritually demanding and convoluted landscape, we will map the construction of sanctity and religion amid growing political tensions between the Maronite Church and Latin missionaries.

A Sanctified Mountain

The place to which Hindiyya came was familiar and alien, similar to the one that her great-grandparents had left but also changed considerably since those times; it shared some things with Aleppo but was quite different in many other ways.

Politically, Mount Lebanon, like Aleppo, was part of the Ottoman Empire. More immediately, its various territories fell simultaneously or alternatively within the administrative purview of the pachalik of Tripoli, Acre, and Damascus. Its inhabitants had to pay taxes, like their counterparts in Aleppo, to one or more of the Ottoman governors; and the ruler of Mount Lebanon had to be approved—albeit as a hollow formality in some instances—by the Sublime Porte in Istanbul. Beyond these broad outlines of similitude rested many significant differences. While the Ottoman government displayed and flexed its power in Aleppo through a garrison of Janissaries and an appointed Ottoman governor, Mount Lebanon was free of both symbols of Ottoman authority. Instead, the political structure was made up completely of local elites, though Ottoman governors made their presence felt frequently during the eighteenth century through military expeditions and imposed levies. At the top of this hierarchy were the emirs (princes) of the mountain, who throughout the eighteenth century came from the Shihab family, who were rural *multazims* (tax collectors) and whose position "was determined by a continual process of negotiation and the reshuffling of political relations" with provincial Ottoman officials.[1]

The political influence and control of the emirs of Mount Lebanon was projected through a fluid network of alliances with other families with titles such as "emir," "*muqaddam,*" and "shaykh."[2] These influential families—like the Jumblatts, Arsalans, and Abi al-Lamas—commanded a large enough political force to make the emir's rule difficult, if not impossible, at times.[3] Among these *muqata'aji* families was the Maronite Khazin clan, which by the beginning of the eighteenth century had gained the *iltizam* (tax-collection authority) for the Kisrawan region (where Hindiyya was to spend all of her life after Aleppo) and had solidified its political prestige after some of its members acquired the role of consuls of France in Mount Lebanon.[4] The ascendancy of the Khazin clan was due, at least in part, to the demographic changes that had come about in Mount Lebanon during the seventeenth century. The same population pressures among the Maronites in northern Lebanon which drove Hindiyya's grandparents to Aleppo led to the migration of Maronites south toward Jubayl, Kisrawan, al-Matn, and the Shuf regions.[5] Over the second half of the seventeenth century this migratory movement turned Jubayl and Kisrawan from a primarily Shi'a Muslim area to a predominantly Maronite Christian territory. This project of displacing the Shi'a of Kisrawan in favor of the Maronites was consciously begun by Shaykh Abu Nadir al-Khazin early in the seventeenth century and completed thereafter by his son Shaykh Abu Nawfal al-Khazin, the same who was appointed consul of France by King Louis XIV in 1657.[6]

The story of the village of Hrajal, high in the mountains of Kisrawan, is illustrative of this project. Sometime around 1720 some of the Shi'a of that village reportedly attacked Ottoman government troops dispatched from Damascus to collect taxes from the area. They robbed and killed them and disposed of their bodies in a small ravine not far from the village. Shaykh Abu Nadir, who had been trying to gain a foothold in the area, took this as an opportunity to expel the Shi'a, with whom he had had a tumultuous relationship. Thus, he traveled to Damascus to inform the pasha of what had transpired. Subsequently, the pasha dispatched troops against the Shi'a of Hrajal; and after three failed attempts,

the increasingly larger force was able to defeat and expel many of them
from Kisrawan. This allowed Shaykh Abu Nadir to start buying the land
cheaply from the remaining Shi'a and to bring in his own Christian peasants and settle them in the area to work the lands and colonize the territory. Henceforth, from 1664 to 1729 about thirty families emigrated from
the north (around Tripoli) or lower parts of Kisrawan and settled in Hrajal. The Christians had become politically and demographically strong
enough by 1671 that they were able to prevail upon the Shi'a families in
Hrajal and build a church there. This trend of dwindling Shi'a authority continued until 1696, when the last of the Shi'a families left Hrajal
and migrated east to Ba'albek in the Biq'a valley. Because of these trends,
Hindiyya arrived at a place and time where Maronites were no longer a
minority (as they remained in Aleppo) but rather the dominant political,
economic, and religious forces in Mount Lebanon.

As a physical space, Mount Lebanon was for Hindiyya also radically
different from Aleppo. Unlike the city of her birth, which was a major
cosmopolitan city in the Ottoman Empire sitting at the crossroads of
many trade routes, Mount Lebanon was a more isolated land of crumpled
topography and limited resources. Strictly speaking, what eighteenth-century travelers and chroniclers described as "Lebanon" was the land that
stretched from the northern mountains overlooking Tripoli to the hills
some twenty miles south of Beirut. Except for Tripoli, Beirut, and Sidon
(all coastal cities), Mount Lebanon was characterized by a geography of
villages and a few towns close enough to almost touch yet separated by
deep ravines and steep mountains. One French traveler, Constantin Volney, described it in this manner:

> When the traveler visits the interior of these mountains, the ruggedness
> of the roads, the steepness of the descents, the height of the precipices
> strike him at first with terror; but the sagacity of his mule soon relieves
> him, and he examines at his ease those picturesque scenes which suc-
> ceed each other to entertain him. There, as in the Alps, he travels whole
> days to reach a place which is in sight of his departure; he winds, he
> descends, he skirts the hills, he climbs; and in this perpetual change of
> opposition it seems as if some magic power varied for him at every step

the decoration of the scenery. Sometimes he sees villages ready to glide the rapid declivities on which they are built, and so disposed that the terraces of one row of houses serve as a street to the row above them. Sometimes he sees a convent standing on a solitary eminence.[7]

The Kisrawan district was not only rugged in topography but also quite sparse in population. Writing of the first half of the nineteenth century, Dominique Chevallier listed some 12,000 inhabitants occupying thirty-three villages.[8] One hundred years earlier the population was most likely smaller.

In sharp contrast to the relative opulence and grandeur of Saliba al-Jdaydeh (Hindiyya's neighborhood in Aleppo), these villages were quite humble. They were hardly distinguishable from the surrounding terrain as the walls of the Lilliputian homes were minimally dressed rocks and their roofs, an earthy mixture of mud and thatch. David Urquhart, a nineteenth-century sojourner in Lebanon, described the house where he had to spend one night as a crowded hovel that contained a few pieces of pottery and little else. He went on to state that "the rest of the villages in this area were, if not worse, no better than the state of this village."[9] Another traveler, F. Bart, lamented that "ces habitations [of peasants] pourraient jouir d'une vue splendide. Mais presque toutes n'ont qu'une chambre sans fenêtre, servant à tous les besoins du ménage" (The homes [of peasants] could enjoy a splendid view. However, practically all of them are made up of one windowless room that is used for all the household needs).[10] With few notable exceptions, the villages which dotted the western slopes of Mount Lebanon were made up of small clusters of similarly modest houses. 'Ayntura, for example, had "15 or 20 houses, at most, surrounded from all sides by well ploughed high mountains, except the western side where the mountains are not quite as high which makes looking at the sea highly delightful since it is one and a half-hour from the village."[11] Even the wealthiest of the inhabitants of Kisrawan in the nineteenth century had accumulated assets worth little more than 10,000 piasters or, taking into account a century of inflation, barely the price of Hindiyya's house in Aleppo.[12] Amid this rather modest existence, monastic orders (especially the newly established Lebanese Maronite order) were prospering. Partly this was due to the money that prospective monks and nuns brought with them from Aleppo. It was also partly funded by the contributions of local and Aleppan Catholics to the project of building up monastic orders; and finally, it was the centralized and collectivized management of land and crops which increased the wealth of convents and monasteries in Mount Lebanon.

The rugged topography, sparse population, and impoverished housing which distinguished Mount Lebanon from Aleppo and the predominantly Maronite population of the mountainous region were factors used to represent it (mainly by outsiders) as a sanctified wilderness. Such a reputation was constructed out of the confluence of European and local images of these mountains. It was cultivated by the rather unique position of Mount Lebanon as a place where Christianity could be practiced freely, especially relative to the surrounding Ottoman lands, its proximity to the Holy Land, and the claims that it housed the only long-standing and faithful Catholics in the Levant.[13] In the words of Pope Leo X to the Maronite patriarch Butrus of Hadath in 1510, the Maronites were the "lily among thorns." They were the true church to whom Christ refers—at least in the Christian interpretation—in another psalm from the Song of Songs: "Come with me from Lebanon, my spouse, with me from Lebanon."[14] Missionaries in the Levant carried forth this historical image in constructing Mount Lebanon as a space of naturalized religion, primitive in its sincerity, untouched by time, and thus for them a remaining tenuous link to the times of Christ and the apostles.[15] For instance, in 1671, Sylvestre de Saint-Aignan, a Capuchin missionary, wrote a book about Mount Lebanon that he titled *Description abrégée de la sainte montagne du Liban et des Maronites qui l'habitent* (*Abridged description of the holy mountain of Lebanon and the Maronites who live there*). After describing the mountainous region as paradisiacal, he turned his attention to the Maronites who inhabited it. "They are," he wrote, "very zealous for the religion, good, dcvout and simple in their words, happy in their conversation, civil and charitable, but austere in their manner of living because they imitate the Ancient Fathers."[16] However, he added, with a biblical reference, that they are in need of missionaries because "their souls can be compared to an excellent vine that has not been cultivated and thus has become sterile because of that abandonment."[17] Père Joseph Besson, a Jesuit missionary to Syria in the second half of the seventeenth century, wrote a more complete articulation of this view in his book *La Syrie et la Terre Sainte au XVIIe siècle (Syria and the Holy Land in the seventeenth century)*. In the section dedicated to Mount Lebanon he began by noting that the "inhabitants [of Mount Lebanon] are naturally very good and religious . . . here at the frontier of the holy land where the blood of Jesus Christ has kept these Christians vigorously Christian and abiding by the rules of the ancient Fathers."[18] Continuing with an arboreal reference similar to Saint-Aignan's, he remarked that Mount Lebanon constituted "a good land capable of bearing excellent fruit albeit it remains hardly cultivated." Its people, he wrote, never blasphemed, always pronounced the name of God, kissed the hand of any priest they met and asked for his benediction; and "the women" were very modest, rarely appearing in public.[19]

Seventy years later, in 1721, Père Petitqueux of the Jesuit mission house in Tripoli related to his superior a similarly hallowed description of Mount Lebanon. He described a trip he took to Qannubin, high in the northern part of Mount Lebanon, near Bsharri, the natal village of Hindiyya's grandparents. He began by recounting the travails of the trip: frighteningly deep ravines, cold winds, clinging to the rocky faces of mountains, lashing rains, and sleeping exposed to the elements. Certainly, this was born out of an understandable inclination to complain of real difficulties. But it also dramatically emphasized his presence in a space which hearkened the reader back to the days of the early fathers of the church and their austere settings. This tableau, evoking a different time and space than that of Enlightenment Europe, was completed with Petitqueux's arrival at Nahr Qadisha, or the "Holy River." Bounded on both sides by great boulders,

> these rocks enclose deep caves which used to be the cells of a large number of hermits. . . . It was the tears of these holy penitents which gave the river its name. The view of these caves and this river amidst this frightening desert inspire compunction, love of penitence and compassion for these sensual and worldly souls.[20]

In emphasizing the "natural" state of the Christians in the "wilderness" of Mount Lebanon, Latin missionaries were resorting to two familiar

5. *Mount Lebanon* from Reverend Thomas Hartwell Horne, B.D., *Landscape Illustrations of the Bible Consisting of the Most Remarkable Places Mentioned in the Old and New Testaments,* vol. 1 (London: John Murray, 1836). © Tate, London 2011.

tropes. The first centered on the concept of the "natural man." Unlike the Augustinian construct—popular among Protestants and conservative Catholics like the Jansenists—which construed the "natural man" to be sinful and as such the enemy of God, most Jesuit theologians had by the end of the sixteenth century come to believe that human beings inherently seek the good and God. This "state of pure nature" was first clearly articulated by the Spanish Jesuit Luis de Molina.[21] Subsequent refinements of this idea culminated in the thesis that "man was born at once exempt from original sin, deprived of supernatural life and subject to death and all other miseries of life."[22] As a concept, natural theism became the intellectual underpinning of the global Jesuit missionary endeavor. The works of José de Acosta (*Historia natural y moral de las Indias,* 1590), Matteo Ricci (*The True Meaning of the Lord of Heaven,* 1603), as well as their fellow Jesuit François-Joseph Lafitau (*Mœurs des sauvages Américains: comparées aux mœurs des premiers temps,* 1724) employ this idea in describing the indigenous populations of South America, China, and "New France," respectively, to their audiences in Europe. To all three Jesuit missionaries, pagan cultures (i.e., non-European ones) expressed a "primordial religious yearning that could be satisfied only by Christian revelation."[23]

Yet the population of Mount Lebanon was neither pagan nor in need of Christian revelation. As Père Besson wrote in *La Syrie et la Terre Sainte*, "Some may think that I am . . . describing here a golden age . . . of twelve centuries of Christianity at the edge of the Holy Land where the blood of Jesus Christ can nourish the faith of these Christians in the tradition of the Fathers of the Church."[24] Such impressions obtained from the Latin missionaries' own narratives left them with the task of self-consciously explaining their raison d'être and justifying what may have struck audiences in France as a superfluous mission, taking resources and energy from more pressing projects. Justifying their presence in the Levant was especially necessary against a backdrop painted by the voluminous *Jesuit Relations* sent by missionaries from far more arduous and "exotic" missions in the "savage" territories of "New France" and Central America.[25] The justification came in the form of shining the religious Enlightenment upon these "natural" Christians, a project that was in fact part of the larger Jesuit theology. For instance, using the Aristotelian stadial model of the world, Père Le Jeune explained to his readers that the evolution of the world can be divided into three parts.

> In the early ages, houses were made simply to be used, and afterward they were made to be seen. In the third stage, men of intellect, seeing that the world was enjoying things that were necessary and pleasant in life, gave themselves up to the contemplation of natural objects and to scientific researches; whereby the great Republic of men has little by little perfected itself, necessity marching on ahead, politeness and gentleness following after, and knowledge bringing-up the rear.[26]

According to this positivist notion of spiritual development and to Jesuit missionaries in the Levant, what was missing in Mount Lebanon (and among Middle Eastern Christians in general) was textualized knowledge and rational religion. While naturally "good," these Levantine Christians were seen by missionaries as corrupted by their proximity to the Muslim and Druze communities and religions. Supposedly, generations of such interactions left local Christians with an irrational approach to religion, characterized by ignorance of the "mysteries" of the faith and a spiritual inertia that kept them from seeking enlightenment about the articles of Catholic faith. Père Besson, for example, concluded his observations about the Maronites of Mount Lebanon by noting that they only lacked religious "enlightenment" to make them completely orthodox Catholics.[27] Later, on the eve of the Maronite Council of 1736 in Mount Lebanon, one of the most influential Latin missionaries, Père Fromage, penned his thoughts about the Christians of Mount Lebanon to a fellow Jesuit priest in France. Of them he wrote that "while they may not be more enlightened than other people, they may at least take pride in being more docile and faithful. . . . The faith of our Christians is pure."[28] In other words, the repeated emphasis on the "natural" state of faith in Mount Lebanon, which is notably absent from depictions of Christians in Aleppo, was meant to justify the presence of missionaries in an area already populated by Christian communities to an eighteenth-century European audience steeped in a rationalized form of Catholicism with a "demarcatable system of doctrines–scriptures–beliefs."[29] Mount Lebanon was depicted as a wild space that defied Cartesian geography, full of naturally faithful people who lacked the most rudimentary religious knowledge. To paraphrase C. John Sommerville, for the missionaries the population of Mount Lebanon practiced Christianity but did not think about it and, thus, did not know it as a "religion."[30] Put another way, Levantine Christians approached Christianity as a religious culture but not as a religious doctrine and faith. Within this context missionaries saw—and represented—themselves as an essential tool for flattening the convoluted and wild religious landscape (where Christians as well as non-Christians intermixed and exchanged habits and traditions) into a cultivable plot clearly delineated and identifiable by sect (Maronite, Melkite, Armenian, etc.).[31] They saw their role as one of imposing discipline on a chaotic religious culture and delimiting the boundaries of any particular church (but most notably the Maronite one) while rationalizing its hierarchy, liturgy, and teachings in concordance with the Roman Catholic Church. In the words of Père Besson, "The forest must be cleared, and its trees must be pruned."[32] In crystallizing this modernizing project, missionaries focused most notably on women, whom they saw as both symbolic of the ignorance rampant among Levantine Christians and central to the process of edifying and uplifting the local population. Père Besson considered the state of women among Mount Lebanon's Christians to be worse than the plagues of Egypt. The exclusion of women from public religious spaces and ceremonies, out of misplaced modesty, and

> their lack of devotion and extreme ignorance, which is notably greater than that of men, with all that pertains to the mysteries of our faith, lead to the loss of the youth who do not receive any instructions from their parents. It must be said that the pitiful circumstances of the children are the fault of the mothers. I am astounded that Christian women of Syria, who previously were celebrated in their piety, and were faithful followers of Jesus Christ during his life, have now become so degenerate.[33]

In employing this paternalistic and essentializing tone, seventeenth- and eighteenth-century edifying letters of Latin missionaries were similar to the "secular" Orientalist texts of the nineteenth century. They constructed a binary of an "irrational" and "traditional" Eastern Christianity juxtaposed against a "rational" and "modern" Western theology.[34] This is a theme that we will encounter repeatedly in this book.

Yet ambiguity about this construction certainly existed. For instance, in 1657 one Franciscan missionary in Aleppo converted to Islam, unleashing a crisis among the missionaries and the Catholic community at large.[35] Less jarring but equally ambiguous is the doubt that some missionaries evinced in letters to their superiors about the utility of their work. In 1635 Père Manillier wrote his Jesuit superior, M. Vitelleschi, from Aleppo to tell him that after ten years in Aleppo he still had not mastered Arabic, that his eyes were failing, and that he would be happy to be replaced.[36] Moreover, the debate which occurred over the course of the seventeenth century about the aims and means of missionary work is further evidence of the tensions that coursed through missionary activity, goals, and ideology—and which are glaringly, if understandably, absent from the majority of the edifying letters sent by missionaries to France. Eusebe Renaudot, a French scholar of the Eastern churches, wrote at the behest of Pope Clement XI a critique of the Latin missionaries in the East. His treatise detailed the reasons behind what he termed the confused state of missionary work in the Levant. These included "the ignorance of the missionaries and those who govern the missions . . . [and] the bad behavior [of missionaries] . . . who suppose that the Orientals are so ignorant that one can convince them of whatever one wishes."[37] At least two French consuls who served in Aleppo during the seventeenth century thought that the Jesuit missionaries were overly aggressive in their efforts to convert local Christians and wrote letters to their superiors to this effect. By the first half of the eighteenth century, these disagreements, discussions, and uncertainties about the modernizing project had all but disappeared—at least in the writings of missionaries—and were replaced with a zealous confidence and at times arrogance toward what they considered to be their Christian flock.

But it was not only Latin missionaries who saw Mount Lebanon as a uniquely Christian space in the midst of the land of the "Turks." For some of the Maronites of Aleppo, Mount Lebanon was a Mecca of sorts. It was the seat of the patriarchate and, until the end of the seventeenth century, the seat of the bishop of Aleppo. It was also a place where building a convent, ringing a church bell, and other public manifestations of religiosity were not subject to the limitations placed (not always consistently) on Christians in other parts of the Ottoman Empire, including Aleppo. Most importantly, though, Mount Lebanon was seen as a sanctified mountain that was closer to God, which in its imagined sectarian and natural "purity" was distant from the worldliness and even corruption of the city and its society.[38] For instance, the record of the Lebanese order begins the history of this monastic order in the following manner: "The history of the Lebanese Monks from the start of their monastic order in the blessed Mount Lebanon."[39] The cedar trees in the northern and highest part of the mountainous range were referred to as *arz al-rabb* (God's cedars) not by locals so much as by Maronites from Aleppo. Jirmanus Farhat, the eighteenth-century Maronite cleric and literatus from Aleppo, wrote several poems evoking the sanctity of this wilderness. In one poem, composed in 1709, eulogizing Dayr Qizhaya (Monastery of Qizhaya, or "Treasure of Life") he wrote, "The wilderness of Lebanon has been honored by a hermitage [Qizhaya] . . . I see in the stem of every cedar around it a temple . . . and its monks are lines of angels facing lines of angels." In another poem penned while he was in Rome in 1711, he spoke of his yearning for the

"Holy Valley" of Qannubin where Dayr Qizhaya is located. His panegyric painted rarified images of flowers and fields, of brooks composing hymns to the heavens, and of mountains "whose tops are proud fortresses distant from the humiliating bondage of the cities."[40]

This juxtaposition between the ensnaring materialism of the cities and the liberating sanctity of the "wild" mountains was, among other things, an image that attracted a stream of religious men and women from Aleppo to Mount Lebanon, including Hindiyya. The wealth of Aleppan Christians allowed for this return migration by underwriting the purchase of lands, construction of monasteries and convents, and financial support of nuns and monks. Ideologically, this movement was an embodiment of a rejuvenated and emboldened Middle Eastern Christianity that increasingly sought to accentuate its distance and difference from the surrounding Muslim milieu. Generationally, this movement was constituted in large part by the sons and daughters of Aleppo's Christian bourgeoisie, who saw religious vows as a way to be independent from the expectations and limitations of their parents' world and to reject the materialism of Aleppo's elites. These sentiments are evoked in Jirmanus Farhat's dedicatory poem in his *Bulugh al-arab fi ʿilm al-adab* (*All you really wanted to know about the craft of literature*):

> I place my teacher over my father in merit,
>> Though my father gave me pride and honor,
> For the former trained my spirit, and the spirit is the essence,
>> While the latter trained my body, and the body is shell.[41]

This tug between the materialism of the father's bourgeois world and the spiritual realm of the Maronite "shaykh" Yaqub al-Dibsi was equally present in the lives of other young Aleppans seeking a religious life. Abdallah Qaraʾli, one of the founders of the Lebanese order (a Maronite monastic order), related in his memoirs that

> when I came of age there arose in me a passion for the monastic life. My father, Mikhail, opposed this because he feared that I knew little about people and living far from home. I remained tormented with my thoughts; sometimes I would become immersed in the world and forget

monasticism, and at other times I would entertain myself by studying books and reading until I was twenty-one years of age.[42]

Once he came of age his inner turmoil subsided rather quickly. In 1693, he secretly met with Jibrail Hawwa (Hindiyya's cousin), and they made a pact to leave for Mount Lebanon to become monks. After writing that he asked for his father's permission (given provisionally), Qara'li never mentioned him, even when he traveled frequently back to Aleppo during subsequent years as monk and then bishop.

Affluence, religious effervescence, opportunity, and generational tensions, then, drove a stream of Aleppan Catholics to Mount Lebanon, seeking the religious life. Among the earliest of these were Jibrail Hawwa, Abdallah Qara'li, and Yusuf al-Tibn, who came to Qannubin from Aleppo in 1695 to ask Patriarch Istifan Duwayhi for permission to establish the first "modern" monastic order.[43] After questioning whether "soft" city residents, like themselves, could handle the rigors of mountainous living and toil, he granted them leave to establish the order. Not long afterward, in 1710, a group of Melkite monks from Aleppo established a new monastic order in Mount Lebanon; and they came to be known as the Shuwayrite order (after Shuwayr, the village in central Mount Lebanon where they built their first monastery). In 1716 Wanis al-'Attar and Yaqoub Yusuf al-Armani left Aleppo for Mount Lebanon, where they asked Qara'li of the Lebanese order for help in establishing the first Armenian Catholic monastic order.[44] A group of Aleppan women, known as the *'abidat* (devotees), followed suit in 1732 and established a religious order known also as the Shuwayrite order. Thus, by the time Hindiyya arrived in Mount Lebanon in 1746 for the purpose of establishing her own religious order, the Sacred Heart of Jesus, she was following a well-trodden path.

A Troubled Beginning

As with many of the endeavors that preceded hers, Hindiyya's project was riddled with tensions from the outset. By all accounts, her stay in Dayr Ziyarat al-Adhra was religiously, spiritually, and materially a trying affair. Hindiyya described the beginning of her experience there to Fr. Desiderio (the inquisitor) in this unpromising way:

The Armenian woman and I were accepted into the convent but the Greek woman went back after a few days to Aleppo. However, our stay in the convent did not go well because at that time there were only two inhabitable rooms while there were nine people, including the two of us and the nuns who were there before us, and we disturbed each other because we all lived together.[45]

For Hindiyya, who had left Aleppo at least in part to search for solitude, this was certainly not a good beginning; the rude accommodations must have also presented an unpleasant contrast to the 'Ujaimi household she had left.

In her testimony to Fr. Desiderio, the assistant to the prioress of Dayr Ziyarat al-Adhra, Sister Theresa, concurred that Hindiyya "did not like to be with many people, so we cleared a house for her and the prioress [Rosa Rosalia al-Khazin] ordered me to stay with her because she liked me and we had two other sisters."[46] It is not clear what this house was or where it was located, but it seems that it was still too small and crowded for Hindiyya because by February 1747 a separate cell was built for her. Sister Theresa said in her deposition that Hindiyya's room was built before any other, and "we tied a white sheet beneath the ceiling so that dirt would not fall on her from the ceiling because she really liked cleanliness and we decorated around her bed with pictures and holy relics."[47] While Hindiyya recalled persecution and pressure as the cause of her unhappiness, Sister Theresa attributed the matter to the shock of spartan circumstances and hard work. She gave one example relating to silk thread spinning, which the nuns did to raise money for the convent. She noted that "as for [Hindiyya's] trials, one day she saw her silk [thread] cut . . . and many times we had seen things like that happen and we would fix it . . . but she complained that a sister had cut it, and she became very angry and cried." During the "great fast," which lasts for forty days preceding Easter, Sister Theresa mentioned that she cooked for Hindiyya "a vegetable and meat stew." But, Hindiyya "said that she saw in it *abu brays* [Mediterranean gecko] and she became upset and said 'why do you do this to me' . . . the prioress came and looked at the food and saw in it a string of meat and she said to her 'if I was not fasting I would eat it.'"[48] Theresa's details about the meat stew and the reaction of the prioress were clearly meant as indications of the material extravagance and religious indulgence of Hindiyya, which set her apart as someone not accustomed to the rigors of rural or, more critically, monastic life.

This echoed the skepticism of Patriarch Duwayhi some fifty years before about the three Aleppan supplicants seeking to establish a Maronite monastery and religious order in Mount Lebanon. And, as will become clear later, it anticipated the tensions that emerged between Aleppan and mountain monks and nuns throughout the eighteenth century. However, within this context and since this testimony was provided by someone whose religious order and companionship Hindiyya ultimately rejected, it has to be taken with a grain of salt. While Hindiyya may have indeed been unhappy because of undesirable living conditions, she was also despondent because she was being pressured to join the Jesuit religious order against her will. Hindiyya told Fr. Desiderio that

> For the first while, they [the nuns in 'Ayntura] barely looked at me. But after a few days they were nicer to me. And then after two or three weeks they began to try to convince me to become a nun like them . . . I would answer them that I did not have that calling and as the days went by they persecuted me more, to the point where they would not let me rest. . . . Then the prioress, who constantly persecuted me, said to me once when I told her that I am not inspired [to join the convent]: "If you do not have this inspiration then I will give it to you. Get used to the idea for you will be a nun whether you like it or not."[49]

According to Hindiyya, matters only got worse when Father Gueynard, the Jesuit founder, spiritual director, and confessor of the 'Ayntura convent, returned from Damascus: "He admonished and frightened me a great deal [by telling me] that I will go to hell if I do not become a nun [in 'Ayntura]."[50] During her stay in that convent, Hindiyya recounted that she felt tormented repeatedly by Father Gueynard and the prioress. At times they supposedly tried to entice her with promises of being appointed as an assistant to the prioress or teacher to the novices. At other times they threatened her with expulsion from the convent or forcible imprisonment in one of its buildings.

Because of these pressures or the relatively harsh physical environment of 'Ayntura, or perhaps both, Hindiyya became bedridden for five of the eight months she spent in the convent. Sister Theresa recalled those times by stating in her affidavit that there were "days when she was in good health and days when she was sick and she worked little."[51] Along with her physical weakness or illness, Hindiyya became increasingly dejected over her stay in 'Ayntura. She said that throughout those times Jesus appeared to her several times to console her, alleviate her fear, and strengthen her resolve in refusing to join the 'Ayntura convent. But Father Gueynard, like Venturi in Aleppo, proclaimed such visitations to be the temptations of the devil who was trying to ensnare her soul. Thus, Hindiyya was buffeted by uncertainty about her visions and her ultimate goal of establishing the new religious order dedicated to the Sacred Heart of Jesus. At night her "guardian angel" would appear to dissuade her from succumbing to the pleas and threats of the nuns and Gueynard. "If you . . . [become a nun in 'Ayntura] to escape your agony then your action will not appeal to God, and if you do so because you have given up [on establishing the new religious order] then that would be a sin; either way do not succumb."[52] In the morning, either Father Gueynard or Mother Rosa al-Khazin or one of the unnamed nuns in Hindiyya's narrative of this episode would beseech or bully her. And so it went for the weeks and months of her sojourn in Dayr Ziyarat al-Adhra.

Finally, sometime in late April, Hindiyya asked Father Gueynard to write and ask Father Venturi to come to 'Ayntura from Aleppo. In the hope that Venturi would convince Hindiyya to join the convent, Gueynard acceded to her wishes, and his fellow Jesuit priest arrived some days later. Upon his arrival, rather than agree to join the convent, Hindiyya told Venturi all that had transpired—or at least her version of the events—and begged him to take her out of 'Ayntura and send her to Dayr Mar Hrash, which at the time was the seat of Maronite bishop Jirmanus Saqr, who had succeeded Bishop Qara'li in that post in 1742. Hindiyya's desire to transfer to seek the help of Bishop Saqr may have been due to a vision she had where Christ "showed me a monk from the Lebanese Order. . . . My Lord said to me: 'do not fear, for this monk is called Ibn Saqr and he will accompany you in establishing the Order of My Heart, and he will help you.'"[53] Or it might simply be an attempt to get one step further from Jesuit control since no mention of Saqr is made in her *Secret of the Union* autobiography, which chronologically preceded the account of this vision. Either way, the Maronite bishop does not seem to have agreed to accept Hindiyya in his convent—at least not in the beginning. Hindiyya thought this was because Gueynard, who had given her an ultimatum of either becoming a nun in 'Ayntura or going back to Aleppo, was going around to the surrounding convents telling those responsible not to allow Hindiyya to enter. Once the deadline passed, Gueynard made good on his threat and "he expelled me from the convent . . . I was afflicted with fever unable to stand and not knowing where to go since I was thrown into the middle of the road with no one to help me."[54] Frightened and alone, she beseeched God for salvation, which came in the form of Venturi, who put her in an animal pen while he sought the assistance of a woman and her son who lived in a village between 'Ayntura and Hrash. Upon their return to the stable, they took Hindiyya back to their house, where she stayed for two days and two nights. While she remained there, Father Venturi tried to convince Bishop Jirmanus to allow Hindiyya into Dayr Mar Hrash but again to no avail. Instead, he managed to secure for her a begrudging invitation to stay with some Melkite nuns who themselves were in exile in a house neighboring the convent.

Sister Theresa's rendition of what transpired toward the end of Hindiyya's stay in 'Ayntura was as different from Hindiyya's as her preceding explanation of the Aleppan's unhappiness at the convent. Hindiyya appears in this alternative narrative less inspired to reject the offer to join the Jesuit convent and more calculating in her goal to establish a new religious order. Theresa told Fr. Desiderio that there was never any pressure on Hindiyya to join their convent. To prove her point, she gave him, as part of her testimony, a copy of a contract supposedly concluded between Hindiyya and the nuns of 'Ayntura on February 11, 1747. It stipulated that in exchange for the two hundred piasters which she gave to the convent Hindiyya "can stay and live among us and she is not obliged to take religious vows or change her secular clothes or observe the Rule of the convent."[55] Quite expectedly, Theresa never mentioned coercion in her testimony; rather, she painted a picture of an overly sensitive Hindiyya. In one instance, Theresa recounted, "Father Gueynard [after Hindiyya had been insisting on only speaking with Venturi] said to her among other things that some of the girls in Aleppo get too attached to their confessor and they get sad when he leaves. She thought that he was talking about her but I do not think so and she became angry."[56] Sister Theresa's speculation notwithstanding, Hindiyya was not mistaken in taking the barb to be meant for her since there were no other Aleppan nuns in the convent.

In Sister Theresa's testimony Hindiyya does not appear as a meek soul, lonely, powerless, and uncertain but for the grace of God. Instead, we find a Hindiyya who stubbornly rejected what she deemed as lesser authority and was resolute in her vision of her future. In that vein, Theresa reported that Hindiyya predicted that the Jesuit religious order in 'Ayntura would collapse and she would take it over because "God willed it so." As we will see later, her predictions may also have derived from the tensions that had long existed between Latin missionaries and local churches. Theresa said that Hindiyya had to dissuade her and other novices from learning the rule of the convent and taking their vows in the hope that they would join her in establishing the new order. To entice Theresa, she promised her that within the new convent dedicated to the Sacred Heart of Jesus order she would be her assistant, and Hindiyya would not accept "just anyone into the convent, but she would bring only young and virtuous Aleppan women." Hindiyya became rather upset when all the novices including Theresa took their vows; and subsequently, Theresa told Fr. Desiderio, Hindiyya was so afraid that her actions would be uncovered and Gueynard and Venturi would be cross with her that she "made me [Theresa] hold the cross and swear not to divulge to anyone what . . . [Hindiyya] did and told [me]." Theresa concluded her testimony by saying that it was the failure of this subversive project and the ensuing isolation that prompted Hindiyya to leave the convent. Even her departure was described differently. It was just as sudden but not initiated by a deadline set and threat carried out by Gueynard. Rather, Hindiyya had previously visited Dayr Mar Hrash, and Bishop Jirmanus, the prioress, and all the religious women treated her with "love and deference." (This seems unlikely since by Venturi's account Bishop Saqr was not willing to accept Hindiyya into an overcrowded convent.) On the day of departure, while all the novices were in the church "praying and taking their vows," Father Venturi supposedly entered the convent with a man and together they packed Hindiyya's belongings and took them and her to Dayr Mar Hrash. "And after that I do not know what happened to her."[57]

A Lonely Perch

Whether she left of her own free will or was expelled (or some combination of the two), Hindiyya became free from Jesuit and—largely but temporarily—from other clerical authority and oversight. She also became far lonelier throughout the two following years during her stay at Dayr Mar Hrash. It is the freedom and loneliness of this period that transformed her from a visionary to a prophetess through a crucible of trials that evoked the experiences and vitae of earlier prophets and formative religious figures. Her relationship with Christ quickened and intensified, her sense of purpose became ever grander and clearer, and her resolve to be the instrument of Christ in establishing a new religious order became firmer. In the depth of her despair she clung to Christ as her only solace.

Hindiyya's stay at Dayr Mar Hrash was hardly any better than her residence in 'Ayntura. In fact, the situation and accommodations at the Maronite convent of Dayr Mar Hrash appear, at least from Hindiyya's bourgeois perspective, far more trying. From the outset she felt that she was received as nothing but an added burden by the nuns and even Bishop Jirmanus Saqr. This may have been partly due to the fact that the convent was already a small, crowded space and Hindiyya was left to reside with seven other Melkite nuns in a nearby house that was part of the convent's properties. She recounted to Fr. Desiderio, "I would stay with one [Melkite] nun every four days until she became fed up with me, and I would have to move with someone else because I did not have a room of my own."[58] Her tale is corroborated and even compounded in the *al-Sijill Shuwayri,* which is the record of the Melkite monastic order in Dayr al-Shuwayr of Mount Lebanon. For the year 1748 an entry in this record noted that "the Maronite nun Hindiyya would sleep in one room with the two Melkite sisters, Mariam and Agatha."[59] They, along with five other Melkite *'abidat,* were—as mentioned cursorily earlier and will be detailed later—displaced against their will from their convent, Dayr al-Ziyara. Food was scarce, with only water, "rotten bread and sometimes . . . soup" to be had by Hindiyya and the devotees. Aside from the chronic illnesses which afflicted at least two of them, the atmosphere must have been rather depressing. It could hardly be otherwise with eight women crammed into a small space, all feeling powerless and despondent in the face of ecclesiastical authorities who either actively denied them the right to make decisions about their religious future or thoroughly ignored them. Thus, even more than at the ʿAyntura convent, Hindiyya was deprived of the dear commodity of solitude and, more critically, support for her vision.

Thus, she escaped into the "wilderness." Hindiyya described her days in Dayr Mar Hrash to Fr. Desiderio as follows:

> God knows how much I suffered. Suffice it to say that just to get some rest I would spend my days in the forest near the convent . . . alone and terribly frightened from the dogs and animals that I would see. But God comforted me with some visions, and with my guardian angel whom I would see at times. But for that I would surely have died.[60]

The place where she fled was not the romantic landscape imagined and depicted by Latin missionaries and Aleppan monks. Rather, for Hindiyya—a woman reared in the leisure of Aleppo's urbane environment—it was a frightening wilderness filled with trials and "demons." It was a place which in its dreadful wildness only compounded her sense of anguish over the "difficulties, insults, persecutions, pains and illnesses [suffered] in this convent, and the neglect which befell me from all including his eminence the bishop [Jirmanus]."[61] But, like Moses on Mount Sinai or Muhammad on Mount Arafat, this very isolation and anguish brought her closer to her God and intensified their relationship quite beyond its beginnings in Aleppo, for in her wilderness Hindiyya came ever closer to being physically, mentally, and spiritually united with Christ.

"I am with you, my friend Hindiyya, do not be afraid."[62] Christ thus addressed Hindiyya as she struggled with her frustrations with where she lived, with the absence of any support for her project, and with her loneliness in her endeavor. She begged Jesus and the Virgin Mary repeatedly to be released from the responsibility of the divine gift and blessing bestowed upon her. "I would say to him many times: 'instead of this gift allow me to be invisible and far from people so that I can love You, and the misfortunes that befall me can no longer keep from loving You.'"[63] But the visions only increased, and the heavenly personae only multiplied. Christ began to communicate with Hindiyya more frequently each day as she meandered in the woods beyond the convent. At times, he spoke to her without showing himself, while at others he manifested himself. On other occasions, the Holy Ghost and the Virgin Mary "consoled" her and encouraged her to persevere against all odds. If that was not enough, Christ even presented Hindiyya with a host of saintly intercessors supposedly working on her behalf and for the establishment of the proposed Sacred Heart order. These included, much to the later irritation and incredulousness of Vatican inquisitors

> Our lady, the Sultana of Heaven, the Virgin Mary, the mother of our God. Saint Michael the archangel. Saint Joseph, the fiancé of the Virgin. Saint Peter the most important of the Apostles. Saint John the Beloved. Saint Ignatius the Martyr, and the Patriarch of Antioch. Saint Teresa [de Avila], Saint Catherine of Siena, Saint Gertrude and Saint Francesca Romana.[64]

This illustrious list of Catholic protagonists appeared in a 1758 letter that Hindiyya addressed to the nuns of her then established Sacred Heart order and at a time when the order was struggling for its survival against attacks by the Jesuits and skepticism from the Vatican. Even in earlier documents dating back to 1748 and 1749—that is, before the establishment of the order—Hindiyya was beginning to place herself along a saintly genealogical line that endowed her with the authority and power sorely lacking from her earthly and earlier life. Thus, while in Aleppo she had vaguely alluded to the presence and ostensible support of saints and other heavenly bodies, this latter visitation was far more specific in identifying the individuals and their role as intercessors on her behalf. Her days in the "wilderness" of Mount Lebanon were thus crystallizing her role as more than a visionary; rather, as something higher in the rankings of divine personages.

Reaffirming this transformation were the words that Christ purportedly spoke to her during their repeated communion amid the rocks and trees surrounding Dayr Mar Hrash. It began with him insistently repeating to Hindiyya that she could not turn away from the gift he bestowed upon her, nor could his will, embodied in this gift, be turned back by her or any other person for that matter. Indeed, he told her,

> My Sacred Heart delights in your sadness and difficulties because you endure it with patience. I look upon you and enfold you with my love at all times because you submit your will to My divine will even during these times that are difficult for human nature to endure. O, Hindiyya, these difficulties that you are experiencing will dissipate but My love for, and contentment with, you will never disappear.[65]

Thus, even as Hindiyya was rising—or elevating herself—in religious stature to rival the likes of Catherine of Siena or Teresa de Avila, her relationship to Christ was becoming more intensely personal and physical. He told her repeatedly during the year of wandering, "Know that through these difficulties [which you face] you have possessed Me, I the Beloved of your heart. And I have taken possession of your will and your heart, and I now hold them in my hand."[66] Hindiyya responded to this evocative image with one of her own. Mirroring and accentuating earlier visions she had had in Aleppo, the body of Christ and his "wounds" appeared to her in brighter glory. His body shone with such a great beauty that "it appeared to me that every one of his wounds was a mouth showing happiness and joy."[67]

This somewhat alarming image—where agony and joy, violence and love intermingle—was surely reflective of the vita of Hindiyya, particularly of that moment in her life. But it is also part of a discourse that transcended the place and the moment and included myriad other visionary women who lived long or shortly before her in Europe and Latin America. Among them were the same Catherine of Siena, Gertrude, and Teresa de Avila who appeared to Hindiyya in the earlier vision. They, like Hindiyya, saw in their own suffering a necessary emulation of the suffering of Christ and an essential step toward attaining his full love. Fasting, prolonged illnesses, humiliation, bloodletting, rejection, loneliness, and ridicule were all part of the life of the visionary seeking union with Christ. Similarly, the focus on the holy wounds of Christ was quite a common theme in the hagiographies and writings of medieval female saints.[68] The wounds represented the ultimate evidence of the "humanation" of Christ because they stood as evidence of the intersection of human experience with his through the blood of suffering issuing from them. Thus, the very agony they symbolize is the source of salvation, which itself is the manifested love of God for humanity. But while these themes had become common in medieval Europe and thereafter, within the context of the Eastern Christian milieu they were incredibly novel in their graphic depiction of the physicality of divine love. Hindiyya was thus blazing a lonely path to reach the heights of love with her beloved Christ.

However, despite Hindiyya's protestations to Christ that she desired neither divine gifts nor glory but only his forgiveness and love, her ever-quickening communion with him was bringing her at least earthly versions of the power and glory she was declining. The duet of love and lovers played out in the "wilderness" culminated in a promise of a divine gift that intertwined body and knowledge, corporeality and divinity. Christ spoke to Hindiyya thus,

> Accept with your earthly will and submit to what I say to you because I will give you a new gift I have never given before and I shall never give again. . . . With this gift you can with My infinite authority comprehend—as much as I desire—the contents of My divine heart which are infinitely expansive knowledge beyond the comprehension of those beings I have created.[69]

With this promise Hindiyya was no longer an ordinary visionary. By itself, the uniqueness of the divine gift—at least as she described it—elevated her beyond those who preceded her and anyone who would come after her. Accordingly, none among the host of saintly men and women whom the Roman Catholic Church beatified and revered was presumably endowed with such a heavenly gift. Such a remarkable pretension was powerfully augmented with the regulated access that Christ gave Hindiyya to the "infinite" knowledge of his heart, which exceeded any earthly knowledge including that accumulated within the church by clerics and theologians. As Katharine Firth noted for Protestant apocalyptic authors, this unbounded knowledge promised Hindiyya a recovery of the mastery which Adam enjoyed over the physical world in the Garden of Eden.[70] This theme was repeated, elaborated, and accentuated in later visions and times. But even in its initial limited scope it afforded Hindiyya a religious authority which potentially transcended the hierarchy of the church and counterbalanced the setbacks and powerlessness she was experiencing back in the ramshackle abode she shared with the seven *'abidat*.

She was to need such a heavenly counterweight as her last earthly ally was taken away from her sometime in the late spring or early summer of 1748. She told Fr. Desiderio,

> then I faced a crisis which shocked me. . . . One day Father Venturi [her Jesuit confessor] came to me and told me that he was obliged in obedi-ence to his superiors to leave 'Ayntura, and so he could no longer come to hear my confessions. This deeply saddened and depressed me because I was to be deprived the support of the only man who cared for me.[71]

Venturi returned to Rome to explain to his superior, General Francesco de Retz, his continued support for Hindiyya and belief in her visions in the face of the skepticism of his fellow (French) Jesuit missionaries about her sanctity. Bishop Jirmanus Saqr reported that Father Gueynard had been secretly writing letters to the Jesuit authorities in Rome criticizing Ven-turi and his "naïve" belief in Hindiyya. In 1750 the Capuchin missionary Gabriel de Quintin wrote to a colleague that Venturi had been reviled by other Jesuit missionaries because he helped Hindiyya leave 'Ayntura—and thus the spiritual direction and oversight of the Jesuits—for Dayr Mar Hrash.[72] Despite this animosity and perhaps because he was unaware of the secret missives of Gueynard, Venturi, who was concerned as always to maintain Jesuit direction over Hindiyya's visionary career, sought to convince her to confess to Father Gueynard.

However, Hindiyya demurred after she heard "an internal voice tell-ing me: 'Do not say that you will confess to Father Gueynard but say that you want to confess to Bishop Jirmanus, and ask Father Antonio [Ven-turi] to ask him [the bishop] to do you this favor.'"[73] Bishop Jirmanus Saqr accepted and told Hindiyya that he was willing to hear confession any time she desired. This was the moment when Hindiyya's spiritual and physi-cal isolation began to subside and when she broke completely from the spiritual direction of the Jesuit missionaries of Syria and Mount Lebanon. Although it would seem that she was simply shifting benefactors—Jesuit

missionary to Maronite cleric—and submitting to a new religious authority, in fact she had just taken the step to greater independence from ecclesiastical authority and begun to reshape the nature of Catholicism in the
Levant and its relationship to the Vatican and missionaries. Whether this
was by design or inspiration is, of course, impossible to assess and irrelevant to the momentous changes that were about to unfold.

A Reluctant Ally

For about nine months Hindiyya confessed to Bishop Jirmanus Saqr
in Dayr Mar Hrash. "I did not reveal my thoughts to him and I did not tell
him anything about what was happening to me. I simply and briefly confessed my sins to him."[74] And "he did not utter a single word to me outside
confession."[75] Her hesitation can be explained as a normal guarded and
timid start of a new intimate relationship to replace her long-term, and
troubled, association with Antonio Venturi. As with the beginning of that
earlier relationship, she may not have been sure how long this one would
last, she did not know Bishop Jirmanus, and she could not have been certain how he would react to her visions of Christ and divinely inspired
missions. On the other hand, his aloofness is striking. Jirmanus Saqr was
himself a native of Aleppo, and given the constant interaction between
Aleppo and Mount Lebanon, he would have heard of Hindiyya and her
visions even prior to her arrival in the Kisrawan region. In the small circle
of religious and secular elites in Aleppo, he presumably knew her family,
relatives, and/or acquaintances. This then begs the question as to why he
was ever so reluctant to give Hindiyya shelter and succor when Venturi
first asked in 1748 and why he did not utter a word to her more than necessary in eight months of confessions.

One possible explanation—in the absence of any sources that speak
directly to this—is that Bishop Saqr was embroiled in, and occupied by, a
bitter conflict that had split the Maronite bishops and patriarch into two
rival camps. The troubles began in 1736 at the conclusion of the seminal
Lebanese Council held in Dayr al-Luwayzeh. The unique gathering, which
is still considered a major turning point in the history of the Maronite
Church, was called for by the Vatican. It was convened by the papal nuncio
Yusuf al-Sima'ani, who was originally from Mount Lebanon but had left as

a young boy in 1696 for Rome to attend the Maronite College and stayed to ultimately become the rector of the Vatican Library.[76] The council was attended by all the Maronite religious elites—some of whom came reluctantly and truculently—and key Latin missionaries in Syria and Mount Lebanon. It was intended to resolve the tensions and conflicts that had come to dominate the Maronite Church in the first three decades of the eighteenth century, of which three major issues stood out in particular.

The first was the issue of patriarchal authority vis-à-vis that of the bishops of the church. As Father Philip al-Samrani describes it,

> before the convening of the Lebanese Council, the Maronite Patriarch held all the authority in his sect. . . . He imposed what he wanted. . . . He had the absolute authority in choosing bishops. . . . Thus, there was really only one diocese for the Maronite sect which was that of the Patriarch . . . and the rest of the bishops were nothing more than his deputies.[77]

Even the number of bishops was not specified and varied between nine and fourteen, many of whom were appointed as honorary bishops without any diocese or ecclesiastical authority. Others were appointed bishops of distant dioceses such as Aleppo, Hama, and Homs, without requiring them to set foot in those cities; instead, they resided in Mount Lebanon. The patriarch exercised equally centralized authority and absolute control over the fiscal affairs of the church. For instance, Maronite patriarchs held a monopoly over the consecration of oil and its distribution and required all the clergy to come to the patriarchal seat in order to obtain— in essence, purchase—the consecrated oil in exchange for "gifts" given to the patriarch. The bishops were completely excluded from this spiritual and financial transaction. Moreover, the absence of a clear and set method for nominating and elevating clerics to the bishopric opened the process to extortion by the patriarch (Simonia), corruption, and the interference of secular and religious authorities and elites in the process. For instance, in 1732 Bishop Ignatius Sharabiya signed a document pledging his loyalty to Bishop Ilyas Muhasib. In it, he wrote

> I pledge to Allah and His Eminence Bishop Ilyas [Muhasib], who sought to appoint me bishop, that I will be one with him in effort and opinion,

and that I will give to the Bishop [Ilyas] all that I receive for the monastery and from the diocese that I visit regardless of the amount, except for fifty piasters for my clothes and necessities.[78]

Compounding these widespread irregularities and corruption in appointing clergy was the often explicit interference by the al-Khazin family into the process. For instance, Iliya Harik, a historian of Lebanon, noted that in the eighteenth century six of the eight patriarchs and fifteen of the twenty bishops belonged to the notable families in Mount Lebanon, mostly the Khazin family.[79] Much of the influence that the *muqata'aji* families, like the Khazins, exercised over the Maronite Church through the first half of the eighteenth century derived from the weak financial situation of the church and its reliance on such families for the construction of churches, monasteries, and convents and for other religious endowments. To a lesser extent, in the politically tumultuous Mount Lebanon, the church was dependent on these families for security and protection of property and person.

The third major issue was the tension between two differing visions of the Maronite Church. To some extent this came out of a generational split between a younger group of clerics (born in the late seventeenth or early eighteenth century) and older clergy (born in earlier times). But it is perhaps more accurate to describe it as a conflict between those who sought to reform the church along more institutionalized and "modern" lines and those who can be construed as more traditionalist, seeking to preserve the existing structure and independence of the church. What characterized the first group is that they had for the most part attained a higher degree of education either locally in Aleppo or by studying abroad in Rome. Many, but certainly not all, were the children of the Maronite bourgeoisie emerging at the periphery of the church's geographic expanse. Their background made them less prone to see the traditions of the church in Mount Lebanon as sacrosanct and more inclined to see them as the accretions of outdated practices emanating from an illiterate and superstitious milieu. Among those we find Abdallah Qara'li, along with many others of the founders and members of the Lebanese order who came from Aleppo, as well as Yusuf al-Sima'ani, who was based in Rome and was Qara'li's main ally. Not surprisingly, Latin missionaries, including Père Fromage, were strongly on the side of these reformers as they hoped they would succeed in bringing the Maronite Church into closer compliance with the reforms issued by the Council of Trent between 1545 and 1563.

These various historical dynamics came to a head at the Lebanese Council in 1736.[80] Over several tumultuous days in June of 1736 in a monastery in Kisrawan, the simmering tensions erupted into a full-blown argument pitting Patriarch Yusuf al-Khazin and his party against al-Sima'ani, several of the bishops who belonged to the Lebanese order, and the Latin missionaries. The arguments centered on the issues of *al-mayroun* (consecrated oil), specifying the number and boundaries of each diocese and assigning a fixed bishop to oversee its affairs, and finally separating nuns and monks into different religious houses as opposed to the joint living arrangement then prevalent in Mount Lebanon.[81] This last issue had been the subject of several letters written before the Lebanese Council, and it had come to represent the divide between the modernizers and the traditionalists in the church. For example, in 1733 the leaders of the Lebanese order sent a letter to the Propaganda Fide enumerating the various reforms required from their perspective to modernize the Maronite Church. "The most needed of these, and it is a very important and necessary matter, is for you to send a strict order to separate the monks from the nuns and to prohibit their cohabitation in the same monastery."[82] Al-Sima'ani noted in his memoirs that three bishops—Jibrail Duwayhi and Tubiya al-Khazin, both of whom graduated from the Maronite College, and Abdallah Qara'li, who studied in Aleppo—wrote a letter to the Propaganda Fide asking them to outlaw the old tradition of cohabitation between nuns and monks and to implement the rules of the Council of Trent on that matter.[83]

The intensity of the emotions surrounding these various issues sealed the fate of the first council. The fact that it was held in a monastery in Rayfoun which was under the control of the Khazin family only strengthened the hand of the patriarch and his party. "When the bishops refused to go along with the Patriarch's decision to annul the council . . . he sent by night a letter to his nephew Shaykh Nawfal [al-Khazin] and asked for their help. . . . When Shaykh Nawfal and others [Khazins] arrived they began to threaten the bishops to force them to sign whatever the Patriarch asked them for."[84] In such an environment of threats and obstinacy, the council was adjourned, and al-Simaʿani left frustrated in his efforts.

It was reconvened at the end of August after al-Simaʿani mobilized the support of the French consul in Sayda and asked him to put pressure on the Khazin family to refrain from interfering in the affairs of the council. Al-Simaʿani's efforts bore fruit, and the Lebanese Council was reconvened, this time in Dayr Luwayzeh, a monastery belonging to the Lebanese order, itself an indication of the shift in power. The attendees opened the synod on September 30 and concluded their work by issuing twelve decrees after three deliberations. However, the efforts to implement its recommendations and arguments about its legality and even about the text itself continued well into the nineteenth century. Thus, when al-Simaʿani sought to implement first the separation of nuns and monks into different religious houses, he quickly ran into opposition from the patriarch and the Khazin clan. The patriarch then dispatched Father Ilyas Saʿad to Rome to present his objections to the decision of the Lebanese Council, particularly as they related to the three main issues alluded to earlier. The Holy See reached a decision in August 1741 after three years of deliberation. Given that al-Simaʿani had undertaken his mission at the behest of the Vatican and the Propaganda Fide, it is not overly surprising that Pope Benedict XIV's decision was to uphold all the reforms dictated by the Lebanese Council. However, despite this decision, the Maronite Church still found it necessary to hold nine councils between 1744 and 1856, seeking to fully implement the decrees of the 1736 council. In fact, seven of those were held in the first fifty-four years after the original Lebanese Council.

It was against this backdrop of conflict within the Maronite Church that in 1742 Jirmanus Saqr was ordained honorary bishop of Homs or Tripoli (two conflicting stories make it unclear which one he oversaw). He was advanced to this position under circumstances borne by the fallout from the 1736 Lebanese Council. In that year, after the death of Patriarch Yusuf al-Khazin, two bishops—Ilyas Muhasib, who had opposed the council of 1736, and Tubiya al-Khazin, who was one of its main champions—squared off in a struggle over ascendancy to the patriarchate. At a conclave in Kisrawan, the Maronite bishops—with the noted absence of Tubiya al-Khazin, who later claimed that he was not even informed of the meeting—met to elect a new patriarch. At first, Sim'an 'Awwad was elected, but he turned the position down. Subsequently, in a second vote, Ilyas Muhasib was elected. Upon hearing of these proceedings, Tubiya al-Khazin ordained two new bishops, one of whom was Jirmanus Saqr, and held his own conclave, which elected him patriarch of the Maronite Church. Thus, when Patriarch Yusuf al-Khazin passed away in 1742, the two professed enemies, Ilyas Muhasib and Tubiya al-Khazin, each declared himself the rightful successor to the seat of the patriarchate. This anomaly, which threatened to tear the Maronite community apart, invited the swift intervention of the Vatican. By unprecedented decree, which the Vatican was at pains to define as exceptional and unique, both elections were annulled and Sima'an 'Awwad was appointed as the new patriarch of the Maronite Church. As part of this imposed resolution, Jirmanus Saqr's ordination to the bishopric was legalized.[85]

The troubles which beset the Maronite religious establishment—and occupied Jirmanus Saqr—did not subside with the ascendancy of Sima'an 'Awwad to the patriarchate. Rather, between 1742 and 1748 another crisis erupted, this time within the Lebanese order. In many ways the issues and protagonists who were behind the fissures in this conflict were similar to those of the 1736 Lebanese Council and the crisis of the patriarchate. The Lebanese order was divided into two fractious camps, Halabi (Aleppan) and Baladi (Mount Lebanon), with the first being dominated by members who came from the major cities in the eastern Mediterranean (Aleppo, Beirut, Damascus, Sidon, and Tripoli) and the latter mostly from the villages of Mount Lebanon. The immediate issue was the claim by the Baladi faction that the Halabis not only dominated the administration of the monastic order but had also accumulated enormously burdensome debts due to mismanagement. But underlying these frictions over political power and economic foibles was the same cultural divide between "traditionalists" and "modernizers" which characterized the Lebanese Council drama of 1736. The Halabis, supported by the Vatican and Latin missionaries, saw themselves as the vanguard of a new cosmopolitan and learned religiosity that stood in marked contrast to the rudimentary and unpolished faith of village priests and monks. The Baladis chafed under such haughty pretensions and harkened to an indigenous authenticity that was pure and

"natural" in its faith. As with the earlier patriarchate crisis, Jirmanus Saqr
was equally embroiled in this conflict on the side of the Baladis and Patriarch 'Awwad, who supported the local monks.

Finally, in 1748 when Hindiyya arrived at Dayr Mar Hrash, Bishop
Saqr was at least peripherally occupied with yet another religious drama
involving Aleppan Melkite nuns seeking to establish their own religious
order in Mount Lebanon. This particular conflict had been unfolding since
1730, when ten Aleppan Melkite religious devotees, under the spiritual
guidance of Jesuit missionaries, sought to establish a convent in Mount
Lebanon alongside the monastery of their coreligionists. Tensions quickly
escalated between the nuns and their Jesuit supporters, on the one hand,
and the Melkite religious establishment, on the other. At issue was the rule
to be followed by the devotees in their convent. (We will return to this in
detail in chapter 4.) The conflict dragged on for nearly a decade and was
finally referred to the Vatican for adjudication in 1740. The Propaganda
Fide issued its final decision on the matter three years later in favor of the
Melkite monks, that the Jesuits did not have the authority to pass the sacrament to the devotees without the permission of the bishop of the diocese
and that the spiritual direction of the convent must be left in the hands
of the Melkite Shuwayrite order.[86] The implementation of this judgment
took another three years for a variety of reasons, but when it was finally
applied in April 1746 "Maria Qari [the leader of the dissenting Melkite
nuns] and her party refused to submit to the authority of the [Shuway-
rite] order and abide by the Basilian Rule. Thus, they immediately left the
convent and went to the Maronite convent of Mar Hrash."[87] They, in turn,
were the ones who convinced Bishop Saqr to allow Hindiyya to stay with
them in the small house adjoining Dayr Mar Hrash.

One can safely say, then, that Hindiyya arrived at Dayr Mar Hrash
at a time when Bishop Saqr was overwhelmed. Hindiyya's concerns and
problems may very well have appeared rather insignificant to him in comparison to the politics that divided the council of Maronite bishops, which
were slowly but surely tearing the Lebanese order into two irreconcilable
factions and which brought into his overcrowded convent seven rebellious women. Hindiyya would have been just one more problem. Thus,
it is not overly surprising to find that he did not heed her at first and did

not "utter one word to me outside of confession." Against this backdrop of tumult and tension, what is more intriguing is why Bishop Saqr suddenly, after many months of neglect, took a keen interest in her. Hindiyya notes the dramatic shift in an almost offhand manner: "after some incident the mother superior of Dayr Hrash found out about my spiritual affairs and she told the Bishop about them and since that time he began to show me some consideration."[88] It is not clear what the incident was or if there really was one, but it seems to have been the moment when Hindiyya's career as a visionary was relaunched.

Speaking in 1753 to the inquisitor Fr. Desiderio di Casabasciana, Hindiyya recounted that "one morning he [Bishop Saqr] said to me after hearing my confession that he wanted me to reveal my thoughts to him, and tell him all that had transpired so that he can better guide my spirit."[89] After their brief conversation, Bishop Saqr directed Hindiyya to recount all her previous life to the mother superior of Dayr Mar Hrash. Despite her professed and somewhat disingenuous protestations for someone who had previously bitterly complained of neglect, he insisted that she reveal her past and thoughts to the mother superior, Rebecca al-Khazin. Her real or contrived submission to his request led to what she had escaped in Aleppo: notoriety and attention, first from the nuns of the convent and then from men and women of the neighboring villages and areas. "Hardly any time went by before, much to my great displeasure, I found myself in greater distress and anguish than in Aleppo because people came in droves to see me and speak with me even when I did not want to see or speak to anyone."[90] In the course of complaining about being the center of a spectacle that made a mockery of her religious vocation, Hindiyya finally divulged to Bishop Saqr the true nature of her visions and calling. She informed him that she had not traveled to Mount Lebanon to become a nun in the convents of 'Ayntura and Hrash but rather to establish the Order of the Sacred Heart of Jesus to glorify God and save the multitudes of souls from certain damnation. "I also hinted a little bit that he was [by divine design] to be my aid in this. Thus, he was moved by great fervor to pursue [that goal]."[91]

Certainly, the grandeur of the vision and project may have moved the religious sentiments of Saqr. In other words, religious enthusiasm and emotions were at least some of the motivations behind Saqr's dramatic change of heart. Growing up in Aleppo at a time of religious revivalism and his affiliation with zealous missionaries, as well as his position as a bishop in the Maronite Church, would seem to indicate some proclivity toward religiosity. To hear, within that context, that he was to be an instrument of God in promoting faith in Mount Lebanon and beyond would have touched and spurred his soul. His eternal salvation would have appeared to him as far more certain if he were to do God's bidding by helping Hindiyya. Contributing to his conversion were the various tales of Hindiyya's spirituality that were beginning to circulate in the Hrash convent. When Hindiyya had fallen ill and was confined to bed (before this episode with the rule), a sister in the convent assigned to serve her began to testify about the self-mortification and stigmata wounds that Hindiyya carried on her body. Previously "naturally lax and negligent in observing the rules," as Saqr described her, Sister Katerina was "edified" by Hindiyya's saintliness and became her first follower and lifelong assistant and companion. Spreading news of Hindiyya's miraculous visions led to nocturnal meetings in Hindiyya's room, where the nuns and novices would pose religious and spiritual questions and she, with the help of her guardian angel, would answer them.[92] The infusion of the convent of Hrash with this new religious energy and deeper spirituality struck Bishop Saqr as a remarkable event, which convinced him of the veracity of Hindiyya's visions.

Yet it is also within the realm of possibility that he saw in Hindiyya the means to transcend the stigma of his questionable ascendancy to the bishopric and his subsequent subservient role to the pretender to the patriarchate, Ilyas Muhasib. In championing the cause of Hindiyya, his tenure would be infused with a far grander meaning and purpose than to simply manage a convent and collect tithes, most of which he paid over to Bishop Muhasib anyway per their agreement, which was similar to the one signed by Bishop Sharabiya.[93] Beyond this personal gratification rested the altruistic dimension of the project that Hindiyya described. At the time that she dropped her "little hint," Saqr was emerging out of thirteen years of contention within the Maronite Church, to which he was party on at least two occasions. Ironically, then, the very preoccupations which led him to ignore Hindiyya for the first part of her stay in Hrash became all the more reason for him to support her cause. As a visionary of God and as the select choice of Christ to establish a new religious order, Hindiyya could, from Saqr's perspective, unify the feuding factions of the Maronite Church and community around her and her vision.

His first step in that direction was to record the rule for the new proposed order, as revealed to Hindiyya "by my Lord." While this may seem a mild development, in fact it was a strong statement of commitment on the part of Bishop Saqr to Hindiyya and her solitary project. As he very well knew from the proceedings of the Lebanese Council, the Vatican did not allow the establishment of new monastic orders and rules for them before its prior consultation and approval. Under those circumstances, penning a wholly new rule—a step meant specifically to establish the Order of the Sacred Heart of Jesus—was a marked departure from the strictures of the Vatican and, at least implicitly, a rejection of its authority to dictate Maronite affairs. In 1753 Hindiyya told her inquisitor Fr. Desiderio that this was the reason that Father Venturi "opposed the Rule completely, and I warned the bishop to avoid discussing the matter with Father Venturi." Therefore, Hindiyya and Saqr agreed to hide the truth from Venturi and to claim that they were simply recording the visions she had received from Christ.

> So we started to write in this manner. . . . They would write what I say that Jesus Christ has shown unto me. . . . Here I ought to tell you another thing, which is that since I did not know how to write I would supplicate God and my guardian angel in prayers [to help me]. My guardian angel would appear and remind me of all that I had to dictate in the colloquy. Then he would come to help me with a visible face standing next to me and I saw him clearly. If he saw that I forgot a word he would tell it to me and so it was that I dictated the chapters of the Rule from beginning until end.[94]

This sequence of events raises the question as to why Venturi was even necessary for the process. If Hindiyya and Saqr did not trust him to support the project and needed a ruse to attain his cooperation and if the guardian angel was ascertaining the veracity of her recollection, then it would appear that Venturi was rather superfluous. In her interrogation, Hindiyya recognized the paradox in her statement because she hastened to add to the above description that he was only there for a "few chapters" and that it was she and bishop Saqr who carried out the majority of the work. But this does not resolve the issue. Rather, involving Venturi was more likely meant to provide Jesuit legitimacy to a project that both Hindiyya and Saqr suspected to be not only ambitious but likely to engender opposition with its audacity. Hindiyya's tense relations with the Jesuit missionaries in Mount Lebanon and their opposition to her project—if carried out independently of their supervision—would surely have been still on her mind. Saqr, who was embroiled in two tendentious conflicts that directly involved the Vatican and the missionaries in Maronite Church affairs, would have also known that a new religious order that did not have the prior approval of the Vatican would not go unnoticed or unopposed. Under these circumstances, Venturi was needed to lend the project an air of Latin Catholic approval, though it is questionable how much legitimacy he could have lent to the project given his recent recall to Rome, where he was censured for his uncritical support for Hindiyya.

With or without divine inspiration and the assistance of her guardian angel, the rule was completed sometime in 1750. Simultaneously, throughout the writing process, Bishop Saqr had been working to secure a convent for Hindiyya and her proposed religious order. For this purpose, he wrote to Bishop Tubiya al-Khazin, the man who ordained him into the bishopric, asking him for a convent where Hindiyya could establish her religious order. Al-Khazin wrote back to Saqr to tell him that he would be willing to provide Hindiyya with one of the monasteries within his diocese that was unoccupied and had fallen into disrepair. At the same time Saqr was pursuing another possibility at the monastery of Bkerki. That monastery had housed the monks of St. Isaiah, but they had fallen onto hard times and had been unable for a while to "keep the place." Their income had fallen short of their expenses—because of their "laziness," as Saqr later claimed—and they had repeatedly proposed selling the property to Bishop Saqr in exchange for building a smaller monastery, which would be attached to the Hrash convent. Thus, in 1750 Saqr approached the monks of St. Isaiah on the basis of their previous offers, and he reported to Hindiyya that they were willing to sell him the monastery, which had seven rooms, for eight or nine hundred piasters. This would have been a bargain despite its small size. A convent that had been built just a decade earlier for Maria Qari and her nine Melkite nuns cost between five and six thousand piasters.[95] It is supposedly at this point that the Jesuits—according to what Saqr told Hindiyya—intervened and convinced the monks of Isaiah to refuse the deal because the price was too low. Saqr, apparently adept at the art of bargaining, did not offer a higher price and told the monks that he would simply accept the earlier offer of Bishop Tubiya al-Khazin. He declined to propose a counteroffer because—again, he informed Hindiyya—he knew that two of the Khazin *shuyukh* contended that they owned the monastery and the monks did not therefore have any right to dispose of it and that, moreover, the *shuyukh* were unhappy with the way the monks had managed the place. Indeed, the same *shuyukh* were already thinking of evicting the monks. Given the precarious bargaining position of the monks, Saqr preferred to wait until they came closer to his price. Saqr's real-estate acumen served him well as the monks did indeed come seeking to sell—with the approval of the Khazin *shuyukh*—the monastery for a total of "five bags," or 2,500 piasters. The negotiations appeared to be almost concluded when the Jesuits "interfered again in this affair and undermined all that was agreed upon."[96] This worldly negotiation was finally sealed with a price tag of 3,500 piasters, which the monks of Isaiah accepted, and a deed that they signed giving the convent to Hindiyya to establish her religious order.[97]

A New Order

"Finally, our Lord Jesus was victorious over all opposition, and we received the monastery and we entered legally into it with the permission and blessing of his Excellency Patriarch Sima'an 'Awwad. That was the twenty and fifth day of the month of February in the year 1750."[98] This is how Hindiyya recounted her entry into the convent of Bkerki to the nuns of her newly established order. She added that Jesus confirmed to her that this was the right place. He spoke to her as she walked around her new convent: "This is the place that I wanted for the establishment of the order of my Sacred Heart."[99] Within this postscript to a long and arduous journey that had brought her from Aleppo to Mount Lebanon in the span of her thirty years of life, Hindiyya was nowhere to be found (nor, for that matter, were the nuns from Dayr Mar Hrash who were accompanying her). Christ had chosen the place, and he overcame obstacles; Patriarch 'Awwad provided church support and legal authority. Her self-elision (out of humility or political calculation) did not last long. A month later—on the Feast of the Annunciation, which fell on March 25, 1750—she was back at center stage. The occasion was the official establishment of the order, when Hindiyya and several nuns took upon themselves the habit and vows of the Order of the Sacred Heart of Jesus. As soon as Hindiyya had made her vows, she saw "with the spirit" the Holy Ghost in the shape of a dove descend upon her chest.

> The rays of its light spread to the head of his Excellency the Bishop [Saqr]—my [spiritual] director—and the church was filled with its divine glory. I also saw the intercessors for the Order [of the Sacred Heart], the heavenly angels, and the archangel Gabriel among the rest. I also saw the male and female saints the founders of religious orders . . . and I saw them singing hymns with beautiful music and indescribable joy . . . to the heart of Our Lord Jesus Christ. They were glorifying His condescension, love and benevolence and the rest of His perfections in allowing for the establishment of the order of His Sacred Heart.

This vision precipitated a deep trance, where Hindiyya was no longer aware of anyone or even herself. She became wholly focused on Christ unabashedly glorifying himself. Among the various things he listed was the glory of his benevolence in giving humanity the supernal gift of his heart, the source of his eternal love, through "the founder of the religious order of My Sacred Heart." It was, as Christ said, an unprecedented gift that was meant to bring believers and those with "lukewarm hearts" back to him through love.

The two events render a remarkably different picture of the role that Hindiyya played in the establishment of the convent and the order. The first attributes everything to Christ and the Maronite Church. The latter makes Hindiyya the central character in the most graphic of manner, with the rays of the Holy Ghost—and the will of Christ—emanating from her own chest and heart to cast its (her) grace upon the Maronite Church as symbolized in the person of Bishop Saqr. While Christ remained the ultimate source of Hindiyya's power-emanating demeanor, the Maronite Church became in this representation a recipient of authority and legitimacy rather than its source. Contradictory though these differing images may appear in our later days, they were in fact coherent elements of Hindiyya's life and calling—and of the Janus-like lives of the visionaries who preceded her. To be a true instrument of Christ, Hindiyya had to subsume her will fully to his, to be meek and humble with no ambitions of her own. Yet this very meekness is what allowed God's will to shine forth, imbuing her with a power and authority that stand in marked contrast to her feebleness and helplessness. This, in essence, was the paradigm of her life and the lives of other visionaries.[100] It projected power and authority unto Hindiyya without making her directly responsible for their implications since she was simply a conduit. It placed her as a singular woman above temporal male authorities, thus turning the patriarchal world of the Catholic Church on its head. These two events, then, represented the very transformation of Hindiyya from a privately devout woman to a visionary whose spiritual experiences and visions could no longer be contained within her body but shone forth upon the world around her. In this sense, walking into the convent of Bkerki high on a mountaintop in Kisrawan, with sweeping vistas of the coast of Mount Lebanon and the Mediterranean sea stretching as far as Cyprus, was a remarkable moment in the life of Hindiyya and of the Maronite Church.

But the moment was brief. Christ quickly added to Hindiyya, as she meandered into her new convent, "Be ready, my friend Hindiyya, to withstand hard trials, diverse difficulties and horrible accusations. . . . You will not have a joy free of grief in this order because I will intermix your rejoicing in the blessings of this order with sorrows always and until the end of your life." With this promise of tribulation, Christ also reminded Hindiyya that "I chose you My beloved as the means to establish the order of my Sacred Heart . . . so do not fear . . . for I am always with you."[101] Indeed, as soon as she set foot in the Bkerki convent, Hindiyya came to be the focus of a campaign by the Jesuit missionaries to discredit her and to dismantle her new order. In response, the majority of the Maronite clergy came to her aid, championing her cause and proclaiming her virtues as a living saint. The alacrity and intensity of the conflict that swirled around Hindiyya and her order were about a woman claiming to speak with authority in the name of Christ. They are testimony to the radical nature and perceived magnitude of her transgressions across gender lines that had been drawn decades before within the hierarchy of the Catholic Church. Thus, despite Hindiyya's fervent prayers throughout her early years in Mount Lebanon "to Christ and our Lady Virgin Mary . . . [to allow her] to disappear and be alone,"[102] she came to be the central protagonist in a very public and political drama to shape and define the substance and contours of Levantine Catholicism.

BKERKI CONVENT

A Living Saint (1750–1756)

Spiritual Madness

Sometime in 1751 copies of a poster satirizing and attacking Hindiyya and her allies appeared across Mount Lebanon and in the city of Aleppo. Commissioned by Jesuit missionaries, the poster was sarcastically titled "A Real Picture of the Heart of the Sinless Hindiyya."[1] The painting—measuring four by three feet, in full color, and crafted with painstaking detail—listed the faults of "The New Cedar of Lebanon" around the representation of a flowering tree. Implanted in a heart inscribed with the words "Arrogance and Egotism," the trunk of the tree stretched upward with the proclamation that a "bad tree cannot bear good fruit." Above this truism and amid the leaves and flowers was a circle of words, which included "chaos, love of silver, spiritual madness, false religion." In its center was emblazoned in red letters "A Definitive Response to All That Is Said, Written and Fabricated by the *Hindawiyyun* [Hindiyya's supporters]."[2] Beneath the tree were two panels. The right one was titled "This Is Mother Hindiyya's Temple," and ranged beneath were the titles ascribed to Hindiyya by her followers: "Absolute Saint," "Sinless since Childhood," "Honor of Lebanon," "Pride of the Roman Church." The left panel proclaimed "This is the door of Bkerki Convent; You can only Enter: By kissing her hands and her footsteps; when bishops submit themselves to her and priests stand with respect for her . . . and finally by donating copious amounts of money."

Clearly, a good deal of time was spent articulating, designing, and then distributing copies of this visually elaborate vitriol against Hindiyya.

6. Jesuit Poster Satirizing Hindiyya. AMPB Hindiyya Papers. Courtesy of Maronite Patriarchate Archives.

By itself the poster would be intriguing enough to make one wonder why Jesuit missionaries saw the need to assail Hindiyya, her order, and her supporters so vehemently. This is especially the case when little over a year before Franz Retz, the superior general of the Jesuit order, wrote Père Venturi instructing him to ask Hindiyya, "that pious devotee . . . to mention me and all the members of our Order in her prayers."[3] However, it is all the more striking because it was not an isolated incident. Beginning in 1750 the Jesuit establishment in the Levant, and some of their Maronite supporters, organized a systematic campaign meant to discredit Hindiyya in the eyes of the Maronite community and the Vatican authorities. The earlier effort by Jesuits to scuttle the Bkerki deal between Bishop Saqr and the monks of St. Isaiah (as described in chapter 3) was the first salvo in this campaign. Matters only escalated thereafter and were spearheaded by Père Marc-Antoine Séguran, one of the founders of Dayr al-Ziyarat al-Adhra in 'Ayntura, where Hindiyya refused to take her vows only four years before. The other main characters in the project to curtail and undermine Hindiyya's rising popularity and influence were Father Gabriel de Quintin, the superior of the Franciscans in the Levant, and Ni'matallah al-Sharabati, a Maronite priest from Aleppo. Besides the voluminous missives that all three (but especially Séguran) addressed to the Propaganda Fide, Séguran traveled to Rome to present the case against Hindiyya personally. Clearly, Hindiyya—herself or what she represented in the eyes of her detractors—was seen as a formidable threat that required years of broadsides.

At the same time the support that Hindiyya enjoyed from Patriarch Sima'an 'Awwad, many of the Maronite bishops (Tubiya al-Khazin, Jibra'il 'Awwad, Istifan Duwayhi, Hanna Istifan), most of the elders of the Khazin *muqata'ajis,* and a widening circle of the Maronite population in Mount Lebanon and Aleppo raises similar questions. Why was there a rush to adopt and proclaim Hindiyya as a saintly woman? What made the Khazin *shuyukh* declare, in a letter addressed to the Propaganda Fide, that "the convents [controlled by the Sacred Heart of Jesus order] are our convents, built by our fathers and grandfathers, and we will allow whomever we want to live in them. . . . As for the Jesuit monks, if they do not cease from these matters [attacks on Hindiyya and her order] harm will come to them and we will cut their legs from our land."[4] Why did several of the elite women of Mount Lebanon (like Teresa al-Khazin) reject Father Séguran's invitation to join the ʿAyntura Jesuit convent and opt instead to take their vows with the Sacred Heart of Jesus order? And why was there a long list of testimonies (which included a Rome-educated Maronite intellectual like Father Mikhail Fadel) attesting to the holiness of Hindiyya and her ability to perform miracles?[5]

The answer to these questions is twofold. The tensions surrounding Hindiyya, her order, and her convent were part of a larger struggle over the dissonant articulation of a new Christianity in the Levant. This was a conflict that emanated from the process of incorporating the "small flock . . . and the small nation," as one Jesuit called the Maronites during the 1736 Lebanese Synod, into the Roman Catholic Church. From the end of the seventeenth century and through the early part of the nineteenth century, Latin missionaries and local Catholic clerics disagreed over what that meant. For most Latin missionaries this implied the curtailment and diminution of the ecclesiastical sway of local clerics whom they regarded as theologically deficient, if not completely prone to dogmatic error. For Maronite and Melkite clergy the closer relations with Rome were meant to augment their own local power vis-à-vis Ottoman authorities and non-Catholic Christians and to support them in their internecine struggles against fellow clerics. They hardly regarded their millennium of religious authority, practices, and traditions to be in need of correction. By dint of her rapidly growing saintly reputation and concomitant authority, Hindiyya came to be the center of this bitter contest over religious authority in the Levant.

Yet, in equal measure, the tensions are testament to the public power of Hindiyya's private and gendered visions and pronouncements. Her project to establish a religious order was grounded in visions that brought her ever closer to Christ and imbued her (at least from the perspective of her supporters) with authority that superseded that of the missionaries and even the Vatican. In this manner, she helped shape a locally rooted conceptualization of Christianity, which stood at times in opposition to the one that Latin missionaries had worked assiduously for over a century to introduce to (and sometimes impose on) the Christian population of the eastern Mediterranean. She also came to embody a distinctly Maronite identity that was turning its back on its Ottoman and Muslim milieu but that still aimed to distinguish itself from Latin Christianity through language (Arabic), culture ("Eastern"), and sacred geography ("Holy Land"). In all of this Hindiyya was a product of preexisting tensions as well as a visionary who sharpened and accentuated the divisions between local and Latin Christianity. Her viability as a saint was contingent on her Maronite and Levantine milieu, and reciprocally the religious validation of the Maronite community was dependent on her viability as a saint.[6] In both ways, she came to be the epicenter of the conflict. To fully understand her position, we need to turn to both sets of historical dynamics in greater detail and to parse their interaction during the early years of the Sacred Heart of Jesus order.

Endless Quarrels

Animosity between local Christians and Latin missionaries did not commence with Hindiyya.[7] In the middle of the seventeenth century the first hint of these confrontations emerged between the Capuchin missionaries and the Maronite Church. The Capuchins were most unimpressed with the state of affairs among the Maronite clergy. As Hilaire de Brenton noted years later,

> Upon arriving in Beirut, Sayda and Mount Lebanon, our [Capuchin] fathers found the Maronite church in a state of extraordinary decadence. The marriage of priests has been the most serious flaw in the Oriental Church. . . . They serve no ecclesiastical function, nor administer any sacrament, even that of penitence, if there is no payment in money.[8]

The Franciscan missionary Sylvestre de Saint-Aignan wrote in 1651 that the devil had convinced local Christians that saintliness and sainthood are brought about by fasting, which ultimately led to the disappearance of confession—central to the post-Tridentine profession of faith and consecration of church authority over all Christian communities.[9] In response to these criticisms, many of the religious authorities in Aleppo prohibited Latin missionaries from giving sermons in their churches or hearing confessions.[10] Patriarch Yusuf al-'Aquri went further in repulsing what he took to be attempts to undermine the ecclesiastical authority of the Maronite clergy on the basis of these criticisms. In 1644 he threatened to excommunicate any Maronite who "confesses to the Latin missionaries, or who takes communion at their hands."[11]

An even more intense conflict unfolded about seventy years later between the Jesuit missionaries and the Maronite clergy in Aleppo. At issue then were the extent and limits of Maronite clerical jurisdiction. Through the end of the seventeenth century, Catholic Christians (Maronites and others) from Aleppo and the surrounding towns and villages would mostly confess their sins and receive absolution at the Maronite Church of St. Elias, the only Catholic church in town. Maronite priests and prelates, in addition, saw their patriarchate as extending to Antioch "and the rest of the East." Such an expansive ecclesiastical authority had gone mostly unquestioned through the eighteenth century because there were few Catholics and the missionaries were either not inclined or, more likely, did not have enough power within the community to counter the Maronite regionalist claim. As these two factors changed, with rising numbers of Catholics and increasingly emboldened missionaries seeking to expand their influence and assure the salvation of souls, the Jesuits sought to delimit Maronite authority.

Jesuit missionaries in Aleppo contended that Maronite priests did not have the authority to hear the confession of members of other Eastern churches (Greek, Armenian, and Syriac). They argued that the acts of the Council of Trent dictated that for the sacrament and penitence to be theologically valid it must be administered by those who have jurisdiction over the souls of the penitents. Failing that, the confession and penitence were to be considered null and void. In fact, the Jesuit superior writing in 1714 continued, "It is preferable for a Catholic, Syrian [Orthodox], Greek [Orthodox] or an Armenian seeking sacrament and penitence to confess to one of their own priests, even if these sects are heretical, than to confess to a Maronite priest." He directed all Catholics who wished to confess their sins to resort to the missionaries because they had the authority to absolve them.[12] Obviously, this not only severely circumscribed the ecclesiastical reach of the Maronite Church but, more critically, subsumed it completely to the authority of the Holy See. Indeed, the Jesuit priests were quite clear about this matter when they wrote, "Only the Holy See, by virtue of the Council of Trent, has the power to permit such jurisdiction [that transcends one sect]. The other Sees [Antioch, Jerusalem, Constantinople and Alexandria] only possess . . . jurisdiction limited to their own territory."[13] Moreover, the Jesuits argued, Maronite clerics committed a multitude of errors in hearing confessions. The Jesuit author of the lengthy diatribe against the Maronite clergy professed horror and outrage at the manner in which Maronite clerics heard confessions, from hurrying through confessions—"hearing in one hour what it would take a day for a disciplined and experienced confessor to hear"—to indifferently absolving anyone of any and all sins to contending that girls below the age of fourteen do not commit sin, "from whence arises infinite sacrileges."[14] The Jesuit author further claimed that Maronite priests were giving absolution without bothering to hear the confessions beforehand and that when they did hear them, they did not always keep their details secret from their wives. More troubling to him—and presumably other Jesuits in whose name he was writing—was his contention that the Maronite clergy had no concept of a "moral theology" whereby they distinguished between the various sins and assigned varying penitences accordingly.[15]

The response of the local clergy was, not too surprisingly, irritation, anger, and protest. As early as the first half of the seventeenth century, they voiced their own qualms about the Latin missionaries. The Maronite patriarch and bishops sought in 1645 to prohibit missionaries from hearing confessions without the express permission of the Maronite Church. Jean-Baptiste de Saint-Aignan noted in 1669 that the local clergy took umbrage at the missionary project for presuming that local Christianity was less perfect or correct than its Latin counterpart. He wrote, voicing their irritation,

Are they [the local community] not Christians? Is it not shameful to abandon the religion of their ancestors to follow that of two or three strangers? Do the local Christians not believe in Christ, do they not revere the holy cross, and are they not baptized? Do they not observe fasts even more austerely than the Latins? Do they not attend mass and hold longer prayers?[16]

But by 1716 the protestations of the local Christians had grown much louder in tandem with the increasingly vociferous critiques leveled by some

Latin missionaries. In an immediate response to the Jesuit missive summarized earlier, a delegation of two hundred Catholic and non-Catholic Christians visited the French consul Lemaire in Aleppo to lodge a complaint against the overly zealous missionaries. They specifically demanded of him to force the missionaries to refrain from proclaiming the local rites and clergy errant, from leading "women and children" astray, and from visiting families and telling lies.[17]

Less than twenty years after this crisis finally settled down, another erupted. This was the 'abidat (devotees) affair, which spanned the better part of two decades (1730–1748) and entangled ten Aleppan devotees, their Jesuit confessors and supporters, the Melkite community in Aleppo, the Melkite Church, and the Vatican. The main character in this religious drama was the leader of the ten religious devotees, a woman by the name of Maria Qari. Like Hindiyya, she was an Aleppan from a wealthy mercantile family who renounced the material world and sought a religious vocation. She grew up amid the same religious effervescence as Hindiyya, pursuing a more individual and rigorous profession of faith through her vocation. In the 1720s she quickly rose to prominence within the Virgin Mary Confraternity established and promoted in the early eighteenth century by the Jesuits, in particular by a missionary with the unlikely name of Père Fromage. By the end of that decade Père Fromage, who had assumed the spiritual direction of the sodality, appointed her as the superior of this confraternity, and she "became an important person in Aleppo. Not only did members of the confraternity seek her prayers and counsel, but also Melkite women and a good number of the notable families of Aleppo."[18]

In 1730 she approached Père Fromage with the idea of establishing a Melkite convent in Mount Lebanon modeled after the monastery founded by two Aleppan monks two decades earlier.[19] Until then, the Melkite devotees of Aleppo would seek seclusion within private homes, where they also met to undertake spiritual studies and exercises. Their intent was to retreat even further from the materialistic world of Aleppo and to dedicate themselves more fully to religious life. But from the beginning the project was fraught with tensions and conflicts that lasted until the end of the 1740s. The first difficulty the devotees faced was to convince their parents to allow them to depart from Aleppo and their supervision. During the eighteenth century this would have certainly been a departure from the ordinary. It was not a custom for young women to leave the houses of their parents unless they were moving to their husbands' homes, and it was most certainly unprecedented for unmarried women to go so far beyond the sphere of influence and authority of their families. Finally, convents had not been part of the Eastern Christian landscape for centuries. Facing such restrictions on gender roles, it was then only the moral weight of the prevalent religious discourse and environment that allowed the 'abidat to obtain permission after months of pleading and cajoling (and Jesuit missionary support). Since the Christian elites of Aleppo had used, among other things, public trappings of newfound religiosity to distinguish themselves as a class, it would have been difficult for them to reject the logical conclusion that their daughters were drawing. In other words, the larger emphasis on an individual spirituality rather than communal religious culture validated the idea of a religious vocation for these ten women, as well as Hindiyya in later years, and allowed them to go beyond the secular norms of society and to legitimately reject its expectations for young elite women.

The second issue was raising enough money to purchase land in Mount Lebanon and construct the convent. "Sacrificing" their dowries, obtaining financial support from the parents, and fundraising among the Melkite elites of Aleppo, the devotees gathered enough money to build eight cells for the future nuns and the associated buildings (refectory, church, kitchen, etc.), which amounted to five to six thousand piasters in total.[20] This substantial financial support further illustrates, perhaps even more clearly, the validation of women's religious vocation in Aleppo. Once these difficulties were surmounted, the 'abidat wrote letters to Abdallah Zakher (a Melkite intellectual and founder of the first printing press), Father Niqula Sayigh (superior general of the Melkite Shuwayrite order), and Athnasius Dahhan (bishop of the diocese), asking for their assistance in building the convent in the Kisrawan district of Mount Lebanon.[21] All three wrote back, congratulating the 'abidat on their choice. For instance, Zakher wrote in August of 1730, "Allow me to offer you my best felicitations for this heroic resolution which you have undertaken in the service of God and your own sanctification."[22]

But these difficulties were minor compared to the issue of authority over the convent and the nuns' spiritual direction. At the outset, the *'abidat* appeared to indicate their willingness to subsume themselves and their proposed convent to the authority of the newly established Melkite religious order. In a letter to Father Sayigh, they wrote, "In return for your troubles and labors in building the convent, we vow to you before God and man that we will dedicate ourselves to God in this convent, and we will place our religious life under the administration, direction and governance of you reverend Father and your holy Congregation."[23] However, their initial letters either neglected the issue of spiritual direction and religious rule or alluded to them in a rather misty fashion. In reality, a majority of the nuns with the support or instigation of the Jesuit missionaries thought to follow the rule of Saint François de Sale (a far less demanding rule than the Eastern rite), to undertake their religious life under the spiritual direction of a Jesuit missionary and, perhaps most importantly, to be independent from indigenous male supervision. On the other hand, the Melkite monks of Dayr Mar Yuhanna al-Shuwayr and their superiors agreed to support the construction of the convent with the understanding that it would be part of their religious order, that it would be exclusively for Melkite women, that the nuns would follow the same Eastern St. Antonius rule, and that their spiritual direction would be undertaken by someone from the ranks of the Melkite monks.

These divergent expectations first became apparent in 1736 when the Aleppan devotees signed four letters in Arabic addressed to the papal legate to the 1736 Maronite Synod, Sima'an al-Sima'ani, to the Propaganda Fide, to Cardinal Belluga, and lastly to the general of the Society of Jesus. In the missive to the Propaganda Fide, the *'abidat* wrote that as "feeble women we beg of you to take us under your protection . . . and to assign us a Jesuit priest who can direct us according to the spirit of the Salesian [St. François de Sales] Rule that we have chosen and adopted."[24] The three other letters were in substance making similar requests to their correspondents and in language equally obsequious in employing the trope of the weak and dependent woman. Once news of the letters, the intentions of the *'abidat*, and the machinations of the two Jesuits Père Fromage and Marc-Antoine Séguran became known to the Melkite monks and community in Aleppo, a storm of protest erupted. In the ensuing months the Jesuit missionaries proclaimed their innocence and laid the blame for the idea at the feet of Sima'an al-Sima'ani, who in turn pointed to the Jesuits as the initiators of this rather blatant attempt at taking control of the convent. Amid all of this, Maria Qari and the other nuns proclaimed their innocence through ignorance. Their defense was that the Jesuits had (mis)informed them that the Vatican was opposed to the establishment of any new religious orders in Mount Lebanon and that they could only fulfill their religious vocation by subsuming their proposed religious institution directly to the authority of Rome. Finally, they claimed that they were not allowed to read the letters and that the explication of Père Francois-Xavier Petitqueux of Aleppo (who was delegated by Père Fromage to convince the 'abidat of the new plan) was incomprehensible because "he is a stranger to the Arabic language."[25] The crisis subsided only after Maria Qari and her fellow devotees signed four new letters addressed to the same correspondents but disavowing their previous letters and proclaiming themselves faithful to their original intent of becoming part of the Melkite religious order.[26] To recommence the construction, the devotees collectively signed a contract with the Melkite monks of Day Mar Yuhanna al-Shuwayr, stating that the convent would be jointly owned by the nuns, their parents (both of whom supplied the capital), and the monks (who supplied the labor). This contractual agreement and the letters of apology to Father Niqula al-Sayigh, Bishop Athnasius Dahhan, and Abdallah Zakher appear to have been sufficient to continue building the convent. By September of 1737 the 'abidat began arriving at the convent, which was consecrated as Dayr al-Bishara (Convent of the Annunciation).

For eight months after the arrival of the devotees, things seemed normal in the convent. However, underlying this superficial calm was an issue left unresolved in all the previous correspondence about the religious rule. When Sofia Qari arrived with the second group of devotees at the convent in October of 1737, she brought a letter from Père Fromage to her cousin Maria. In the letter he exhorted Maria to insist upon following the Salesian rule because it was more suitable "to their condition and to the modern times."[27] However, it was not simply at the instigation of the Jesuits that the devotees began asking to be allowed to use this rule.

Indeed, the very premise of the Salesian rule was free will and independence from legalistic and irrational constraints, and thus by extension from arbitrary hierarchical authority. It was an ideology meant to unfetter the individual from any communal obligation or limitation in order to pursue a relationship with God. For instance, François de Sales wrote in 1617 to St. Jane de Chantal, the cofounder of the Visitation Congregation, "DO ALL THROUGH LOVE, NOTHING THROUGH CONSTRAINT; LOVE OBEDIENCE MORE THAN YOU FEAR DISOBEDIENCE. I want you to have a spirit of liberty, not the kind that excludes obedience (this is freedom of the flesh), but the liberty that excludes constraint, scruples and anxiety."[28] It is unclear how much Maria Qari and the other devotees had read of the writings of François de Sales; however, there is no doubt that their rejection of Melkite ecclesiastical authority echoed the words quoted above. Regardless of the source of ideas, the religious space opened up by tension between the Latin missionary and local modernization projects, as well as the audacity or courage of these nuns, allowed them their collective exclamation of independence.

Beyond this liberationist ideology, the physical rigors and difficulties faced by the nuns—because of the strict Saint Basil rule but also because of the rural environment of the convent in Mount Lebanon—were corporeally real and unwelcome by the devotees, who had grown up in the luxury of elite Aleppan households. Thus, Maria Qari wrote to Bishop Athnasius complaining that all the nuns had fallen ill because of the harsh Eastern rites that demanded absolute abstention from meat. In a following letter to Bishop Athnasius, penned on June 10, 1738, she added that the Eastern rites of Mar Yuhanna were simply too harsh and the nuns were not accustomed to following their strictures in dress (wearing the same rough habit day and night) and prayer (prolonged and numerous prayers).[29] Most significantly, Maria Qari argued in her letter that, contrary to Bishop Athnasius's assertions, deprivation and abstinence are not of the essence in the monastic life in the East. She added that strict and harsh monastic rules had alienated the current nuns and scared away potential ones. Thus, these rules were obstacles keeping the religious from seeking and attaining the love of Christ, which after all, for the ʿabidat, was the whole premise of monastic life. In this manner, she shifted from complaining of particular difficulties to questioning the very basis of monastic Christianity as stipulated by the Melkite cleric. Her knowledge of an alternative vision of monastic life (Salesian), as well as the existence of an alternative, Latin, and self-avowedly superior source of religious learning, allowed the 'abidat to raise fundamental questions about the newly established Melkite monastic order. In questioning the Melkite tradition, Qari and the devotees were proposing a "modern" interpretation of religion that rejected blind imitation of an invented past for a reasoned adjustment to new realities, which would serve the higher purpose of individual love for Christ and each other.

The responses of Bishop Athnasius, Abdallah Zakher, and Father Sayigh were equally vehement in their rejection of the demands of the nuns. Bishop Athnasius wrote on June 13, 1738, "The Rule of which you speak [St. François de Sales] is diametrically opposed to our Eastern rites and customs. . . . To allow you to eat meat would be to go against all the Rules that govern the religious institutions of the East."[30] In this self-conscious formulation, meat became the dividing line between two different Catholicisms that were historically, culturally, religiously, and institutionally separate. Moreover, for Zakher, Athnasius, and Sayigh the real culprit behind the *fitna* were the Jesuit missionaries who were aiming to take control over the convent and to undermine the Eastern rites among Christians in the Levant in their unrelenting attempts to Latinize Middle Eastern Christianity. Neither the prohibition nor the attempt to shift the blame away from the nuns dissuaded the latter from their position. In fact, Maria Qari refused to accept the letter (and thus instructions) of Bishop Athnasius and insisted that they would continue to follow the Salesian rule and take confession and even sacrament with the Jesuit fathers. Finally, she informed him that she would be bringing the case to the attention of the Apostolic See for arbitration.

With that declaration, the case went from being a local affair to being a far larger question on the authority of the Melkite Church and clerics vis-à-vis that of Latin missionaries. Equally, it tested the extent to which a bishop can oblige nuns to submit to his will and how much independence the latter could exercise. Finally, referring the matter to the Vatican—on the presumption that it was the universally accepted penultimate church authority—implicitly and explicitly subsumed the local Melkite Church to that authority, thus tying it closer to a European-centered conceptualization of Catholicism. Bishop Athnasius was, of course, obliged to accept Rome's authority since the Melkites had relied on that same authority in proclaiming their independence from the Orthodox Church in Syria only few years before. Nonetheless, he simultaneously sought to assert his authority as a male Levantine Christian cleric until the moment a decision was handed down from the Propaganda Fide. In September he wrote to the devotees, "We—in deference to the Sacred Council and to your weakness [as females]—allow you to wait . . . until you receive the answer. Since you cannot behave according to your whims nor live as seculars . . . you are obliged by regulations like obligatory prayers . . . and abstention from eating meat."[31] Maria Qari's response was to take off the novice's habit. Regardless of the pleas of Bishop Athnasius to the contrary, Maria Qari and Maryam Ni'matallah remained determined, and the other 'abidat supported them by refusing to take the sacrament from any Melkite priest appointed by the bishop.

The crisis only escalated thereafter. Père Marc Séguran, the director of the Jesuit mission in Syria, intervened more openly than ever before. In the preceding months he and Père Fromage had sent the devotees secret letters exhorting them to remain steadfast in their demand for the Salesian rule. However, by November 1738 he decided to appeal directly to the patriarch of the Melkite Church for fear that the Vatican's decision would be long in coming and the devotees might succumb to the authority of Bishop Athnasius in the intervening time, especially since three of them had already broken with the rest of the 'abidat and declared their allegiance to the bishop. Since the patriarch had been at odds with the Shuwayrite order because of their own refusal to subsume themselves to his ecclesiastical authority, Séguran hoped that the patriarch would side with the devotees. His expectation was fulfilled. The patriarch obliged Séguran's request and penned four letters: one to the devotees, expressing his sorrow at their suffering at the hands of the bishop; two to the bishop, stripping him of any authority, under the threat of excommunication, to manage the spiritual affairs of the devotees or interfere with them; and the fourth providing Père Séguran with full authority to oversee Dayr al-Bishara. Subsequently, the affair of the devotees became the focal point of a tug of war between Patriarch Kirallis and the Jesuits, on the one hand, and Bishop Athnasius, Abdallah Zakher, and the Shuwayrite monks, on the other. This conflict entailed asking the Maronite Bishop Qara'li, the only Christian judge in the eastern Mediterranean, to adjudicate between the two parties, which he did in favor of the devotees. It was also carried out in long and detailed reports sent by each of the protagonists to the Propaganda Fide to bolster their claim not only regarding this issue but also in terms of the extent and limits of ecclesiastical authority.

But perhaps the most compelling manifestation of this conflict was the war of words that erupted between Père Fromage and Shammas Abdallah Zakher. Just in the sheer ink expended, this episode was remarkable. For example, in one letter Abdallah Zakher wrote two hundred pages in response to a thirty-page missive sent to him by Père Fromage. In substance, this bitter exchange is most telling of the transformation in the relationship between missionaries and local Christians. Zakher and Fromage had been close collaborators in promoting Catholicism in the Levant for the previous twenty years. They had worked on translating and editing a multitude of religious texts together, they had conceived and implemented (primarily Zakher) the establishment of an Arabic printing press that was ultimately located in Mar Yuhanna al-Shuwayr, and they had fought together against the Greek Orthodox "schismatics." In fact, Zakher was taking refuge in Kisrawan specifically because he was being pursued and persecuted by his Greek Orthodox opponents in Aleppo. However, that relationship collapsed around the issue of the Aleppan devotees, which Zakher saw as an overstepping attempt by the Jesuits to control local Christian affairs and which Fromage regarded as a legitimate part of Latin missionary activity in the Levant. In a letter dated January 22, 1740, Père Fromage wrote to chastise Abdallah Zakher as a rebellious student who

> thought himself to be the imam of philosophers and theologians. Indeed, you think too highly of yourself. Is it not sufficient that God through the Jesuits has brought you out of the darkness of heresy? . . . The Jesuits have not taken anything from your knowledge, but rather it was you who have taken all that you know and illustrate in your writings. . . . The

Jesuits will let you bark until you are hoarse, because they know that you will dwindle and disappear . . . while they will persevere and remain with the grace of God.[32]

Zakher took nine months to reply, in a meticulously argued rebuttal written in a two hundred-page manuscript. Among his arguments was the sarcastic dismissal of Fromage's claim that the Jesuits brought knowledge to him—and, by extension, to all Eastern Christians. He wrote, "With what science did you enlighten me? With your eloquence in Arabic . . . ? You have to admit that what little you know comes by the grace of God from me and from reading my books. Did you enlighten me with logic and philosophy when you know not a word of these sciences in Arabic and I do not speak Latin or French."[33] Zakher then enumerated the errors of the Jesuits in the matter of the devotees. Among those was the second entry, where Zakher accuses the Jesuits of "causing harm to the [Shuwayrite] monks and the devotees equally and for no other reason other than to achieve your goal of absolute control over the convent."[34] Fromage never had the chance to respond—or even read—this letter because he passed away on December 10, 1740. But the rift remained as the Jesuits continued to presume that they had higher authority because they represented Rome and they had brought religious enlightenment to the benighted souls of the Levant, while the local Melkites assumed the role of authentic Christians with Arabic language and Eastern rites as the distinguishing characteristics in the face of missionary incursions into their sphere of authority.

Ultimately, the Propaganda Fide issued its final decision in the matter three years later, in 1743. In that final report it was decreed, among other things, that the devotees must adopt the rule of Saint Basilius because

that is the Rule of monks and nuns in the four Eastern Patriarchates. However, since some of the devotees wish to adopt the Augustinian Rule and the Salesian ordinances . . . then some spiritual exercises and Salesian ordinances may be added to Saint Basil's basic Rule that would be in accordance with the Eastern rites and the circumstances of the country.[35]

In addition, the report concluded that the Jesuits did not have the authority to pass the sacrament to the devotees without the permission of the bishop of the diocese, and the spiritual direction of the convent must be left in the hands of the Shuwayrite order. The implementation of this judgment took another four years for a variety of reasons, but when it was finally applied in April 1746, "Maria Qari and her party refused to submit to the authority of the [Shuwayrite] order and abide by the Basilian Rule. Thus, they immediately left the convent and went to the Maronite convent of Mar Hrash."[36]

A New Chapter

Following on the heels of these two and other crises, the clash between Latin missionaries and the *Hindawiyyun* would seem to be another chapter in the struggle over defining Levantine Christianity.[37] Certainly, in part at least, it was an exacerbation of existing tensions and another instance of the contention surrounding the murky subject of religious jurisdiction. On the one hand, by 1750 the various Levantine Catholic churches had all acknowledged, at various times, the ultimate authority of the Holy See "over the earth" and the Pope "who is the successor to Saint Peter . . . and the true Vicar of Christ . . . and the father of all Christians."[38] Latin missionaries understood this submission to be, by extension, an acknowledgment of their authority over local churches as representatives of the Holy See. But, as Bernard Heyberger argues convincingly in *Les chrétiens du Proche-Orient,* the Vatican gave "Oriental" churches latitude in pursuing their own rites and advised (and at times forbade) missionaries against intervening in local affairs. Then again the Propaganda Fide had clearly delegated Latin missionaries to bring Eastern Christians into closer conformity with the teachings of the post-Tridentine church. The confusion about the extent and limits of religious authority in Bilad al-Sham is hardly surprising amid these conflicting expectations and pronouncements.

These tensions were also the product of an expanding, energized, and self-conscious Maronite community seeking to articulate more clearly an independent identity and primacy among Catholic sects in the Levant, even as it integrated itself into universal Catholicism. At the most basic level the demographic growth and concomitant wider geographical dispersal of Maronites in the Levant was prompting church leaders and clerics to lay claim to an ever-expanding ecclesiastical territory. But it also necessitated a more coherent definition—centered on Mount Lebanon as a reified Maronite religious and political space—of a community spread thin across wider spaces. It was not only in Aleppo that the Maronite community was growing around the turn of the eighteenth century but also in Jerusalem, where the community doubled in the span of fourteen years between 1702 and 1715 and new communities were established in Nazareth, Acre, and Ramallah around the same time. In Mount Lebanon, the community was quickly and aggressively expanding beyond the traditional northern redoubt of the *tai'fa* to the central and even southern reaches of the small principality. This prompted church clergy to assert their authority, in the seventeenth and eighteenth centuries, over an ever-growing geographical territory. For example, Patriarch Istifan Duwayhi in 1700 wrote Cardinal Carlo Barberino to complain about the Franciscan brothers who were supplanting his authority over the community in Acre and to affirm that his authority preceded that of the missionaries.[39] One part of the argument, as we saw earlier, was that the domain of the patriarch of the Maronite *ta'ifa* included the See of Antioch "and the entire East."

A more critical element in the assertion of Maronite primacy over missionary and local Uniates alike was the history of the communities that were being produced from the early 1600s and well beyond our time period. Clerical Maronite writers such as Ibrahim al-Haqillani (d. 1664), Istifan Duwayhi (d. 1704), Marhaj ibn Nirun al-Bani (d. 1712), and Yusuf al-Sima'ani (d. 1768) wrote histories of the Maronites that sought to establish the *ta'ifa*'s perpetual orthodoxy.[40] This was premised on a historical claim that Maronites constituted the only *ta'ifa* to be steadfastly Catholic since the time of its founding by St. Maroun at the end of the fourth century. This idea was first advanced by the Maronite bishop Ibn al-Qila'i (d. 1516), who had written a defense of the Maronites in a short vernacular history titled *Madiha 'ala Jabal Lubnan* (*Ode to Mount Lebanon*). Against accusations he heard in Rome while a student there (1471–1492), he painted an idealized image of Mount Lebanon as a place of heroes and kings who were always steadfast in their Catholicism, at least until the Jacobites arrived and began to corrupt that purity.[41] His glorification of that past is captured by his notion that "God lived among them [the Maronites]."[42] His vision of that golden age—where "Heretics they did not have and no

Muslim lived among them and if a Jew was found his grave was soon covered by crows"[43]—was an aspiration for a distinct and unified Maronite identity centered in Mount Lebanon. About two hundred years later, Istifan Duwayhi wrote a far more elaborate history proclaiming the orthodoxy of the Maronites and setting them apart from their milieu. Educated and trained as a historian and polemicist at the Maronite College in Rome, Duwayhi's book *Tarikh al-Mawarinah* (*History of the Maronites*) narrated the story of the *ta'ifa* all the way back to St. Maroun. In this seminal—and highly creative—work Duwayhi not only agreed with Ibn al-Qila'i that the Maronites were never Monothelites or Monophysites but went further to argue that the Maronites were descendents of the Mardaites, also known as the "Jarajim" in Arabic chronicles.[44] The significance of this questionable family tree emerges from the fanciful genealogy Duwayhi gives to the Mardaite founder of the Maronite Church: Hanna (John) Maroun. According to Patriarch Duwayhi, Hanna Maroun's mother was a Frankish princess descendent of the Carolingian line. This is clearly "an anachronism . . . as the Carolingians did not appear in Western Europe until the following century."[45] For Duwayhi this bloodline was evidence that the Maronites were always tied to the Roman Catholic Church, not only by belief but also by an ancestry that led them to reject Monothelitism and exposed them to persecution by the Byzantine emperor Justinian II (685–95, 705–11).[46] Continuing along this narrative line, it was persecution in the seventh century that drove Hanna Maroun and most of his followers to the mountains of Lebanon, where they could safely remain faithful to Rome in their Catholicism.

Histories published by other contemporary Maronite intellectuals provided similar narratives asserting primacy and perpetuity in Catholicism against heretical Jacobites and vacillating Melkites. They also established the Maronites as the earliest defenders of Catholicism in the eastern Mediterranean, long before Latin missionaries set foot in the region and even prior to the establishment of these proselytizing religious orders. These histories were integral to a narrative that affirmed, against contrarian missionary assertions, Maronite religious jurisdiction over the Levant and even beyond to Egypt, Cyprus, and the "East" in general. The narrative also gave Maronites a source of authority that extended far back to the early fathers of the church, thus predating the rise of Rome as the center of universal Catholicism. While maintaining that Maronites have always had an uninterrupted link to Rome, these narratives elevated the patriarchate of Antioch to a critical and central role in the history of Catholicism. Finally, these works sought to unify and homogenize the dispersed and diverse community of Maronites into a normative cultural framework of Maronitism. In these histories Maronitism emerges as an identity that stands between East and West, a bridge or a buffer depending on the historical period and context. It was an identity that was Arab in language and heritage even as it claimed for Maronites a non-Arab ethnicity (the Marada); it was "European" in Catholic faith even as it sought to "Easternize" Catholicism by harkening back to the Middle Eastern historical roots of Christianity. Within this context, Hindiyya and her project were a reassertion of a historical legacy substantiated by revelations from Jesus. Mikhail Fadel, a graduate of the Maronite College and commissioned in 1750 by Patriarch 'Awwad to investigate (and hopefully substantiate) Hindiyya and her claims, expressed this sentiment most clearly.

> Christ revealed the devotion to His Sacred Heart, to attract the tepid hearts of humanity, first in the land of France in the sixteenth-century through a nun called Margaret Marie Alacoque. Seven years after her death the Church confirmed this devotion in 1696 and then again in 1717, but it was an incomplete devotion. In our times, it has been completed through the fundamental reality of the agonies of the Aleppan Maronite Hindiyya al-'Ujaimi because the Savior of humankind inspired her with the devotion to His Sacred Heart in a manner that combines the monastic way with popular devotion. From His mouth He taught her a wondrous book that contains rules, ordinances, rites. . . . Would the Exalted Divine, who endowed this land and people with all of his blessings, not single them out for this particular blessing and thus make them the origin above all the rest of the world?[47]

In other words, Hindiyya embodied the central principles of Maronitism. She was at once grounded in a local and popular culture of Christianity while seeking to situate herself within a European lineage of visionary women and projecting her vision as a universal message to humanity. Seen in this light, it is then neither surprising nor accidental that she came to be at the center of the struggle between Maronite clergy and Latin missionaries.

Finally, the energy expended by Jesuit missionaries on this matter can also be linked to the deep sense of betrayal some of them may have felt over Hindiyya's rejection of their spiritual authority and cooption of the very religious order they sought to establish as part of their apostolic project. (This was especially the case of Père Marc-Antoine Séguran, who was one of the founders of the convent of Dayr Ziyarat al-Adhra in 'Ayntura and the most vitriolic in his attacks on Hindiyya as well as on the Melkite monks in the preceding 'abidat affair.) At a time when the Jesuit order was under attack in France and Spain, when it was competing with other Latin missionaries in the Levant, and when it had lost control over female religious institutions to local Catholic churches in Aleppo and Mount Lebanon, the Hindiyya affair would have been the proverbial straw that broke the camel's back. Perhaps incensing them most was the fact that they were the ones who introduced the confraternity for the adoration of the Sacred Heart of Jesus into Aleppo. They were also the ones who cultivated, educated, and spiritually sustained and nourished Hindiyya— and many other women—in Aleppo as part of their campaign to popularize Latin Catholic catechism and precepts. Such intimacy likely bred an equally deep-seated hostility from the spurned priests.

The New Cedar of Lebanon

But if one is to use the amount of ink scribbled on this matter as a measure of sorts, then it becomes clear that the Hindiyya affair unleashed far greater passions than previous incidents and elevated the tensions to unprecedented heights. Hundreds of pages in French, Italian, and Arabic stretching across the span of almost thirty years of a controversy that embroiled Latin popes, cardinals, bishops, and missionaries and a host of local Maronite and other Catholic clergy and laypeople is evidence that the Hindiyya affair was not simply another episode in a long-standing conflict. It was unprecedented in intensity and language, and the context by itself does not completely account for this. Rather, Hindiyya's womanhood (as articulated in a variety of ways), her gendered language of Christian spirituality, and her project of a relatively autonomous and certainly new female religious order were central to the intensity of the conflict. Her words, actions, and visions crystallized and focused the various latent tensions into a struggle over religious authority and knowledge in the Levant. For Jesuit missionaries, and some clerics in Rome, Hindiyya unhinged the relationship between the local church and Rome because she transgressed the boundaries of religious roles assigned to women by the post-Tridentine church. She posited an alternative source of knowledge (the "eternal wisdom" of Christ) that challenged (and, in the minds of some, trumped) the textually based temporal learning of the doctors of the church. For Hindiyya and the *Hindawiyyun* she—specifically as a meek and unassuming woman—was the vessel of authentic Maronite faith and religion through whom Christ sought the salvation of the world. More to the point, while always seeing herself as unworthy, Hindiyya still represented herself—and was characterized by supporters—as a unique messenger of Christ. Or, as Christ put it to her, "I have never before called any being with this noble and exalted name, which is the 'daughter of my heart.'"[48] To fully explore the centrality of gender to this conflict and the way in which it reshaped it, we need to examine in greater detail the whirlwind of arguments generated by Hindiyya after her entry into the Bkerki convent in 1750 and through the first inquisition in 1754.

Returning to the poster described at the beginning of this chapter, we can surmise one common trope in these arguments: Hindiyya was a woman transgressing the religious boundaries articulated by the Catholic Reformation and imported and advocated by Latin missionaries. On the limited real estate of an eighteenth-century hand-drawn poster, only the most damning of accusations could have been allocated space. Thus, the painted images and written words are the best summary of what some missionaries found troubling about Hindiyya, her visions and project and the movement she unleashed. The choice of a tree as a central motif in the poster was itself a not so subtle allusion to Eve, the archetype of the arrogant and deceitful woman, and the original sin which blighted the history of humanity. Spelling out this allusion were the textual accusations. Out of the literal and metaphorical heart of the poster, where the Jesuit authors had written "Arrogance and Egotism" to describe Hindiyya's character, blossomed the list of faults they found with the "New Cedar of

Lebanon." At the very top was the label ascribed to Hindiyya's visions: "spiritual madness." Arranged beneath it were "disobedience of superiors," "disobeying church rules and laws," "false religion," "constant lying," "love of silver," "unceasing arguments," and fostering "enmity between people." Not only did she stand in juxtaposition to the precepts of a good Christian, which was troubling enough, but what was repeatedly emphasized was her reversal of the "natural" order of clerical authority. She did not simply break away from the mold of a meek and humble woman or the prototype of a good Catholic woman, and surely of a visionary submitting her will fully to Christ, but she had the temerity to disobey her male superiors. Indeed, the authors of the poster raved in red ink that men, priests, and bishops were prostrating themselves before her.

In short, Hindiyya represented for Séguran and other missionaries a break with the precepts that the post-Tridentine Catholic Church had sought to impose on nuns. These were normative prescriptions formulated in the last year of the Council of Trent (1563) and focused on physically, administratively, and theologically controlling and enclosing female spirituality and religious life. This trend became widespread throughout Catholic Europe, where the church demanded ever more that women should "work more diligently, dress more modestly, obey more speedily."[49] Even Teresa de Avila, who was canonized in 1622, could not escape the inquisitorial disapproval of the male hierarchy of the church. One papal legate described her as a "disobedient, and stubborn *femina* who, under the title of devotion, invented bad doctrines . . . teaching as a master against Saint Paul's orders that women should not teach."[50] Around the same time Mary Ward's Institute of Mary (also known as The English Ladies), which disregarded the enclosure restrictions on nuns, ran afoul of a church establishment bent on enforcing its Tridentine rules on nuns. Her insistence on an active apostolate garnered her enemies and derision as her "Ladies were derisively described as 'noxious weeds,' and labeled the 'galloping girls' who did not know their place."[51] Finally, in 1630 Mary Ward was condemned as a heretic and her order suppressed. Forty-two years later the archbishop of Paris, Hardouin de Péréfixe, was chastising Marguerite de Sainte-Gertrude Dupré, a nun at the convent of Port Royal de Paris, for refusing (along with the other Port Royal nuns) to sign a formula condemning the *Augustinus*

(1640), a theological study by Cornelius Jansen, the late bishop of Ypres. When his patience ran out—rather quickly, one might add—he yelled, "Keep quiet, listen to me: do you not know well that I have the right to command you and that you are obligated to obey me?"[52] Closer to the time and circumstances of Hindiyya was Pope Benedict XIV (r. 1740–1758). A Jansenist by temperament and sympathies, he had a rather dim view of women, particularly those who claimed to have visions. His authoritative oeuvre on the subject of beatification, *De Servorum Dei Beatificatione et Beatorum Canonisatione,* laid out a rigorous and almost impossible set of conditions for the church's acknowledgment and acceptance of valid visions and miracles. In particular, he saw women as prone to flights of fantasy that they interpreted as visions and "was suspicious of expressions of spiritual autonomy" and of "popular" claims of authority to teach religious truths outside the boundaries of church-approved doctrine.[53]

Of course, these examples demonstrate the "obstinacy" of nuns in rejecting strictures and normative behavior in the midst of spiritual revival ironically encouraged by the same establishment. However, they also illustrate that some within the church's male hierarchy in general were equally "obstinate" and tenacious in seeking to delimit the role of nuns and female auxiliaries within the church. Women were to be physically and theologically secluded within the walls of the convent and subject to male priestly oversight. Hindiyya did not comply with any of these expectations, which Latin missionaries carried with them from the seminaries of France and Italy. She refused to stay in Aleppo under the supervision of the Jesuit missionaries and to remain in their confraternity. She would not submit to the will of Father Gueynard in the Jesuit convent in 'Ayntura. She insisted on establishing a new religious order against the counsel and admonition of her Jesuit spiritual director. Moreover, she proclaimed that the Jesuits had angered Christ for which they would be punished by their dissolution. But what irked Latin missionaries the most were two events that after 1750 took her the furthest away from the norm of behavior for a Catholic woman. First, against strictures limiting the establishment of any new religious rules after the Council of Trent, she claimed that Christ had dictated to her a new rule for her convent. Then, for all intents and purposes, she was proclaimed a living saint by her followers.

The storm of activities was unleashed on November 6, 1750, when Hindiyya sent a letter to the Propaganda Fide petitioning the council to confirm the rule of her new religious order. Writing in the formulaic language of supplication, she nonetheless made promises of glory that were not quite in tune with the humble preamble.

> Hoping that your benevolence and zeal will move you to work with us, your [female] servants, to confirm the rule of our confraternity with the Holy See. . . . Do not keep your succor from me and my sisters so that this confraternity will spread to all, and the glory of the Heart of our Lord Jesus Christ will shine forth. I expect Christ will repay in the most felicitous of manners all who assist in the establishment and dissemination of this confraternity.[54]

Shortly thereafter, Patriarch Butrus 'Awwad wrote the secretary of the Propaganda Fide with the same request as Hindiyya. He couched his request in theological and practical terms. "We inform your brotherly eminence that our Lord Jesus Christ has seen fit to endow us with a great blessing in these times because He established in our sect the female Order of the Sacred Heart of Jesus through the beloved virgin Hindiyya." The linguistic equation of the secretary with the patriarch established an equal level of authority between Rome—if not the Holy See—and Bkerki, rather than subordinating the latter to the first. If the implication of the preamble was lost on the cardinal, the patriarch made sure to invoke the supreme authority of divine will to undermine any opposition to his, and Hindiyya's, request. Supplementing his recourse to Christ's wishes, Patriarch 'Awwad noted that the Maronite community did not have as of yet a rule for nuns, "and the girls cannot adhere to existing rules followed in the land of Christians [Europe] because of the [cultural] differences."[55] He did not specify what those differences were, yet the brevity of his allusion assumes unquestioningly the existence of two distinct "Eastern" and Latin religious cultures embodied, in this case, in what "girls" can and cannot follow.

Finally, Father Mikhail Fadel, who was commissioned by Patriarch 'Awwad in the summer of 1750 to investigate the claims that Hindiyya was deluded by Satan—spoke glowingly about her religious rule, "which will bring about the salvation of humanity." He affirmed that he "did not find in her or the rule of her Confraternity any hint of satanic delusion or lies or anything that goes against religion and Christianity or that is below perfection and evangelical standards." To the contrary, he continued, "I have determined that she is absolutely good and pious and elected by the Savior of the world so that He can be glorified through her, and to attract through the tepid hearts of humanity and ignite in them the fire of love for His divine heart." He concluded his report by saying,

> We have determined that Christ himself [has dictated] from His own mouth directly to his noble servant [Hindiyya] the Confraternity Rule. This is not only because of the true and steadfast testimonies which we have received, but also because of the Holy Ghost and Divine Knowledge that are to be found in it [the Rule] and which transcend the understanding of a simple virgin ignorant of all human knowledge as is [Hindiyya].[56]

This report accompanied the portfolio of letters (including Hindiyya's and the patriarch's and a third signed by twelve of the sixteen ordained bishops) that was sent to the Propaganda Fide. It was the most explicit in not only authenticating the rule as divinely inspired but also establishing Hindiyya's credentials as an extraordinary religious woman and a living saint. To assuage any hint of religious impropriety on the part of Patriarch 'Awwad, Fadel began his report by noting that "It is not the purpose of His Holiness to proclaim and affirm her [Hindiyya's] sainthood at this time because it is well known that this cannot take place in her lifetime and it is solely the purview of the Holy See to do so." Yet he proceeded in the eight subsequent pages to enumerate at length characteristics that can only be labeled as saintly. He started with the godly virtue of a perpetually strong and vibrant faith attested to by people from Aleppo to Mount Lebanon. Then, he addressed her "special talents and supreme exalted blessings which His Majestic Self endowed her with since her childhood." Among these was her ability to effortlessly subjugate her "animal instincts" since the age of five and the replication of Christ's agonies in the "virgin at various times and especially on Fridays." These talents also enabled her to comprehend the hidden meanings of scriptures, "strange languages, as well as veiled and unveiled matters in the past and future. Thus she had the spirit of prophecy through her constant union with her maker in thought, invocation and will."[57] Other endowments were witnessed by those around Hindiyya, including signs of the stigmata, the appearance of the Sacred Heart in a cup of Hindiyya's blood, and the smell of incense and visions of angels and saints hovering around her during her trances. Hindiyya's gifts radiated grace to those around her, moving many, through tears of repentance and contrite hearts, to return to a pious existence that shunned sin and embraced the tenets of Christian faith with abandon. All of these were elements common in the vitae of visionary nuns like Teresa de Avila and Catherine of Siena, who were recognized and beatified by the Vatican as saints.

Augmenting these attributes were the most critical of saintly markers: miraculous works. Fadel spoke of

> countless strange miracles [wrought by God through Hindiyya's hands] that are: making the blind see, the dumb speak and the deaf hear, and curing the lame and crippled; purifying the lepers and criminals and bringing those on their deathbeds back to life; making the milk of nursing mothers flow forth and growing the breasts of those women who did not have them . . . exorcism . . . and saving some souls from the jail of purgatory . . . curing the sick, even animals, from their ills and diseases and multiplying bread and other foods when necessary.[58]

In case Fadel's abridgement—panegyric, really—of Hindiyya's miracles was not sufficient, the portfolio also included more detailed accounts by clerics and laypeople of her divinely empowered intercession. For example, in a petition penned on May 2, 1751, Bishop Jibra'il 'Awwad, Father Yusuf of Qaytuli, a couple of the village's "doctors,"[59] and the superiors of nearby Aleppan and Lebanese order monasteries testified to either having witnessed a series of miracles or to having heard witnesses recount their eyewitness accounts of miracles. They swore that "The arms and legs of Butrus ibn Abi Jirjis 'Issa from the village of Sina had been paralyzed for a long time, so he visited the convent of Mother Hindiyya and was cured completely." Another account recounted that "Anis imm Kana'an Karam from the village of Jizzeen was deaf and could not hear anything, so we

matters collectively and individually as if they are true, and you also commanded that it should be read to the people of the Maronite church in Aleppo.[74]

This behavior, the pope continued, led "many believing men and women, who are either imbeciles, fools or deceived, to honor this girl in ways that are illegitimate and unacceptable," and it caused a great deal of tumult and turmoil in the Maronite community. Such actions not only went against sanctified church law, according to Benedict XIV, but also showed disobedience to him and his "eminent authority," by which he had previously confirmed and ordained 'Awwad as Antiochian patriarch. He further chastised 'Awwad for "forgetting or refusing" to inform and consult the Holy See about such weighty matters, when he is "absolutely required to do so."[75]

After seeking to reestablish the hierarchy of church power in the relationship between the Vatican and the Maronite clergy with his blunt discourse, Pope Benedict XIV abrogated to himself another source of authority: learned knowledge. He wrote Patriarch 'Awwad prefacing his edict about Hindiyya:

> We are the ones who have sufficient experience and learning in these matters because of the number of books we authored about this issue [visions and beatification], and . . . we have not only learned from the years of attacks by heretics and schismatics against the Catholic Church but also from the hidden tricks and tyranny of Satan.

The implication, one would have to assume, was that Patriarch 'Awwad and the Maronite Church as a whole lacked those sources of knowledge and, more importantly, that these sources were normative in their superiority. (The tone and assumptions underlying this statement are reminiscent of those made by Père Fromage to Abdallah Zakher a decade before, positing textual knowledge as the foundation of orthodox faith.) After this preamble, he passed his judgment on the matter: "We advise you, esteemed brother, we exhort you and we order your eminence," to remove Hindiyya to another convent, to dissolve the Sacred Heart order, to return the Bkerki convent to the St. Isaiah monks, to destroy all written or printed records and books relating to Hindiyya and the order as "we have deemed them forbidden texts," and to announce the edict to all Maronites.[76]

As Bernard Heyberger notes, the alacrity and manner with which Benedict XIV reached his decision are remarkable. Rather than call a general or particular congregation to discuss this matter, as was normally the case, the pope appears to have made the decision unilaterally. Heyberger attributes this to the low regard which Benedict XIV had for the "slowness and ineptitude of such assemblies."[77] However, this rushed decision was also a reflection of Benedict's aversion to private revelations, especially among women, which he saw as "fanaticism, fantasy and hysterics."[78] For two decades before he ascended the throne of St. Peter as Benedict XIV, Prospero Lambertini was dedicated to infusing Christianity with scientific certainty and rationality, to defend it against superstition. In his tenure as archbishop in Bologna, his native town, he actively supported dissection of human bodies at the university for the purpose of advancing the *scienza* of the physiology and pathology of the human body. His keen interest in science, particularly medicine, was central to his career as a canonist lawyer frequently assigned the role of Promotor Fide, or "devil's advocate," in beatification trials. His work at these trials, which required a breadth of historical, physical, and theological knowledge, culminated in the monumental treatise *De sevorum Dei beatificatione et beatorum canonizatone.* In large part his treatise, which became and remains the standard work in beatification trial, was based on the work of the physician Paolo Zachias (1584–1659) entitled *Questiones medico-legales.* Most pertinent to his decision about Hindiyya was his conclusion that the heart "was a mere muscle and therefore it could not function . . . as the domicile of emotions, the virtues and the soul." It is for that reason that "despite the repeated interference of major secular leaders, the pope refused to recognize the tremendously popular Devotion of the Holy Heart" in Europe.[79] Thus, when, as Pope Benedict XIV, Lambertini decreed the dissolution of Hindiyya's religious order, he was continuing his lifelong work of building an Enlightenment church based on "science" and averse to "superstition." His dismissive and imperious tone in addressing Patriarch 'Awwad was the distillation of those travails dedicated to establishing a church where a male-gendered mind and reason are separate from, and predominate, the fallen female body and its suspect senses, which lead to unbridled imagination, a sure path away from orthodoxy.[80]

The response of the Maronite religious and secular leadership was a unanimous rejection of this separation as well as of the content of the edict. In contrast to Pope Benedict's disembodied tone, the patriarch, bishops, and Khazin *shuyukh* wrote emotionally charged letters to him and the cardinals of the Propaganda Fide. In tone, these missives alternated between pleas for reconsideration and angry denunciations. They were a mixture, not always rhetorically elegant, of juridical argumentation about religious authority and evidence and impassioned defense of a bruised and gendered honor. The bishops' letter to the cardinals in the Propaganda Fide is the best example of this. Written around the middle of June 1752, the letter begins by recounting the list of accusations against the patriarch. After the paragraph-long introductory précis, the bishops immediately shift the blame for the upheaval within the community to the unwelcome interventions of the Jesuit missionaries. It was their opposition to Hindiyya and her religious order and their scandalous and libelous tactics, including the poster, which led to tensions and conflicts. They did all of this because "they were afraid that her rise will undermine and dissolve their convent [in 'Ayntura]."[81] Jesuit shameful behavior was only emboldened, according to the bishops, by the pope's letter, which "puzzled the faithful and the heretics and which grieved us because it was based on the words of biased people."[82] This rhetorical thread intertwining legalistic analysis and communal emotions was continued in the protestation against accusations that the patriarch had acted independently and was overstepping his authority in allowing and encouraging the portrayal of Hindiyya as a living saint. Here, the bishops professed incredulity at such an idea when "our Patriarch knows full well, because he is distinguished in theological sciences, that canonization can only be conferred by the Holy See after death [of the saint]." They then added not only that the honor and respect conferred upon Hindiyya are within the bounds of reason but that "the [Maronite] people who have accepted and continue to accept great blessings from God through Mother Hindiyya, thank God and praise the

Holy [Roman] Church which still contains within it the Holy Spirit as it always has."[83] While Pope Benedict XIV was advocating a church where the space for divine revelations was increasingly narrowed and hemmed by science and orthodoxy, the bishops embraced Hindiyya's revelations as central not only to the spiritual sustenance of the Maronite community but also as a vital and historical element of the Roman Church.

The tone of the letter became decidedly more impassioned, emphatic, and even angry when the bishops turned their attention to defending the "honor" of the nuns of the Sacred Heart of Jesus order. They noted that the nuns had sent their rule to the Holy See to be examined and corrected in case of omission or error and that the sisters of the order were willing to accept those changes. "So how can his Holiness suppress it, instead of correcting and confirming it, when he had no legal cause." Compounding the injustice in the eyes of the Maronite elites was the scandalous suggestion that the nuns should go back to their parents' homes after the proposed dissolution of their order. At one point or another, all of the letters dispatched to Rome gasped at such a notion. For instance, the bishops noted that the "girls are ready to shed their own blood" rather than be forced to leave their convent. Twenty-three signatories on the Khazin letter to the cardinals exclaimed that no human mind can fathom how "the girls" were to be expelled after they had taken their vows in the Bkerki convent. "Such a thing has never happened in the past and it will not happen now . . . for how can we obey an edict that runs contrary to our honor and religion."[84] This rejection of the pope's edict and authority was unanimous. Patriarch 'Awwad wrote, "The destruction of the confraternity according to the order of His Holiness is unjust and baseless and we do not feel constrained to implement it, even if it could be implemented to begin with."[85] The bishops echoed the same sentiment and added that the pope's edict had exposed the Maronites to accusations of heresy by other Christian sects, an intolerable state of being when the Maronite Church had positioned itself as steadfastly Catholic for centuries before any other group in the Levant. They concluded their letter by stating that the pope can write "one thousand insistent letters" and his edict will not be implemented. If this rejection of the pope's authority was not clear enough in its implications, all Maronite correspondents stated that insistence on the implementation of the edict will drive a possibly irrevocable wedge between the community and the Roman Catholic Church.

"Virgin Hindiyya"

In the face of uncompromising and widespread opposition, the pope was forced to take at least a few steps back from his decision. However, his retreat was equivocal. To reopen the Hindiyya affair, the Propaganda Fide convened a special congregation, which, after deliberation, appointed Friar Desiderio di Casabasciana, who was intimately acquainted with the Levant and its Christian communities, had cordial relations with the Maronites, and "did not have great sympathy for the Jesuits."[86] In 1753 Desiderio spent the months of April through September in Mount Lebanon interviewing/interrogating Hindiyya and the nuns of the Sacred Heart order before compiling a largely favorable report for the Vatican. Yet, shortly after his return to Rome in early 1754, Benedict XIV asked Cardinal Gall and Friar Isidoro Mancini to scrutinize the constitution of the Sacred Heart order and the claims of sanctity swirling around Hindiyya. In his report Mancini produced an overwhelmingly negative assessment of Hindiyya. These starkly different conclusions and recommendations attest to the different personalities of the inquisitors and to the divergent theological currents and approaches within the Catholic Church itself. Where the inquisitors also diverged was in the voice they accorded Hindiyya. In Desiderio's voluminous report, Hindiyya was a subject who spoke in the first person to the point where her multipage answers dwarfed the one-sentence questions. Even in his analysis Desiderio allowed Hindiyya and her sympathetic nuns space for articulating their own defense through lengthy quotations and paraphrasing of their arguments. Mancini, on the other hand, treated Hindiyya as an object of inquiry—and derision—throughout his report, hardly, if ever, giving her words space. Rather, he placed her actions and visions under his inquisitorial microscope in order to "scientifically" discern her errors.

But, regardless of their tone, both reports were almost exclusively focused on Hindiyya. Previously, the letters and arguments were carried out by an all-male cast, effectively marginalizing Hindiyya as a deluded woman or one in need of protection. In contrast, Desiderio's and Mancini's reports were centered on Hindiyya almost to the exclusion of all other actors. Placing her again at the heart of the narrative could possibly have been, at least partially, an attempt at placating the Maronite Church and community. Rather than cast doubt on the theological knowledge, authority, and traditions of the Maronites as a whole, both reports narrowed their attention to an individual woman. This was a clear departure from the wide-ranging criticisms leveled by Pope Benedict XIV at Patriarch 'Awwad and the Maronite Church as a whole. Yet this shift was not simply one of political expediency. Rather, both authors implicitly recognized that at the heart of the independent streak characterizing Maronite revivalism in the eighteenth century was gender, in the abstract, and more specifically Hindiyya. One saw her as a meek, obedient, and saintly woman, while the other depicted her as the embodiment of women's propensity to religious flights of fantasy, ignorance, and even feeblemindedness. Each in his own way focused on gendered tropes of womanhood to reach a different conclusion. But both took Hindiyya's story out of the larger Maronite context, sundering (consciously or otherwise) the link between her and the Maronite Church and delimiting her influence and role. In their narratives she became a solitary woman.

Desiderio structured his report of the "Virgin Hindiyya" around the characters ascribed to idealized Latin Christian female behavior. These included humility; virtue; obedience; extraordinary patience; meekness; deep love for others, Christ, and God; as well as emulation and veneration of the Virgin Mary. (Such self-effacing characteristics did not constitute the model of Levantine Christian womanhood and certainly not the behavior of most women if one is to judge by the various bits and pieces of evidence presented in earlier chapters.) In order to prove his conclusion that Hindiyya was genuinely a devout woman, he presented evidence, both that he witnessed and about which he was informed, to substantiate these characteristics. Desiderio began and concluded his report with a proviso about the limitations of his conclusions. In part, he ascribed these limitations to exaggerations inherent in testimonies by Hindiyya's nuns and her spiritual directors, Bishop Jirmanus and Père Venturi. But more frequently he referred to the limitation of his human observation to discern what is earthly and what is divine. For instance, in writing about

Hindiyya's virtues, Desiderio noted that he was "most careful" to closely observe and examine her virtuous deeds, which he attributed to the "desire to please only God and no one else." He quickly added, "However, because it is very difficult to know the intent [of Hindiyya] I do not dare say that her motivations are super-natural [divinely inspired], rather I submit my judgment to someone who is more qualified."[87] Desiderio concluded his report with a similar disclaimer. He wrote, "I declare that what I relate is what I saw with my weak understanding and I do not know if I am deluded and accordingly I submit everything to the judgment and review of someone more qualified to look into these matters."[88]

In between these two bookend proclamations, Desiderio wrote some fourteen pages of barely restrained panegyrics that gave examples and evidence of these virtues and sought to "scientifically" prove that Hindiyya's visions were from God rather than self-induced or, even worse, from the devil. Thus, Maryam the Greek told Desiderio of a time when someone called through a window to Hindiyya, saying "O Saint Hindiyya take pity on me and pray for me oh Saint of God." Hindiyya's response—purported evidence of her extreme humility—was to weep long and hard because she "is the greatest sinner in the world, full of more errors than the devils of hell."[89] Desiderio corroborated this story with his own "stealthy" observations of Hindiyya cleaning the "dirtiest places in the convent." Her obedience was similarly illustrated by stories recounted by Bishop Jirmanus and Hindiyya herself and then confirmed by her willing and repeated submission to the orders and will of Desiderio and his secretary, Fr. Raymondo.

Hindiyya's saintly patience was subsequently lauded by Desiderio for her willingness to withstand severe illnesses and pain without complaint but rather with joy. Tales of her self-mortification, which started in childhood, continued through her adult years and, augmented by bloodletting, were considered truthful by Desiderio because of the multitude of testimonies including those by Hindiyya's brother Niqula al-'Ujaimi and her assistant Katerina. Her modesty was, on the other hand, not ascertained only by secondhand reports of aversion to speaking to men but also because she "was shaking with embarrassment" when Desiderio asked to see her hands and her feet for evidence of the stigmata. Her "love for strangers and especially the poor sick women" was recounted by Katerina,

Maryam, and Lucia the Greek to Desiderio. For example, Katerina told him the story of Sister Gertrude, who suffered greatly from pain in her swollen knees. In trying to heal her, Katerina prescribed a medical treatment. The day after, Gertrude appeared completely healed, which "astonished" Katerina, who had not expected the illness to dissipate so quickly. Upon questioning this unlikely recovery, Gertrude indicated that "Mother Superior healed me." Upon further investigation, Katerina noticed that the same disease had manifested itself in Hindiyya's knees. So "I [Katerina] said to her, this is Gertrude's illness and she has been healed and you took upon yourself her malady. So she answered me 'it is alright for I do not do anything while if she is sick then the whole convent will suffer.'"[90] Following the pattern of his report, Desiderio then reaffirmed this with a story of his own. His was about Hindiyya's insistence on administering to the sickest of the nuns, particularly Sister Madelana, who suffered from tuberculosis. At the behest of other nuns in the convent, Desiderio approached Hindiyya to ask her to keep her distance from Madelana, to avoid catching the disease. "She answered me immediately: 'what love would I possess if I ignored this poor sick woman? I beg you father, for the love of Jesus Christ, not to order me [to cease caring for her].'"[91]

Admirable as Hindiyya's love for her nuns (but not so much for men) was in the eyes of Desiderio, he found her love for Christ to be exemplary in its abandon. While her love for the "poor sick woman" was an act of charity—perhaps leavened with pity—her relationship to Christ was passionate, ecstatic, and bodily. As characterized by the report, once triggered, her emotions for Christ spiraled quickly out of control into enrapture, "so much so that the heat of love would inflame her body and she would feel a burning pleasure" that was physical enough to send forth vapor from a wet handkerchief placed by Desiderio on her chest. The novice nun Sa'ada and sisters Lucia, Maryam, and Maryam the Greek all affirmed Hindiyya's burning love for Christ with a story about a discussion centered on St. Philip Neri. During one of the free hours in the convent, Hindiyya asked Sister Matilda to read the hagiography of St. Philip Neri. When Matilda reached the point in the story that spoke of St. Philip Neri's intense love for Jesus Christ, she stopped and asked Hindiyya if she loved Christ as much as the saint, an inherent equation of stature and not just emotion.

Hindiyya demurred at the comparison to a saint, saying "'I am a wretched sinner and therefore cannot love Jesus Christ as much as Saint Philip Neri who was a great saint.' But as soon as she finished her words she went into rapture [because of her intense love]."[92] Of course, the irony of the story is that even as Hindiyya rejected a comparison with a saint out of (false or real) humility, she physically demonstrated the similitude of their love and their spirituality.

Whether Desiderio was aware of the implication of the story is not clear from his report. However, he certainly believed that her love was extraordinary, as attested to by his own story. "On the 25th of June, 1753 I and my secretary Raymondo went to Hindiyya's room and we found her amidst the usual dialogue that the sisters normally practiced each day." The start of this story is striking because it is the only place where Desiderio specifies the exact date in his report, lending an air of certainty and solidity that stands in stark contrast to the malleability of previous tales. The tableau of a group of nuns engaged in rational discourse on a daily basis is also remarkably different from the other "domestic" images put forth by Desiderio about the sisters of the Sacred Heart. The shift in his narrative to a more exacting tone was perhaps due to the fact that he wanted to describe his own "scientific" observation of the most intangible aspect of religious attributes: ecstasy of love. The discussion on that day was about the agonies of Christ, in particular whether the lashing he received or the crown of thorns was more painful. Reflection on the agonies suffered by Christ was a common enough exercise by those men and, more so, women who sought to comprehend the magnitude of his sacrifice and love for humanity by way of approximating his suffering in their own deprivations.[93] For Desiderio, however, this was a moment when he could observe an instance of Hindiyya's enraptures, about which he had heard much from the sisters in the convent. For the purpose of inducing such rapture he prolonged the discussion with Sister Lucia while surreptitiously watching Hindiyya struggle to maintain control over her body. "But she could not resist and she left her body in my presence remaining kneeling submissively as she was [before] to the point that she moved me to humble myself."[94] Desiderio noted that his purpose in including this incident is not to prove that Hindiyya went into rapturous states but to "permit a just judgment to be passed on Hindiyya's love for God Almighty and her devotion to the agonies of the divine Redeemer."

This conclusion and the injection of a "scientific" experiment into the religious inquisition formed a segue for the second part of Desiderio's report, which was dedicated to analyzing his accumulated observations. Desiderio began this section by noting that none of the divine gifts attributed to Hindiyya was outside the bounds of theologically recognized "*gratis data*," or gratuitous graces given by God to individuals regardless of their moral merits and life. Therefore, he continued, in and of themselves these gifts were not evidence of whether Hindiyya is a virtuous woman or not since God can choose to give them to the pious as well as to sinners. Leaving behind this ambiguity, he proposed to systematically examine "first the raptures by themselves . . . then the gifts in combination with the raptures, and then the gifts by themselves."[95] To begin his methodical exposé, Desiderio first argued that the raptures were real because he observed Hindiyya on multiple occasions, felt her temperature (which seems to have been an important indicator), and tried waking her up from her stupor. Second, he argued that these raptures "cannot be brought about by natural causes because I found her of happy, not sad, countenance and free of those illnesses that may lead to unconsciousness." Moreover, she was never weak or disoriented after returning from her raptures as would have been the case, according to Desiderio, had they been caused by a disease.

Finally, Desiderio argued, these events could not have been evil in source because they did not fit the criteria established by the "doctors of theology" for discerning diabolical possessions. Those normative measures included whether the raptures happened to an evil person especially during a sinful act, if the body moved "indecently or with tremors," if the person could not recall what he or she said during their absences, if she or he emitted "horrible sounds" that strike fear in the hearts of those present, if the rapture diminished his or her love for God, or if these raptures took place in public spaces. In other words, raptures and visions had to be private, contained affairs before they could be considered divinely inspired. Hindiyya, according to him, did not display any of these objectionable elements. To the contrary, she manifested the very opposite behaviors, proving—as far as Desiderio was concerned—that she was not a woman seeking public attention and power but really a privately pious woman whom God had graced with divine gifts. For instance, he wrote, "I noticed that Hindiyya was very careful to cover herself with the *niqab* [veil] or to disappear into hidden areas for fear that even her sisters would witness her raptures."[96] To affirm her piety and goodness, Desiderio assured his readers that Hindiyya did not seek to transgress gender boundaries but rather was content—and even desperately sought—to retreat into the most private spaces possible, effacing herself from any public view. In other words, he implied, she behaved in a manner that befitted religious women: inconspicuous and passive.

Her obedient nature was further evidence that she was not a "rebellious" woman. Her raptures were not voluntary departures from this world but submission to the will of God. Bishop Jirmanus illustrated this element of enrapture one day when Hindiyya fell to the ground unconscious at noon "in an uncomfortable position under the hot sun." So, Desiderio, solicitous of her well-being, asked the bishop to order Hindiyya to return from her rapture, which she promptly did. Jirmanus then quickly ordered her to return to her state of rapture, and she again submitted her will to his command. Desiderio approved of the first order—which he had prompted, after all—as evidence that the rapture was induced by God. To independently duplicate and verify this experiment, he and his secretary "ordered her on several occasions in Arabic and Italian to return to consciousness from her rapture and she always obeyed."[97] Desiderio did not hint at any unease over wielding such control over Hindiyya's body, yanking it back and forth between consciousness and unconsciousness. Indeed, he seemed to be indicating to his superiors that the very ease with which he and two other men were able to lay control over her body was proof that she was not in league with the devil and that she remained submissive to the authority of the church and its male hierarchy. This, in addition to the signs of the stigmata, or what appeared like a stigmata, that he and Raymondo saw on her hands on one occasion, as well as the pleasant and delightful odor they smelled after purported visitations by her guardian angel and her beautiful and unusual countenance after her raptures were all proof that Hindiyya's visions and raptures could not be but divinely inspired.

Friar Isidorios Mancini was not so sanguine in his evaluation of Hindiyya. "If the alleged gifts are examined it would be sure evidence that the spirit of God does not animate this virgin."[98] From this generalized condemnation, Mancini set about arguing that if measured by the standards established by the Catholic Church, Hindiyya was at best a deluded woman, if not one possessed by the devil. He attributed her delusions to the fact that "this virgin is constantly ill, has a strong imagination and she persists in disciplining and restraining her body with perpetual fasts and self-mortifications that go beyond the norm." Quoting Cardinal Giovanni Bona's treatise on discerning spirits, Mancini argued that this method of extreme asceticism "dries the brain and dissipates the soul" and leads women especially to delusion. Further evidence against Hindiyya was mustered from the writings of François de Sales, who contended that a surfeit of visions is enough to raise suspicions about their validity. Accordingly, "the countless raptures, visions and revelations" that Hindiyya had only increased the possibility of delusion in the mind of Mancini. The medical aspect of Hindiyya's visions only strengthened his conviction. In making this case Mancini turned to the scholarship of Pope Benedict XIV to prove his point. He cited Benedict's magnum opus, *De Servorum Dei Beatificatione et Beatorum Canonisatione,* to show that "because the brain's energy is focused on contemplating divine matters . . . the body forces must surely be arrested and [the body] will cool down, turn yellow and become weak."[99] Saint Teresa de Avila's book *Interior Castle* confirmed that the symptoms of rapture were a drop in temperature and failure of body parts and that the face "will turn yellow and become dry similar to the look of a dying or dead person."[100] Hindiyya's postrapture flush and radiant face obviously did not fit the criteria Mancini accepted as the standard dictated by the scholarly authority on the subject and by one of the most renowned female visionaries in Catholic history. This was hardly the stuff of science, but the resort to that trope was meant to establish the Vatican as the ultimate arbiter in rationally discerning spirits.

Nor was he convinced that Hindiyya's visions and revelations were divinely inspired. Rather, he regarded them for the most part as "unbelievable, childish and unsavory." Mancini took offense at the notion that saints and angels—"even high ranking ones," including St. Michael—were constantly singing hymns to Hindiyya and that even Christ joined in every now and then singing a little ditty titled "'Glory to My Flock,' I mean to that group of women [the nuns of the Sacred Heart]." He fulminated in the face of Jirmanus's testimony that Christ would send a goldfinch every morning to stand by Hindiyya's room singing spiritual hymns for hours. Another claim by Antonio Venturi of divine grace led Mancini to exclaim in an exasperated tone, "What a naïve man!" In this instance, Venturi had testified that the Holy Ghost perfumed Hindiyya's body "with a real and tangible balsam, and he [the Holy Ghost] descended upon her while praying in the form of dew drops some of which fell upon the confessor as well." If Venturi was a simpleton for Mancini, Jirmanus and Hindiyya were liars. He quotes Jirmanus repeating Hindiyya's claim that Christ had told her that, when established, the Sacred Heart confraternity will be unprecedented and remarkable in its goodness, and in the benefit it will bring to humanity. "This equation is a lie from every perspective because there are in the Church countless blessings, and they are far better and greater then this new women's society."[101] Mancini's petulance was not simply driven by bragging rights, but because left unchallenged Hindiyya's claim potentially placed her in a position of grace that transcended any other within the Catholic Church—past, present, or future. With such unique grace came an unparalleled authority that threatened not only to allow Hindiyya (and through her the Maronite Church) greater independence but even to shift the center of theological and ecclesiastical gravity from Rome to Bkerki. While such a possibility was far-fetched, the fact that Mancini took the underlying claim seriously is an indication of how disturbing Hindiyya had come to be for Rome.

What scandalized Mancini further were "matters that defy decorum and propriety . . . (and it is a customary arrogance in women like that) I mean that Christ placed each of his holy hands on each of Hindiyya's hands, and each of his legs and torso on Hindiyya's legs and torso and his head on her head. I mean that Christ lay on top of the virgin!"[102] Even Francis of Assisi and Catherine of Siena were not privileged by such an intimacy with the body of Christ.[103] What offended Mancini is not so much the union with Christ but the very physicality of that union. In other parts of his report he highlighted this troubling departure from the more traditional disembodied connection with God and Christ. Thus, toward the end of his statement he ridiculed Bishop Jirmanus as an extreme simpleton for stating that "when receiving the Eucharist Hindiyya and the nuns taste the flavor of milk, flesh and blood in a material manner."[104] The irrationality of such an experience put it even beyond the pale of imagination and made it a fictional fabrication on the part of impressionable women and ignorant confessors.

Finally, Mancini took serious issue with the gift of knowledge that was supposedly bestowed by God upon Hindiyya. It is claimed, he noted, that "the Holy Ghost gave this virgin the 'gift of tongues,'" the ability to discern difficult theological secrets like the Trinity and incarnation, as well as the "ability to explicate books even on mathematical, philosophical and natural sciences."[105] Mancini found such assertions on the part of Hindiyya's confessors to be absurd because, according to his reasoning, God only bestows gifts that fit the "situation and status" of the person. So, he asked rhetorically, "what status and situation does this woman have— when her life is said to be limited to isolation and contemplation—that would make her worthy"[106] of such gifts. The tone Mancini employed was dismissive on several levels. He dismissed Hindiyya as a woman, he rejected the possibility of combining bodily and intellectual knowledge, and finally he dismissed her as living in a world isolated from the center of Catholic learning, where he was sitting and writing his report. The first of these verbal waves of the hand was a common enough theme in the annals of the Catholic Church. As Grace Jantzen illustrates in her book *Power, Gender and Christian Mysticism,* women were regarded from the very earliest days of the Church as irrational carnal bodies standing in direct opposition to, and corrupting, the male spirit and mind.[107] In 1486 the authors of the notorious *Malleus maleficarum,* the two German Dominicans Heinrich Kramer and Jakobus Sprenger stated this attitude quite bluntly when they wrote that "a woman is more carnal than a man, as is clear from her many carnal abominations."[108] More generally, as Carolyn Bynum notes, men and women in the later Middle Ages saw "'woman' or 'the feminine' as symbolizing the physical part of human nature, whereas man symbolized the spiritual or rational."[109] These same attitudes toward women continued to prevail around Mancini's time, as evidenced not only by his disregard for the "woman" Hindiyya but also by the temperament of Pope Benedict XIV, for whom he was compiling his report. According to this tradition, women could not be trusted in religious matters because their very nature—as descendents of Eve—made them inherently sinful, much more so than men. Hindiyya was not an exception in the estimation of Mancini.

Furthermore, Hindiyya's claim to have acquired, as a woman, the most "rational" of sciences through bodily experience and emotive visions transgressed the sharp divide that many philosophers and theologians had invested years constructing, particularly in the seventeenth century with its project of modern science. René Descartes was certainly not the first to articulate this idea, but his *Meditations* "provide the first real phenomenology of the mind, and one of the central results of that phenomenology is . . . the enormous gulf that must separate what is conceived as occurring 'in here' from that which, correspondingly, must lie 'out there.'"[110] In other words, Descartes posited a deep alienation between the mind and the body and between rationality and the senses. Cartesian objectivism regarded cognitive relations with the outside world as remarkably fragile and contingent, leaving the individual with an interiorized, self-centered consciousness as the only stable source of knowledge. This divide between body and mind was highly gendered, with the unreliable senses and body depicted (in a long tradition stretching to Aristotle, Plato, and St. Augustine) as female. Sandra Harding argues that this scientific model of knowing represents "a super-masculinization of rational knowledge."[111] Karl Stern equally notes that what "we encounter in Cartesian objectivism is the pure masculinization of thought."[112] And it was not only philosophers like Descartes who posited this dualism between a feminized body and a masculinized soul; this posited radical ontological difference between the two was one of the main aspects of the Catholic Enlightenment. For example, Nicolas Malebranche, a central figure in that movement, explained "at the start of Book Two . . . that one of the principal impediments to the discovery of truth was 'the delicacy of the brain fibers . . . usually found in women . . . [which] gave them great understanding of everything that strikes the senses.'" Malebranche was not writing admiringly of this ability. Rather, "he employed Descartes's psycho-physiological model to demonstrate that, as a rule, the power of women's imaginations made them intellectually and morally weaker than men."[113] Friar Mancini, a product of the Catholic Enlightenment himself, held to this epistemology. In refuting a claim of Hindiyya's infallibility (something only the Virgin Mary presumably possessed), he quoted Cardinal Bonna that "throughout this life the body and soul are in conflict . . . which binds the soul with the chains of sin." Thus, Hindiyya's proclamation that her senses and emotions were conduits to deep intellectual knowledge undermined the epistemological premises of Mancini's faith, rendering her a liar and a heretic.

Mancini's dismissal of Hindiyya as a woman and a heretic was not novel in 1754. Other visionary women—and to a lesser extent men—had been subjected to such marginalization long before, and after, her. However, the third aspect of Mancini's rejection of Hindiyya as a visionary is somewhat different. He found her "life of isolation and contemplation" unworthy of any heavenly favors and surely not philosophical knowledge, for it was a life of no consequence to human history. The isolation of which he spoke referred to her cloistered life, focused as it were on contemplating the passion of Christ and his love for humanity. For Mancini this was obviously a waste of time and effort that could perhaps be better employed in apostolic work: teaching, caring for the sick, and plowing the fields. But at the same time, he was implying that the Levant itself was an isolated and unlikely place for learning and scholarship. Mancini intimated that the clearest evidence of Hindiyya's delusion or mendacity was her claim that God would elevate the villages and cities of the Levant to the same level as, or even above, learned Rome. Such a preposterous notion was simply unfathomable from his perspective. In his mind the Catholic world was mapped with Rome at its center, emanating the light of Christian knowledge—and hence faith—outward to the corners of the world.

(In)Conclusion

After his scornful dismissal of Hindiyya and her two confessors, Mancini concluded that those who think they can attain their salvation through mystical experiences and visions, rather than learning the scriptures with the "natural light of the mind" like the rest of humanity, have to be humiliated, chastised, and disciplined. While inclined toward Mancini's draconian conclusions, Pope Benedict XIV and the Propaganda Fide needed to temper the tone of that blunt condemnation. They sought to exercise their ecclesiastical authority over the Maronites without further alienating a community already in open rebellion over the matter of Hindiyya and the order of the Sacred Heart. Hence, the letters sent to Patriarch 'Awwad were remarkably different in tone and content from earlier haughty missives. For example, Pope Benedict spent the first two pages of his March 14, 1754, dispatch in part expressing his joy at receiving news about the good health of the patriarch and the reconciliation of the Maronites with the Jesuits. The remainder of those two pages was dedicated to assuring the patriarch of the Vatican's concern and love for the Maronites and their church as evidenced by an earlier letter the pope had sent affirming the orthodoxy of St. Maroun against Melkite claims that he was really a Monophysite. Then, he added,

> As for the matter of our dear daughter in Christ, the Aleppan virgin Hanna 'Ujaimi, we see it as part of your duties to teach and support her through wise and devout confessors and to send her away from people . . . in order to safeguard her virtue from the shadow of pride which would expose her to [moral] dangers, and for fear that she will become a cause for the renewal of division, conflict and insult.[114]

Benedict's short paragraph at once embraced Hindiyya within the Catholic "family" while at the same seeking to dispatch her to the far reaches of the community. It vaguely acknowledged the authority of the patriarch over her (and by extension all Maronites) while providing clear instructions of what was expected of him. By blaming her for the divisions and tensions which had brought the case to the attention of the Vatican in the first place, the rift between Rome and Bkerki was reduced to the troubles caused by one woman and not a struggle over the future of the Maronite Church. The cardinals' letter sent a few months later exhorted Patriarch 'Awwad to follow the counsel of the pope and provided the rationale for that decision by summarizing Mancini's points. It then concluded with the specific instruction that "His Eminence decided that this deluded virgin (as she must be assumed to have been until now) should be turned over to the [sole] care of Father Carlo Innocenzo [di Cuneo]."[115]

The attempt to contain historical, deep, and troubling questions about the relations between the Vatican, Latin missionaries, and the Maronite Church and community in the person of Hindiyya is not overly surprising. It allowed for a face-saving formula for all involved (except, of course, for the "naïve" Jirmanus Saqr and Antonio Venturi) and a retreat from the brink of a rupture in those relations. The metaphor of "family" optimistically swept aside any dysfunctionality as mere quibbles between those whose universal love in Christ should transcend local jealousies and indignations. The directive to remove Hindiyya to the netherworld of Maronite religious life left the "honor" of Maronite elites intact by withdrawing the earlier demand for the departure of nuns from the convent of Bkerki. At the same time, referring to the "dear daughter" by her baptismal name, Hanna, rhetorically broke the link between her and the *Hindawiyyun* or between her and the Maronite community at large. Hindiyya was to be rendered once again a solitary woman, her self-professed (and widely accepted) linkage to Christ severed, and her mind, body, and soul disciplined and restrained within the boundaries of orthodoxy administered by the Vatican's emissary, Brother Innocenzo. In other words, her transgressions across gender boundaries were to be reversed. This, the Vatican hoped, would normalize the relations between the Maronites and the Roman Catholic Church.

However, Hindiyya was not a hapless compliant "Aleppan virgin." For all the claims and displays of obedience reported by Desiderio and others, she had lived most of her life rejecting worldly authority when it stood between her and Christ. Her infatuation with Christ (and with the power emanating from that relationship) for the previous thirty years led her to defy her mother and the mores of Aleppan elite society; shun her father, sister, and Jesuit priests; and turn away from the embrace of Maronite nuns intent on dissuading her from her aim. Throughout those years she was willing to roam the literal and metaphorical wilderness rather than abandon the plan she believed Christ had charted for her.

Such a tenacious soul was not easily diverted, even if by order of the Vatican. Her reaction to the counsel of the Propaganda Fide was recorded in the *Secret of the Union* through a conversation with Christ. She wrote, "A hieromonk and a priest told me that the Sacred Congregation decided that I am deluded, and that Satan appears to me and he is the one who is deluding me." His response was to thunder that his justice and anger will bear down upon those "who come in sheep's clothing" but who in their arrogance delude themselves and place doubt into simple hearts. If this was not a clear enough indictment of the Vatican's decision, then the subsequent remark left no doubt as to whose voice she was to follow. Jesus, the Nazarene, said, "Have I said that priests should be obeyed against my divine will and my love?"[116] After a series of similarly rhetorical questions meant to dissuade Hindiyya from giving heed to what mere mortals say against her, "He disappeared from my sight and I felt a peace descend upon my conscience and my body too."[117] The resolution of her inner turmoil and doubt was to draw ever closer to Christ and to turn her back on those who castigated her and her visions.

In the summer and fall of 1755 Hindiyya did exactly that. She refused to submit to the will of the Vatican, and she shunned the papal legate, Brother Innocenzo. In part, she was able to do so because Innocenzo was a reluctant emissary who complained of advanced age and poor health and wished the pope had sent someone else in his place.[118] But aside from the physical ailments that weakened his resolve, Innocenzo faced determined opposition to his efforts to interrogate, teach, and confess Hindiyya. In other words, she would not submit to his authority. This opposition coalesced rather quickly when he proved himself unimpressed by Hindiyya's claims to divine grace and gifts of visions. For example, Katerina, Hindiyya's assistant, asked him on July 30, 1755, to come and witness Hindiyya enraptured; the demonstration was so underwhelming and unconvincing to him that he subsequently refused to accept any future invitations to similar séances. Nor was he any more convinced by Hindiyya's claims that a nun in Bkerki, a Sister Mubaraka, was imprinted by the stigmata of Christ. Hindiyya reciprocated by refusing to confess to him. In September and October, when he asked to hear her confession, she replied that she neither understood his Arabic nor trusted him.[119] Her intransigence and resort to the familiar complaint of a linguistic barrier to negate Latin religious authority, coupled with the machinations of those around her, drove Innocenzo to the crestfallen conclusion that his efforts were futile and hopeless. On January 10, 1756, he wrote the Propaganda Fide that his efforts to discipline Hindiyya had come to naught and that his continued presence in Bkerki was useless. By the beginning of February he was on his way out of Lebanon, defeated in the face of sustained resistance on the part of Hindiyya and her nuns as well as Bishop Saqr.[120]

Innocenzo's disheartened departure was footnoted by a complete disregard for his report to the Propaganda Fide. After an initial vigorous attack on Hindiyya, her confessors, and Patriarch 'Awwad, Pope Benedict XIV appears to have lost interest in that affair since he did not even bother dispatching any further letters about the subject to the patriarch. The flurry of earlier communications came to a grinding halt with nary an explanation. At first blush this gradual but ultimately radical shift can be explained away by a sense of fatigue similar to Innocenzo's. The pope, after all, had a world of Catholicism to manage and Hindiyya was but one character. (It is also certainly possible that the man was nearing the end of his life—he died in 1758—and was just tired of spending so much energy on any singular issue.) However, it is also indicative of a baroque Europe, where passion and reason mingled in every aspect of religious life, including that of the pope himself. While he dedicated a good deal of his life to rationalizing the Catholic faith, he could still write at the conclusion of his brief for the sanctification of Giuseppe da Cupertino, "in an intimate union with God, the heart enflamed out of Love of God, and it was almost torn apart by this sweet love, whereupon ecstasies and raptures occurred."[121] He embodied the tensions between visionary and scientific knowledge, between a textualized religion and a mystical faith based on an impassioned search for a union with God. Perhaps the quick fading of the Hindiyya affair could also be attributed to the emergence of Pope Clement XIII, a mild-mannered prelate who was preoccupied with trying to impose the will of the church over European territories. Or maybe, as Bernard Heyberger suggests, Hindiyya and her visionary ambitions were more palatable because the cult of the Sacred Heart was finding renewed favor in the halls of the Vatican, ultimately leading to official recognition (with a proper feast, mass, and offices) in 1765.[122]

Regardless of what caused this reversal from intense opposition to benign neglect, the outcome for Hindiyya was the same. Even without official recognition of her as an authentic visionary, she had clearly triumphed in her insistent effort to establish a religious order dedicated to the Sacred Heart of Christ. As a young woman she had struggled against the dogged opposition of secular and religious patriarchal hierarchies, local and beyond the shores of the Levant, and had come out the victor. That is remarkable in any century but surely even more so in the eighteenth century, when she stands out as a rather unique example. Her success was not only that she established a new religious order with bylaws dictated by Christ or imagined by her but also that she emerged as a central religious figure who towered above all around her, even as she protested (sometimes too loudly) that she had no aspirations for a public presence and authority. Through her visions and calling she made bodily knowledge of Christ the ultimate source of religious knowledge and, hence, stature and power. Whether reviled or adulated, she conspicuously occupied a pinnacle position in the struggle between the Vatican and the Maronite Church. Her persona as well as her efforts crystallized an emerging sense of Maronitism distinct from other Catholics but also novel in its modern image of an invigorated and individualized faith premised on a far more intense relationship with Christ. Throughout, she shed unrelenting light upon the gender contradictions inherent in a post-Reformation Catholic Church that stoked spirituality—particularly among women—even as it sought to contain the effervescence within ever more restrictive and domineering hierarchy. She—unwittingly or purposefully—rejected another gender dichotomy which placed reason (an abstract faculty ascribed to men) above and beyond emotion (a sensory faculty identified as feminine). Following in the footsteps of earlier female visionaries (the most recent of whom was Marguerite Marie Alacoque in France), she pushed the concept of the physical union with Christ to its extreme when she proclaimed that embracing his body meant channeling an infinite and supernal source of knowledge. Thus, the gender paradoxes were at once central and transcendent in Hindiyya and her visions.

Being poised at such a pinnacle must have been a heady affair, but it also meant teetering on an edge. Being free to pursue the adoration of Christ's heart as a means to universal salvation also meant that Hindiyya was essentially unfettered from the supervision of anyone or any limitations on her claims to authority. From such a position Hindiyya began a descent into hell.

5

PURGATORY

Angels and Demons in the Convent (1756–1778)

Is it true that you composed a prayer to discover those in the Satanic
Fraternity?

—Fr. Pietro di Moretta to Hindiyya[1]

In 1787 Constantin François Volney, who sojourned in Mount Lebanon
two years before, began his narration of the demise of Hindiyya in the following portentous fashion:

> A factor, travelling from Damascus to Bairout [*sic*], in the summer, was
> overtaken by night, near this convent [Bkerki]; the gates were shut, the
> hour unseasonable; and, as he did not wish to give any trouble, he con-
> tented himself with a bed of straw, and laid himself down in the outer
> court, to wait the return of day. He had slept but a few hours, when a sud-
> den noise of doors and bolts awaked him. From one of the doors came
> out three women, with spades and shovels in their hands; who were fol-
> lowed by two men, carrying a long white bundle, which appeared very
> heavy. They proceeded towards an adjoining piece of ground, full of
> stones and rubbish, where the men laid down their load, dug a hole into
> which they put it, and, covering it with earth, trod it down with their
> feet, after which they all returned to the house. The sight of men with
> nuns, and this bundle, thus mysteriously buried by night, could not but
> furnish matter of reflection to the traveller.[2]

The bundle was the body of Nassimeh Abou Badran, who died one night
in June 1777 during exorcism by Elias Burkana the Aleppan, a monk in the

convent of Bkerki. The subsequent discovery of the body of Nassimeh by the distraught father, Antoun Abou Badran, as well as the body of another nun, Wardeh the Aleppan, became the premise for a renewed papal inquisition into the life, words, and work of Hindiyya and her religious order.

Once unleashed, this process (which lasted from 1773 through 1783) refracted the tensions and passions within and outside the convent of Bkerki that led to the tragic deaths of those two nuns. As with practically every instance before, the explanations for what transpired were centered on Hindiyya—even as she deflected attention to others—and reflected the views of two opposing camps. One group—including dissident *Jabaliyyat* nuns of the Bkerki convent, some Maronite clergy, and the Propaganda Fide—saw the deaths as testament to the delusions of grandeur harbored by Hindiyya and the falsehoods of her revelations which had beguiled and misguided secular and religious Maronite notables.[3] They regarded Hindiyya's proclaimed physical and spiritual union with Christ (compiled in the manuscript titled *Secret of the Union*) as the height of her arrogance and hubris and the cause behind the Maronite Church's departure from Roman dogma. It was *Secret of the Union,* they contended, which allowed Hindiyya to rule her nuns, and even those outside the purview of the Bkerki convent, as an autocratic abbess who would brook nothing less than blind obedience and faith in her pronouncements and actions because they emanated from Christ. Thus, the Maronite priest Sim'an al-Sim'ani wrote to Cardinal Borgia, the secretary of the Propaganda Fide, that "all without exception must obey Hindiyya because she is united with Christ."[4] In summarizing the Propaganda Fide's position on this issue, Cardinal Borgia noted that

> It can be concluded that the Bkerki convent has suffered for a long time from a great disorder ... because of the blind exaltation put forth—and which everyone is expected to put forth—for all that Mother Hindiyya says or does ... and to believe and state that she is objectively and subjectively united with our Lord Christ and that her sanctity is greater than that of the Virgin Mary.[5]

The criticisms leveled at Hindiyya's perceived transgressions can be further separated into two categories. One was, at least partially, a common enough problem within convents and monasteries. As historian Craig Harline points out in his book *The Burdens of Sister Margaret,* "Factionalism versus common love, dissent versus obedience, the rights of the individual versus the demands of the community, the drawing of the line between temporal needs and extravagance . . . have always been the central tensions of monasticism."[6] The relationship between the *Halabiyyat* and *Jabaliyyat* in the Bkerki convent seems to have started out as tepid and deteriorated thereafter into hostility, jealousy, and mistrust. According to the testimonies of some of the *Jabaliyyat,* this was exacerbated by Hindiyya's undisguised preference for the nuns from her hometown and by her open disdain for those who came from the rural countryside. Another explanation for the tensions was more predicated on class divisions. Hindiyya was accused by some nuns of favoring those who brought with them a sizeable dowry to the convent and whose parents seemed better placed socially and economically to help extend the influence and scope of the Sacred Heart of Jesus order. What deepened these fissures were accusations of hypocrisy leveled by some dissident nuns at Hindiyya. In contrast to the very austere life and demanding spiritual exercises that Hindiyya expected her nuns to follow, she was accused of leading a pampered life of rich clothes, elaborate meals, lax religiosity, and even sexual and social improprieties. Regardless of the veracity of these accusations, they allow us to map out the social and economic landscape of religious life. More to the point, they permit us to understand the dialectical relationship between the ideal and the reality of monastic life as defined by religious women and men in Mount Lebanon.

From the perspective of the Propaganda Fide, Hindiyya's transgressions were not only about her alleged abuse of power over her nuns. Rather, what the Holy Roman inquisitor Pietro di Moretta and the cardinals in Rome found most disturbing was that Hindiyya had simply upended the Catholic Church's gendered structure of authority. As early as 1753 a secret report sent from Rome to then patriarch Istifan 'Awwad noted that the cardinals of the Propaganda Fide took strong exception to parts of Hindiyya's "Christ-inspired Rule." In particular, they rejected her assertion of the right and authority of the nuns of the Sacred Heart order to elect their own bishop, which they found to undermine the priesthood authority enshrined in various synods.[7] Some twenty years later the cardinals delegated by Pope Pius VI to investigate Hindiyya and her order were equally perturbed by her transgressions of the norms of church hierarchy that they saw as animated by her claim of physical and spiritual union with Christ.[8] For example, the cardinals reported—with what one assumes had to be horror—that she heard confessions, absolved men and women of sin, and went so far as to distribute the Eucharist, "claiming to give of herself as Jesus Christ did at the last supper." They added with utmost disapproval that her male acolytes follow her "blindly," call her "Sultana of the Heavens," and claim that her *Secret of the Union* allows her knowledge and power of intercession that is beyond anything contained in the books and teachings of the Roman Catholic Church.[9] Through these and counternarratives we can discern the competing definitions of religious authority within the context of divergent attempts to shape Catholicism in the Levant. Even more than the contentions of the 1750s, the horrendously sad events of the 1770s lay bare the tensions between local and Roman articulation of authority and highlight the intimate role that gender played in this struggle for power. It also brings into relief the strain between the Tridentine ideal of the convent as a private space of cloistered women who are ostensibly dead to the world and the central role that Hindiyya came to play in the public religious life of Catholicism in Bilad al-Sham. Not only had she become integral to the hierarchy of the Maronite Church but the Bkerki convent had become a focal point of religious pilgrimage and the Sacred Heart confraternity had formed a widespread network of men and women disseminating Hindiyya's ideas and teachings.[10]

The *Hindawiyyun* also contended that *Secret of the Union* was at the heart of the conflict coursing through the convent of Bkerki and leading to the disorders across Mount Lebanon and beyond. Most of the Aleppan nuns in the Sacred Heart of Jesus order, Patriarch Yusuf Istifan, a majority of the Maronite clergy, and practically all of the Khazin shaykhs believed that Hindiyya was the target of the devil, who was threatened by the power of good unleashed through her union with Christ. In accounting for the deaths in the Bkerki convent, Patriarch Yusuf Istifan decreed them to be a just punishment from God because "the Masonic Satanic fraternity entered this blessed convent through the disobedient nuns in order to destroy it and the great blessing it has brought about [through the Secret Union]."[11] Various testimonies provided by some nuns from the convent and dispatched to the Propaganda Fide in defense of Hindiyya corroborated the patriarch's statement and embellished it with lurid tales of sexual, gastronomical, and ritualistic trysts. Whatever one is to make of these testimonies—and they are highly problematic, not least because they were always witnessed by allies of Hindiyya—they underscore the *Hindawiyyun*'s argument that it was not Hindiyya who sowed trouble and dissent but rather it was her devil-worshiping opponents who were to blame. For instance, Domitilla, daughter of Mikhail ibn Jiryis the Damascene, stated that she had entered the "satanic fraternity through the diabolical traps of Nassimeh and Wardeh . . . who established this cult in order to kill our Mother Hindiyya and destroy the Order of the Sacred Heart of Jesus."[12] Likewise, and in his defense, the monk Elias Burkana stated that he beat Nassimeh (but did not kill her) in order to extract from her the location of papers containing the vows of a "Masonic satanic fraternity" she supposedly established with her sister, Wardeh, in Bkerki to kill Hindiyya and take over the convent.[13]

The tale of satanic cult and rituals in the narratives of the *Hindawiyyun* is a palimpsest. Its layers recount not only the events but also the underlying social, theological, and gendered assumptions that led to elaborate accusations of demonic possessions and exorcisms. As much as the reported nefarious activities of the devil and his conventual minions may have been a smokescreen to hide the violence committed against nuns in Bkerki (as maintained by those opposed to Hindiyya), they still draw us a map of the anxieties of the time. Interwoven through the narratives are hints of barely contained passions (physical and emotional) which animated tales of debauchery, sin, and retribution. Sexuality (opposite and same-sex) within the convent—freed as it was from societal restraints by the passion inherent in *Secret of the Union*—comes to the fore repeatedly and vociferously in these narratives. Needless to say, for a convent full of "virgin" women who had taken solemn vows of chastity, this was not the expected norm of behavior nor was the cuckolding of their divine groom Christ through illicit affairs an act of piety. While sexual acts may have taken place—as they did in some convents in Europe and

Latin America—these scintillating tales offer us a window into a subject normally hidden from historical view by taboo-induced silence. Our voyeuristic peek into this private sphere will show how sexuality was publicly construed as part of social relations but also as a manifestation of anxieties about the changing religious and secular worlds. Thus, rather than a private enclosure of "virgins," this chapter will approach the Bkerki convent as a lens which refracts the tensions of the larger society, even as its occupants shaped ideas about religion, sexuality, and gender roles. With this in mind we can now take a closer look at the source of the trouble: *Secret of the Union.*

"What Is This *Secret of the Union*?"

The short answer to di Moretta's dismissive question is that *Secret of the Union* was the apogee of Hindiyya's career; the physical and spiritual culmination of an emotionally tumultuous relationship between her and Christ; and a source of authority, knowledge, and power which made her in effect a living saint. But, of course, there is a much more detailed and telling answer.

We know of *Secret of the Union* from three sources. The first is the document with that title ostensibly dictated by Hindiyya to Bishop Jirmanus Saqr and then after his death to Bishop Jirmanus Diyab. It narrates the religious vitae of Hindiyya from infancy to the moment of union with Christ. The second source is a summary narrative by an anonymous but sympathetic author of the immediate events leading to and subsequent to the union. Finally, we have the inquisition of Pietro di Moretta as a hostile probing into the story of the union. On the basis of these sources, we can follow Hindiyya's passionate affair with Christ and its physical and metaphysical climax. We can also begin to understand the power unleashed by this union.

Secret of the Union begins the story when Hindiyya was but a child in Aleppo. It does not explicitly provide any timeline but hints at the dates of particular events from the context in which they are located within the narrative. From the outset Hindiyya is depicted as dubious of her visions, a trait befitting a pious and humble woman. Addressing Christ in one of her visions in Bkerki, she asked, "Do you not know that those who oppose

me are many . . . and they make me doubt [my visions]. And even without anyone planting doubts in me I greatly doubt and fear that I am possessed and deluded thus veering off the path of salvation."[14] Christ, the
Virgin Mary, and Hindiyya's guardian angel spent the following four to
five pages soothing her doubts and encouraging her to embrace the gift
which Christ sought to bestow upon her. Vaguely rendered, the gift was
"this secret union" that through the "motion" of Christ's living and sacred
body would expand Hindiyya's understanding "to an unbelievable extent
and in a manner that cannot be understood by any being."[15] Despite these
various reassurances, Hindiyya was still apparently unconvinced because
she subsequently asked the "one I used to see" (her moniker for Christ)
for further proof.[16] At this juncture the autobiographical record and di
Moretta's inquisition converge to tell a similar tale with different tones.
In both accounts she challenged Christ by saying, "If you are Christ the
Son of the Living God . . . then you will imprint your holy wounds on the
body of the stupidest nun in our convent [Bkerki], who does not have any
obvious virtues and who does not know spiritual matters."[17] He did accept
her conditions and "the stigmata was implanted onto Sister Mubaraka."[18]
Remarkably, Hindiyya informed di Moretta that after a while the whole
matter passed from her mind because Christ had not given her a definitive
promise and because Sister Mubaraka hid her stigmata for a long while. A
similar version appeared in her response to di Moretta's inquiry but with
a different prologue. That record notes that before recounting her demand
of Christ, Hindiyya cried profusely and told di Moretta that she never
wanted this gift; in fact, she wished death before seeing these visions "but
what could I do."[19] Her proclaimed lapse of memory and reluctance are
understandable given that she was trying to defend herself to di Moretta
against accusations of hubris and arrogance. But they are also in tune with
the normative vitae of female visionaries, who were frequently represented
as nothing more than vessels of the will of Christ or God. To be otherwise would transcend the gendered role of women, especially in the post-
Tridentine era.

   Paradoxically, even in her purposeful retelling Hindiyya could not
obscure the active role she had in the relationship with Christ. Not only did
she—like St. Gertrude of Helfta (1256–c. 1307), the German Benedictine

and mystic writer—speak to Christ but she in fact contended with him, as we can see from the challenge she posed above.[20] Christ's response is equally indicative of their grappling relationship, which was less about her submission to divine will and more like the demands of an insistent lover whom she did not quite trust yet. After she demanded evidence through the implantation of the stigmata, Christ reappeared to threaten her with eternal damnation and unparalleled torment if she insisted on doubting him and rejecting the secret gift. However, later he relented and tried another approach. He told Hindiyya during a subsequent visitation, "I, with my unlimited condescension, have moved the heart of your simple [naïve?] spiritual director to tell you of his own will to obey my command and my decisions."[21] The contradictions inherent in this solution are legion. There is first the paradox of free agency manipulated like a marionette by the power of Christ, and then there is contradiction between a spiritual guide who is supposed to be adept at deep theological matters being labeled a simpleton. But most remarkable is the tension between Christ's haughty words, which describe his power and authority in very "masculine" terms, and the fact that he continuously supplicated Hindiyya to accept his will. (At the same time, she demonstrated the strength of her will and power to resist by retreating behind the normative "feminine" language of weakness, self-deprecation, and fear.) Hindiyya noted the irony of the situation (or perhaps she sought to explain away the paradox for outside observers) when she later asked Christ the following pointed question: "If you are our Lord Jesus Christ and you want to give me a gift then why are you asking me to accept it by my choice and by submitting my will [to yours]." Christ's response, rendered in very convoluted text, was that it was only by facing difficulties and struggles through her own free will that she could fully comprehend and feel the gift he was about to give her.[22]

Placated somewhat by this answer, she nonetheless remained, by her account, resistant to abandoning herself to the "one who appeared" to her. Hence, and despite the pleas of her own confessor, Bishop Jirmanus Saqr, to obey the will of Christ and accept the gift, Hindiyya took a different approach to justify her hesitation. When Christ appeared to her after their last discourse, she asked him coyly, "I know with my [mental] weakness and limited intelligence that you are pleased with those who follow the guidance of the priests." Then, she added that a priest quoting Galatians 1:8 warned her that the personage in her "false fantasies" is Satan, the chief of the devils. Christ's response to the accusation Hindiyya cast upon him through the mouth of the priest was to dismiss priests, in general, as arrogant souls. "He who speaks to me looked upon his body and his gaping wounds . . . and angrily said . . . : 'Did I say that priests should be obeyed against my divine will and active love? . . . I condemn whoever doubts me and keeps you from . . . accepting the Secret Union.'"[23] This unequivocal dismissal of any male clerical authority who stood in the way of Hindiyya brought her "mental and physical peace." It also brought with it the beginnings of unfettered passions. She wrote that his assurances allowed her the confidence to reflect at length on his appearance, "and I would feel in my soul and heart the impact of that vision . . . and sometimes my heart would be so deeply stirred with love [for Christ] that I would lose consciousness."[24]

Her stirrings of love were not enough to abandon all ecclesiastically dictated restraints. So, Christ had to appear in yet another vision to admonish and threaten her with dire straits if she did not obey. In this instance he sounded like a petulant suitor. Jesus chided her,

> I am the eternal wisdom who condescended with love perfected with gentleness toward your soul which is created by me, and I showed you love with an unfathomable humility which has astounded the spirits in heaven . . . and still you shun in disgust what I have made manifest unto you through this free gift which I bestow upon you through my infinite wisdom.

In the face of such a display of divine hurt feelings, Hindiyya relented somewhat but spoke again of the opposition she was facing from ecclesiastical authorities. This time it was not simply a monk or priest but the highest of authorities who, she claimed, kept her from accepting the divine gift of physical and spiritual union with Christ. Two priests, whose names were not recorded, informed her that the pope and the Propaganda Fide commanded her to reject her delusions and flee from the person she encountered as she would to avoid adultery. This tug of war within her heart, mind, and soul was torment so severe "I do not know where I am at times, and sometimes I become numb walking around as if I am asleep even though I am awake."[25] His response was to smile and say, "I am glorified by this naïve credulity." Then he commanded her to gaze at the wound on his side so that her understanding would expand. She marveled at seeing a human heart but one that was perfected with absolute purity and that contained within it a secret. While the form was human and thus limited in its dimensions, at its center was a great expanse unbounded and unending, leading to infinite and divine knowledge. The contradiction between the human vessel and the divine infinite was the ultimate symbol—for Hindiyya anyway—of the union of the man and the god in one entity. Animating the union was divine love channeled from the infinite and emanating from the finite to alleviate the suffering of humanity and atone for its sins.

It was a moving sight that pushed Vatican opposition and possible opprobrium to the peripheries of Hindiyya's concerns. Her soul soared in ecstasy from this vision, but she told Christ, "I fear offering up my body [to feel this] and my fear is tormenting me." Her fear derived from the intense feelings she knew would overwhelm her body in an erotic fever that surely resembled adultery. Thus, she beseeched him to give the gift of this secret union (physical and spiritual) to someone who desired it or to at least let her experience his love in her soul and not materially. In response, and as if to confirm her trepidation, Christ became more explicit in words and actions. He addressed her, "With my righteous will . . . I want you to be my bride by giving this gift solely to you . . . in order to move the souls and hearts of . . . [men and women] so that they may return to me in penitence, and to illuminate minds with just truths that make human beings submit in worship to the love of its Creator and Atoning One, which is I."[26] With this one sentence, Christ implied several things. Hindiyya was to be uniquely endowed with this gift of the union, and the union had to be both material and spiritual. Moreover, he made clear (or at least clearer) for the first time the purpose of his courtship of Hindiyya. What was at stake was purportedly the salvation of humanity, a task that could be accomplished only when Hindiyya willingly became the vessel of his divine will. Such an ambitious goal also implicitly meant that existing mechanisms— most notably the Catholic Church—were not sufficient. Short of dismissing the ecclesiastical authorities of Rome and Bilad al-Sham as irrelevant to the salvation of souls, this turn of phrase catapulted Hindiyya to the stratosphere of religious authority. It did so through a bodily experience, which Hindiyya described quite explicitly: "I felt that with his eyesight he penetrated my soul, heart and body with a strong thrust that made me feel blood flowing in my veins and sense every bone and joint in my body."[27] As Grace Jantzen has observed for other visionaries—such as Mechthild of Magdeburg, Gertrude the Great of Helfta, Catherine of Siena, and St. Teresa de Avila—Hindiyya described a literal passionate encounter of the body and soul, rather than an allegorical mystical experience.[28]

As with any smitten lover, Hindiyya's thoughts frequently turned to Christ from this point onward. Thus, one day while pondering the secret of the Eucharist and its embodiment of Christ and his mercy toward the unworthy "man," Hindiyya went into a state of rapture "as if I no longer existed in this world." Christ then appeared to her as he was the day he died: a meek body insulted and tortured and ultimately crucified. Once again he gently chastised her even as he drew parallels between his struggles and hers. Speaking of his humility, he said, "I am the one who concealed the power of the union of my human and divine nature in the secrets of my agonies so that I would appear to my enemies and despisers as a simple human being, as a criminal."[29] Hindiyya, of course, also had enemies who cast doubt on her and her visions and who sought to dissuade her from fulfilling her promise as a visionary woman. In fact, as Christ observed, her qualms about fully embracing him were born out of her fear of those enemies and the doubts they implanted in her mind. With echoes of Gethsemane, Christ told Hindiyya that she was the only one who could bear the cross of his gift and she could not pass the bitter cup along to another as she had repeatedly pleaded with him to do. Lest the weight of that pronouncement be too burdensome, he quickly assured her that he would sustain her against his and her enemies. To underline the power of his promise, shafts of light came forth from all of his wounds to open an ever-expanding gap—in what is not clear—filled with the images of the creation and the universe with its planets and stars. Hindiyya was suitably and predictably dazzled with this kaleidoscope of images, which symbolically stood for her own expanding knowledge. What makes this even more powerful was that her knowledge was also expanding across the body of Christ. In a symbiotic movement, she came to understand the universe as a body of intellectual knowledge through intimately knowing the body of Christ. With such a heady brew she came ever closer to the tipping point of losing herself within Christ.

After dismissing the objections of ecclesiastical authorities to her planned divine betrothal and, thus, her ascendancy to a paramount place of religious authority, Hindiyya was left with but one barrier between her and her beloved: the sin of pride. There is a double entendre to this word as employed in *Secret of the Union*. It was pride as in conceit over obtaining an unequaled gift from Christ, but it also denoted the power which derives from becoming one with Christ in body and spirit. The discourse of Christ on this subject and Hindiyya's questions about this matter form a foundation for justifying the latter transformation of a private mystical experience into a source of public power. With this in mind, it is worth our while to follow the dialogue between the two lovers as they circle each other in an ever-shrinking orbit. The conversation started with Christ appearing to Hindiyya somewhere in the Bkerki convent, and this time he asked her to reflect on his crown of thorns, which "I had accepted . . . for the sins of all humanity." From here he launched into a soliloquy on the sin of pride. From the outset he made it clear that for him it was one of the vilest of sins, one that placed the sinner furthest away from the love of Christ and that brought upon the sinner the unmitigated wrath of God. "I detest any instance when the actions of an arrogant person pierce the hearts [of others] because it is the opposite of infinite merits and my unbounded humble condescension through my [human] embodiment and my sacred life." This stark juxtaposition was followed with admonishment to Hindiyya to avoid at all costs the sin of pride. The instructions were simple: "Listen to what I tell you," Christ said to Hindiyya, "and possess it with your understanding, memory and heart, and with your free agency humble your will."[30] To illustrate the fate of those who are too proud to submit to his will—and because Hindiyya still begged him to give his gift to someone else—Christ carried her soul to hell, where three angels surrounded her. They pointed out the "hideousness" of the devils that only became so after rejecting Christ's will because of their pride. After highlighting the agonies of hell, they warned her, "If you continue in your opposition and refuse . . . to accept this gift [union with Christ] then you will be in this dark pit."[31]

This was hardly a choice: either eternal damnation in the fires of hell or the sweet pleasure of physical and spiritual union with the body of Christ. And that was exactly the point. Hindiyya saw and represented herself as being compelled to accept the union because to do otherwise would be to commit the sin of pride. Thus, uniting with Christ was not motivated by a willful soul—as her opponents claimed throughout her visionary career— but by its very opposite characteristics: humility and total submission of her will. The anonymous narrative describing the union of Hindiyya and Christ underscores this point quite explicitly. Over two pages of the manuscript (in elegant handwriting and far more eloquent Arabic than *Secret of the Union*) Christ attributes all of Hindiyya's actions from childhood onward to himself. "I made you think of me, I—your creator and god— even before you could speak . . . and your heart yearned for me before you were even [mentally] aware."[32] Indeed, the long-running saga of *Secret of the Union* and the greatly truncated answer to di Moretta's inquiry both emphasized Hindiyya's continual resistance to, and rejection of, Christ's gift because she feared transgressing the precepts of the church and rising above the station allocated to women in post-Tridentine Catholicism. It is against this backdrop that we have to read the subtext of Christ's discourse on pride. Those who sought to dissuade Hindiyya were going against his will because of their own arrogance and belief in themselves rather than submission to divine desires. If the nuance of this subtext was too subtle, his following statement bluntly put forth the same judgment. "My holy anger will pierce the arrogant souls which, dressed in lamb's clothing and through the error of their pride, lead my sheep astray."[33]

Then, he delivered his final assurance to Hindiyya that coming into him physically and spiritually is not prideful but the obedient fulfillment of his plans. In the summary narrative of *Secret of the Union* the author has Christ saying,

> O Hindiyya . . . I am the pride of your heart. I am the one who has captured your mind. I am the one who has captured your thoughts. I am the one who has attracted you to me. I am the glory of your soul and the light of your heart. Do not fear. You have the right to be proud of my sacred name and me because when you pronounce the name of the crucified

Jesus of Nazareth your soul will become proud. Sometimes because of this [feeling of pride] you are afraid of becoming haughty. Your pride is coming from me so let your soul glory in me and do not be afraid because I am your god and savior. I make humble hearts victorious.[34]

Hindiyya's doubts and worries were thus thoroughly assuaged as she was rendered an object of the desires of Christ, who sought to be her consort and to "frequently visit her."[35] Simultaneously, her path to mystical union and its attendant religious power were cleared from any remaining hurdles by this configuration of the relationship. Christ could then tell her forthrightly: "My daughter Hindiyya, I want you . . . to kiss my body . . . and fear not for it will purify your soul and heart and distance your senses from all that which displeases me and goes contrary to virtue."[36]

With that invitation Hindiyya entered timidly into her union with Christ. She recalled, "I kissed his body with fear, confusion, and shyness."[37] Upon contact, she felt an emotional reaction she had never felt, her heart raced with love, and she began to speak with him "in words I never uttered before because I did not know them." She continued in this blissful stupor for hours oblivious to her surroundings, only to awaken to a mixture of fear and pleasure brought about by unbeckoned recollections of the illicit moment. She alternated for days, according to her, between being intoxicated by the passions coursing through her being at the mere thought of her kiss and guilt for allowing herself those forbidden pleasures. Whether playing coy or truly torn, Hindiyya still allows us a glimpse into the tensions deriving out of sexual desire in an environment bent on controlling those urges and the bodies from which they emanate. In other words, union with Christ was not only about gaining knowledge and authority beyond the walls of the convent but also about liberating the female body from the social and religious enclosures. This theme of sexual freedom, and even revolution, is fully articulated a short while later in the narrative. Nevertheless, to arrive there she still felt compelled to attain permission and support from the patriarchal figure in the convent: Bishop Saqr. Given her propensity to disregard male authority if it went contrary to her visions or desires, it is safe to assume that she sought Saqr's blessing as a way to shift responsibility for what had transpired. From this it becomes evident that this was a distinctly transgressive act and that she was aware of its ramifications.

Her conundrum between pleasure and guilt and her awareness of the immensity of what was to transpire led her to confess to Bishop Saqr the story of her furtive kiss and the persistence of "the person I see" in seeking to repeat that experience. After having dismissed Hindiyya during their first encounter in 1748, Bishop Saqr had become one of her most ardent supporters. Certainly, and as noted earlier, this was because his affiliation with a visionary with a fast-rising renown brought him prestige and power (and sanctification after death). However, he also believed that Christ was gracing the Maronites with a divine gift. Amid an emerging narrative of Maronite exceptionalism with a constructed timeless identity, Saqr saw Christ's visitations to Hindiyya as a reward for the Maronites' persistent Catholic faith in the face of centuries of persecution—imagined and real. Therefore, his palpably impatient response to Hindiyya was that she should indulge in the love of Christ and kiss his sacred body without any fear or concern. For good measure, he added, "When you see him tell him to forgive my sins and to stoke my heart with his love and to make it shun sin . . . I tell you all this so that you will set aside your self-torturing doubt."[38] (Of course, the promise of a direct supplication of Christ's favor may have had something to do with his reassurance and encouragement.) If Saqr's impatience with her hesitation was subtle, Christ by that time had lost all patience. A few hours after the bishop had nudged Hindiyya toward consummating her courtship with Jesus, Christ castigated her. "Why do you doubt me," he thundered, "when I have taken pity on your weaknesses time and time again and have repeatedly given you peace from your doubts . . . and yet you persist in doubting me in one form or another. . . . If you continue to oppose my will and desire then you will meet a horrifying end and suffer frightening afflictions."[39]

In the face of impending doom, Hindiyya fled to her bishop—in her seemingly endless vacillation—to tell him that her resolve to obey Christ always dissipated hours after his disappearance, leaving her with an ephemeral memory and soon overwhelmed with her fear of trials that awaited and doubt that persisted. Her propensity to "forget" Christ and his promises, proofs, and assurances is puzzling given the numerous apparitions and conversations she had had with him from her childhood years in Aleppo and through this period in the 1750s and beyond. It is also bewildering in light of the power and authority with which Christ sought to endow her. It is less mystifying if understood as a mechanism of self-preservation. As the narrative of the journey that took her from anonymity as an ordinary child and young woman in Aleppo to prominence as a visionary embodying a resurgent Maronite Church, *Secret of the Union* appears as a probing device that tested the limits of what is permissible. The choreography of her pas de deux with Christ was one of a few steps into the forbidden sublime followed by a quick retreat back to the ordinary. Her hesitation may have been meant to provide an element of plausible deniability given the storm of opposition kicked up by Latin missionaries, local secular and religious opponents, and the Curia. Less cynically, it may have been the reluctance of a very pious young woman brought up to regard extramarital sexuality as sinful and who was fighting hard against the temptation of her flesh because of a real fear of hell. A combination of the two is equally within the realm of possibility.

In any case, this last encounter set the ground for establishing bodily knowing as the primary means of theology not only for Hindiyya but also for all who sought to know God and his truth. This was not a minor twist in a thickening plot but a major shift that posed a challenge to the theological foundations of the post-Tridentine church, to over one hundred years of Latin missionary propaganda in Bilad al-Sham, and to patriarchal authority. These themes are displayed prominently in the response of Bishop Saqr to Hindiyya's latest bout of doubt. The benevolent elderly bishop (as portrayed in *Secret of the Union*) calmed her fears by telling her, "I believe that this [person] is Christ the living son of God . . . even if I were ignorant and did not know through study and philosophy, my heart is still moved when you speak sometimes of our Lord Jesus Christ whom you see . . . I understand that He is Christ and I believe in Him."[40] The tradition of rational thought that had come to dominate the official theology of the Catholic Church by the eighteenth century was subsumed to the quickening of the heart. In other words, a prominent male cleric not only gave Hindiyya his stamp of approval for the proposed union but also allowed for a higher level of knowing that transcended the foundational teachings of the Vatican—and Hindiyya was the conduit of that knowledge.

This appears to have finally unfettered Hindiyya from the last remaining vestiges of doubt and concern about the reactions of the local and distant church clergy. The long-awaited moment arrived when Christ appeared, demanding of Hindiyya to freely submit to his will and give her body and soul to him. "He said this and opened his arms to embrace me." Dashing all caution to the wind and with the pleasurable memory of their first kiss, Hindiyya said, "'I give you my soul and body. . . . My beloved I freely offer you my worthless senses as you desire.' As I said these words to him he embraced me with unlimited tenderness, and with this embrace he penetrated my body and soul with his deified body."[41] The summary of *Secret of the Union* was more specific about this moment, albeit with a differing date.[42] Its author noted that, "on the fourth of February, 1759, Mother Hindiyya felt the body of Jesus Christ unite with her body . . . and she saw clouds of light emanating from him and she felt as if her whole body was on fire." Christ then invited her to kiss his sacred body and to sing a hymn to each of its parts.[43] Such erotically suggestive imagery leaves little room to doubt that Hindiyya was in the throes of physical as well as emotional passions. Hindiyya's subsequent breathless soliloquy only confirms the orgasmic nature of the moment.[44] With her body out of her control and the agonies of pleasure coursing through her veins, Hindiyya poured forth a poetics of 'ishq (ardent love) that was focused on the body of Christ. His was a sublime body emanating divine wisdom, endowed by radiant and enlightening transparent purity, whose *every* part was perfect. He was her beloved, the center of the passions of her heart, the pleasures of her emotions, and the anchor of her knowledge. As her longing (lust) for him melted her heart and sapped her energy, she begged him to give her strength to love him more. In Abu Nawassian fashion (the medieval Arab-Persian poet known for his *khamriyyat,* or poetry of wine and love), Hindiyya declared Christ to be her bountiful wine, who intoxicated her soul and quenched the passions of her heart. She marveled at every aspect of his body, in its human perfection, and was moved to tears by its divine beauty.

In large part this and subsequent moments of spiritual and physical ecstasy and rapture came to define the life of Hindiyya privately and publicly. She became more "heavenly and unaware of earthly matters," lost— so her vita relates—in her love for Christ, seeking to feast upon his body every minute and to perpetually kiss his divine body with her mouth.[45] Yet the pleasure was mirrored and inextricably linked with excruciating agonies that became Hindiyya's constant companion through the rest of her life on earth. In *Secret of the Union* she concluded her account of her union with Christ by noting,

> Ever since my senses were moved by . . . [the union with Christ] through the impulse of [his] body I have not had any comfort. . . . And I no longer sleep as I used to . . . for if I sleep after my prolonged periods of insomnia I lay as if I am awake. . . . I feel agony every minute [of my life] because of the difficulty I find with my material senses because the movements of his body [within my body] are purely spiritual causing pain to my material body. . . . And I only mention little of my great many agonies.[46]

As Christ came to inhabit and move Hindiyya's physical being, he subjected her to pains that were meant to duplicate his own agonies on the Cross. Angels were dispatched by Christ to place a crown of thorns on her head, practically choking her, and to force her to drink a cup of vinegar. Jesus went further by extracting from every part of her body "thin veins" that sent shock waves of pain coursing through her. Such torturous agonies were inflicted upon her in order to purify her being and make her a perfect vessel for the will of Christ and a mechanism for saving souls. This was a common enough phenomenon among visionary women. As Carolyn Bynum notes, both Catherine of Siena (d. 1380) and Catherine of Genoa (d. 1510) "felt that it was in the excruciating pain . . . that they fused with the agony of Christ on the cross and offered such agony for the salvation of the world."[47] Thus, *imitatio crucis* (imitation of the agonies on the Cross) was conceived by (mainly female) visionaries as the only way to truly become one with Christ and feel his eternal love. In other words, as Bynum remarks in speaking of religious women in the thirteenth and fifteenth centuries, "if the agony was also ecstasy, it was because of the . . . union with Christ's limitless suffering, which is also limitless love."[48]

Placed within the context of eighteenth-century Vatican theology, Hindiyya's account is remarkable at three levels. First, as J. Giles Milhaven and Ulrike Wiethaus have separately observed for medieval European women, bodily knowing was seen by most Catholic theologians as a spiritual palliative at best but more frequently as a delusion. In either case it was a subjective experience that could add nothing to the accumulated religious learning because it was irrational in that it did not emanate from the mind, the sole link to divine knowledge per Roman Catholic theologians from the thirteenth century and thereafter. Milhaven argues further that bodily knowledge was highly suspect among medieval and even modern theologians because it eschewed the universal for the particularity of the moment. Or as Aquinas put it, "truly worthwhile knowledge is knowledge of the universal, moving to know yet more of reality."[49] However, for Hindiyya—even more than for previous female mystics—the very subjectivity of her union with Christ is the foundation for a universal objective knowledge. Touching his finger, kissing his mouth, or becoming one with him physically was a means of expanding her vision and knowledge of his plan of salvation for humanity. The sensuality of touch—which for Aquinas was the lowest kind of knowledge—was the main trope in Hindiyya's relationship with Christ. His constant promptings for her to feel him and kiss him and her yearning—albeit halting at first—to touch his perfected human body were the forces that led to the tactile experience of intertwined bodies and, thus, sublime knowing. The overt sexuality of that moment and subsequent encounters further compounded the error inherent in bodily knowing because for Thomas Aquinas and subsequent theologians moral wisdom is corrupted by physical pleasure.[50] It is obvious then that Hindiyya's experience and its oral and popular articulation stood in stark opposition to Roman Catholic dogma as textually enunciated by its male doctors and disseminated by the Propaganda Fide through Latin missionaries. In this she echoed Catherine of Siena's observation that "Christ wrote the eternal truth on his own body, not with ink but with his blood."[51]

Within its Ottoman context Hindiyya's encounter with Christ is equally noteworthy but for a different reason. Her narration of the courtship and its consummation incarnated a novel definition of gender roles and a new model for male–female interaction. It is not so much that the story contained subtle or overt allusions to sexuality that had been hitherto absent from literature, popular art, and public life. Quite the contrary: sensual erotic poetry, bawdy puppet theater, bathhouse prostitution, and quasi-scientific treatises on sex abounded in Ottoman cities throughout the sixteenth, seventeenth, and eighteenth centuries. For instance, in his article "Hiding Sexuality," Dror Ze'evi catalogs some of this material. A fifteenth-century medical manuscript on hygiene dealt openly—with explicit imagery for visual aid—with the proper way for intercourse, masturbation, and same-sex sexual practices. The sixteenth-century guide *Kābusname* detailed the physiognomy of the most suitable male partner for intercourse. More accessible than medical guidebooks was the genre of erotic literature. The most widely known (and reprinted) of these was *One Thousand and One Nights,* which explored wide variations of sexual encounters in allegorical and not so subtle ways.[52] One of these was the "Story of Qamar al-Zaman and the Princess Budur," where two women, Hayat al-Nufus and Budur, carry on a barely concealed lesbian relationship.[53] However, other poems, stories, and popular guidebooks abounded. In the Ottoman world of the sixteenth century, the most prominent of these books is Kemalpaşazade's *Ruju' al-shaykh ila sibāh fi al-quwwa 'ala al-bāh.* "This exemplar of erotic literature in the mid-sixteenth century was since copied and used by quite a few Ottoman authors until the nineteenth century. Kemalpaşazade's book . . . describes comprehensively all forms of man-to-woman sex, aphrodisiacs, contraception, and similar issues."[54] Khaled el-Rouayheb documents a plethora of eighteenth-century poetry from Damascus, Aleppo, and Cairo that documents pederastic and homosexual acts in a variety of contexts extending from Sufi mystical orders to coffeehouses and baths.[55]

Shadow theater and other forms of public performance also made sexuality in all of its forms a topic for discussion and contestation. The *Karagöz* figure in Ottoman shadow plays acted as a character that could bypass the norms of morality and utter sexual obscenities, describe outrageous sexual encounters, and openly ridicule and dismiss sexual propriety.[56] Prostitution was another venue of public sexuality widespread throughout the cities of the Ottoman Empire. Elyse Semerdjian's research in the seventeenth-century sharia court records of Aleppo makes it clear that prostitutes lived in residential neighborhoods and that they were quite visible, whether through their activities or because they "lengthened their tongues" at their neighbors, a euphemism for verbally flaunting their profession.[57] Alexander Russell, the English physician who lived and chronicled life in Aleppo during the eighteenth century, noted that in 1764 the governor of Aleppo ordered the closure of the coffeehouses after sunset because of the problems with prostitution and drunken behavior. In 1767 he reissued the order, with little effect.[58] The point of all this is that sexuality in all of its facets was a well-articulated subject of public discourse in the Ottoman Empire before and during Hindiyya's lifetime.

The novelty of Hindiyya's narrative, then, does not lie with its explicit exploration of sexual themes but rather with something else. To wit, practically all discussions of sexuality and sex within the Ottoman Empire during this time period were carried out by men and for men. As in the examples provided above, women's voices were represented almost exclusively as subjects of the narrative. In contrast, Hindiyya was not only the main protagonist in *Secret of the Union* but, more importantly, the narrator/author of an encounter that was meant to be disseminated among her nuns as well as female and male laypeople. Certainly, Christ (and to a much lesser extent other male figures) had roles within the unfolding sexual–religious drama. However, Hindiyya was unambiguously in control of the dialogue because she was the *hakawati,* or storyteller. Equally telling is the fact that she also controlled the tenor of the conversation with Christ. Her repeated rejection of his advances and his perpetual frustration with her hesitation elucidate, at the least, a relationship of equals. When one takes into account that the male figure is a deity, her role within—and beyond—the relationship is magnified to be the dominant one, notwithstanding all her proclamations of feebleness of mind and will. This position was clearly in contradistinction to the prevailing equation of power within mainstream male–female relations. For example, in looking at the relationship between master and disciple in Sufi orders, Margaret Malamud notes that, "Guides were often . . . described as fathers who served as sources of authority and discipline. Novices . . . were consistently enjoined to behave in a manner that closely matched the subordinate behavior women were urged to display toward fathers and husbands: they should be submissive, respectful, and deferential."[59] Therefore, Hindiyya's *Secret of the Union* represented a break from the prescriptive norms of behavior, first through Hindiyya's role as author and second by endowing her with the power over the liaison. This reversal in accepted gender roles not only was contained within the story but became the blueprint for Hindiyya's relationship with the male-dominated ecclesiastical and secular worlds.

Arrows of Burning Love

Despite its obviously personal nature, the passionate climax of the union of Christ and Hindiyya—and its subsequent physical, emotional, and spiritual tremors—was not a purely subjective experience. From the outset, it was an objective set of events that transcended Hindiyya and touched those around her in an accidentally and intentionally ever-widening circle. The first obvious links were to Bishops Jirmanus Saqr and then Jirmanus Diyab, who were consecutively her spiritual directors. It was Bishop Saqr to whom she turned in her moment of doubt in 1755, and he was the one who exhorted her to heed the command of Christ and accept the union. Years later, in May 1769, Bishop Diyab signed an affidavit attesting to the veracity of her claims. He testified that the books she dictated—*Book of Marian Praises, Book of the Treasure of the Kingdom [of Heaven], Rule of the Monastic Order for Girls and Men, Book of Revelation of the Hidden Secrets,* and her vitae, among others—were brought forth when she perceived the body of Christ within her soul and body. "Her utterance of these sayings is evidence which confirms the gift of the aforementioned union, for others to believe in it, and to absolve her of any doubt."[60] At the tail end of this document, Bishop Arsenious Shukri of Damascus wrote in September of the same year to testify to the truth of Diyab's declaration and Hindiyya's claims.

Within Bkerki, Hindiyya's bouts of rapture, induced by her perpetual and sensual amorous union with Christ, became a fixture in conventual life. Moreover, the power and knowledge emanating from that union and embodied by her were central tenets in the communal existence of the nuns and monks there. Textually, the nuns and monks were the subjects of many of her writings. For example, in June 1758 Hindiyya dictated a letter addressed to "the daughters of the Heart of Jesus and his sons." This was a normative text meant to shape the collective historical memory of Hindiyya's personal journey to her role as the first and foremost daughter of the heart of Jesus. In the process it elucidated the hierarchy of power within the convent by positing total obedience and self-effacement vis-à-vis the will of Christ as embodied on earth by Hindiyya. In narrating Christ's selection of Hindiyya as his conduit to the establishment of the Sacred Heart order and the subsequent difficulties she faced because of her tenacity in pursuing the fulfillment of his will, the letter made it clear that Hindiyya was unique in her elevated stature. At one point, Christ tells Hindiyya, "O daughter of My heart, embrace My divine heart with love and fear not, kiss it with respect because I . . . will give you an unreachable gift [the union] . . . that I have not given to anyone before and will not give to anyone after [you] . . . [For that] I have not allowed you to fall to any deadly sin that would keep you away from Me and My love."[61] The implications of Hindiyya's elect status were spelled out toward the conclusion of the letter. Hindiyya began this last section by pleading with the nuns and monks—whom, she opined, Christ had honored by allowing them into the Sacred Heart order—to love the order and its rule with all their heart and might. After this prelude, she quoted Christ as instructing them to abandon all material things, to leave the world behind, to safeguard their chastity, and to "obey absolutely with honesty, naïveté, and total surrender in order to be easily saved from the trials of the world, the body, and the devils." A few lines later, Christ made the subject of their required obedience crystalline clear. He said, "I . . . want the daughters of My heart and His sons to obey their superiors even if they [the leaders] hate them and oppose them."[62]

Legally, the rule actuated this concept by allocating the abbess nearly absolute control over the matters of the convent. The very first clause in the rule established its inspiration and thus authority. "We must, O daughters of the Heart of Jesus, first to know and believe that the spirit of our order—which my divine spiritual Guide Jesus has led me to establish—exists only through the love of his Sacred Heart and its glorification." With the tight linkage between Christ, Hindiyya, and the well-being of the order thus established, the fourth clause in the rule spelled out the implications in terms of authority and power. It starts out by bluntly stating, "My beloved sisters you must completely obey with all respect and love your superior, and to accept her as a loving and beloved mother, and to even take her in the place of Christ and to [regard her] as if she was him." The totality and absoluteness of this requisite obedience unfolded with subsequent instructions. Thus, to disobey the abbess was to disobey Christ, nuns were to obey her in everything—but sin—and to be ready to die for holy obedience just like Christ did, they were to obey her if she denied them receipt of the Eucharist, they could not send or accept a letter before she read it, they were to obey willingly and not resentfully, and they were not to question her policies and management.[63]

Beyond the walls of the convent, news of Hindiyya's union with Christ and the miracles it wrought spread quickly. Propelling the ripples of reputation and influence was, in large part, the unquestioning support that Yusuf Istifan gave to Hindiyya and her proclamations upon his elevation to the seat of the Maronite patriarchate. To understand this critical relationship between Patriarch Istifan and Hindiyya we have to look at his history. We need to do so particularly against the backdrop of a Maronite Church contending with internal factionalism around issues of reform between those who sought to institutionalize its organization and those who held on to the kinship-based and communal authority; tensions surrounding his relationship to the Vatican over boundaries of respective authority; the larger political struggles within Mount Lebanon; and the rise of the Maronite community in the eighteenth century to a position of political, demographic, and economic prominence.

Yusuf Istifan was born in 1729 in the town of Ghusta into a clerical family. His father was a lay priest, and his four brothers chose to join the priesthood as well. His two uncles, one also named Yusuf and the other Yuhanna, were bishops within the Maronite Church, with the first overseeing the bishopric of Beirut and the monastery of 'Ayn Warqa where Yusuf Istifan the patriarch later established a prominent Maronite college in 1789. In 1739, when he was but ten years of age, his uncle Yusuf sent him to pursue a religious education at the Maronite College in Rome, where he spent the next eleven years of his life. Of the 280 students who studied in the college over the course of its two hundred years, Yusuf Istifan was one of only three who graduated cum laude. His education focused on the humanities, with courses in Arabic, Syriac, Latin, Italian, philosophy, and theology.[64] While we do not have biographical details beyond this general outline, we can surmise some relevant points from the culture which pervaded the college, particularly after the reforms by Cardinal Felice Zondadari in 1732. One of the striking characteristics of life in the college was the control surrounding the lives of the Maronite seminarians. Students had to contend with a rector and prefect of the college who oversaw and shaped their spiritual and academic instruction, with strict restrictions over their movements within and outside the seminary and rigorous observance of prolonged daily prayers and masses. This daily intellectual and spiritual regimen presented the seminarians with a modern disciplining religious environment markedly different from the more fluid life left behind in the villages of Mount Lebanon. Set, as it was, amid the overwhelmingly impressive urban splendor of Rome and the Vatican, the ten-year sojourn left Yusuf Istifan with the lasting impression that the success and growth of the Maronite Church required an equally institutionalized organization directed by a strict hierarchy of authority—a Maronite Vatican, if you will.

Another pertinent aspect of Yusuf Istifan's education in Rome was the emphasis after the reforms of 1732 on the acquisition of linguistic and cultural fluency in Arabic and Syriac. This new requirement—which dedicated every afternoon to the teaching of grammar, rhetoric, and the humanities in both languages—was enacted to ascertain that upon their return to the Levant the graduates of the college would be able to effectively communicate religious ideas to their people. To that end Jirjis Benyammine, the ex-bishop of the town of Ehden in the north of Lebanon, was placed in charge of a special program to better prepare the students for their future tasks. Aside from reading and writing in both Syria and Arabic and learning the "costumes and traditions" of the Maronites, the students were expected to read and understand the Quran and other "Muslim and Turkish texts." Those who excelled in their studies were trained in disputations and debate to rationally convince "schismatics and infidels" of the Catholic truth and the errors of the others' faiths. Finally, they were to be provided with missionary tools, from learning how to deliver rousing sermons to effectively communicating Christian doctrine to the illiterate commoners among their people. These were augmented after graduation with a year of assisting in passing the sacraments and celebrating mass in Syriac. This regimen was intended to construct and maintain a Maronite identity among the seminarians who stood intellectually and theologically aloof from the mixed sectarian milieu of the Ottoman provinces and cities. While this identity was theologically and organizationally meant to be intimately linked to the mother church, the emphasis on Syriac and Arabic language and culture led Yusuf Istifan to develop a Maronitist self that rivaled in religious heritage and history the Roman Catholic Church. In later years he would sum this up with the notion that the Maronite Church subsumed itself to the Vatican in dogma but was not subject to it in organizational authority.

Upon his return to Mount Lebanon in 1750, Yusuf Istifan quickly sought to parlay his Roman theological training into a career that garnered him the highest clerical rank and that allowed him to implement his vision of the Maronite Church as the preeminent Christian establishment in the Middle East. Both ambitions set him on collision courses with various vested interests within Mount Lebanon and outside its boundaries. In brief, the various episodes coalesced around two major events. The first occurred between 1754 and 1766, when he was still a bishop (he was ordained in August 1754 at the age of twenty-five), and it entailed his opposition to Patriarch Tubiya al-Khazin's attempts to circumvent the pivotal 1736 Lebanese Council's edicts on the number of dioceses and manner of appointing bishops. Yusuf Istifan's tenacious resistance was most evident in his refusal, among all the bishops, to sign a document giving Patriarch al-Khazin a free hand in temporarily abrogating the aforementioned edicts.[65] He was partly motivated by personal animus because in 1757 Patriarch al-Khazin had removed Yusuf Istifan from overseeing the diocese of Beirut and the convent of 'Ayn Warqa and gave it back to his uncle. However, his removal—and conflict with, first, his uncle and, second, Patriarch al-Khazin—was due to their disagreements over the modernizing policies he wanted to implement in the diocese of Beirut. One author summarized the clash in the following manner: "Bishop Yuhanna Istifan was a naïve simpleton advanced in age, and Bishop Yusuf Istifan was famous for his knowledge and his hard-work among all the other bishops."[66] Bishop Yusuf Istifan's energetic attempts to implement reforms within the diocese—by elevating merit above kinship, by professionalizing the clergy through educational reforms, and by rationalizing the organization and dogma of the church—smacked of innovation as far as his uncle was concerned. Patriarch al-Khazin, who himself was not highly educated, was equally disturbed by Yusuf Istifan's policies, which implicitly, if not explicitly, threatened his power and undermined his authority. The juxtaposition and conflict between Patriarch al-Khazin and Yusuf Istifan were manifestations of a generational shift taking place within the Maronite ecclesiastical establishment. In this formulation, Istifan was championing a reform movement meant to overturn the ancient regime of Maronite clerics.

While Yusuf Istifan's vehement opposition to the old guard garnered him the enmity and approbation of Tubiya al-Khazin, ironically it also positioned him as the preeminent patriarchal candidate upon the death of the patriarch.[67] Thus, on June 9, 1766, the Maronite bishops, including his previous archenemy Mikhail Fadel, met and unanimously elected him as patriarch. Shortly after his ascension to the patriarchal seat and his confirmation by the Vatican, Yusuf Istifan crystallized his nascent vision for the Maronite Church through two major proclamations made in 1768 within four months of each other.

Significantly, the first major patriarchal pronouncement pertained to Hindiyya and the cult of the Sacred Heart of Jesus. In June 1768 Yusuf Istifan wrote the Maronite community at large "about the matter concerning the holiday of the Sacred Heart of Jesus." Addressing all Maronites— clergy, *shuyukh, 'ayan,* and commoners—as equals before his patriarchal voice, Yusuf Istifan quickly identified the focal point of his circular: the love of Christ toward humanity. "Who amongst you," he wrote rhetorically, "is so insensitive that he cannot feel the arrows of this burning love, and whose heart does not melt in the face of this divine heart?"[68] Thus establishing Christ's divine heart as an indisputable mechanism of salvation that no one could ignore, the patriarch quickly turned to historical precedent to prove that the worship of the Sacred Heart emerged during the earliest days of Christianity. Speaking unequivocally, he wrote,

"Who is impudent enough to say that the worship of the Sacred Heart is a modern innovation? It is the oldest type of worship and the most honorable spiritual exercise in the church of Christ, and it is the basis of the religion and the symbol of salvation." Subsequently, "we order all of you, indeed we decree with the power of holy obedience, that you celebrate this beloved day as a special holiday every year on the second Friday after Corpus Christi."[69] He went on to order all bishops and archbishops "of our Patriarchal See" to declare a celebratory holiday and prescribed attending masses and fasting for four days before the Friday and promised complete absolution of the sins of those who confessed on that day. In a later show of support, the patriarch sent a letter to the inhabitants of the town of Bayt Shabab warning them against allowing a religious confraternity to be established there other than the one dedicated to the Sacred Heart of Jesus, "because that would be great deception . . . used by Satan to take you away from the love of Christ."[70] In between these two proclamations, Yusuf Istifan toiled tirelessly to promote Hindiyya and the order and confraternity of the Sacred Heart of Jesus.

With his resounding support and promotion, Patriarch Istifan signaled the intertwining of two matters. He threw his support behind Hindiyya while simultaneously pronouncing himself to have near absolute authority over the Maronite ta'ifa. By proclaiming an ancient pedigree and unrivaled salvational prowess for the worship of the Sacred Heart of Jesus, he substantiated Hindiyya's claims and propagated her influence and that of her visions and religious order. Equally, in content and style this missive was intended to elevate the patriarch above all other Maronites. His erudite quotations bespoke of his theological training, his tone in elegant Arabic prose brooked no dissension, and his directives projected Istifan's authority (vis-à-vis bishops and the Vatican) to declare a religious holiday, to permit the consumption of meat on a Friday, and to grant indulgences. Bernard Heyberger convincingly argues that Yusuf Istifan supported Hindiyya then and throughout his life because, like his two predecessors, he saw in her the means to unify a fractious community divided along kinship lines and beset by political and economic power struggles.[71]

The tumult besetting the Maronite community was brought about by new fault lines created and old ones exacerbated during the second half of the eighteenth century caused by a variety of factors. On one level, Mount Lebanon suffered an economic decline because of "the overall economic recession in the Ottoman Empire as a result of the depreciation of Ottoman currency, the disruption of Asian trade due to the Ottoman–Persian wars, and the increasing tax demands of state officials."[72] Demographically, the Maronites were the fastest-growing community; and as noted in chapter 3, this population bubble led to their expansion into areas previously populated mainly or exclusively by 'Alawis and Druzes. This population movement rendered the management of the affairs of the dioceses more complicated than ever as families and individuals moved across demarcation lines. More to the point, the wider dispersal of the Maronite population made the old diocese system, whereby bishops lived in their natal towns among their kinsmen rather than in their dioceses, an outdated and obsolete form of ecclesiastical governance. Finally, Mount Lebanon was in the throes of a tectonic shift in political power at two levels. New, politically powerful families were displacing, to one degree or another, the old *muqata'aji* families. Thus, Maronite *muddabirs* (managers) of the Shihabi rulers of Mount Lebanon, in this period represented by Sa'ad al-Khuri, rose in prominence and sway at the expense of the Khazin clan, which had dominated Maronite politics throughout the previous century. One arena of this contention was control over the affairs of the church. Another change occurred within the relationship between the secular and religious authorities. The Lebanese Council of 1736 began this process in earnest by forbidding secular authorities from intervening in the election of Maronite patriarchs and bishops.[73] In the midst of these dislocations, Yusuf Istifan envisioned a central steadying role for the church that at once would give it greater independence from secular authorities, while making it the final arbiter in the quarrels of the community. Within this context, his desire to institute the Sacred Heart of Jesus as the penultimate source of salvation and holiday, and by extension make the Bkerki convent and its mother superior the focal point of Maronite religious life, would surely have helped Patriarch Istifan to achieve his goals of unrivaled authority for the patriarchal see.

Yet this utilitarian reason does not completely account for Yusuf Istifan's wholehearted adoption of Hindiyya and her cause. What is missing are the religious and spiritual reasons that animated the patriarch's decision, which were the first-person emotions, sentiments, and passions that were as real as his worldly calculations. Easy though it may be, as latter-day observers we cannot dismiss the reality that inhabitants of this eighteenth-century drama thought and acted according to their religious convictions—that is, according to their belief in, and understanding of, a God on whose behalf they acted upon the earth. Rationalizing everything—as modernists are apt to do—into categories of objective and observable facts renders only a partial story and bifurcates the historical individual into irredeemable halves of self and other, when in reality their actions are the marriage of reason and emotion, individual and community, body and mind. In other words, we have to allow that the union which Hindiyya proclaimed—reconciling herself to Christ and, thus, humanity to God— was a real historical dynamic pursued by others seeking redemption in the world for themselves and others.

Patriarch Yusuf Istifan, a very devout Christian by all accounts, was not different in this regard. Aside from assiduously practicing prolonged and arduous spiritual exercises (fasting, long sessions of prayers, meditation, and limited sleep) throughout his life, he concerned himself from the outset of his clerical career with the spiritual well-being of the Maronite people. Thus, in the 1750s he initiated a program to inculcate the youth with a stricter notion of Christian values. In his brief tenure as bishop of Beirut, he wrote a long missive to the priests of the diocese exhorting them to deliver Christian instruction to all the youth to assure their salvation. This remained a lifelong concern of his which pervaded many of his circulars to the Maronite community. In 1766, for instance, he wrote that a great number of Maronite parishioners did not fast or pray as they should to attain salvation.[74] In addition, he acquired a reputation for performing some miracles, particularly expelling devils from the bodies of the possessed. Another inkling of his sincere belief in Hindiyya comes from a letter he wrote on August 8, 1768 (a month before he convened the 1768 Ghusta Council), to Hindiyya seeking her prayer on his behalf. This was a private letter addressed only to Hindiyya and, thus, did not have any public political purposes. After wishing upon her divine grace and heavenly blessings, he apprised her of his troubled state of mind caused

by the "enemy of good" who stood behind the recent trials and tribulations facing the Maronite community. He then wrote, "Our only hope is
in His Sacred Heart and in your prayers. We ask of you pray unto Him to
provide us with a quick and safe exit [from this crisis]."[75] In this and other
documents, Patriarch Yusuf Istifan avowed his sincere faith in Hindiyya's
connection to Christ and in the power of that union to bring about good in
the world. When read against the backdrop of his own religious biography,
this letter appears not as a Machiavellian calculation but as the aspiration
of a religious leader to bring his people peace, prosperity, and salvation by
bringing them closer to God. Regardless of what one thinks of his concerns and without romanticizing his motivations or accepting his beliefs,
we can—and, indeed, should—still allow that his deep faith played a role
in his support for Hindiyya. Only by acknowledging that he did accept
the supernatural visitations of Christ to Hindiyya as real events with tangible implications for the spiritual well-being of the Maronite community
can we fully comprehend why he would support her even as the Maronite
community was being torn asunder by the tensions surrounding her.

But Yusuf Istifan was not the only one championing the cause of
Hindiyya and elevating her above all others including himself. News
disseminated by the *Hindawiyyun* of the miracles performed in Bkerki
through the power of the *Secret of the Union* was another engine of fame
that attracted popular attention, belief, and devotion and made Hindiyya
famous beyond Mount Lebanon and as far as Aleppo, Marseilles, Geneva,
and Rome. One measure of this spreading influence can be seen in letters, like that of Patriarch Yusuf Istifan, written to Hindiyya seeking her
help, prayer, and advice. The obsequious tone and the text of these letters
are telling signs of the transformation of Hindiyya's private visions into
a source of public power and authority. One of those letters was written
in 1768 by Arsenious Shukri, the bishop of Aleppo, and addressed to a
nun in the Bkerki convent. He asked the nun to transmit his apologies
to Hindiyya and Bishop Jirmanus Diyab for the delay in obtaining a list
of items needed for the Bkerki convent, which he attributed to the difficult economic times facing the city and lack of philanthropic zeal. But he
assured his correspondent that "the parishioners in Aleppo will do their
best to fulfill their promises because they seek the beneficence" of Mother

Hindiyya's intercessions and prayers. He concluded by praying for abundant peace to be bestowed upon "Her Excellency, Our Mother the Saint."[76]

Farther away, a priest from Marseilles, France, named Rousseau wrote Hindiyya in 1769 a letter seeking her inspired advice about his future. He related to her that seven months earlier he had heard, from some Maronite monks passing through the city, about her union with Christ and that she had established a convent dedicated to the Sacred Heart of Jesus. From this introduction, which included news of the cult of the Sacred Heart in France and Italy, he then asked her to intercede on his behalf with God so that he would be inspired to decide between going on a mission to "foreign lands," to stay in France "where faith is greatly persecuted," or to join a French monastery renowned for its holiness.[77] Not only is the fact that Hindiyya's reputation reached as far as Marseilles remarkable, but it is equally interesting that a priest would seek her distant advice and supplication with God. This is even more the case when he was in the immediate vicinity of miracles wrought by the cult of the Sacred Heart, like the one which purportedly saved Marseilles from the plague.[78] At the least, then, we can safely conclude from this example that Hindiyya's reputation was successfully promoted through the religious networks linking the Mediterranean Catholic world. Pushing the point further, we can also posit that the spiritual aura of the "Holy Land"—particularly when contrasted with the author's note about the secular persecution of faith in France—would have imbued Hindiyya with a more potent reputation than local visionaries and adherents of the cult of the Sacred Heart.

At a far higher ecclesiastical level, Hindiyya and her project garnered attention and support from Pope Clement XIII (r. 1758–1769) on two separate occasions. Through the intercession of Patriarch Tubiya al-Khazin and Patriarch Yusuf Istifan, the Sacred Heart of Jesus confraternity was granted papal indulgences in 1759 and then again in 1768. For example, in August 1769 Cardinal Andrea Corsini, prefect of the Congregation of Indulgences, wrote a letter announcing that Pope Clement XIII gave complete absolution to all "Christians, men and women, for the day in which they join this confraternity [Sacred Heart]." In addition, the pope gave a seven-year absolution to all members of the confraternity who visited the Bkerki convent four times a year on days determined by the bishop of the convent, absolution for sixty days in return for "acts of worship and piety," and finally complete absolution from sins for all brothers and sisters of the confraternity who visited the convent on a date specified by the nuns of the convent.[79] These indulgences were powerful tonics which imbued Hindiyya, her order, and confraternity with supernal authority. In short, both the letter from Father Ross in Marseilles and Cardinal Castelli's transmission of papal favors—along with the many other complimentary notes she had received directly or indirectly—reaffirmed Hindiyya's sense of self-importance and strengthened the *Hindawiyyun*'s belief in the validity of her calling and purpose. One manifestation of this conviction is to be found in the anonymous vitae of Hindiyya, where the author asserted in a clearly exaggerated manner that "God spread her name until her news reached the lands of the West, India, and the furthest cities and became famous throughout the world."[80]

A more objective measure of the transformation of Hindiyya's private visions into public influence is found in the wealth accumulated by the Bkerki convent and its growing number of affiliates. Throughout the 1750s and 1760s, at a time when Mount Lebanon and Aleppo were suffering from a severe economic downturn, Hindiyya's religious order appears to have flourished. This good fortune was not the outcome of hard work in agricultural production (as was the case with the monks of the Lebanese order three decades later) but rather was primarily sustained by a steady flow of donations spurred by the ever-growing saintly reputation of Hindiyya. The sources were either the dowries brought into the convent by novice nuns seeking to attach themselves to Hindiyya's religious mystique and aura or donations given to Hindiyya by clerical and lay supplicants and admirers. The last will of Gregorious Shukrallah, the Syriac Catholic bishop of Jerusalem, is one example of the magnitude of, and motivation for, donations to Bkerki. Written in September 1769, the will was witnessed by a host of notables including the Shihabi *umara'* Mansour, Musa, Yusuf, Sai'd Ahmed, As'ad, Haydar, and Murad. The roster of political and religious elites signing their names to the will is an indication of the prominence of the dying bishop as well as the importance of the document within the textual landscape of Mount Lebanon. Not only were these signatories legitimizing the endowment of Hindiyya's religious establishment with this particular revenue, but their names and titles explicitly and publicly championed the idea of lavishing gifts on her order. The directives of the will itself strengthen this impression. Bishop Shukrallah's first dying wish was to be buried "in the hallowed grounds of the Bkerki convent, the convent of Her Excellency Mother Hindiyya, the founder of the order of the Heart of Jesus." He then bequeathed all his clothes; "the big clock in the house"; silver utensils; two rings and two seals; all the oil, *saman,* wine, and wheat he had; 550 piasters "to Mother Hindiyya"; and his house in Zuq Musbih (Kisrawan) as a *waqf* (religious endowment) to the convent.[81]

In addition to similar large bequests, the *'awam* provided the convent with a steady flow of donations, sometimes for prayers and supplications on behalf of penitents and other times to purchase some of Hindiyya's blood or hair in the hope of miraculous cures for loved ones.[82] Women seeking to take their vows in the order of the Sacred Heart of Jesus also brought a sizeable income to the convent. An account of the monies bequeathed by these women to Bkerki during its first two years of existence gives an idea of the magnetic pull of Hindiyya's vision among the wealthier families in Aleppo and Mount Lebanon. In total, the thirty-five women who joined the convent between 1750 and 1751 brought with them over 10,000 piasters. While few brought in less than 100 piasters, the majority contributed hundreds of piasters, and five (including Hindiyya herself) added 1,000 piasters each to the communal pot. What is noteworthy in this list of financial contributions by the original founders is that, but for two exceptions, the donations were in cash. There was not any land given to the convent as a *waqf,* which would potentially provide a continuing, even if modest, source of income. While in later years a few individuals did endow Hindiyya's order with land and houses by way of providing for the convent and nuns in perpetuity, the donations remained limited. In other words, from 1750 and for two decades thereafter the expenses of Bkerki were paid by donations and not work by the nuns, a situation that contrasted sharply with the great majority of monasteries and convents, where labor produced income.

A final illustrative set of figures is provided by a letter sent in October 1780 by some ex-nuns of the Bkerki convent seeking financial compensation after their ejection from the convent by the papal legate Pietro di Moretta. While we will look at the precipitating events in detail later, here it suffices to note that the letter listed the assets of Bkerki convent as follows: 30,000 piasters worth of land and cattle, 20,000 piasters in furniture, and 10,000 piasters which "Hindiyya had put aside to build a new [and magnificent] church" dedicated to the Sacred Heart of Jesus. A priest by the name of Sim'an al-Sim'ani recalled that when Sa'ad al-Khuri, the *muddabir* of Amir Bashir, occupied the Bkerki convent in October 1777, his troops took away close to "three thousand bags." This was ten times, or 600,000 piasters, the amount quoted by the nuns.[83] While quite likely an exaggeration, its inflated magnitude is testament to the public perception of Bkerki's wealth and Hindiyya's affluence and influence. In comparison, eleven other monasteries in Mount Lebanon generated a total revenue of 134,906 piasters between 1696 and 1738. Put another way, by the 1770s the Bkerki convent had accumulated over two hundred times the annual revenue of one of these Lebanese order monasteries.[84] Even Patriarch Yusuf Istifan was hard-pressed to collect more than 2,500 piasters every year from the tithes in all eight Maronite dioceses extending across Bilad al-Sham.[85] In other words, Hindiyya's religious order (especially with the addition of four monasteries by 1769) was by far the wealthiest religious establishment in Mount Lebanon. Such extravagant wealth would have surely appeared unseemly—or at least peculiarly conspicuous—within an environment where holy poverty was expected to be the religious norm among monastic orders. Rising so high above all other establishments was an invitation to scrutiny and enmity and may very well have contributed to the efforts to undermine Hindiyya's order.

"The Powers of Hell . . ."

Hindiyya's spiritual visions and worldly power thus swirled one around the other—the first attracting monies that helped spread her fame, which only begat more donations that reaffirmed her sanctity—into a perfect storm which elevated her stature beyond anything comparable in the history of the Maronite community. Never had a woman—and rarely had a man for that matter since St. Maroun, the sixth-century founder of the sect—acquired such acclaim, religious authority, and sway over large swaths of the Maronite *ta'ifa (sect)*. Certainly, none before her had attained during her or his lifetime a saintly reputation premised on a direct connection to Jesus from whom she or he obtained new knowledge, salvation for the believers, and the powers to perform miraculous works. Yet Hindiyya's meteoric rise to unprecedented power precipitated an equally spectacular and sheer descent. The unleashed spiritual passions and seemingly limitless power of Bkerki excited eddies of jealousies and conflicts within the convent as well as beyond its walls. These tensions coalesced around conventual factions and devolved into internecine struggles that diminished the religious pretenses of the inhabitants of Bkerki and exposed them to harsh outside scrutiny. Local and Roman authorities, deeply suspicious and some even resentful of the power of Hindiyya, grasped this opportunity of discord and concomitant reports of ill deeds to dismantle the edifice she had spent nearly three decades building into an extraordinary center of religious influence in Bilad al-Sham.

One of the first cracks in the edifice was a falling-out between Bishop Jirmanus Diyab, who ostensibly oversaw the spiritual direction of Bkerki, and his nephew Arsenious Diyab, who served as a monk and artist there. The acrimony began in 1769 at Bkerki and quickly enmeshed a growing number of individuals until it reached the Vatican in 1771. It emanated from a power struggle within the convent over the position of confessor between Niqula al-'Ujaimi, Hindiyya's brother and a priest in Bkerki, and Arsenious Diyab.[86] However, this detail is lost within the story told by Arsenious and his supporters and the counternarrative elaborated by Bishop Diyab, Patriarch Yusuf Istifan, and various monks and nuns from Bkerki. Regardless of their veracity, these two tales are revealing of the tropes defining the tensions surrounding Hindiyya. Arsenious Diyab's argument was presented in a petition he submitted to the Propaganda Fide on October 10, 1770. He complained of the harsh treatment he had received at the hands of his uncle, Bishop Diyab, and Patriarch Istifan, who locked him up in a cell for a few days. He wrote that this persecution was brought about by his refusal to accept the holiness of Hindiyya and the validity of her visions. He accused her partisans of asserting that she ranked above St. Joseph (Jesus' father) and claimed that Hindiyya stated that once in heaven she would sit to the left of Christ facing the Virgin

Mary. At the 1768 funeral of Bishop Jirmanus Saqr, the spiritual director of Bkerki prior to Jirmanus Diyab, the bishop of Damascus, Arsenious 'Abd al-Ahad, reportedly declared that "Hindiyya ranks higher than all the angels and apostles, and she was only outranked by the Virgin Mary."[87] Arsenious's refusal to acquiesce to this characterization of Hindiyya as well as a subsequent sermon he delivered on the feast of St. Joseph wherein he proclaimed to all attendant that the saint, and not Hindiyya, would sit on the left of Christ garnered him severe rebuke from his uncle, dismissal from his clerical duties, and finally expulsion from Bkerki. Between 1769 when this took place and the presentation of his petition almost two years later, Arsenious went about gathering sympathy and support for his position primarily from dissident Maronite bishops, like Mikhail Fadel, who were already at odds with Patriarch Istifan over other matters.

Patriarch Yusuf Istifan and other *Hindawiyyun* told a very different tale. In a patriarchal encyclical dated September 25, 1769, blame for the acrimony was placed squarely on the shoulders of Arsenious Diyab. As the patriarch publicly announced to all the Maronite "nation," Father Diyab's "wild" claims were utterly unfounded for two reasons. First, all the sworn testimonies taken by the patriarch and his representatives from the fifty monks and nuns in Bkerki attested that Arsenious never mentioned in his sermon anything about where St. Joseph is seated in heaven. Thus, the patriarch concluded, there would be no need to penalize Arsenious for something he did not do. More to the point, the patriarch added incredulously,

> Are the bishops, Patriarch, monks and nuns inanimate objects who do not feel, or animals who do not reason, or mad people who cannot differentiate that they would dislodge saints from their ranks and remove them from their seats of glory in order to place in their stead those who are still alive[?] It behooves them to wait and be patient as you [the audience of the circular] no doubt will. We desire from the bottom of our hearts that God will preserve the life of our venerable mother [Hindiyya] for a long time. And then, after her death, we will seek to place her in the station she deserves in paradise.[88]

Even in dismissing as patently absurd Father Diyab's suggestion that Hindiyya was treated as a living saint, Patriarch Istifan left the door wide open for seeking her beatification, which, of course, only reaffirmed to the Maronite *ta'ifa* her extraordinary piety and divine gifts. In place of the "poisonous lies of this snake," Patriarch Istifan attributed the tumult within the convent to Father Diyab's "arrogance, stubbornness and worldliness."

Arsenious's sister, Marguerita Diyab, elaborated on this opaque accusation. In a letter addressed to Cardinal Castelli and dated May 22, 1773, she wrote—or at least signed her name to—a long expository of her brother's life of errors and sins. From his childhood, she noted, he was afflicted with arrogance, disobedience of his father, and the desire to control and dominate his siblings and environment. Thus, "our God struck him from an early age with the disease of deafness in order to break his pride and imbue him with humility." Rather than succumb to divine judgment, as Marguerita implies would have been fitting of a "true" Christian, Arsenious left Aleppo against the wishes of his father and traveled to Bkerki seeking to be healed by Hindiyya. However, he failed to regain his hearing and instead—"because his pride kept him from returning to the world"—he took his vows to become a monk in the monastery. Once inside the order of the Sacred Heart, Marguerita added, Arsenious continued his ways of disobedience and bullying those around him, including the two consecutive bishops of the convent, and Mother Hindiyya, "who treated him with gentleness that is beyond that of parents." Finally, matters came to a head when the nuns of Bkerki elected "another priest" to be their confessor and bypassed Father Arsenious because he was young, "without virtue," and deaf. "I cannot explain enough how intensely the fires of my brother's . . . jealousy erupted and how he opposed this matter." According to Marguerita, then, it is this event and his own psychology which prompted him to "declare war on Mother Hindiyya."[89]

However, Father Arsenious was not swayed by either his sister's unflattering characterization or by the patriarchal directive for him to desist from publicly "speaking ill or good of Hindiyya." He continued his campaign to elicit support by first approaching different bishops and then by appealing to the Propaganda Fide to set up a council to investigate his allegations on the promise that "he will reveal dangerous and essential matters pertaining to Hindiyya and all the forbidden acts she performs which lie to, and deceive, the Church of God." The cardinals of the Propaganda Fide were initially unimpressed with Father Arsenious's tale of persecution and directed him to "be quiet" and submit himself to the authority and orders of his patriarch, while asking the latter to show mercy to him.[90] Nonetheless, Cardinal Castelli, the secretary of that same congregation, noted in a letter to Patriarch Istifan that he needed to be careful and alert in the matter of Hindiyya, to combat myths and delusions, and to fully implement the orders Pope Benedict XIV had issued to his predecessor about her spiritual direction. So, while they unequivocally supported the authority of Patriarch Istifan to discipline monks, priests, and even bishops, they were wary of the power garnered by Hindiyya through means that stood outside the hierarchical authority of the church and defied its dogma.

Compounding their worries was another conflict dividing the Maronite Church where Hindiyya was once again a presence, albeit not by choice. The quickly hardening division was precipitated by a tug of war between Patriarch Yusuf Istifan and some dissident bishops over the limits of his authority in matters pertaining to the ecclesiastical and financial management of the dioceses. This was a recurring theme in the history of the Maronite Church dating back at least a century, and chief among the decisions of the seminal 1736 Lebanese Council were ways to rationalize and institutionalize the thorny relations between patriarchs and bishops. But until Yusuf Istifan was elected patriarch in 1768, these resolutions remained ink on paper as familial and patronage politics of Mount Lebanon continued to dominate the distribution of positions and power within the church. In fact, Pope Clement XIII sent Yusuf Istifan a letter in August 1767 exhorting him to implement without delay the edicts of the Lebanese Council, with a particular emphasis on the absolute demarcation of the dioceses into eight separate ones.[91]

Hence, in part to implement the 1736 regulations but also to unify the disparate Maronite *ta'ifa* under his authority, Patriarch Istifan convened the 1768 Ghusta Council in September of that year.[92] The council was conducted in five separate sessions, and its resolutions were signed by all the Maronite bishops but for three who were absent and who delegated attending clerics to sign their names on the final document. In all, the decisions taken were meant to establish unambiguous hierarchical control over Maronite religious and, to a lesser extent, social life. For instance, the religious purview of monks was confined to the boundaries of their monasteries; women were prohibited from entering monasteries, and only nuns were to enter convents; believers could not own a religious book that was not authorized by the church; promotions to higher clerical ranks were to be made only after the candidate passed qualifying exams in theology and dogma; Maronites were forbidden from consorting with "heretics"—that is, non-Catholics—in prayers and sacraments or to accept them as god-parents.[93]

While these and other sundry items received some attention, two other matters were repeatedly and more forcefully emphasized in the summary of the Ghusta synod. The first was declaring anathema any attempt to resort to secular authorities in matters pertaining to church governance. In the second and fifth sessions the matter was brought up again and the decision affirmed that "Whosoever resorts to secular rulers in legal cases or decisions pertaining to the Church, or seeks their help to attain a clerical position will be immediately excommunicated with divine curse on him and all who help him in any way, and this as dictated by all the sacred laws, especially our Lebanese Council, to protect the liberty of the Church."[94] Wresting greater church independence from secular authorities was one of the hallmarks of the eighteenth century, and this legal prescription was another facet of a process gathering momentum in its waning decades.[95] At a more personal level, this thrice-repeated clause was obliquely aimed at Patriarch Istifan's old nemesis Mikhail Fadel, who had taken over the Beirut diocese from him during the time of Patriarch al-Khazin, through the intervention of Amir Yusuf al-Shihabi.

Organizing the dioceses and establishing the financial and institutional relationships between the patriarch and the bishops was the second issue to garner a great deal of time and attention in the council. As noted earlier, at the insistence of the Vatican and born by the desire of Patriarch Istifan to subsume the dioceses under his authority (and undermine those who opposed him when he was bishop), the Ghusta Council decreed the establishment of only eight dioceses.[96] However, since there were already more than eight bishops, the decision was to be implemented after some seated bishops passed away. In the intervening period, some dioceses were divided to accommodate the eleven sitting bishops. The divisions were not haphazard by any means but rather intended to delimit the sphere of influence of bishops who had stood against Yusuf Istifan in his days as bishop of Beirut. Most pertinently, the diocese of Beirut was split, limiting Bishop Mikhail Fadel to the city itself while assigning all other areas to Bishop Athnasius, to whom Beirut the city would revert upon the death of Fadel. Moreover, Patriarch Istifan reluctantly allowed Bishop Arsenious Shukri to remain in charge of the diocese of Aleppo because he was instructed by the Propaganda Fide to do so. Finally, he took away from Bishop Antoun Muhasib (who oversaw the diocese of Jubayl and Bsherri) the wealthy area of al-Matn, "which he had wrested illegally" and controlled through the support of Amir Yusuf al-Shihabi and his two *muddabirs,* Sa'ad al-Khuri and Sima'an al-Bitar.[97]

Shortly after the conclusion of the Ghusta Council, six dissident bishops met in a town in Kisrawan to air their grievances against the patriarch. When Yusuf Istifan threatened them with excommunication for contravening the rules of the Lebanese Council, they—keeping with what had become by then a well-worn pattern—resorted to the Propaganda Fide in a petition they signed in November 1769. In this first complaint the bishops wrote that the patriarch had overstepped his boundaries in making the aforementioned decisions about the dioceses. They added that he was far too strict in his attempt to collect tithing, and he was not willing to reside in Qannubin, the traditional seat of the patriarchate and insisted instead on living in his natal village of Ghusta, a stone's throw from Bkerki. In August 1771 the Propaganda Fide waved off these charges as spurious, counseled the bishops to obey their "legal leader," and warned them sternly of accusing the patriarch of simony. Like Arsenious Diyab, the bishops were dissatisfied with this answer and composed a second petition addressed to Pope Clement XIV with similar accusations. While the pope and Cardinal Borgia, prefect of the Propaganda Fide, exhorted them in two separate letters to obey and submit to the will of their patriarch, both promised them that the cardinals of the Propaganda Fide would look into this matter. This promise was not animated by any of the bishops' complaints about the patriarch's behavior toward them; in fact, those were dismissed. Rather, what Pope Clement XIV and Cardinal Borgia found alarming enough to necessitate a formal investigation was a new complaint by the bishops that Yusuf Istifan had permitted the eating of meat on the Friday commemorating the Sacred Heart of Jesus.

In other words, it was Hindiyya and her project of a new vision-induced Maronite dogma that mostly troubled the pontiff and his subordinates. This is not to say that they were not concerned with resolving the other matters but rather that they saw those as organizational questions which could be massaged into a resolution of sorts. On the other hand, Hindiyya and the innovations she brought about, particularly as a woman, raised fundamental theological questions about the orthodoxy or heresy of the Maronites from a Roman Catholic perspective. Yusuf Istifan's unrestrained support for Hindiyya was also profoundly disturbing to Rome because it supposed and practiced an uncomfortably high level of Maronite ecclesiastical independence. Hints of this had appeared before the crisis between the patriarch and dissident bishops unfolded. In August 1769 Yusuf Istifan commissioned Bishop Mikhail Fadel (before their fallout) to write a treatise on the question of whether the Holy See had endowed Maronite patriarchs with the authority to minister to non-Maronite Christians throughout the patriarchate of Antioch. As we have seen in chapter 4, this was a question that pitted Latin missionaries against Maronite priests in Aleppo during the early part of the eighteenth century. However, Mikhail Fadel's scholarly essay was more thorough and replete with historical references meant to establish a long-standing precedence for Maronite universal oversight over Christian affairs in the area roughly equal to Bilad al-Sham. His conclusion was that Rome could not remove that right from Maronite patriarchs—Yusuf Istifan in this case—except for "a clear and heavy error."[98]

Vatican concerns led to the dispatch of two consecutive papal legates to investigate and resolve the matters at hand. The first was Valeriano di Pratto, guardian of the Holy Sepulcher in Jerusalem, who arrived in Bkerki in the summer of 1773. Di Pratto achieved very little, in part because of his even-handed approach to the intransigence of the protagonists in this crisis and mostly because he did not seek to impose his decisions through local secular authorities. His equanimity and even-handedness are manifest in the tone and observations of his report to Rome, which he dispatched on September 10, 1773. He first identified money as the source of the rancor between dissenting bishops and the patriarch. After several fruitless sessions, he concluded, "There is no doubt that the complaints presented [by the bishops] to the Sacred Congregation [Propaganda Fide] are exaggerated. If the necessary tax [tithe] is agreed upon then all those upset with the Patriarch would be happy with him as were three [bishops] to whom he left a small portion of the tithe."[99] However, such a straightforward resolution was not to be, despite di Pratto's shuttle diplomacy between the feuding factions. The patriarch insisted that tradition, the Lebanese Council, and the papal bull of Pope Benedict XIV all affirmed his right to collect the tithe in toto and then redistribute 10 percent of each diocesan total to its respective bishop. The bishops were willing to raise the amount of money they paid the patriarch each year (up to 2,900 piasters per annum) but were adamantly opposed to his proposal to send his own delegates to collect the monies directly from the dioceses.

Di Pratto was even less successful in three other matters he raised with Patriarch Yusuf Istifan. The patriarch would not rescind the encyclical allowing Maronites to eat meat on the Friday commemorating the Sacred Heart of Jesus; he would not dismantle the altar built on top of the tomb of the departed bishop of Bkerki, Jirmanus Saqr; and he refused to stop offering patriarchal indulgences to those affiliated with the Sacred Heart of Jesus confraternity or to those celebrating the Feast of the Sacred Heart. In all three instances, he cited a long genealogy of patriarchal authority independent of the Vatican, established "eastern" traditions, and precedent set by papal recognition of the wide latitude inherent in the authority of Maronite patriarchs. The fact that all three cul-de-sac topics were related to Hindiyya only reaffirms the intimate link Yusuf Istifan drew between establishing his patriarchal independence and Hindiyya's visions, project, and stature.[100] Moreover, these constituted parts of an argument that was later crystallized by Hindiyya in her assertion that the pontiff had authority over the Maronites only in matters of faith.[101] The corollary was that the Maronites were independent in running their organizational affairs. Yusuf Istifan and Hindiyya thus developed a symbiotic relationship, where her union with Christ sanctioned the patriarch's desire for greater authority and Maronite autonomy and the patriarch unstintingly supported and defended her. In this manner, Hindiyya's private visions played a central role in shaping a new conception of Maronitism as a religion and culture. The only crack in the solid wall of resistance which di Pratto faced was the flight in 1773 of two nuns from Dayr Sahel 'Alma, a convent newly affiliated with Hindiyya's order of the Sacred Heart. The two nuns, Marie Mukarzal and Thérèse al-Khazin, had previously fled from the Bkerki convent and taken refuge with relatives in 'Ayntura before the patriarch forced them to enter the Sahel 'Alma convent. Responding to the request of the patriarch to help return them to their convent, di Pratto dispatched Fr. Raymond (the translator and scribe for the first inquisitor, Father Desiderio, who interrogated Hindiyya in 1753) to interview them. On the basis of their testimonies, di Pratto decided that they had exaggerated their claim of persecution by Hindiyya and the patriarch to elicit sympathy but that there was no doubt that Hindiyya was deluded and those who "manage her affairs are not innocent of deceit." With that, di Pratto concluded his mission and left Mount Lebanon without being able to resolve any of the issues.

Pietro di Moretta, the second papal legate and a Franciscan friar who had spent some years in Bilad al-Sham as a missionary, was far more forceful and successful than di Pratto. This was partly due to the fact that he came to Bkerki in 1775 armed with the "Seven Edicts" which the Propaganda Fide had issued upon di Pratto's return to Rome in a council held on June 8, 1774. Every one of the seven orders faulted Patriarch Yusuf Istifan for refusing to acquiesce to di Pratto's counsel and by extension submit himself and his religious community to the authority of the Vatican. For instance, he was directed to annul his permission to eat meat on the holiday of the Sacred Heart and to desist from offering indulgences. The remaining decrees were meant to resolve the conflict between him and the dissenting bishops by limiting his authority to interfere in diocesan affairs and by assigning him a set tithing revenue equal to 2,500 piasters. With such an unequivocal rebuke to the patriarch in hand, Pietro di Moretta arrived in Kisrawan in an uncompromising mood. Patriarch Istifan was equally adamant that the Propaganda Fide's orders were illegitimate because they were issued before the patriarchal delegate (Arsenious 'Abd al-Ahad) dispatched to Rome with supporting documents could present his case and because they unjustly contradicted the rules of the

Lebanese Council. For these reasons, Istifan asked di Moretta to hold off on announcing the decrees to the Maronite multitudes until the Propaganda Fide could hear his side of the story.

Di Moretta was not inclined to do so. While he may have been partial to the patriarch personally, as Bernard Heyberger contends, the papal legate left Rome with a negative predisposition toward Maronites in general, and Hindiyya in particular, whom he regarded as the source of all the troubles.[102] He had read Mancini's 1753 damning assessment of Hindiyya and the subsequent report of Carlo Innocenzo. In fact, just three months after his arrival in Kisrawan di Moretta wrote the Propaganda Fide with his recommendations for resolving the conflict within the Maronite Church. His first part of the cure was to dismiss all the nuns from the Bkerki convent "because it appears that the source of all evil is Hindiyya and her convent." On the heels of this recommendation he also suggested the dissolution of "Hindiyya's order, the primary cause of the discord."[103] Second, he appears to have very quickly taken the side of Bishop Mikhail Fadel and the *muddabir* Sa'ad al-Khuri and to be willing to use secular authority to force the patriarch to submit to his will. Father Ignatius de Pappiano, the superior of St. Antonious monastery where di Moretta was staying in Kisrawan, noted this bias in his own memoir of these events. He wrote "the [Papal] legate refused the request of the Patriarch [to postpone the declaration of the decrees] at the behest of Bishop Mikhail Fadel the famous enemy of the Patriarch, with whom the legate had established a strong alliance."[104] To implement the decrees and his personal recommendations, di Moretta asked for a letter from the pope to Amir Yusuf al-Shihabi— "accompanied with an appropriate present like a sword"—asking for the latter's support in implementing the decrees and recommendations. He also solicited a letter to be sent to Sa'ad al-Khuri thanking him for his support and exhorting him to continue offering di Moretta help.[105]

A standoff ensued, with the balance of power seesawing between patriarch and legate. The stalemate finally began to break in favor of Pietro di Moretta, Bishop Fadel, and Sa'ad al-Khuri when the nearly seamless façade of Bkerki developed larger cracks. The most notable of these was Father Niqula al-'Ujaimi's defection and subsequent testimony to Pietro di Moretta. A mercurial character with inflated pretensions, Niqula al-'Ujaimi alternated between supporting, opposing, and then again defending his sister. For example, in January 1773 he signed an affidavit swearing that all of Hindiyya's writings were supernaturally inspired by Christ and that he played no role in composing any of the works.[106] In June of that same year he sent a letter to a correspondent in Rome asking for his help in obtaining papal confirmation of Hindiyya's rule. He wrote,

> I am certain that if I send you just one of the books composed by Mother Hindiyya about different topics—such as theology, philosophy, astronomy, natural sciences, religious advice about virtue and sin, and hymns—and this book was accurately translated into Latin then it alone would be sufficient to prove that the mentioned Rule uttered by Mother Hindiyya is without a doubt inspired by Christ our Lord.[107]

Additionally, he was chosen by and served as the confessor of the nuns of Bkerki, which was reportedly the cause of Father Arsenious Diyab's tumultuous departure from Bkerki and ensuing campaign to undermine the convent and its founder. Yet by 1775 his relationship with the occupants of the convent and Hindiyya had soured. He told di Moretta that his sister had become cross with him because he would not show her the same level of adulation as her lifelong assistant Katerina and Bishop Jirmanus Diyab. For that reason, she began to turn the nuns against him and to dissuade them slowly from confessing to Niqula. This gradual alienation, or perhaps the desire to be in the good graces of the Vatican's delegate and his powerful supporters, drove Niqula to turn on his sister. In his affidavit he fleshed out some of the vague accusations of hubris that had been a constant cloud over Hindiyya's head. After a preamble in which he affirmed his continuing belief that the spirit of God did reside in Hindiyya, Niqula confessed that he was puzzled because he could not overcome the contradiction between that spirit and his sister's underhanded actions. These included living a pampered life, physical abuse of a nun called Khadimat al-Saleeb, insulting nuns from poor families, and overlooking the mistakes and sins of sisters from rich or powerful families.[108]

This testimony—along with earlier revelations by Arsenious Diyab, the two escaped nuns, and a priest from Bkerki—only increased the pressure on Hindiyya to open the doors of Bkerki for a full investigation. Yet that only came about two years later, when some nuns within the convent staged a revolt of sorts whereby they rejected Hindiyya's claims of infallibility and protested the harsh treatment reserved to the *Jabaliyyat* sisters. Emboldened by the pressing inquisitorial gaze of Pietro di Moretta and the growing chorus of religious and secular support around him, Nassimeh and Wardeh Badran (two of the pioneer residents of Bkerki) openly refused to follow the orders of Hindiyya and her assistant Katerina. To quell the rising tide of internal opposition, Hindiyya threw the two of them into subterranean cells. Their rich Beiruti father, Antoun Badran, heard of this in a letter smuggled to him, so he traveled to Bkerki around the beginning of May 1777 and demanded to meet with his daughters. When he was turned away, he appealed to Patriarch Istifan to investigate the matter. Confronted with a powerful and irate father and already feeling besieged and weakened by the relentless attacks from Pietro di Moretta and Sa'ad al-Khuri, the patriarch had little choice but to travel to Bkerki and inquire into the matter.

There ensued a battle of testimonies gathered, dictated, and dispatched to the Propaganda Fide, which were more politically motivated and constructed than they were records of any particular fact or truth. The *Hindawiyyun*'s narrative rested on the premise that an alternative satanic/Masonic confraternity had infiltrated Bkerki with the intent of killing Hindiyya and destroying the Sacred Heart order, all to foil Christ's plan. Her biographer summarized the point in this manner:

> They saw this Eastern planet that shed light on all [for good] and so they wanted to destroy and eradicate it. Thus, they accused her of being a witch, and an adulteress with an illegitimate son. . . . When that failed and the devil saw that his efforts to destroy the Order were for naught . . . he directed his minions to enter the convent . . . and poisoned her one thousand and three hundred times.[109]

To support their contention, the *Hindawiyyun* gathered over two hundred pages of affidavits that collectively formed an orchestrated effort to inundate the cardinals of the Propaganda Fide with "evidence" of malfeasance on the part of Hindiyya's accusers and opponents. The handwriting on these testimonies—copies of which exist in the Maronite patriarchate archives in Bkerki as well as those of the Propaganda Fide—shows that they were transcribed by two anonymous individuals. The great majority of them were witnessed by three ardent Hindiyya supporters: Bishop Jirmanus Diyab; Father Touma, a superior general in the Lebanese order; and Father Youssef, who was identified as a preacher in the Maronite Church of Aleppo. While the majority were formally witnessed final drafts, some appear to be little more than rough drafts replete with crossed-out words and rephrased sentences. A few, dated December 1776, were attacks on Niqula al-'Ujaimi, who was at the time siding with di Moretta (later he switched his allegiance back to his sister). However, practically all were witnessed sometime between January and July of 1777, with the largest number coming in May and June close to the time when Patriarch Yusuf Istifan came to Bkerki at the behest of the aggrieved Antoun Badran. One final piece of evidence which points to the organized nature of this effort at defending Hindiyya is a document that listed the various codes to be used in writing up the affidavits. It anonymously directed writers to substitute, among other things, "the known bishop" for Mikhail Fadel and "the known delegate" for di Moretta. From there it went on to list more than twenty other coded names to be used in generating affidavits.[110]

The story these testimonies collectively told is a paradoxical mixture of outlandish claims and ordinary facts. They almost invariably began with the proclamation "I . . . testify to the truth before God." The names listed after the first-person pronoun included those that supposedly belonged to the satanic confraternity or less frequently those tempted to join by its ringleaders, Nassimeh and Wardeh Badran. The confraternity was sometimes called satanic and at other times *Bannayyin* (Masons) in a conflation of the two threats to Catholicism. In a draft of their "confession," Nassimeh and Wardeh labeled it "the innovation of [Martin] Luther," who blasphemed against God and the church and sold his soul to the devil, thus adding Protestantism to the mix of enemies.[111] The center of this fraternity was identified as Beirut and its founder, a Franciscan missionary by the name of Fr. Rafael. Here again the narrative conflated two elements. In reality, there was a competing religious confraternity established in Beirut by Fr. Rafael and Bishop Mikhail Fadel, dedicated to the Virgin Mary. It had spread rather fast in the region and challenged the Sacred Heart confraternity for members, influence, and resources. Even before matters came to a head in 1777, Hindiyya was instructing her followers about the danger of this alternative religious organization. In a Sacred Heart confraternity meeting in February 1769 she told those in attendance, "The other confraternity in Beirut is founded on deceit and is rejected as evil and vile by His Sacred Heart because their purpose is to destroy the Sacred Heart Confraternity, and they persecute it through internal means."[112] And in 1771 Patriarch Istifan dispatched a circular to the people of the town of Bayt Shabab exhorting them to reject the new Virgin Mary confraternity because, he implied, the hand of *ibliss* (Satan) was behind that innovation.

By 1777 the accusations about satanic motives and connections were unambiguous and outrageously elaborate. Nassimeh and Wardeh purportedly beguiled various nuns to join them through words, sexual advances, and magic. Khuduʿ Qaythani said that "Nassimeh and Wardeh . . . talked with me about spiritual matters . . . [interspersed] with stories about fornication like [the story of] a bishop who committed sin with a virgin and other sexually exciting matters . . . my heart was inclined toward them with great love until I became very attracted to them and I began to feel hatred toward our Mother and her teachings."[113] Maryam al-Fattal testified that "Wardeh would say to me: 'My Soul, My Heart.' When she would say that to me I would be attracted to her and my heart would lean toward loving her, and sometimes I would kiss her face and embrace her and she would kiss and embrace me."[114] Other testimonies detailed a campaign of words that Nassimeh and Wardeh supposedly carried out to sully the reputation of Hindiyya. They gossiped among each other that she was possessed and her assistant Katerina was the devil incarnate; they proclaimed that she fornicated with Bishop Diyab, among others; and they complained that she was starving them to death. In other reports, the respondents painted an image of the dissident nuns as irreverent in their behavior around Niqula al-ʿUjaimi, talking and laughing with him for hours. In response, Hindiyya's brother appears in these testimonies to berate his sister and her claims to the nuns, to acclaim the sanctity of Nassimeh and Wardeh, and to seek favors (food, flowers, and sex) from the nuns. For those who were not moved by these approaches, Nassimeh and Wardeh placed magical "papers" in their drink and food to bind their soul to the devil—or, as Domitilla put it, "I entered the Satanic Fraternity through the devilish trap of Nassimeh and Wardeh." And when that failed they "threatened to kill the women who did not follow them."[115]

Once enrolled in the confraternity, the acolytes were allegedly taken through three stages of initiation, each bringing them closer to the presence of the devil himself. The first one entailed traveling "with the help of evil spirits" to various spots on the face of the earth. Five of the fourteen nuns—Nassimeh, Wardeh, Segunda, Angela, and Tufuliya—were initiated into the second level. Each of them cut her hand and dripped her blood on a small idol, offered it sacrifices and incense, and "changed their names, so that Nassimeh's name became Khadijeh, Wardeh's Fatima, Segunda's Ammoun, Angelina's Na'ameh, and Tufuliyya's Rabiya."[116] This Islamization of the names and its equation of satanic worship with Islam was a common theme running through many of these testimonies. For instance, one testimony indicated that the "satanic sisters" prayed toward the Qibla, or the direction of the Ka'aba. Another spoke of Bishop Mikhail Fadel, who was accused of being a member of this devilish gathering, changing his name to "Muhammad"; and another cleric chose "Mustafa" as his name. Finally, Wardeh recounted under duress that her sister Nassimeh had a child whose name was "Sayyid Muhammad." Allegations of Christian impurity extended beyond Muslim affiliations to include other groups. Wardeh Badran's "testimony" listed Muslims, Jews, Arabs, and North Africans among the host of people attending one particular orgy two nights before Rufina, another Sacred Heart nun, died. Segunda's affidavit against Nassimeh and Wardeh told of a "large banquet . . . in a place full of *saraya* [Ottoman seraglios], halls and large houses. In that place I saw different types of people [including] Jews, Muslims, Matawli, Franj, Druzes and Christians." In fact, even those testimonies which attacked Hindiyya described her as worse than "Muslims, Jews . . . and idolaters."[117]

Certainly, the mention of the amalgamated "other" was meant to impress upon the cardinals in Rome how un-Catholic the dissident nuns (or Hindiyya and her supporters) were. The inclusion of Jews, Muslims, Druzes, Arabs, and North Africans accentuated the importance of Hindiyya's order and project through the host of its enemies and located it within the narrative of Roman Catholic division of the world into heresy and true faith. Aside from its display of xenophobia, the list of the devil's guests was also a subtle rejection of Roman Catholic authority. The participation of "Franj bishops, priests, monks and nuns" in the carnal banquets cast aspersions on Western Christians and their authority to condemn Hindiyya or interfere in Maronite affairs. Yet the elaborate tale that was constructed represented a public display of anxieties, on both sides, about the fragility of Maronite coherence and purity. The banquets and orgies taking place in identifiably Ottoman cosmopolitan spaces erased boundaries that were deemed by some as essential for the construction of a coherent and separate Maronite identity.[118] Hindiyya left Ottoman Aleppo and its mixed neighborhoods and markets, seeking the textually sanctified space of Mount Lebanon. Intellectuals like Patriarch Istifan Duwayhi wrote histories that extracted Maronites from their Ottoman and Eastern Christian milieu and isolated them in the villages and towns of Mount Lebanon away from the corrupting and nefarious influence of Muslims and heretic Christians. Even more ambitiously, the *Hindawiyyun* had made Bkerki the Jerusalem and the Vatican of the Maronites. It was the one point where Christ spoke, through the intermediacy of Hindiyya, to his chosen people and where Patriarch Yusuf Istifan sought to concentrate religious authority and power. From this perspective, the testimonies of these nuns were a fabricated litany of the threats facing this utopian world and a catalog of the real anxieties of its occupants about the impending doom of their independent community.

Two other tropes of anxiety emerge from the descriptive and prescriptive words of these testimonies: one is about sexuality and the other concerns food. In reality, they were the manifestations of the same dynamic at work within and outside the convent of Bkerki: passion. There is no doubt that Hindiyya's Christ-inspired rule and personal advice to the nuns of her convent stressed chastity and self-denial.[119] For example, Hindiyya's rule had one chapter (chapter 5) with twelve articles dedicated to maintaining chaste bodies and thoughts. Another included directions for modesty, including refraining from laughter and sleeping in "chaste" positions. Contact with strangers, especially men, was prohibited; the convent was sealed to outsiders; and food was to be administered in modest portions. Prayers, prostrations, spiritual exercises, and reflections punctuated daily life to the point where they would have occupied the better part of the day if they were followed faithfully. All in all, then, the nun was to subject her body, mind, and soul to severe restraints that were meant to invite the presence of Christ and repel Satan. Yet these restrictive texts stood in marked juxtaposition to the unfettered spiritual and physical passion made manifest in *Secret of the Union*. Moreover, the nuns were repeatedly directed to spend long hours contemplating the seminaked body of Christ in order to understand his love and sacrifice on their personal behalf. It is not too surprising then that the tension between the two polarities was exacerbated by reports from both sides about flagrant—and, in the case of Hindiyya, hypocritical—disregard for the sanctified space of Bkerki.

Along these lines, Philippia, Milad al-Massih, and Rufina "admitted" that they felt oppressed by the rule and went against it repeatedly. They told their Maronite inquisitor, "We slept together in the same bed, embraced and touched each other . . . during bed time and other times as well, and because of this dirty thoughts would enter my mind."[120] Sister Khuduʿ related that after her induction into the satanic confraternity, "I became like an animal in committing sins . . . and after I gave myself to Satan, Nassimeh and Wardeh committed the sin of fornication with me."[121] Maryam, Hindiyya's niece, added more details to the description of the same-sex trysts between dissident nuns. "Wardeh would teach her companions to commit the sin of fornication with me, and when Wardeh would do these things she would lift the shirts off the nuns and touch with her hand the beastly place and they wanted her to do that . . . and she would say lurid things and mention the thing which is the sin of fornication by its name and . . . and laugh as if it is an act of virtue." In fact, Wardeh, Niqula al-ʿUjaimi, and Khadimat al-Saleeb were quoted repeatedly as stating that it is not sinful for the nuns to have sexual relations. In the purported words of Wardeh, "This is not a sin, for if it was then our Mother [Hindiyya] would not be doing it all the time!"[122] Beyond these "admissions" of lesbian relations, the testimonies were also replete with confessions of sexual meetings with men. Francesca bint Touma admitted to repeatedly having sex with Niqula al-ʿUjaimi in the confession box after her enrollment in the satanic fraternity. The ever-present Maryam declared in her June 21, 1777, testimony that Nassimeh and Wardeh arranged sexual affairs between men like Bishop Mikhail Fadel, Fr. Rafael the missionary, and Father Niqula and the "virgin nuns" in order to please "Our Master the Devil." But the most profligate behavior was reserved for Nassimeh and Wardeh, the only two nuns to reach the third level within the confraternity, where they consorted directly with the devil. Nassimeh was reported to have over one hundred lovers, while Wardeh had a more modest retinue of fourteen men. This extravagance was necessary to produce two nonexistent children: Muhammad, who was Nassimeh's son, and Layla, who was Wardeh's daughter. They were to be taken to the "Land of the English," where they would be raised, presumably in the heretical faith of Protestantism; and once they came of age, they would produce together the Antichrist.

Impossible sounding as these fantastical tales are, and were to some contemporaries, they emanated from real sources. The threat felt by Hindiyya and her followers from dissident nuns, Pietro di Moretta, Mikhail Fadel, and others was the catalyst for concocting stories of decadent behavior which included not only sex but also gluttony, theft, and attempts to poison Hindiyya.[123] However, it was not simply that those who wrote these affidavits threw in every possible transgression they could think of, and then some. The stories themselves were reflections of the anxieties about sensuality and sexuality unbridled from normal social constraints. The enclosed private space of nuns living in intimate proximity to each other, and to some male clerics, was very different from habitations in Ottoman villages, towns, and cities. While the latter afforded their residents little, if any, privacy from the prying eyes and ears of relatives and neighbors, the conventual space, de jure and de facto, provided almost total privacy from the outside world. Sheltered from overbearing societal scrutiny, these convents became the focus of ribald humor flimsily disguising discomfort—and some voyeuristic jealousy—over potential misdeeds within their walls. The line between piety and chastity, on the one hand, and profligacy and wickedness, on the other, was regarded as thin indeed.

In the minds of some observers it was rendered even thinner in Bkerki by the exaggerated celebration of the spiritual passions and physical ecstasies of Hindiyya. For the *Hindawiyyun* that line was erased, and the bodies of dissident nuns became enslaved by the devil through carnal desires, when they doubted and then moved away from the protection of the *Secret of the Union*. The religious enthusiasm stoked by seventeenth-century Latin missionaries, which flowered into the conjoined spiritual and physical ecstasy of Hindiyya, was thus transmogrified into debauchery of mind and body because the nuns rejected Hindiyya's authority. Holy sensuality devolved into debased and satanic sexuality when some Sacred Heart sisters neglected the requirement of holy obedience. For those who opposed Hindiyya it was the *Secret of the Union* which permitted her and her followers to transgress vows of chastity in the name of holy obedience to Christ and his wishes. For instance, in response to a question by Pietro di Moretta during the 1778 inquisition Hindiyya affirmed that Christ was united with her as a god and as a human. To this the incredulous di Moretta responded, "How can Jesus Christ unite with you with His human essence?"[124] The commentary of Father Sim'an al-Sima'ani was far more virulent about this matter. He wrote the Propaganda Fide in November 1777 that "a new tyrant has emerged from hell . . . I mean Hindiyya. For she is an unparalleled monstrosity of heresy who has for the past twenty-nine years deceived the Maronite sect under the veil of worshipping the Heart of Jesus Christ. . . . It is certain now that she is a heretic, idolater, murderer . . . and an evil from the devil himself." Without any evidence to support him, he added, "Her assistant Katerina has killed at the behest of Hindiyya four nuns because they were pregnant."[125] Thus, sexuality and Satanism—devil of the flesh and the devil from hell—were intertwined in both narratives, and Bkerki—the Maronite Jerusalem and Vatican—became Sodom and Gomorrah.[126]

On still another level, these narratives tell of a real fear of evil, the devil, and hell which permeated the society at large. In other words, we cannot simply see them as stories concocted for defending (or accusing) Hindiyya and preserving her Sacred Heart order. The very same seventeenth- and eighteenth-century religious revival which stoked the spiritual fires in Bilad al-Sham and exhorted all to come unto Christ produced far more frighteningly detailed images of hell. If Christ was to be a real, tangible presence in the daily life of penitents, then the devil was also there in equal measure. The two were flipsides of the same supernatural power competing for the souls of men and women. The painting of the

Day of Judgment in the Armenian Church of Forty Martyrs in Aleppo stands as an example of that duality. It is evenly split between depicting the host of angels and saints at the feet of Christ and the demons of hell herding sinners into the pits of brimstone filled with scenes of agonizing torture. Hindiyya dwelt at length about her visit to hell and the depiction of its horrors. In her 120-page treatise on hell and its agonies, she wrote, "All the damned will feel in reality their punishment by fire, darkness and worms and hideous demons." She then explored the darkness of hell, the everlasting fires which scorch the bodies of sinners, the never-dying worm which "devours the immaterial spiritual soul," and the demons that inhabit various levels of hell, each of which is reserved for particular types of sinners.[127] Demonic possession was considered a common enough phenomenon in the Middle East to warrant specialized exorcists and normative procedures for expelling the evil spirits out of the bodies of the afflicted. Among Muslims and Christians confinement of the possessed, treatment with cold water, beatings, bleedings, and amulets were all common cures for possession.[128] Similarly, the painting of the body of dissident Bkerki nuns with red dye, the sacrifice of animals to idols, and the transportation of body and soul through the night to subterranean rendezvous with the devil cannot be seen simply as disturbed flights of fantasy. To many contemporaries these would have been regarded as real events with real consequences.

Against this backdrop, possession and exorcism must be read as metaphors of the conflict between Hindiyya and the Maronite Church, on the one side, and Satan and his subordinates, on the other.[129] As Hindiyya acquired greater power to bring lost souls back to Christ, her followers and advocates became convinced that Satan was more intent on destroying her. From the perspective of the *Hindawiyyun* this was the only reasonable explanation for why dissident nuns would seek to circumvent Hindiyya's authority, doubt and ridicule her power, and perform abominable acts that ran contrary to the normative behavior expected of them. Had Hindiyya been an inconsequential individual in the eschatological play leading to Revelations, then the devil would not have bothered with his elaborate scheme which enlisted every possible enemy of God. Put another way, these episodes were regarded and believed as testaments to the piety and chastity of Hindiyya, and this only strengthened the resolve of Patriarch Istifan and others to defend her and sustain her project of salvation for the Maronite nation and beyond.

To circumvent this palpable power of the devil and protect his vision for, and control over, the Maronite Church and community, Patriarch Istifan sought to dismantle the satanic confraternity. After listening to the various testimonies presented in 1777 in Bkerki, he issued a one-sided forceful edict on the matter. The monastic habit and picture of the Sacred Heart of Jesus were to be removed from Nassimeh and Wardeh, the daughters of Antoun Abou Badran, and Angela, daughter of Kamil. They were to be placed indefinitely in separate cells and prohibited from speaking to anyone, including their parents. This draconian sentence was justified on the grounds that they were hopelessly beyond redemption. Kamila, Milad al-Massih, Rufina, Tufuliya, and Khadimat al-Saleeb were condemned to silence for one and a half years, to confinement in their cells, and to a diet "befitting of penitent sinners." Clara, Philippia, "and the other disobedient nuns" were sentenced to silence and only thirty minutes of daily supervised contact with the "public."[130] Patriarch Istifan, with Hindiyya's encouragement, was seeking to silence dissidence and shore up the crumbling remains of their project by redrawing stricter boundaries between the privacy of the convent and the public space.[131] But all of this was for naught.

On June 10, 1777, news of the death of Nassimeh escaped the convent of Bkerki and reached her father. This time around, Antoun Abou Badran (dissatisfied with the earlier verdict of Patriarch Istifan, which faulted his daughters) asked Amir Youssef to intervene with troops to force the occupants of Bkerki to reveal the whereabouts of Nassimeh and Wardeh. After the soldiers forced their way into the convent, it soon became obvious that Nassimeh was dead and Wardeh was imprisoned in piteous conditions in a subterranean cell. Both had been tortured by Elias Burkana, a monk affiliated with the Bkerki convent, supposedly to extract from them the locations of the "satanic papers" that were meant to poison and kill Hindiyya and to drive the devil out of them.[132] Once the walls were breached and the violent deaths of Nassimeh and another nun, Rufina, discovered, events quickly cascaded out of the control of the patriarch.

Amir Youssef—to put his hand on the riches of Bkerki, to stamp down the tumult, to prosecute the perpetrators, to ingratiate himself with the Vatican, or all of the above—camped his troops in the convent and demanded that Patriarch Istifan remove Hindiyya from the convent and bring her and her collaborators to justice. After months of refusing to cooperate with those orders (enabled by the preoccupation of Amir Youssef with the threat of the Ottoman governor Ahmed Pasha al-Jazzar), Patriarch Istifan ran out of options. By the winter of 1778 the convent of Bkerki was emptied of its previous occupants, and Pietro di Moretta installed himself there as a symbol of reestablished Vatican authority over the center of Maronite independence. Hindiyya was evicted and, after brief sojourns in various parts of Mount Lebanon, ultimately sent to Dayr Mar Hrash, the residence of Bishop Mikhail Fadel and ironically the place where she had commenced her remarkable career. Her assistant Katerina escaped, never to be caught again, while she was being transported to a convent in south Lebanon, near Sayda. Similarly, Elias Burkana escaped his captors. The remaining nuns and monks of the now dissolved Sacred Heart of Jesus order were sent disgraced to their homes in Mount Lebanon and Aleppo.

Yet, while the physical, religious, and financial infrastructure of Hindiyya's alternative vision of Christianity was effectively dismantled, her legacy was far harder—if not impossible—to take apart.

6

EPILOGUE

Hindiyya, Alone and Everywhere (1778–1800s)

While the terrible deaths in the convent were decried, the second inquisition of Hindiyya and its surrounding events were less focused on attaining justice for the nuns and more directed at casting aspersions at Hindiyya, dismantling her order, and clipping the wings of Maronite ecclesiastical independence. In a 1783 two-page "confession" by Hindiyya, conspicuously lacking her signature and bitterly contested, six issues were expounded. The first pertained to the location of her ever-elusive books, and the second was her purported repudiation of *Secret of the Union*. Only the fourth and briefest of the document's paragraphs touched on the subject of the "nuns who were killed," and then it was simply to lay blame—in strikingly unemotional tone—for their violent deaths at the feet of the embattled Patriarch Yusuf Istifan and Bishop Jirmanus Diyab.[1] Sim'an al-Sima'ani's long diatribe against Hindiyya, composed in November 1777 and dispatched to the Propaganda Fide as part of the case against her, emphasized first and foremost Hindiyya's heresy laced with witchcraft and idolatry and interwoven with demonic evil. While he mentioned the murder of the nuns (whose number he inflated to twelve) as evidence of her ill deeds, they only appear as a distant afterthought to her larger crime of deluding and dividing the Maronite community.[2] The reams of testimony by nuns opposed to Hindiyya described at length her hubris but said little of the death of the nuns. Pietro di Moretta's interrogation of Hindiyya dwelt on questions meant to prove her delusion and theological error, while the exorcism of the two nuns was relegated far less space.[3] Finally, the report and judgment of the Propaganda Fide on the Hindiyya affair—passed at a council held in Rome on June 25, 1779—dedicated its twenty-four pages to detailing her error, the derivative nature of her books, her impious and worldly behavior, and her dangerous and unrestrained influence over the Maronite community through fraudulent claims of saintliness.[4]

This almost exclusive obsession with discrediting Hindiyya's theological works and miraculous claims and undermining her widespread influence is understandable. For the Vatican to allow what it regarded as unorthodox ideas and practices to persist within any Catholic community under its purview would have been to fail at its self-appointed role of shepherding the universal Christian flock. In other words, the horror evinced by cardinals and papal legates at Hindiyya's transgressions constitutes to one extent or another a genuine reaction to acts that went beyond the constructed norms of the Catholic Church. Thus, as much as we should take Hindiyya's claims of union with Christ seriously, we have to accept that the ecclesiastical authorities, to varying individual degrees, may very well have acted according to their faith. Recognizing this as a historical reality does not preclude critical inquiry into the dogged pursuit of Hindiyya all the way to the grave and beyond. Rather, and as I have stated previously, Hindiyya presented an alternative source of religiosity that threatened Vatican power. Moreover, she was the lightning rod for an increasingly self-confident Maronitist movement that was constructing an identity and organization equidistant from Rome and Istanbul and separate from its immediate Ottoman mixed milieu and Western Roman Catholicism. Hence, to marginalize Hindiyya and force her followers to repudiate their support for her pretensions was to reassert Vatican primacy in Maronite affairs. On the other hand, it is equally important to note that Hindiyya's disgrace and demise was a mechanism that some Maronite clerics, like Bishop Mikhail Fadel, sought to employ to undermine their rival, Patriarch Yusuf Istifan. In other words, ecclesiastical politics at various levels were central to the campaign against Hindiyya and her supporters.

Yet there was another equally important dimension to this postscript in the narrative of Hindiyya. In attacking Hindiyya, Roman clerics consciously sought to restore a patriarchal gender order—crystallized during the 1736 Lebanese Council—which prescribed the symbolic and institutional submission of nuns to the male hierarchy of the church. The council, convened at the insistence of the Vatican at a formative moment in the history of the Maronite Church, gave the Maronite patriarch, local bishops, and priests absolute oversight in matters ranging from the establishment of female convents to the admission of novices, confession, distribution of the Eucharist, financial management of the order, and election to religious offices. And while the council of 1736 envisioned and advocated an energetic public apostolic role for the Maronite clergy, it sought symbolically and practically to render religious women invisible and silent behind conventual walls.[5] Nonetheless, even as it was being constructed, this patriarchal order was disrupted by the rise and assertion of religious women's voices throughout the eighteenth century. Hindiyya was by far the most prominent, and perhaps dangerous, voice among them. Hers not only had reached a large swath of Catholic communities in Bilad al-Sham but was imbued with divine power that attracted hosts of people to her convent and convinced many to join the religious fraternity she established in the name of the Sacred Heart. While the Melkite 'abidat, whom we encountered earlier in this book, publicly proclaimed their right to manage their own affairs and adopt the religious rule of their choice, their struggle remained more or less contained within the confines of religious institutions. Hindiyya, by contrast, became a female public figure whose reputation, divine gifts, and powers (and therefore influence) were widely known among the 'awaam, or commoners.

This success cannot be solely attributed to the support of Patriarch Istifan and many in the Maronite religious establishment or to the dissemination of tales (fabricated or otherwise) about her miracles and saintly behavior. Manipulation of public sentiment could succeed only if there was a readiness, even hunger, among individuals in villages, towns, and cities to believe that Christ could and would manifest himself to a woman in Bilad al-Sham. The idea that malevolent and good spirits, demons and angels, if you will, coursed through quotidian life was not anomalous to the religious worldview of peasants and city folks alike.[6] Supernatural events were within the realm of reason and would not have raised many eyebrows. Additionally, the local and foreign missionary projects which produced a spiritual revival in Aleppo and Mount Lebanon (and

partially account for the rise of Hindiyya) stoked the religious enthusiasm of men and women and rendered them open to the possibility that
Christ would visit the "Holy Land" from whence he came. Ironically, the
preexisting gender order itself made it quite believable that Christ would
speak through a woman. After all, that order expected (without success
evidently) women to be meek, lowly, ignorant, and powerless—the very
character traits of those whom Christ would favor most with his love and
presence. In other words, Hindiyya's transgressions across religious gender lines were made publicly acceptable and sustainable by the gender
roles stipulated by that very same system. Moreover, Hindiyya's proclamation of bodily knowledge—physically and emotionally gaining access to
universal and divine knowledge—rung true in a society where reason and
sensibility were not alienated from each other but rather coexisted in the
same system of knowing.[7] Even when women's knowledge was not necessarily valued as equal to that of men, the process and substance of knowing were not divided into irreconcilable feminine (body) and masculine
(mind) realms. By embodying and empowering this syncretic approach
to knowing, Hindiyya's vision and project resonated with her local audience and stood in contradistinction to a Roman Catholic theology growing increasingly Cartesian in its dogma. Thus, the Propaganda Fide and
local opponents of Hindiyya were not battling simply one woman but a
movement unleashed by her Christ-sanctioned visions and magnified by
a populace seeking salvation through an embrace of an alternative and
distinctly feminine form of Levantine Christianity.

"A Worldly Woman . . ."

The Propaganda Fide's 1779 report captures this gender dimension in
the language it employed and the issues it raised. This final report was
based on hundreds of pages of testimonies, petitions, and communications
dispatched by foe and friend of Hindiyya after the untimely deaths of Nassimeh and Wardeh the Aleppan. From the outset the report highlighted
the reversal in the gender order as the source of the problems afflicting the
Maronite community. Cardinal Boschi read to the gathered Cardinals, "It
is evident that the aberration—and the sterility of its cure—derive from
the absolute authoritarianism which the famous Mother Hindiyya has

imposed upon the Maronite Church for many years, and the blind obedience of the Patriarch [Istifan] to her every whim and order." What permitted this travesty were Hindiyya's books, which the report condemned
as poor imitations of preexisting theological works, "brimming with poisonous knowledge" that fooled even those who were more learned, like
Bishop Fadel, into leaving the straight path. This opaque allusion to the
story of Eve and the "wiliness" of women—bringing about the fall of righteous men through intellectual forbidden fruit—was reinforced in a subsequent statement. In trying to explain away the mass support Hindiyya
had come to enjoy, the report noted that Hindiyya, "with her duplicity,"
and her assistant Katerina, "an attractive prostitute without a conscience,"
bewitched the minds of the "simple people" with tales of rare miracles. It
was these two elements, according to the report, which brought fame, fortune, and supplicants to Bkerki and perpetuated the "idiocy and heresy"
of Hindiyya's perfect—material and spiritual—union with Christ.[8]

In dismissing as sacrilege Hindiyya's intimacy with Christ and the
concomitant power imparted to her through that union, the cardinals in
Rome repeatedly pointed out its unacceptable physicality.

> The teachings of Hindiyya . . . are these. . . . She is actually and not just
> incidentally united, member to member, with Jesus Christ . . . that she
> continuously and substantially senses the body of Jesus Christ . . . and
> that by the power of this union and this sensibility she is the sole bride
> of Jesus Christ who orders her to kiss Him as is said in the sacred Song
> [of Songs] "Let him kiss me with the kisses of his mouth."[9]

The quotation is from the Song of Songs 1:2, and it is a woman beseech-
ing her lover for passionate kisses that are sweeter than wine. Thus, it is
intriguing—to put it mildly—that Hindiyya (since the attribution is to
her statements) placed Christ in the position of a supplicating woman,
while she becomes the male lover kissing "his" beloved. The cardinals
were naturally most perturbed by these "heretical myths." It was not only
that Hindiyya went about the Bkerki convent passionately and tangibly
kissing Christ but that she also transposed the gender roles of their amorous relationship. Mirroring this reversal, the report depicted Hindiyya

as overturning the predominantly male Catholic body of knowledge. In particular, the report noted that Hindiyya claimed that God was spreading through her "a new canon of love which uncovers new divine secrets that nullify all the [established] sciences."

In the face of such outrageous claims, the cardinals proceeded to textually right the gender order by emphasizing the worldly feminine traits of Hindiyya, which, to their minds, precluded not only any connection to the divine but also access to religious knowledge. Rather, they stipulated, these traits which stood in juxtaposition with female monastic characteristics were the mark of a fallen woman who was closer to the devil (Eve) than God (Mary). In the composite picture painted by the report, Hindiyya was depicted as without any virtue whatsoever. On the basis of the testimonies of the *Jabaliyyat* and her brother, Niqula al-'Ujaimi, the cardinals decried Hindiyya as "arrogant, miserly, frivolous . . . and gluttonous." It is worth quoting the full description of her purported worldly ways for what it tells us about the Vatican's construction of female monastic religiosity and attempts to impose that ideal upon Eastern Christians.

> In her food and clothing she is more like a sultana and a worldly woman than a nun, for there is not a single luxury, rare or precious item in Kisrawan—even in Beirut, Tripoli, Damascus and Aleppo—that is not acquired regardless of cost for the service and comfort of the Mother. Her room is adorned with fine china, gold watches, musical instruments, as well as expensive and beautiful fabrics. Her bed is soft and comfortable covered with Indian products [?] and seven different furs . . . all lined with silk and velvet. She has sixty delicate shirts dyed with cochineal [the color of royalty] and a large amount of goods imported from France, Cairo and Ankara. She is used to changing her robes twice a day, and her shirt every hour. . . . Her opulence in food rivals her extravagance in clothing. Outside the periods of fasting (and it is not known that she has ever fasted) she indulges in the most delicious of meats, chicken, game birds. . . . She only ate bread made of clean gleaming flour while the rest of the nuns ate it hard and black. . . . While she diligently tried to convince everyone that she has not tasted alcoholic drinks, in fact she drank copious amounts of it, as well as coffee mixed

with ambergris and rose water. . . . Some say that contrary to the habits of nuns in the East she let her hair loose and put make-up on her face. She went to such lengths of extravagance that she ate while the nuns sang for her, and in the evening two nuns would enter her room to swat away the flies.[10]

One is tempted to see in this hints of Orientalist imagery: a morally corrupt and slothful sultana lying amid an orgy of carnal senses, complete with her own harem of attending nuns. Such imagery was readily available in seventeenth- and eighteenth-century European travel accounts and novels, which depicted the "East" as a world of sensual delight and lustful pleasure.[11] As we have seen earlier, Latin missionaries, papal legates, and Roman cardinals were not culturally immune from similar Orientalist attitudes toward Eastern Christians even as they avowed a dogma of universal brotherhood in Christ. But, while shades of the dreaded "Turk" were interlaced into this disparaging description, Hindiyya's greater sins were in embodying the "other" in a different constructed binary.[12] She stood in opposition to the Tridentine monastic ideal of nuns, imported by Latin missionaries, enshrined in the 1736 Lebanese Council, and variably adhered to by some Maronite nuns. These strictures included chastity, asceticism, hard work, observance of religious rules, submission to male clergy, and most importantly invisibility from the public eye, surrounded by walls and vows of silence. By contrast, the report represented Hindiyya as a bewitching temptress; her uncovered hair and makeup—the hallmarks of prostitutes in both the Ottoman and Roman worlds—branded her as sexually loose. (In Katerina's case, subtlety was eschewed as she was plainly labeled a bewitching prostitute.) In other letters and reports, the diminution of her status was achieved simply by the dismissive title "the woman Hindiyya" or "the woman Hanneh." For example, the "Letter of Repentance" dispatched from Rome to Patriarch Yusuf Istifan on September 29, 1781, for his signature began, "I, the undersigned, having been enlightened by divine grace and guided by the decrees of the Roman Apostolic Holy See, the mother of all churches and their teacher from whence emanates throughout the world the light of Truth, admit and confess my previous errors and my false belief in the delusions and sanctity of the deceitful Hindiyya, that is Hanneh 'Ujaimi."[13] With few exceptions, she was no longer referred to as "the nun" or "Mother" Hindiyya, titles which elevated her out of the fallen secular womanhood into an asexual and, to a certain extent, nongendered status. She was a woman who lied, cheated, craved attention, accumulated wealth, subjugated men to her will, and luxuriated in the fruits of her labor. And while she remained within the walls of her convent, she brought the world into that sanctuary by transforming it into an emporium of material luxuries. In short, she was the antithesis of the post-Tridentine nun, a "woman who is worse than an idol-worshipper."[14]

With such absolute condemnation the cardinals of the Propaganda Fide proceeded to try to put Hindiyya in her place. On July 17, 1779, they passed their sentence on her and it included three decrees.[15] The first affirmed that Hindiyya was certainly deluded and had engaged in rebellion against the church and its teachings. Her visions and teachings, in particular her claim that her body and soul were united with the body and soul of Christ, were deemed as corrupt lies and deviancies that were, in the least, heretical innovations. The newly appointed vice patriarch, Bishop Mikhail al-Khazin, was directed to force Hindiyya under the threat of excommunication to recant verbally and in writing the *Secret of the Union* and the existence of the Masonic cult within Bkerki as ungrounded fabrications. As punishment for her transgressions she was to be turned out of Bkerki and sent to another convent, where she was to remain confined for the remainder of her life under the watchful eye of a spiritual director appointed by the vice patriarch and approved by the Propaganda Fide. The vice patriarch was also to track down and gather all of Hindiyya's writings and compositions—whether authored by her or written in her name—in order to keep them from circulating and spreading heresies. While the first decree set about disassembling Hindiyya's spiritual foundation, the second one dismantled her religious institutions. Thus, the order of the Sacred Heart of Jesus and its associated confraternity were abolished. The Bkerki convent with its properties and income was to be used for the "good of the Maronite nation," while the other three convents were to revert to the Antonian order. The monks and nuns of all four convents were to be given the option of either returning to

their homes—without being absolved of their vow of chastity—or enroll-
ing as religious men and women in the Antonian order. Finally, the third
decree divested Yusuf Istifan of his patriarchal and episcopal authority
and ordered him to travel to Rome to stand ecclesiastical trial for some of
his actions in the Hindiyya affair.

"I Am Innocent of All . . ."

The implementation of these decrees generated a paradox for the Propaganda Fide: Hindiyya as a person was shunned and incarcerated, but
Hindiyya as an idea of Maronite spiritual and ecclesiastical distinctive-
ness, independence, and authenticity persisted. Pietro di Moretta and his
Maronite allies (Mikhail Fadel, Mikhail al-Khazin, and Sa'ad al-Khuri) were
able to quickly dissolve the religious order and confraternity, expel the nuns
and monks out of Bkerki, confine Hindiyya to one convent after another
until the end of her life in 1798, and keep her from making public pronouncements. Yet, for all their immediate accomplishments and repeated
assurances of success to the Propaganda Fide, they could not stamp out
Hindiyya's influence or undo the transformation she helped bring about
of the Maronite Church into a self-consciously and fiercely independent
Eastern church.[16] Several factors frustrated the efforts of the Propaganda
Fide and its erstwhile Maronite collaborators. In part this was due to the
ineptitude and heavy-handed approach of Vice Patriarch al-Khazin, whose
unpopularity even within his own family of Khazin notables kept him from
rallying the Maronite community behind him.[17] It can also be attributed
to the advanced age of Mikhail Fadel, who had grown fatigued from the
struggle with Yusuf Istifan to the point that he no longer could attend to
the affairs of his diocese in Beirut. The departure of the combative Pietro di
Moretta back to Rome in the summer of 1780 completed the dissolution of
the ecclesiastical triumvirate that led the charge against Hindiyya.

But a far more potent factor was a widespread desire within the
Maronite community to transcend the divisions and tighten the ranks of
the believers. As much as Hindiyya was the central character in earlier
times, the "deluded woman" became—after her condemnation by the Propaganda Fide—a convenient female scapegoat for all the troubles besetting the ta'ifa. Thus, a narrative was constructed in the wake of her demise

whereby her expulsion out of the community defeated heresy, restored normalcy in the gender order, and removed any need for Vatican oversight and involvement in Maronite affairs.

This approach is best characterized by Sa'ad al-Khuri, the advisor to Amir Yusuf al-Shihabi, who was chiefly responsible for carrying out the decrees against Hindiyya. On one level, he appears to have lost interest in the whole affair after the closure of the Bkerki convent, acquisition of some or all of its wealth, and dismissal of Hindiyya. His personal animus toward Hindiyya may very well have been satiated by these vindicating steps. However, he was also loath to prolong the disorders which had beset the Maronite community as a result of this whole affair and tarnished the prestige of the Maronite Church. He made this clear in July 1782 when Patriarch Yusuf Istifan returned to Mount Lebanon, after two years of residence/exile in Carmel, in order to defend himself against the accusations of heresy leveled against him in absentia by Bishop Mikhail Fadel and Bishop Mikhail al-Khazin. Patriarch Istifan was welcomed warmly by Amir Ahmad and Sa'ad al-Khuri to the palace in Dayr al-Qamar. The latter then sent the two bishops a letter rejecting their frenetic plea for the expulsion of the patriarch and demanding that they convene a church council wherein the patriarch could tell his side of the story. He wrote pointedly,

> [the Patriarch] was accused of what blackens his name, the name of his *ta'ifa*, and the name of the patriarchs before and after him. The Maronite patriarch was accused of divulging confessional secrets and "writing for himself a deed in hell." And now he wants to prove his innocence, so tell us what we should say to him?! . . . We have no right to prohibit the Patriarch from proving his innocence, and if you reject this meeting then shame and humiliation will befall the *ta'ifa*. . . . Be certain that in addition to all our work and concerns this matter weighs us down more than the highest mountains [and] to reject [the council] after the arrival of the Patriarch would [cause] great evil and damage [to the Maronites].[18]

This last comment made palpable his exasperation with the bishops and the whole affair; a little over a year later he was far more public and vociferous, with similar sentiments directed then at the Vatican. This latter episode reflected a widespread resentment within the Maronite community of the incessant demands of the Propaganda Fide for further evidence of compliance with its decrees and the prolonged punishment of the patriarch. It began in October 1783 with a letter from Pope Pius VI to the Maronite clergy, notables, and commoners announcing the dispatch of Pietro di Moretta (now with the honorary title of Bishop Craveri) on a second mission to Mount Lebanon because "the earlier deceits have not been rejected, our orders have not been obeyed and the fires of the Bkerki intrigues have not been extinguished for there remain sparks of that old fire."[19] Di Moretta undertook the trip after appointing Father Yusuf Tayyan, a graduate of the Maronite College in Rome, as his secretary. But rather than travel directly to Mount Lebanon, di Moretta asked Father Tayyan to proceed there without him and to obtain letters of safe passage from "Amir Yusuf al-Shihabi and his brother Amir Ahmad, from the inspector general of the Beirut Customs house, from all the notables of the *ta'ifa* and if needed from the *wali* of 'Akka Ahmad Pasha al-Jazzar."[20] Whether out of paranoia or grounded fear for his safety, di Moretta's long litany of adamant requests (which also included sending the letters unopened to the French consul in the city of Sayda so that they could be authenticated, supplying him with a convent and coverage of all his expenses) makes it clear that he felt unwelcome back in Mount Lebanon. His onerous and obdurate demands made Rome's letters all the more difficult to accept and soured the general mood about this new mission. Thus, when Father Tayyan presented the letters in March 1783 to Sa'ad al-Khuri, Patriarch Yusuf Istifan, and other seculars and clerics, the response was explosive. Tayyan wrote as follows:

> Here the pen cannot describe the astonishment that came over everyone as I read the Papal letters and rescripts within it, the faces changed and a great clamor arose followed by absolute silence. Shaykh Sa'ad al-Khuri began to complain at the top of his voice . . . saying: I have suffered sorrows and hardships to carry out Rome's orders. . . . It pains me to hear my *ta'ifa* accused of disobedience, and to be accused of continuing in its allegiance to Hindiyya. . . . How can the Holy Father say we have not obeyed his commands?[21]

Out of this tempestuous meeting was born a campaign of letters—from Amir Youssef, Sa'ad al-Khuri, the Khazin *shuyukh*, Patriarch Yusuf Istifan, all the Maronite bishops, and a host of other Maronite notables—to Pope Pius VI and the Propaganda Fide, protesting the unjust accusations leveled at the *ta'ifa* and demanding the immediate reinstatement of Yusuf Istifan as the Maronite patriarch. All in all, the community—as represented by the tenor and substance of the letters of these elites—was neither interested in pursuing the Hindiyya affair any further nor willing to acquiesce much longer to what it regarded as unreasonable and intrusive impositions by Rome. The pendulum had swung back toward assertion of Maronite independence from Rome.

But here again there is an additional explanation for the persisting legacy of Hindiyya even when her immediate voice was silenced. While the institutions of Hindiyya's project were shuttered and some community leaders publicly condemned her enthusiastically and others reluctantly, the foundational framework of her project remained intact for practical and less tangible reasons. On the practical side, neither Hindiyya nor Katerina would admit to any wrongdoing, and Hindiyya insisted to the last days of her life that she was only following the commands of Christ. Thus, di Moretta's interrogation of Hindiyya was riddled with her intransigent answers that either deflected responsibility or demurred behind the façade of physical and mental weakness from answering to the inquisitor's satisfaction. The following exchange is illustrative of this trope in Hindiyya's responses.

> *Question 23:* Is Jesus Christ, or the one whom you say is within you, united with you only as a God or as a human as well?
> *Answer:* If the person united with me is truly Jesus Christ then he is united with me as a god and as a human.
>
> *Question 24:* How can Jesus Christ unite with you with what is essentially [his] human [side]?
> *Answer:* My illness does not allow me to explain this; if I could I would, for this requires a detailed explanation, and the subject is too difficult for my brain to delve into it now because I have no energy.

Further on, when confronted with statements she had made proclaiming that she was answerable only to the patriarch and that the Holy See had authority over the Maronites only in matters of dogma, Hindiyya dismissed these as the utterings of an agitated woman who was deeply depressed and did not know what she was saying. Still later in the inquisition, Hindiyya denied any role in allowing for eating meat on the Sacred Heart holiday or in uncovering the satanic confraternity. In both cases, she claimed for herself the role of a weak woman unable to deflect Bishop Jirmanus Diyab or Patriarch Yusuf Istifan from either decision. When di Moretta pressed her on the matter, suggesting that other witnesses had contradicted this assertion, Hindiyya let a flash of combative frustration peek through. She retorted, "Father, if you want me to tell [you] what the others have said then I will, but the plain truth is that Bishop Jirmanus [Diyab] asked me several times to sign and affirm with the convent's seal the existence of this [satanic] confraternity and I refused."[22] This streak of stubbornness and strength came through again a few months later. In a letter written on December 29, 1778, di Moretta reported in exasperated terms that "Hindiyya and Katerina remain to date without [the rite of] confession because they insist on denying everything and His Eminence the Patriarch, who does not care about the latter [Katerina], continues to support Hindiyya . . . for fear of losing a great saint."[23]

Much to the chagrin of the Propaganda Fide, Hindiyya's insistence on her innocence and the validity of her visions persisted long after these two incidents. Pope Pius VI's stern letter to the Maronite ta'ifa, quoted earlier, was in part driven by the long and futile wait for a confirmed written confession from Hindiyya. The Propaganda Fide repeatedly and impatiently wrote Vice Patriarch Mikhail al-Khazin asking for a copy of Hindiyya's signed confession, which never materialized, and chastising him for his incompetence in this and the management of the Hindiyya affair. For example, in September 1781 Cardinal Antonelli, who had taken over as secretary of the Propaganda Fide after Cardinal Castelli had passed away, wrote Bishop Mikhail al-Khazin, "As for Hindiyya we have not received a copy of her letter of repentance. In the proceedings of the Mayfouq Council it was noted that it was sent to the Holy See, therefore it is your duty to send another original copy of that [letter]."[24]

Notwithstanding the repeated requests, Hindiyya's letter of repentance was never sent and the only "confession" alluded to earlier was problematic, not least because it was not signed by Hindiyya and its legitimacy was undermined by the insistence that it was obtained under duress. Patriarch Yusuf Istifan confronted this issue in a letter to the Propaganda Fide defending himself against the accusations of his two Maronite arch-enemies. One of the various arguments he presented detailed how Bishop al-Khazin tortured Hindiyya "with beatings, starvation, cold, and threats of burning, scalping and killing her" to force her to testify against the patriarch.[25] In a rare instance when we hear her voice directly, Hindiyya herself sent a letter in 1784 narrating her seven years of perpetual torture at the hands of the vice patriarch and his minions all in an ineffectual effort to make her confess to her errors and delusions. She described her travails as follows:

> Until now I have neither been able to take the holy sacrament nor enter a church despite my unceasing pleas. The Vice Patriarch has allowed a priest to hear my confession in these last years but will only allow him to absolve me from my sins if I confess that I am guilty of all the accusations that were hurled at me. This is something that I cannot do short of being a hypocrite . . . because my conscience still maintains that with the grace of my God I am innocent of all that I have been accused of.[26]

Of course, these assertions of counterfeited confessions obtained under duress could as likely be self-serving as factual. Nevertheless, they do serve to illustrate the lack of any documented admission of guilt on the part of Hindiyya and, more importantly, the failure of the Vatican to categorically define her as a heretic in the minds of the Maronite populace. In other words, the persistence of these counternarratives cast a long shadow of doubt on the Vatican's assertions and allowed the *Hindawiyyun* to mutter—albeit under their breath—proclamations of innocence.

Hindiyya's books formed another element that was infinitely frustrating to the Propaganda Fide, especially as an indication of both the limited ability of its cardinals to enforce their decrees and the continuing support Hindiyya enjoyed among some segment of the Maronite community.[27] For all the requests to seize the writings of Hindiyya, the books were never located, even after a decade of searching. The hunt began with the first sentence in the Propaganda Fide's 1779 decree. When the soldiers of Amir Yusuf, at the request of Sa'ad al-Khuri, entered and searched the

Bkerki convent, they could not locate the books; and the rumor was that Hindiyya's "lover," Antoun Jammati, had made away with the books and disappeared into the "mountains."[28] Pietro di Moretta confirmed the subsequent difficulty in locating the books when he informed the Propaganda Fide that "As for Hindiyya's books it is impossible to reach them because they are carefully hidden."[29] Some three years later Cardinal Antonelli demanded that Vice Patriarch Mikhail al-Khazin redouble his efforts to locate the books and to threaten with excommunication "once again anyone who has or knows the location of the books."[30] Almost a decade later—a year after Hindiyya passed away in the convent of Sayyidat al-Haqli—the Holy See asked Jirmanus Adam, the Maronite bishop of Aleppo and the papal legate, to renew the search for Hindiyya's books and to announce to the community that anyone who comes forth with the books or information on their whereabouts would be absolved of all sin.[31] The fact that neither the threat of excommunication nor the promise of absolution of sins was enough to convince those who possessed the books to relinquish them is an indication of the continuing popularity of Hindiyya and her spiritual and religious thoughts, at least among those who possessed the books.

Neither Hindiyya's persistent denial of any wrongdoing nor the safekeeping of her books in the recesses of one or more hiding place provides an appreciable measure of her continuing influence in Bilad al-Sham. Far more convincing evidence of the potency of her legacy is to be found toward the end of the eighteenth century back in the city of Aleppo. Around that time a new sect emerged among the young women of the Maronite, Melkite, and Syriac Christian communities devoted to the worship of the Sacred Heart of Jesus. This was not a matter of happenstance in foundation or ideology. Rather, it was intimately linked in both ways to Hindiyya and the feminine mystical spirituality she had articulated in her written works and through her public proclamations, religious institutions, and personal behavior. The founder of the new religious sect of the Sacred Heart was Marguerita Batishta, a young Maronite woman from Aleppo. She was a contemporary of the Aleppan Sacred Heart nuns who were expelled from Bkerki in 1778 and made their way back to their natal city. Her exposure to Hindiyya's ideas reportedly came about through her intimate acquaintance with these nuns. Father Boulus Hatem, an Aleppan Melkite priest and one of the main critics of this new sect, claimed,

> In this manner she adapted all of Hindiyya's teachings from the afore-mentioned nuns, and she began to proclaim this novel [spiritual] path attracting to it some clerics, and particularly the Lazarist Father Nico-las Codice . . . and then some young women particularly Marguerita Najm from the Melkite sect, who replaced her [Batishta] after her death as the leader of this sect and in claiming sanctity, visions and discern-ment of spirits.[32]

Whether she plagiarized Hindiyya or followed in her spiritual steps to receive her own revelations, the connection between the two histories is incontrovertible. Either consciously or by divine intervention, she was continuing the tradition of Hindiyya; and the activities of this new sect were read by supporters and opponents alike against the fresh backdrop of the Hindiyya affair.

This impression is reinforced by the substance of the new sect's teach-ings. While we cannot fully explore these here, it will suffice to highlight the main points—proclaimed by Marguerita Najm and condemned by the Vatican—to illustrate the genealogical connection between Hindiyya and the Batishtaniyyat (as the new sect was known). Adherents of this sect contended that, contrary to the teachings of the Roman Catholic Church, new revelations and visions from God are not only possible but necessary for modern times. As human beings had become in the nineteenth cen-tury more enlightened and educated, it stood to reason that God would provide more elevated means of salvation and a higher degree of knowl-edge than what was available in "older times for simple people."[33] These revelations were supposedly obtained by the select, who followed the seven steps toward a mystical union with Christ and then propagated the new knowledge amid their acolytes in open and secret meetings.[34] This union not only was manifested in spiritual ways but was a physically tangible connection with the divine that liberated women like Marguerita Najm from bondage to human and ecclesiastical laws and from the limitation of existing sacred books.[35] For instance, on the basis of her union, Najm permitted her female followers to travel alone at all hours of day and night, to refuse to perform housework as beneath them, to reject marriage as an outdated institution, and supposedly to participate in sexual rituals meant to simulate union with Christ.[36] The brushfire popularity of this new sect testifies strongly to the continuing popularity of Hindiyya and the mystical enthusiasm she promoted during her lifetime. Or, as Father Nicolas opined, the new sect perpetuated the wholesome principles of Hindiyya's devotion to the Sacred Heart of Jesus without falling prey to the base material motivations "which permeated the Bkurki [sic] convent."[37]

This conjoining of the past and present of the Sacred Heart cult was also obvious—albeit in less salutary terms—to the Vatican. In 1818 the Congregation for the Doctrine of the Faith, which was examining the sect of the Batishtaniyyat at the request of Ignatius 'Ajouri, Melkite bishop of Aleppo, announced its condemnation of the confraternity. In pronouncing its sentence (which was never fully implemented and required another council meeting in 1830), the congregation began by referring to the 1779 Propaganda Fide verdict against Hindiyya and her Sacred Heart order and confraternity. It noted that the decree ordering the annulment of the religious order and its associated confraternity was not limited simply to Hindiyya but extended to anyone else who followed her in setting up an unauthorized religious association of any kind, especially one dedicated to the Sacred Heart of Jesus.[38] The official pronouncement went on to link the troubling aspects of the new cult with all the errors and heresies of its predecessor in an implicit acknowledgment that fifty years after the fact Hindiyya and her ideas were still a prominent factor in the construction of Levantine Christianity.

Religion, Gender, and History

This acknowledgment is a fitting conclusion to the narrative of Hindiyya as it captures a central motif coursing through the history of Christianity in Bilad al-Sham during the long eighteenth century. At a time when the male hierarchs of the Vatican, Latin missionaries, and local Christian clerics alternatively cooperated and competed to define the ideas and institutions of a new apostolic church in the region, women and gender became central to the unfolding historical drama. Presaging the nineteenth-century secular modernizing efforts aimed at liberating women within the confines of the house, eighteenth-century Latin missionaries and the Vatican sought to unleash the spirituality of Maronite women within the strict constraints of Tridentine religious dogma and institutions. This was done in the hope of converting (religiously and culturally) a new genera-tion of Maronites, Melkites, and other Eastern Christians to the precepts of Roman Catholicism through the inculcation of concepts of individual and enthusiastic spirituality in mothers and wives. On the other hand, the Maronite Church (and other religious sects) saw women, particularly Hindiyya, as the vessels of an "authentic" and ancient Christian sect equal in stature to Rome. A new generation of educated reformers (like Duwayhi, Farhat, Qara'li, and Yusuf Istifan) emerged across the breadth of the eigh-teenth century intent on asserting a distinct and dominant identity for the Maronite Church within the Levant. Through constructed histories they laid claim to ancient ecclesiastical rights and perpetual orthodoxy—reaching to the earliest days of Christianity—to buttress their argument for a modern Maronite Church whose patriarch was not subservient to the pope. From this perspective the imperious (or even humble) intrusion of Latin missionaries into the Maronite domestic sphere (to hear confessions, absolve sinners, and dispense catechism) as well as the incessant attempts of some to oversee female religious houses and associations were regarded by many Maronite and Melkite clergy with suspicion, resentment, and sometimes hostility.[39]

The contestations of these two competing visions permitted some women to construct and advance their own alternative visions of Chris-tianity.[40] The Melkite 'abidat, the Maronite Hindiyya, and the religiously mixed Batishtaniyyat represent this trend stretching across one hundred years. While Hindiyya was by far the most important (in duration and impact) member of this movement, they all claimed for themselves the freedom to manage their own affairs with minimal male supervision and the right to define their religious practices and beliefs. Hindiyya went even further. Prompted by lifelong visions of Christ, she founded a new and unsanctioned religious order and confraternity, which broadcast her self-centered ideas about a new revealed Christianity to the populations of Mount Lebanon and Aleppo. In doing so she directly challenged the authority and dogma of the Vatican and its emissaries and local allies in

Bilad al-Sham and garnered growing support among many commoners and clerics seeking salvation, evidence of the beneficence of God toward Maronites, and an indigenous source of religious power to counter the Holy See.

This project of reorienting Christianity could only have been undertaken by Hindiyya and other women because of the confluence of two simultaneous historical dynamics. These were the rise of a prosperous mercantile elite Aleppo and the construction of an invigorated "modern" Christianity across the Levant. Hindiyya—along with Maria Qari, Marguerita Batishta, and other religious women from Aleppo—embodied the impact of these two forces. They were, with few exceptions, all daughters of affluent and religious families. They grew up in a materially comfortable environment that afforded them the luxury of choosing the contemplative life. They had the physical space and leisure in their larger homes to read, reflect, and pray in relative solitude; they had servants who freed them from the requirement of labor for survival; and they had the financial security of significant dowries that obviated the need for marriage—and allowed some to even criticize marriage as spiritual bondage. At the same time they grew up in a period when Latin missionaries were introducing the discourse and practice of a Christianity that encouraged individual search for a relationship with Christ outside the boundaries of local communal practices. Finally, the spread of literacy and accessibility of religious literature and iconography provided Hindiyya and others (who were literate) with some ability to develop their own corpus of religious knowledge and to locate new models of female religious behavior.

These historical conditions were indeed conducive to the rise of religious women's voices amid the entangled debates on the future of Christianity in Bilad al-Sham, but by themselves they do not explain the power those voices attained. Rather, the gender-based paradox inherent in Christianity was the wedge that allowed Hindiyya, among others, to insert herself forcefully into those debates, all the while claiming to be an "innocent abroad." This paradox emanated from the fact that the new Christianity disseminated by Latin missionaries and local reformers espoused universal equality more forthrightly than ever before, even when most—if not all—of those men considered women to be naturally inferior to them in mental acuity and social stature. Hindiyya used this gendered characterization of women as the weaker vessel to explain why Christ would choose her as a conduit for his revelation of the cult of the Sacred Heart and to eschew any responsibility for the repercussions arising from the pursuit of those visions. As the meekest and most ignorant of God's creatures, women—in this case, Hindiyya—would naturally be chosen above prideful, learned men to hear and see Christ. Christ reiterated this to Hindiyya on numerous occasions, and she in turn assumed those characteristics whenever subjected to the inquisitorial scrutiny of local clerics or the Propaganda Fide. Hindiyya and the *Hindawiyyun* defended her claims of divine inspiration by constantly noting that a woman—an unlearned one at that—was incapable of concocting the profound truths coming forth in her multitude of visions and writings.[41] But for rare flashes of assertive anger, Hindiyya maintained this façade to the outside world through the last letter she sent to Rome protesting her innocence. Ironically, then, Hindiyya explained away her rise to religious prominence and relatively unfettered power by adopting the cultural persona of the lowly and weak woman. Even when—and perhaps because—she was a central public figure in the struggle over the future and shape of the Maronite Church, she maintained the demure demeanor of a woman whose only concern was her private relationship with Christ. Only by allowing for this gender dimension can we truly comprehend the magnitude, vehemence, and substance of the Propaganda Fide's response to Hindiyya's challenge and its limited success in erasing her legacy.

More poignantly, Hindiyya's feminization of the Christian experience stands as a testament to the power of religious sentiments and passions in shaping the course of human history. While it is difficult to ascertain the sincerity of the sentiments animating the events surrounding her life, there is little doubt as to the reality and magnitude of their impact on the history we have traced across the eighteenth century. Her union with Christ, the throngs of supplicants beating a path to her conventual door, the tumultuous events in Bkerki, and Vatican responses are a few examples of episodes driven by religious passions and not just religion as a social or political force. Together these and other events were central to the process of constructing a new Christianity in Bilad al-Sham, where spiritual enthusiasm and individuated faith occupied a more central role in the lives of the faithful and the workings of church and community. In turn, the emergence of a new model of Christian faith and institutions was inextricably linked to the transformation in the politics of the Maronite community and its relationship to the Ottoman and European worlds. Through the *Secret of the Union* and her own bodily experience of Christ, she conjoined the divine (religion) and the human (history) in the face of a Roman Catholic project of religious modernity that sought to push the two apart and place itself as the ultimate intermediary between God and Levantine Catholics. She fused the subjective (feminine) and objective (masculine) into a unitary religious experience that was a central dynamic in the history of the Maronite *ta'ifa* as well as a distinctive thread in the chronicles of the Roman Catholic Church. In her own self she reintegrated somatic experiences with rational thought, proclaiming that unity (and her union with Christ) as the only true means for the redemption of humanity. Hindiyya's gendered narrative, then, is a rapprochement between history and religion, one which transcends their rivalry in explicating the human condition and infusing meaning into the human experience.

NOTES

BIBLIOGRAPHY

INDEX

NOTES

1. Introduction

1. ASCPF, CP Maroniti, vol. 136, 437–38.

2. The two main Catholic communities which I will be focusing on in this book are the Maronites and the Melkites. Later, we will explore at length the eighteenth-century historical narrative of the Maronites, so here it will suffice to note that most Maronites trace their religious origin to Mar Yuhanna Maroun, a fifth-century ascetic monk living around the Orontes River between Emesa and Apamea. "Originally, most of these Maronites had inhabited the valley of the Orontes, but they had always been on poor terms with the Byzantine Church and its Syrian followers, the Melchites [sic] . . . The available evidence indicates that the final exodus of the Maronites to Mount Lebanon occurred at some point between the tenth and eleventh centuries." Kamal Salibi, *A House of Many Mansions: The History of Lebanon Reconsidered* (Berkeley: Univ. of California Press, 1988), 13. Their Christian and Muslim contemporaries considered them to be Monothelites; that is, they believed that Jesus Christ had two natures but only one will—a charge which Maronite historians and clerics, since the fifteenth century, have consistently denied as they affirmed their perpetual orthodoxy and adherence to the Chalcedonian creed of two natures and two wills (human and divine).

For example, a chronicler during the Crusades, William of Tyre, related the conversion of 40,000 Maronites in 1182 from Monothelitism after they "had for five hundred years adhered to the false teaching of an heresiarch named Maro." William of Tyre, *De Bello Sacro*, XX, viii. Maronite apologists argue that either William of Tyre uncritically copied the *Annals of Eutychius,* an Egyptian Melkite who calumniated the Maronites, or those 40,000 had gone astray from the body of the Maronite community. Similarly, the very existence and identity of Saint John Maro, the purported founder of the Maronites, is deeply contested. While Maronite chroniclers like Monsignor Yusuf al-Dibs insist on his existence and central role in the foundation of the Maronite sect sometime between 685 and 707, his name is not to be found in the Episcopal records of Antioch from that time period.

But regardless of the veracity of Maronite hagiographies for this early period, the Maronites entered into permanent and uninterrupted communion with the Catholic Church in Rome after the Lateran Council of 1516. By that time their population center was definitely in the northern parts of Mount Lebanon, with scattered smaller communities in Syria, Cyprus, and Palestine. For a more detailed history of the Maronites, see Matti Moosa, *The Maronites in History* (Syracuse: Syracuse Univ. Press, 1986). You can also refer to the encyclopedic work of Butrus Daw, *Tarikh al-Mawarinah al-dini wa-al-siyasi wa-al-ḥaḍari,* 5 vols. (Beirut: Dar al-Nahar, 1970–76)

The term *Melkite* refers to Middle Eastern Christians who accepted the teachings of the Council of Chalcedon. The word comes from the Syriac word *malko,* meaning imperial or "king's men," and it was coined pejoratively by non-Chalcedonians (Jacobites and Nestorians). The Melkite Church was organized into three historic patriarchates— Alexandria, Antioch, and Jerusalem—in union with the patriarch of Constantinople. In 1724, after the death of the Antiochan patriarch Cyril V (who had submitted to the authority of the Roman Holy See in 1718), the community splintered into two parts. In Damascus one group elected Seraphim Tānās as patriarch, who took the name Cyril and ultimately had to flee to Mount Lebanon because of his affiliation with the Vatican. The second patriarch was the Greek candidate Silvester the Cypriot. See Robert Haddad, "The Orthodox Patriarchate of Antioch and the Origins of the Melkite Schism" (PhD diss., Harvard Univ., 1965), for details about this split. The focus of this book will be on the Greek Catholic wing of the Melkite Church, which by the 1740s had become the larger part of the community.

3. I am using the term *Bilad al-Sham* as a shorthand for the geographical territory encompassing modern-day Lebanon and Syria. I will also use the term *Levant* for the same area for no other reason but variety.

4. Wilfred Cantwell Smith, *The Meaning and End of Religion* (San Francisco, Harper, 1978), 38.

5. Here, I am thinking of the pioneering scholarly works of anthropologists Elizabeth Fernea and Cynthia Nelson; historians Beth Baron, Marilyn Booth, Nikki Keddie, and Judith Tucker; and Arabic literature scholars like miriam cooke, who brought women and gender studies in the Middle East to the fore.

6. See, for instance, Ussama Makdisi, *Artillery of Heaven: American Missionaries and the Failed Conversion of the Middle East* (Ithaca, N.Y.: Cornell Univ. Press, 2008); Nancy Stockdale, *Colonial Encounters among English and Palestinian Women, 1800–1948* (Gainesville: Univ. Press of Florida, 2007); Heather Sharkey, *American Evangelicals in Egypt: Missionary Encounters in an Age of Empire* (Princeton, N.J.: Princeton Univ. Press, 2008). Heleen Murre-van der Berg, ed. *New Faith in Ancient Lands* (Boston: Brill, 2006) is an edited collection of articles on Western missionaries in the Middle East that combines the latest work of European and American scholars like Ellen Fleischmann, Anthony

O'Mahony, Roland Röffler, and Uwe Kaminsky. As for works focusing on the history of Christians in the modern Middle East (sixteenth century and thereafter), there is the outstanding work of French historian Bernard Heyberger, whose corpus of articles and books on Christianity in the Middle East makes him by far the dean of this field of studies. Among those are *Les chrétiens de Syrie, du Liban et de Palestine aux XVIIe et XVIIIe siècles* (Rome: Ecole française de Rome, 1994a) and *Hindiyya: mystique et criminelle, 1720–1798* (Paris: Aubier, 2001). Bruce Masters has also written some outstanding works on this subject. See, for example, his *Christians and Jews in the Ottoman Arab World: The Roots of Sectarianism* (New York: Cambridge Univ. Press, 2001). More prosaic studies of the topic in English include Habib Badr, Suad Abou el Rouss Slim, and Joseph Abou Nohra, eds. *Christianity: A History in the Middle East* (Beirut: Middle East Council of Churches, Studies and Research Program, 2005).

7. A quick perusal of the Middle East Studies Association's annual programs over the past decade confirms this stark reality, with nary a panel dedicated to the history of modern Christianity before the 2009 program. Similarly, the American Academy of Religion's annual programs provide a sharp contrast between the plethora of panels on Islam in the Middle East and only the rare paper on modern Christianity there.

8. For an excellent study of protestant missionaries in Mount Lebanon, see Makdisi, *Artillery of Heaven.*

9. Febe Armanios and Nelly van Doorn are among the few scholars who have focused on women and gender in Middle Eastern Christianity. See, for example, Armanios's "The 'Virtuous Woman': Images of Gender in Modern Coptic Society," *Middle Eastern Studies* 38, no. 1 (Jan. 2002): 110. For a sample of van Doorn's work, see "Imagined Antiquity: Coptic Nuns Living Between Past Ideals and Present Realities," in *Living for Eternity: The White Monastery and Its Neighborhood,* ed. Philip Sellew. Proceedings of a symposium at the University of Minnesota, Minneapolis, Mar. 6–9, 2003.

10. Daniella Kostroun, "A Formula for Disobedience: Jansenism, Gender, and the Feminist Paradox," *Journal of Modern History* 75 (Sept. 2003): 486.

11. This was a similar formulation to Hildegard of Bingen's "poor little figure of a woman" and Julian of Norwich's "though I am a woman, ignorant, weak and frail." Caroline Walker Bynum, *Holy Feast and Holy Fast: The Religious Significance of Food to Medieval Women* (Berkeley: Univ. of California Press, 1988), 227.

12. Ibid., 279.

13. Elizabeth Petroff, *Medieval Women's Visionary Literature* (New York: Oxford Univ. Press, 1986), 6.

14. For a full exploration of the exclusion of the senses from Western thought, see Constance Classen, *Worlds of Sense: Exploring the Senses in History and Across Cultures* (London: Routledge, 1993).

15. David Hume, *A Treatise of Human Nature* (London: Clarendon Press, 1896), 269.

16. Gerda Lerner, *The Creation of Feminist Consciousness: From the Middle Ages to Eighteen-Seventy* (New York: Cambridge Univ. Press, 1994), 66.

17. For a good discussion of the idea and ideation of modernity, see the introduction in Keith Watenpaugh's *Being Modern in the Middle East: Revolution, Nationalism, Colonialism and the Arab Middle Class* (Princeton, N.J.: Princeton Univ. Press, 2006).

18. Jon Butler argues that professional historiography, in general, has kept religion at arm's length, particularly in matters relating to the great core of religious life: the supernatural world where humans do not dominate causality. Jon Butler, "Theory and God in Gotham," *History and Theory* 45 (Dec. 2006): 47–61.

19. David Shaw, "Modernity Between Us and Them: The Place of Religion in History," *History and Theory* 45, no. 4 (2006): 4.

20. Rosalva Loreto López, "The Devil in Seventeenth-Century Puebla Convents," *The Americas* 59, no. 2 (Oct. 2002): 183.

2. Aleppo: The Making of a Visionary (1720–1746)

1. ASCPF, CP Maroniti, vol. 118, f. 725, "Interrogation of Hindiyya," question 1.

2. There are two main hagiographies of Hindiyya. The most complete one was written by Father Antonio Venturi, Hindiyya's last Latin confessor. It is located in the archives of the Propaganda Fide. ASCPF, CP Maroniti, vol. 118, "Alcune notizie da server il libro Primo della vita della serva di Dio Hendi Ageimi." The other is titled *Sirat Hayat al-Umm al-Batoul Hindiyya* (*Vitae of the virgin Mother Hindiyya*), and it is found in the archives of the Maronite patriarchate in Lebanon (Hindiyya Papers, vol. 1). It is written in Arabic, with a readable but less than perfect handwriting. It may have been a draft since there are many corrections to the manuscript and marginalia. The author is anonymous, and the manuscript is incomplete; but from its striking similarities to the Italian hagiography, it is most likely a translation of Venturi's work with some amendments.

3. The only recorded exception is the 1748 register of the Mar Hrash convent, where it was noted that "Hannah al-'Ujaimi called Aprexia from Aleppo" became a novice at the convent.

4. Michel al-Hayek, "al-Rahibah Hindiyya: Amaliha wa rahbanatuha," *Al-Mashriq* 74 (1965): 525. Al-Hayek suggested that her name derives from her brown skin, and he alludes to the legend that she had traveled to India. Among her detractors who used her name to sully her image were the Jesuits who, in an anti-Hindiyya poster they commissioned, derided her as "Hindiyya the black," writing her name in black amid a red-ink sentence to emphasize their point even further. Bernard Heyberger also notes that the Capuchin Gabriel de Quintin "in trying to blacken the 'saint' noted falsely that her baptismal name is Hindiyya." Heyberger, *Hindiyya*, cf. 6, 41.

5. Antoine Rabbath, *Documents inédits pour server a l'histoire du Christianisme en Orient (XVI–XIX siècle)*, vol. 2 (Paris: A. Picard et Fils, 1905–11), 95–96.

6. Ibid., 22.

7. Tripoli was the capital of the Ottoman district which included much of the Maronite mountain villages and territory. Istifan al-Duwayhi, *Tarikh al-Azmina* (Beirut: Dar Lahad Khater), 143.

8. Ibid., 152.

9. Ibid., 155–58.

10. Ibid., 157v.

11. Between 1672 and 1695 the number of adult Jews in Aleppo rose from 450 to 875, with most coming from the migration of Sephardic Jews into the city in pursuit of economic opportunities. Bruce Masters, "Aleppo: The Ottoman Empire's Caravan City," in *The Ottoman City Between East and West*, ed. Edhem Eldem, Daniel Goffman, and Bruce Masters (Cambridge: Cambridge Univ. Press, 1999), 39.

12. Pedro Teixeira, *The Travels of Pedro Teixeira,* trans. William Sinclair (London: Bedford Press, 1902), 121.

13. Ibid., 120.

14. Ibid., 71.

15. *Livre* is the name for the French unit of currency, like the English pound and the Venetian ducat. Of course, the market of these various currencies was not exactly the same, and it certainly changed over time; but it was close enough to provide a good comparative basis. 'Adel Ismail, *Documents diplomatiques et consulaires relatifs à l'histoire du Liban et pays du Proche Orient du XVIIe siècle à nos jours,* vol. 3 (Beirut: Université Libanaise, 1975), 203.

16. Masters, "Aleppo," 35.

17. *Dragoman* is the Latinization of the Arabic word *turjman,* or translator.

18. Ferdinand Tawtal, "Watha'iq Tarikhiyya 'an Halab fi al-qarn al-thamin cashar," *Al-Mashriq* 41 (1958): 268–69. Tawtal quotes a document which appeared in a book by the bishop of Aleppo, Jibrail Hawshab, dated October 16, 1758, in which the Latin missionaries convened and decided to put pressure on the Catholic dragomans to force them to pay their share of the community's taxes. The missionaries were to visit the consuls and Jirjis 'Aida and demand that all dragomans, protégés, and coterie should attend a meeting on October 18 to resolve this issue and to inform them that noncompliance may lead to excommunication.

19. Masters, *Christians and Jews, 77.*

20. Among these were the 'Aida and Fakhr families. Masters, "Aleppo," 58.

21. AMPB, Hindiyya Papers, vol. 1, "Sirat Hayat al-Umm al-Batoul Hindiyya," 4; ASCPF, CP Maroniti, vol. 118, "Alcune notizie da server il libro Primo della vita della serva di Dio Hendi Ageimi," 134.

22. AMPB, Hindiyya Papers, vol. 1, "Sirat Hayat al-Umm al-Batoul Hindiyya," 5.

23. The other seven were Tumayat, Zuqaq al-Khall, Zuqaq Arbacin, Kanisa, 'Abd al-Hayy, Basatina, and Qastal Harami. André Raymond, "The Population of Aleppo in the Sixteenth and Seventeenth Centuries According to Ottoman Census Documents," *International Journal of Middle East Studies* 16, no. 4 (Nov. 1984): 457–58.

24. Abraham Marcus, *The Middle East on the Eve of Modernity: Aleppo in the Eighteenth Century* (New York: Columbia Univ. Press, 1989), 319–21.

25. Alexander Russell, *The Natural History of Aleppo* (London: G. G. and J. Robinson, 1794), 33.

26. Ibid., 45.

27. Bulus Qara'li, "Manshur batryarki qadim," *al-Majalla al-Batriyarkiyya/al-Majalla al-Suriyya* 4 (1929): 376–77.

28. Habib al-Zayyat, "Akhbar al-ta'ifa al-malakiyya fi Halab." *Al-Mashriq* 36 (1923): 32–40.

29. The same Russell who noted the extravagance of dress among Aleppan Christian women wrote that "the dread of ecclesiastic censure has little weight." Russell, *Natural History of Aleppo,* 55.

30. Tawtal, *Watha'iq Tarikhiyya,* 113.

31. Ibid., 110–11.

32. Ibid., 44.

33. Russell, *Natural History of Aleppo,* 175.

34. Ibid., 173. The other pages are 73–90, 115–19, 172–77.

35. AMPB, Hindiyya Papers, vol. 1, "Sirat Hayat al-Umm al-Batoul Hindiyya," 4.

36. Ibid., 5.

37. ASCPF, CP Maroniti, vol. 118, "Alcune notizie," f. 122r, 127v–28v.

38. ASCPF, CP Maroniti, vol. 118, f. 725, "Interrogation of Hindiyya," question 3.

39. Rabbath, *Documents inédits,* 358–74.

40. Ibid., 452.

41. Congregatio de Propaganda Fide, *Collecatanea Sacrae Congregationis de Propaganda Fide: seu Decreta, Instructiones, Rescripta pro Apostolicis Missionibus,* vol. 1 (Rome: Ex Typographia Polyglotta, 1907), doc. 2.

42. Rabbath, *Documents inédits,* 87–88.

43. Bernard Heyberger, "Les chrétiens d'Alep (Syrie) à travers les récits des conversions des Missionnaires Carmes Déchaux (1657–1681)," *Mélanges de l'École Françaises de Rome* 100 (1988): 461–99.

44. Masters, "Aleppo," 54.

45. Charles Le Gobien and Jean-Baptiste Du Halde, *Lettres Édifinates et Curieuses: Mémoires du Levant,* vol. 3 (Lyon: Librairie J. Vernarel), 1819, 211–18.

46. Russell, *Natural History of Aleppo,* 29.

47. Rabbath, *Documents inédits,* 60.

48. Joseph Besson, *La Syrie et la terre sainte au XVIIe siècle* (Poitiers, France: H. Oudin, 1862), 106.

49. Ibid., 105.

50. Ibid., questions 11, 23, 33, and 36.

51. This paragraph quotes at length from Bernard Heyberger, *Les Chrétiens du Proche-Orient au temps de la réforme Catholique* (Rome: École Française de Rome, 1994b), 363.

52. ARCD, Plut, 245 C 1, 2–3. SOCG, 197, f.109r, May 22, 1651, Sylvestre de Saint-Aignan.

53. Père Alexandre de Saint-Sylvestre, "Briève relation des missions des révérends pères Carmes Déchaussés en Syrie et en Perse, Lettre du P. Jean-Baptiste de Saint-Aignan à Colbert, Aleppo 1670," in Rabbath, *Documents inédits,* 436.

54. R. P. Nicholas Poirresson, "Relation des missions de la compagnie de Jésus en Syrie en l'année 1652," in Rabbath, *Documents inédits,* 52–53.

55. Père Alexandre de Saint Sylvestre, "Briève relation," 435.

56. Père Jean Amieu, "Relation de Syrie pour l'an 1650," in Rabbath, *Documents inédits,* 402.

57. Michel Febvre, *Théâtre de la Turquie* (Paris, 1682), 467.

58. Nasser Gemayel, *Les échanges culturels entre les Maronite et l'Europe* (Beirut: L'Imprimerie Y. & PH. Gemayel, 1984), 125.

59. Louis de Gonzague, "Les anciens missionnaires capucins de Syrie et leur écrits apostolique de langue Arabe," *Collectanea Franciscana* (1932): 39.

60. Gérard Troupeau, *Catalogue des manuscrits Arabes de la Bibliothèque Nationale* (Paris: *Bibliothèque Nationale,* 1972), 89. See also Paul Sbath, *Bibliothèque de manuscrits,* vol. 1 (Cairo, H. Friedrich et Co: 1928), 59, no. 95.

61. Troupeau, *Catalogue des manuscrits,* 90, no. 130.

62. Wahid Gdoura, *Le début de l'imprimerie Arabe à Istanbul et en Syrie: évolution de l'environnement culturel (1706–1787)* (Tunis: Publ. du Centre d'Études et de Recherches Ottomanes, Morisques, de Documentation et d'Information, 1985), 167.

63. ASCPF, CP Maroniti, vol. 118, "Interrogation of Katerina," 532r.

64. Sylvie Agemian, "Ne'meh al-Musawwir, peintre melkite 1666–1724," *Berytus* 34 (1991): 205.

65. ASCPF, CP Maroniti, vol. 118, "Alcune notizie da server il libro Primo della vita della serva di Dio Hendi Ageimi," 115r, 119r, 132rv. This new wave of religious artistic production represented a gradual move—in style and themes—from Byzantine iconography to baroque sensibility. In discussing this new iconography, Mahmoud Zibawi wrote, "The Baroque Madona replaced the Theotokos [Mother of God], crushing the serpent under her feet. The inscription identified the icon as that of Immaculate Conception, a Latin concept alien to the Christian East and rejected by Eastern non-Catholic churches." Mahmoud Zibawi, "Les icônes du Proche-Orient," in *Icônes Arabes: art Chrétien du Levant* (Paris: Éditions Grégoriennes, 2003), A27.

66. Heyberger, *Les chrétiens du Proche-Orient,* 359–60.

67. ARSI, Gallia, 96, I, f. 603v. See Gemayel, *Les échanges culturels,* 944–45.

68. While I realize that the term "nahda" is reserved for the nineteenth-century literary and cultural renaissance, I make use of it here as a way to contest the periodization of "modernity" in the Middle East and to suggest that this—as well as other periods—were not only precursors but also significant movements in their own right. I will address this more in chapter 4.

69. This and most of the other information about Farhat has been adapted from Kristen Brusted's unpublished article on him, which she quite generously shared.

70. In total there were twenty-nine students from Aleppo who attended the Maronite College. This made the city the third largest source of Maronite students (after Zghorta and Bsherri in north Lebanon). Most of them traveled to Rome between the late 1690s and late 1780s. Gemayel, *Les échanges culturels,*125.

71. AMPB, Hindiyya Papers, vol. 1, "Sirat Hayat al-Umm al-Batoul Hindiyya," 2.

72. Ibid.

73. ASCPF, CP Maroniti, vol. 118, "Alcune notizie da server il libro Primo della vita della serva di Dio Hendi Ageimi," 725.

74. ASCPF, CP Maroniti, vol. 118, f. 725, "Interrogation of Hindiyya," question 5.

75. Ibid.

76. In a letter which she dictated for the members of the confraternity she established later in her life, she states that he appeared to her when she was 5 years of age. AMPB, Hindiyya Papers, vol. 1.

77. ASCPF, CP Maroniti, vol. 118, "Interrogation of Mother Hindiyya," question 13.

78. Ibid., question 20–21.

79. ASCPF, CP Maroniti, vol. 136, "Sirr al-Ittihad," f. 449.

80. ASCPF, CP Maroniti, vol. 118, f. 725, "Interrogation of Hindiyya," question 61.

81. ASCPF, CP Maroniti, vol. 136, "Sirr al-Ittihad," f. 448.

82. ASCPF, CP Maroniti, vol. 118, f. 725, "Interrogation of Hindiyya," question 58.

83. Ibid., question 12.

84. Ibid., question 38.

85. Ibid., questions 40–56.

86. Bynum, *Holy Feast and Holy Fast,* 295.

87. Revised English Bible, New Testament, Romans 12:1. (Oxford and Cambridge: Oxford Univ. Press and Cambridge Univ. Press, 1989).

88. ASCPF, CP Maroniti, vol. 118, "Interrogation of Hindiyya," question 65.

89. Ibid., question 66.

90. Ibid., questions 25 and 28.

91. Ibid., questions 27.

92. Grace M. Jantzen, *Power, Gender and Christian Mysticism* (Cambridge: Cambridge Univ. Press, 1995), 210.

93. Bynum, *Holy Feast and Holy Fast,* 140.

94. Ibid., 141. Also see Rudolph Bell, *Holy Anorexia* (Chicago: Univ. of Chicago Press, 1987).

95. Bell, *Holy Anorexia,* chapter 2.

96. See plates 25 and 26 in Bynum, *Holy Feast and Holy Fast,* for a visual example of this tendency to see Christ as feeding women through his divine wounds and thus obviating the need for human food.

97. This was a common practice in Aleppo in the eighteenth century, though it was primarily handled by barbers. There is no description of how this was performed on Hindiyya, but the most common process would have been to cut into one of the major veins in her arms. Marcus, *The Middle East,* 267.

98. ASCPF, CP Maroniti, vol. 118, "Interrogation of Hindiyya," question 88.

99. Ibid., question 90.

100. Ibid., question 39. See also AMPB, Hindiyya Papers, vol. 1, "Sirat Hayat al-Umm al-Batoul Hindiyya," 7.

101. Thomas Aquinas, *Basic Writings of Saint Thomas Aquinas* (New York: Random House 1945), 92.1. Jantzen, *Power, Gender,* 195.

102. ASCPF, CP Maroniti, vol. 118, "Interrogation of Hindiyya," question 39.

103. AMPB, Hindiyya Papers, vol. 1, "Sirat Hayat al-Umm al-Batoul Hindiyya," 3.

104. Ibid., 6.

105. Ibid., 5v.

106. ASCPF, CP Maroniti, vol. 118, "Interrogation of Hindiyya," question 59.

107. Margot King, *The Desert Mothers: A Survey of the Feminine Anchoretical Tradition* (Toronto: Peregrina, 1984).

108. Duwayhi's sermon is taken from a book of his collected sermons and reprinted. Tawtal, *Watha'iq Tarikhiyya,* 25–33.

109. Saint Simon the Stylite (c. 390–459) was a Christian ascetic saint who became renowned for having lived for some 37 years on top of a pillar near Aleppo.

110. Agnès-Mariam de la Croix and François Zabbal, *Icônes Arabes: art Chrétien du Levant* (Paris: Éditions Grégoriennes, 2003), A42.

111. Youcim Moubarac, *Pentalogie antiochienne/domaine Maronite, vol. 1* (Beirut: Cénacle libanais, 1984), 214.

112. Rudolph Bell presented that argument in his tellingly titled book *Holy Anorexia.* Bynum, *Holy Feast and Holy Fast,* 5. See also her "Fast, Feast, and Flesh: The Religious Significance of Food to Medieval Women," *Representations* 11 (1985): 1–25.

113. Renunciation of the bourgeois trappings of life, born out of anxiety over newly acquired wealth and status, was also a common phenomenon in Europe during the thirteenth and fourteenth centuries. See, for example, Carolyn Bynum's "Religious Women in the Later Middle Ages," in *Christian Spirituality: High Middle Ages and Reformation,* ed. Jill Raitt, Bernard McGinn, and John Meyendorff (London: Taylor & Francis, 1987), 123–25.

114. ASCPF, CP Maroniti, vol. 118, "Interrogation of Mother Hindiyya," question 12.

115. One historian, Bernard Heyberger, has taken this to mean "sexually" sleeping with the father and has, on the basis of this one comment, provided a Freudian analysis of Hindiyya's life to explain all her subsequent behavior as a product of this formative psychological moment. While the work of Heyberger on Hindiyya, *Hindiyya: mystique et criminelle,* is outstanding in many respects, this central argument is problematic. The notion that Helena would have told Hindiyya to have sex with her father at the age of 7 is a reading of one statement that cannot be sustained by any other evidence from the time period and that seems highly unlikely given that other observers note that even in marriage Christians do not consummate the union until late adolescence. Russell, *Natural History of Aleppo,* 47. A much more plausible reading is that for a prepubescent girl, as was Hindiyya at the age of 7, it was permissible to sleep in the same room with the father without transgressing any sexual taboos. Hindiyya's refusal to do so is not refusal of sexual intercourse, as Heyberger proposes, but rather an adherence to a greater degree of modesty than was the norm among her peers, and that would be a sign of her early vocation. This alternative reading is supported by the recurrence of this same theme in the vitae of other Catholic visionary women and saints. For instance, St. Bona of Pisa's vocation "is already formed by age seven, when she refuses to sleep in the same bed with her mother, although this is the custom." Elizabeth Alvilda Petroff, *Body and Soul: Essays on Medieval Women and Mysticism* (New York: Oxford Univ. Press, 1994), 168.

116. AMPB, Hindiyya Papers, vol. 1, "Sirat Hayat al-Umm al-Batoul Hindiyya," 5.

117. Ibid.

118. ASCPF, CP Maroniti, vol. 136, "Sirr al-Ittihad," f. 448v.

119. In all, Helena and Shukralla had ten children, of whom only four survived their childhood. Antun, Hanna, Ilyas, Qudsiyya, and Antun, Jr., all passed away before reaching their second birthday. Suzanne, the youngest, died when she was 9 years of age. Heyberger, *Hindiyya,* 40.

120. AMPB, Hindiyya Papers, vol. 1, "Sirat Hayat al-Umm al-Batoul Hindiyya," 5.

121. In writing about the popularity of saints' narratives in Europe, Donald Attwater noted medieval people's fascination with the bizarre and the excessive in a pious setting. Donald Attwater, *The Penguin Dictionary of Saints* (London: Penguin Books, 1995), 13.

122. ASCPF, CP Maroniti, vol. 118, "Interrogation of Mother Hindiyya," question 104.

123. ASCPF, CP Maroniti, vol. 136, "Sirr al-Ittihad," f. 448v.

124. ASCPF, CP Maroniti, vol. 118, "Interrogation of Mother Hindiyya," question 104.

125. Seraphim are the heavenly attendants in the court of Yahweh. The only scriptural reference to them appears in Isaiah 6:22, when he is called to be a prophet of God. Two of their wings hold them aloft, two hide their eyes, and the last two hide their feet.

126. ASCPF, CP Maroniti, vol. 118, "Interrogation of Mother Hindiyya," question 104.

127. Pokocke, Richard, *Beschreibung des Morgenlandes und einiger ander Lände* (Erlangen, Germany: Walther, 1771), 221; Tawtal, *Watha'iq Tarikhiyya,* 66.

128. AMPB, Hindiyya Papers, vol. 1, "Sirat Hayat al-Umm al-Batoul Hindiyya," 9; ASCPF Maroniti, vol. 118, f. 330r–333v "De Directioni Nobilis Virginis Alepensis," 134.

129. AMPB, Hindiyya Papers, vol. 1, "Sirat Hayat al-Umm al-Batoul Hindiyya," 12.

130. Ibid., 9.

131. Ibid., 28–29. This rejection of patriarchal authority was not an isolated incident. Hindiyya's brother, Niqula, left to become a Jesuit without his parents' permission. Jirmanus Farhat wrote a poem dedicated to his teacher, Yusuf al-Dibsi, embodying the conflict between patriarchal authority and spiritual yearning. There are other examples of these generational bifurcations and even conflicts, deriving from the cultural transformations in Aleppo that opened new possibilities for young men and women not available to their parents. See chapter 3 for a longer discussion of this issue.

132. ASCPF, CP Maroniti, vol. 118, "Interrogation of Mother Hindiyya," question 71.

133. Ibid., question 107.

134. ASCPF, CP Maroniti, vol. 118, "De Directioni Nobilis Virginis Alepensis," f. 323v.

135. AMPB, Hindiyya Papers, vol. 1, "Sirat Hayat al-Umm al-Batoul Hindiyya," 4–7.

136. ASCPF, CP Maroniti, vol. 113, f. 96rv (Apr. 25, 1750), Gabriel de Quintin to procurer of the French missions. Quoted in Heyberger, *Hindiyya,* 110. The poster is in the Bkerki archives. AMPB, Hindiyya Papers, vol. 1.

137. ASCPF, CP Maroniti, vol. 118, "Report of Friar Desiderio di Casabasciana," 196.

138. ASCPF, CP Maroniti, vol. 118, "Interrogation of Mother Hindiyya," question 71.

139. His letters were written to defend himself from accusations by fellow Jesuits that he was "hoodwinked" by Hindiyya. ASCPF, CP Maroniti, vol. 113, f. 96; vol. 118, "Alcune notizie da server il libro Primo della vita della serva di Dio Hendi Ageimi."

140. AMPB, Hindiyya Papers, vol. 1, "Sirat Hayat al-Umm al-Batoul Hindiyya," 9.

141. Marguerite-Marie Alacoque was a late-seventeenth-century French nun who claimed to have received visions of Christ similar to those of Hindiyya. This included the focus on the devotion to the Sacred Heart of Jesus and the proclamation to both nuns that they would be the instruments for the dissemination of Christ's saving grace and love to humanity. Raymond Anthony Jonas, *France and the Cult of the Sacred Heart: An Epic Tale of Modern Times* (Berkeley: Univ. of California Press, 2000).

142. Attwater, *Penguin Dictionary of Saints,* 13.

143. "Risalat al-Umm Hindiyya al-'Ujaimi ila banat Qalb Yasu'," 9.

144. ASCPF, CP Maroniti, vol. 118, "Interrogation of Mother Hindiyya," question 107.

145. ASCPF, CP Maroniti, vol. 136, "Sirr al-Ittihad," f. 432.

146. ASCPF, CP Maroniti, vol. 136, "Sirr al-Ittihad," f. 447r-v.

3. Mount Lebanon: A Voice in the Wilderness (1746–1750)

1. Richard van Leeuwen, *Notables & Clergy in Mount Lebanon: The Khazin Sheikhs & the Maronite Church* (Leiden, Netherlands: Brill, 1994), 53–54. For the eighteenth century the emirs were Haydar (1706–1732), Milhim (1729–1753), Mansur (1753–1763,

1763–1770), Yusuf (1763–1790). The reason behind the overlap in some of these dates is that the rule of one emir or another was contested successfully, at least for a period of time, by other members of the Shihabi family.

2. M. de Grangé, inspector of the French consulates in the "Eastern" territories, estimated that between fifty and sixty Maronite and Druze *shuyukh* made up the political strata beneath the Shihabi emir. Father Butrus Ghalib, "Taqrir al-sayyid de Grangé," *Al-Mashriq* 28 (1930): 578–87.

3. Emir Bashir II, for instance, was in a continuous power struggle with Shaykh Bashir Jumblatt. He won only through by outbidding his rival for the allegiance of the Ottoman governor of Acre, who was holding Shaykh Bashir hostage and who agreed to put him to death for a sum of about one million piasters. For details on this particular incident as well as on the history of the conflict between these two powerful figures, see Fouad Efram al-Bustani's edition of *Mudhakkirat Rustum Baz*. Also refer to Amir Haydar Shihab's *Lubnan fi 'ahd al-umara' al-shihabiyyin*. Tannous al-Shidyaq reported that in 1782 "the governing amir [Yusuf Shihab] decreed a tax of five piasters on every oka [128 grams] of silkworm eggs, which enraged his Jumblatti brethren against him and they came to Simqanniya [a village near Dayr el-Qamar] and agreed to reject the tax. Then they went to Dayr el-Qamar with the intent of deposing the Amir from the governorship and to kill his mudabbir (manager) al-shaykh Sa'd, and they commenced to shoot off their powder [guns] . . . so that the Amir sent to them a messenger promising to rescind that decree . . . after which they returned to their homes." Tannous al-Shidyaq, *Kitab akhbar al-a'yan fi jabal lubnan* (Beirut: Lebanese Univ. Press, 1970), 405.

4. In May 1657 King Louis XIV sent a letter to Shaykh Abu Nawfal al-Khazin informing him that: "[Since] it has become necessary for the good of our French merchants trading in Baruth [*sic*] to have a person who exercises the duties of Vice Consul, and since it has been brought to my attention that you have a special zeal for the French nation and for the Christian name, then I wanted to write . . . to inform you that it would greatly please me if you would . . . establish the vice consul [position] and render to French missionaries and others the services that you have been providing on many previous occasions." René Ristelhueber, *Les traditions françaises au Liban* (Paris: F. Alcan 1925), 327. The Khazin family maintained its control over the position of vice-consul long after Abu Nawfal, who was followed by his son Abu Qansu, who was succeeded by his uncle Husn, and after that came Shaykh Nawfal.

5. Kamal Salibi, *The Modern History of Lebanon* (Delmar, N.Y.: Caravan Books, 1977), xx; William Polk, *The Opening of South Lebanon, 1788–1840: A Study of the Impact of the West on the Middle East* (Cambridge, Mass.: Harvard Univ. Press, 1963), 129.

6. Bulus Qara'li, *'Awdat al-Nasara ila Jurud Kisrawan* (Beirut: Jurus Press, 1983), 11–30.

7. Constantin-François Volney, *Travels through Syria and Egypt, in 1783, 1784 and 1785* (London: G. G. J. and J. Robinson, 1788), 182.

8. Dominique Chevallier, *La société du Mont Liban à l'époque de la révolution industrielle en Europe* (Paris: Libraire Orientaliste Paul Geuthner, 1971), 61.

9. David Urquhart, *The Lebanon: A History and a Diary* (London: Thomas Cautley Newby, 1860), 233–34.

10. F. Bart, *Scènes et tableaux de la vie actuelle en Orient—Mont Liban* (Paris: Xavier Marmier, 1883), 42. Certainly, there were those whose depictions of Mount Lebanon were more romantic. Most notable was Alphonse de Lamartine, whose book *Souvenirs, impressions, pensées et paysages pendant un voyage en Orient, 1832–1833* (Paris: Hachette, 1875), was naïve in its observations to say the least, full of preconceived romantic images that had little to do with reality. Even contemporaries were aware of that bias. Another French romantic observer was the Viscomtesse d'Aviau de Piolant, who recorded her highly impressionistic recollections about Mount Lebanon in a book titled *Au Pays des Maronites* (Paris: Librarie A. Oudin, 1856). Lebanese folklorists painted equally romantic images of the Lebanese house, and village life in general, but for reasons that are more political. Most of these writers tended to be Maronite Christians who were loathe to admit any relationship between the surrounding Arab culture and that of the Maronite community. Thus, they argued, with a great stretch of the imagination at times, that the Maronites safeguarded intact their Aramaic, Syriac, Phoenician, Marada, or even European heritage. For example, Michel Feghali wrote, "La conclusion que nous pouvons en tirer, c'est que sur ce point particulier, comme sur tant d'autres, la civilisation arabe ou turque n'a réussi, à aucun moment, à s'imposer dans le Liban. Les Libanais, ainsi que le prouvent leur vocabulaire en grande partie syriaque, ont toujours mené la même vie que leurs ancêtres des premiers siècles chrétiens . . . D'où la ressemblance frappante que nous constatons aujourd'hui encore entre les habitants du Liban actuel et les anciens peuples de Syrie: Araméens, Cananéens et Hébreux" (The conclusion we can draw is that on this particular point, as on many others, Turkish or Arab civilization has not succeeded, at any time, in imposing itself on Lebanon. The Lebanese, as proven by their largely Syriac vocabulary, have always led the same life as their ancestors of the first Christian centuries. . . . Hence the striking resemblance that we see today between the actual inhabitants of Lebanon and the ancient peoples of Syria: Arameans, Canaanites and Hebrews). Michel Feghali, "Notes sur la maison libanaise," in *Mélanges René Basset* (Paris: Publications de l'Institut des Hautes-Études Marocaines, 1923), 185–86.

11. Ghalib, "Taqrir al-sayyid," 581.

12. Dominique Chevallier, "Que possédait un Cheikh Maronite en 1859? Un document de la famille al-Khazin." *Arabica* 7 (1960): 72–84.

13. For example, in 1735 Aleppo's pasha issued orders requiring the city's Christians to wear particular colors to distinguish them from Muslims, prohibiting them from frequenting the surrounding gardens, and denying Christian women the right to visit tombs and churches. In 1738 Janissary troops ransacked Christian churches, and the pasha ordered the demolition of some wealthy homes that had risen above surrounding Muslim

ones. The lot of Aleppo's Christians was obviously not one of constant persecution, but these episodes created enough of a sense of insecurity and uncertainty among them to make Lebanon appear as a safe haven. Rabbath, *Documents inédits*, 33–34.

14. For the full text of the bull, see Tobia Anaiss, *Bullarium Maronitarum* (Livorno, Italy: Max Bretschneider Librarius, 1911). The quotes are from Song of Songs 2:2 and 4:8, respectively.

15. Bernard Heyberger and Chantal Verdeil observe a similar trope. For example, they write: "In Jesuit eyes, the Holy Land constituted hallowed ground. . . . It was also a country consecrated by history, evoking certain episodes from biblical Antiquity or the Christian past . . . Palestine was seen as sanctified by sacred history . . . Sidon, where the Jesuits settled, was honored by Christ's visit . . . Egypt was also part of the Holy Land. Speaking of the Virgin's house in Nazareth, Joseph Besson evoked the house of 'Matharée' [Matariyya] near Cairo, where the holy Family was said to have lived." "Spirituality and Scholarship—The Holy Land in Jesuit Eyes (Seventeenth to Nineteenth Centuries)," in *New Faith in Ancient Lands: Western Missions in the Middle East in the Nineteenth and Early Twentieth Centuries,* ed. Heleen Murre-van den Berg (Leiden, Netherlands: Brill, 2006), 21–23.

16. Sylvestre Saint-Aignan, *Description abrégée de la sainte montagne du Liban et des Maronites qui l'habitent* (Paris: Jean-Baptiste Coignard, 1671), 16–17. This is a precursor to similar nineteenth-century ruminations by secular observers. For example, Alphonse de Lamartine wrote of Mount Lebanon that it is "the most religious country in the world." He added, "The very special environment of frequently arid mountains had made the Maronites a simple and austere people, and had also developed their natural tendencies toward mysticism. The grand and sometimes terrible beauty of certain Lebanese sites is well suited for meditation." Lamartine, *Souvenirs, impressions,* 1, 68.

17. Saint-Aignan, *Description abrégé,* 30.

18. Besson, *La Syria,* 104.

19. Ibid., 101–2.

20. For an exploration of the changing conceptualization of time and space within Europe and in relation to other parts of the world, see Johannes Fabian, *Time and the Other: How Anthropology Makes Its Object* (New York: Columbia Univ. Press, 1983). Père Petitqueux, *Relation d'un voyage à Cannobin, dans le Mont Liban, envoyée au Père Fleuriau par le Père Petitqueux, missionnaire jésuite,* vol. 1, *Actes des Apôtres modernes ou missions Catholiques* (Paris: Parent Desbarres, 1854), 103.

21. Luis de Molina, *Liberi arbitrii cum gratiae donis, divina praescientia, providentia, praedestinatione et reprobatione concordia* (Antwerp: Trognæsii, 1595).

22. André Shimberg, *L'éducation morale dans les collèges de la Compagnie de Jésus en France sous l'ancien régime* (Paris: Champion, 1913), 57. Quoted in George R. Healy, "The French Jesuits and the Idea of the Noble Savage," *William and Mary Quarterly* 15, no. 2 (1958): 147.

23. Peter A. Goddard, "Augustine and the Amerindian in Seventeenth-Century New France," Church History 67, no. 4 (1998), 663.

24. Besson, *La Syrie*, 103–4.

25. See Reuben Gold Thwaites' *The Jesuit Relations and Allied Documents: Travels and Explorations of the Jesuit Missionaries in New France, 1610–1791: The Original French, Latin, and Italian Texts, with English Translations.* (Toronto: Burrow Brothers, 1901).

26. Ibid., vol. 7, 5.

27. Besson, *La Syrie*, 107.

28. Père Fromage, "Lettre du Père Fromage . . . au Père Le Camus . . . le 30 Septembre, 1736." in *Actes des Apôtres modernes ou missions Catholiques*, vol. 1 (Paris: Parents Desbarres), 137. Not all European observers had such a sanguine notion of the people residing in Mount Lebanon. A year before Père Fromage wrote his letter, Monsieur De Grangé, inspector of the French consulates in the East, wrote a report to the minister of the navy describing the region. While allowing that Kisrawan is the refuge of all persecuted Catholics in the "East," he had less than salutary words for the Maronites. He noted for instance that "the Maronites are all Catholics, but most [of them] only in name. Generally you find them leaning toward vices and abominations, and on top of that they are ungrateful . . . all their religion is made up of fasting and some works." A little later in his report he mentions a visit to the same Qadisha valley toured by Père Petitqueux but without the spiritual panegyrics. Rather, he describes an illiterate Maronite patriarch receiving him to a very austere table, where they drank "good vinegar" and held a "mute conversation" for an hour. Ghalib, "Taqrir al-sayyid," 583–87.

29. David Scott, *Refashioning Futures: Criticism after Postcoloniality* (Princeton, N.J.: Princeton Univ. Press, 1999), 55.

30. C. John Sommerville, *The Secularization of Early Modern England: From Religious Cultures to Religious Faith* (New York: Oxford Univ. Press, 1992), 9.

31. In the context of early nineteenth-century America, evangelical preachers were arguing that western preachers were necessary not so much to convert Indians but to reclaim the savage settlers who, through contact with Indians and their lives in the western wilderness, had abandoned civilization. See James Buss, "The Winning of the West with Words: Clearing the Middle Ground for American Pioneers" (PhD diss., Purdue Univ., 2006), 64.

32. Besson, *La Syrie,* 107.

33. Ibid., 106.

34. In his article "Reclaiming the Land of the Bible: Missionaries, Secularism and Evangelical Modernity," *American Historical Review* 102, no. 3. (1997): 680–713, Ussama Makdisi eloquently explores a somewhat similar theme within the context of nineteenth-century Presbyterian missionaries in Lebanon.

35. Ambiguity about Islam predates the seventeenth century. For example, Bacon himself regarded Islam (or the "religion of the Saracens") as highly rational—and, thus,

admirable—and not so much antithetical to Christianity as a garbled form of it. See John Tolan, *Saracens: Islam in the Medieval European Imagination* (New York: Columbia Univ. Press, 2002), 226. Riccoldo da Montecroce, a Dominican missionary who set out to the Levant in 1288, wrote a series of letters about his impressions of the "Saracens." Of the 'ulama' of Baghdad, for example, he wrote, "I payed close attention to their law and their works; I was astounded at how, in such a perfidious law, one could find works of such great perfection." Riccoldo da Montecroce, *Libro della peregrinazione; Epistole alla Chiesa trionfante* (Genova: Marietti, 2005), 154–56.

36. Manilier to M. Vitelleschi (Aleppo, Jan. 20, 1635), in Rabbath, *Documents inédits,* vol. 2, 505–6.

37. Eugene Renaudot, "Dissertation sur les missions en Orient (Addressée au Cardinal Filippo Antonio Gualtiero, à Paris entre 1700 à 1706," in *Les échanges culturels entre les Maronites et L'Europe, vol. 2,* ed. Nasser Gemayel (Beirut: L'Imprimerie Y. & PH. Gemayel, 1984), 869.

38. Heghnar Zeitlian Watenpaugh remarks on a very similar division between Aleppo and its environs. In her superb article about the *majdhubs* (those enraptured by God) of Aleppo, she writes, "The hagiographies [of mystical Muslim saints] indicate a conceptual demarcation between the built environment and the wilderness, each endowed with opposite social meaning yet dependent on each other. The wilderness was the domain of the antinomian saint, while the built environment was the domain of conventional Islam." "Deviant Dervishes: Space, Gender, and the Construction of Antinomian Piety in Ottoman Aleppo," *International Journal of Middle East Studies* 37 (2005): 535–65.

39. ALO, "Dayr al-Luwazeh, Sijill al-Rahbana al-Lubnaniya," vol. 13, 29.

40. Jirmanus Farhat, *Diwan Jirmanus Farhat ma' ta'aliq 'aliyhi li-musahhihuhu Said al-Khuri al-Shartuni al-Lubnani* (Beirut: Al-matba'a al-kathulukiya, 1894), 131, 329.

41. Jirmanus Farhat, *Bulugh al-arab fi 'ilm al-adab* (Beirut: Dar al-Mashriq, 1990), 37.

42. Father Joseph Qazzi, *Bidayat al-Rahbaniyah al-Lubnaniya* (Beirut: Markaz al-Nashr wa al-Tawzi', 1988), 25.

43. There had been monks, nuns, monasteries, and convents in Mount Lebanon long before that. Dayr Mar 'Abda al-Mushammar, Dayr Mar Shallita, Dayr Mar Sarkis, and Dayr Mart Mora were among the various monasteries that had been established or renovated in Mount Lebanon by 1690. However, these were all independent institutions where monks and nuns (and sometimes both since they occupied the same buildings) loosely followed one rule or another. More critically, none was dedicated to learning, scholarship, or developing a normative Maronite theology, culture, or knowledge. Rather, their whole purpose was the introverted life of a hermit, seeking God by renouncing the world completely. In contrast, Hawwa, Tibn, and especially Qara'ali and Jirmanus Farhat (who joined them two years later) undertook to establish a new rule that would be rigorously followed, a proselytizing, expanding, and centrally organized monastic order of monks dedicated to learning and teaching.

44. Aghustin Zanadah, *al-Tarikh al-Lubnani, 1714–1728* (Rome: Archives of the Mariamite Order, ms. 29), f. 10.

45. ASCPF, CP Maroniti, vol. 118, f. 725, "Interrogation of Hindiyya," question 108.

46. ASCPF, SC Maroniti, vol. 7, 436, "Testimony of Sister Theresa, Assistant to the Prioress of Dayr Ziyarat al-'Adhra," Aug. 1753.

47. Ibid., 435.

48. Ibid.

49. ASCPF, CP Maroniti, vol. 118, f. 725, "Interrogation of Hindiyya," question 108.

50. AMPB, Hindiyya Papers, vol. 1, "Risalat al-Umm Hindiyya 'Ujaymi ila banat Qalb Yasu'," 14.

51. Ibid.

52. ASCPF, CP Maroniti, vol. 118, f. 725, "Interrogation of Hindiyya," question 108.

53. AMPB, Hindiyya Papers, vol. 1, "Risalat al-Umm Hindiyya al-'Ujaimi ila banat Qalb Yasu'," 9.

54. Ibid.

55. ASCPF, SC Maroniti, vol. 7, 429, Rosa Rosalia al-Khazin, Theresa Yamin, Louisa Clara Khazin, Reem Aneesa Khazin, Maryam Magdalene Kyork, "Copy of Conditions We Wrote for Our Sister Hindiyya When She Was with Us," Feb. 10, 1747.

56. ASCPF, SC Maroniti, vol. 7, 434, "Testimony of Sister Theresa, Assistant to the Prioress of Dayr Ziyarat al-Adhra," Aug. 1753.

57. Ibid., 430.

58. Ibid.

59. Archives of the Melkite Order, Dayr al-Shuwayr (*al-Sijill al-Shuwayri*), vol. 4, notebooknotebook VI, 103.

60. ASCPF, CP Maroniti, vol. 118, f. 725, "Interrogation of Hindiyya," question 109.

61. AMPB, Hindiyya Papers, vol. 1, "Risalat al-Umm Hindiyya al-'Ujaimi ila banat Qalb Yasu'," 13.

62. Ibid.

63. ASCPF, CP Maroniti, vol. 136, "Sirr al-Ittihad," 446.

64. AMPB, Hindiyya Papers, vol. 1, "Risalat al-Umm Hindiyya al-'Ujaimi ila banat Qalb Yasu'," 15.

65. Ibid., 13–14. This promise is similar to ones given by God to other visionaries, like Mechthild of Magdeburg, to whom he said, "If thou wouldst have all that mine is, thou must give me all that thine is." Quoted in Carol Lee Flinders, *Enduring Grace: Living Portraits of Seven Women Mystics* (San Francisco: Harper, 1993), 60.

66. Ibid., 13.

67. ASCPF, CP Maroniti, vol. 136, "Sirr al-Ithad," f. 446.

68. See, for example, Bynum, *Holy Feast and Holy Fast*, as well as her *The Resurrection of the Body in Western Christianity, 200–1336* (New York: Columbia Univ. Press, 1995).

69. Bynum, *Holy Feast and Holy Fast.*

70. Katharine R. Firth wrote that "many continental [Protestant] authors . . . believed in a future Golden Age which would see not only the perfection of religion but also the completion of knowledge." *The Apocalyptic Tradition in Reformation Britain* (Oxford: Oxford Univ. Press, 1978), 175. I am grateful to Zach Hutchins who brought this connection to my attention through his own work on the idea of the Garden of Eden in early American religious thought.

71. ASCPF, CP Maroniti, vol. 118, f. 725, "Interrogation of Hindiyya," question 109.

72. ASCPF, CP Maroniti, vol. 118, f. 95r "Relazione del'operato del P. Desiderio." Cited in Heyberger, *Hindiyya*, 103–4.

73. ASCPF, CP Maroniti, vol. 118, f. 725, "Interrogation of Hindiyya," question 109.

74. Ibid.

75. AMPB, Hindiyya Papers, "Risalat al-Umm Hindiyya al-'Ujaimi ila banat Qalb Yasu'," 15.

76. For a brief biography of al-Sima'ani and a list of his numerous publications, see Gemayel's *Les échanges culturels*, vol. 1, 420–41, 489–507.

77. Father Philip al-Samrani, "Dhukra Majida: Mi'ata sana marrat 'ala in'iqad al-majma' al-Lubnani," *Al-Manara* 7 (1977): 241.

78. AMPB, Yaqub 'Awwad Drawer. Document no. 49, Contract between Bishop Sharabiya and Bishop Muhasib.

79. Iliya Harik, *Politics and Change in a Traditional Society: Lebanon, 1711–1845* (Princeton, N.J.: Princeton Univ. Press, 1968), 69.

80. For an excellent study of the Lebanese Council, see Ghassan al-Ayyash, *Majma' al-Luwayzeh, 1736* (Beirut: al-markaz al-watani lil-ma'lumat wal-dirasat, 1991). Also see Richard van Leeuwen's superb summary of the prelude to the council and its events in his *Notables & Clergy*, 110–27. Pierre Dib's *Histoire des Maronites* (Beirut: Librairie Orientale, 2001), vol. 1, 176–93, includes a section on the council as well. Finally, see Butrus Daw's encyclopedic work *Tarikh al-mawarina* (Beirut, Lebanon: Dar al-Nahar, 1977).

81. See Sabine Mohasseb Saliba's *Les monastères Maronites doubles du Liban* (Paris: Librairie Orientaliste Paul Geuthner, 2008) for the most extensive and thorough study of these mixed monasteries.

82. Daw, *Tarikh al-mawarina*, 22.

83. Bulus Mas'ad and Nasib Wuhayba al-Khazin, Dhikra al-Majma' al-Lubnani," *Al-Manara* 7 (1936): 113.

84. Daw, *Tarikh al-mawarina*, 114.

85. Hattuni, *Nabdha Ttarikhiya fi al-muqata' al-Kisrawaniya* (Beirut: Dar Nazir Abbud, 1997), 152–55; Dib, *Histoire des Maronites*, 189–91.

86. Ioannes Dominicus Mansi, *Sacrorum Conciliorum nova et amplissima collectio.* Vol. 46, *Sinodi Melchitarum, 1716–1902* (Paris, 1911), column 283, no. 12, and columns 280, 310–20, 330, 419–25, 430.

87. Archives of the Melkite Order, Dayr al-Shuwayr (*al-Sijill al-Shuwayri*), vol. 1, notebook XXII, 364–65.

88. AMPB, Hindiyya Papers, vol. 1, "Risalat al-Umm Hindiyya al-'Ujaimi ila banat Qalb Yasu'," 15.

89. ASCPF, CP Maroniti, vol. 118, f. 725, "Interrogation of Hindiyya," question 109.

90. AMPB, Hindiyya Papers, vol. 1, "Risalat al-Umm Hindiyya al-'Ujaimi ila banat Qalb Yasu'," 15.

91. Ibid.

92. ASCPF, CP Maroniti, vol. 118, "Ristretto della Vita della Figlia Endia," f. 353r, 354v, 361r.

93. AMPB, Drawer of Yaqub 'Awwad. Document no. 63, Contract between Bishop Saqr and Bishop Muhasib.

94. ASCPF, CP Maroniti, vol. 118, f. 725, "Interrogation of Hindiyya," question 108.

95. Archives of the Melkite Order, Dayr al-Shuwayr (*al-Sijill al-Shuwayri*), Letter from Abdallah Zakher to Maria Qari and the *'abidat*, Aug. 26, 1730, vol. 1, notebook VII, 101.

96. ASCPF, CP Maroniti, vol. 118, f. 725, "Interrogation of Hindiyya," question 109

97. Despite later claims by the monks that they were forced to sell the Bkerki monastery, the Maronite patriarchate archives has a copy of the contract with the names and signatures of the superior general of the St. Isaiah order and his four deputies, agreeing to the "seven bags" on Mar. 1, 1750. AMPB, Hindiyya Papers, vol. 1, Contract Between Bishop Jirmanus [Saqr] and the Monks of Saint Isaiah.

98. AMPB, Hindiyya Papers, vol. 1, "Risalat al-Umm Hindiyya al-'Ujaimi ila banat Qalb Yasu'," 29

99. Ibid., 30.

100. For example, in the year 1175 the Flemish monk Guibert "wrote to the famed seer, Hildegard, with mingled curiosity and awe. Surely she had received 'rare gifts, till now practically unheard of throughout all ages; in prophecy she excelled Miriam, Deborah, and Judith; but let her recall that great trees are uprooted sooner than reeds, and let her keep herself humble.'" Barbara Newman, "Hildegard of Bingen: Visions and Validation," *Church History* 54, no. 2. (1985): 163.

101. Ibid.

102. ASCPF, CP Maroniti, vol. 136, "Sirr al-Ittihad," 446.

4. Bkerki Convent: A Living Saint (1750–1756)

1. At the bottom left part of the poster were the signatures of Father Suenesra and Father Tierramage and an affidavit testifying that they had examined and approved this "picture," which was composed by "Professor Liyachim."

2. The use of "Hindawiyyun" can also be construed as a dismissive label that distances her and her supporters from Christians and Christianity, in the same way that "Mohametan" was meant to place Muslims outside the rubric of monotheistic faith.

3. Quoted in Bulus al-Ghustawi, *al-Majali al-Tarikhiyya fi tarjamat hayat al-rahibah al-shahirah Hindiyya* (Beirut: Matba'at al-Tawfiq, 1910), 18.

4. ASCPF, SC Maroniti, vol. 6, 642.

5. ASCPF, CP Maroniti, vol. 113, "Report of Mikhail Fadel," 104–14.

6. Here, I am paraphrasing Frank Graziano's comment about the relationship between St. Rose and the Catholic community in Lima, Peru. See his *Wounds of Love: The Mystical Marriage of Saint Rose of Lima* (New York: Oxford Univ. Press, 2004), 7.

7. There were also tensions between the various missionary communities in Aleppo. In the early part of the seventeenth century, the Franciscans, who were the first missionaries in the Levant, deeply resented the implantation of Capuchin missionaries with the support of Louis XIII, the king of France. In one letter the Capuchins argued that "Since [the Franciscans] do not learn Oriental languages to be of service to the Christians of [this] country, they are jealous of the esteem with which everyone holds the Capuchins because of their good example, their zealousness and their learning." Gemayel *Les échanges culturels*, vol. 2, 716. When the Jesuits arrived in Aleppo, the tensions between all three missionary companies only got worse. For example, the French consul in Aleppo, Mr. d'Avrieux, wrote on June 19, 1680, to the French ambassador in Istanbul, Vicomte Guilleargues, complaining of the bitter rivalry. In a fatigued tone he wrote, "Sir, the disagreements that have broken out here between the Jesuit Fathers and the Fathers of the Holy Land, since the arrival of Reverend Father Nau [Jesuit] have exhausted me to the point that I am far beyond ill." Quoted in Heyberger, *Les chrétiens du Proche-Orient*, 247.

8. Hilaire de Barenton, *La France catholique en Orient* (Charleston, S.C.: Nabu Press, 2010), 155–56.

9. SOCG, 197, f.108v, Sylvestre de Saint-Aignan, May 22, 1651.

10. The Franciscan missionary Jean-Baptiste de Saint-Aignan, noted in 1669 that Latin missionaries are generally not able to preach and deliver sermons because of the "jealousy of the Oriental clergy." SC, FRANCIA, 3, f.114v, 1667. SOCG, 423, f.176r–195r, Jean-Baptiste de Saint-Aignan, Mar. 20 1669.

11. Quoted in Gemayel, *Les échanges culturels, vol. 2*, 732.

12. ARSI, gal. 96, "Mission Constantinopolis I Syriensis (1651–1770)," 595.

13. Ibid.

14. Ibid., 603.

15. Ibid., 601–16.

16. SOCG, 62, L103rv, 108r, Michel de Rennes, May 21, 1645, Sayda. SOCG, 423, f.176r–195r, Jean-Baptiste de Saint-Aignan, Mar. 20 1669. Quoted in Bernard Heyberger, *Les chrétiens du Proche-Orient*, 368.

17. This particular conflict generated over 100 pages of letters and counterletters to the Vatican. See SOCG, 578, f.179r–240r, Alep (1711), and for the missionary perspective see the account given by the Carmelite missionaries in Rabbath, *Documents inédits*, 44–50.

18. Letter from Shammas Theodore-Jean Qari to Abdallah Zakher, Archives of the Melkite Order, Dayr al-Shuwayr (*al-Sijill al-Shuwayri*), vol. 1, notebook VII, 96–97. For a more detailed study of the history of the *'abidat*, see Akram Khater, "God Has Called Me To Be Free: Latin Missionaries, Aleppan Nuns and the Transformation of Catholicism in 18th Century Bilad al-Sham," *International Journal of Middle East Studies* 40 (2008): 421–43.

19. These two were Sulayman Kusri and Jirjis al-Samman, and in 1710 they established the monastery of Dayr Yuhanna al-Shuwayr, which grew fairly quickly to include about twenty-five monks and priests by 1720 and whose financial fortunes grew as well. See Athanasiyus Hajj, *al-Rahbaniya al-Basiliya al-Shuwayriya (al-Halabiya-al-Baladiya) fi tarikh al-kanisa wal bilad* (Beirut: Matabi' al-Karim al-Hadithah, 1973), 88–97.

20. In comparison the income of the Melkite monastery in the village of Shuwayr amounted to 480 piasters in 1724 and double that in 1725. Purchasing a piece of land in Mount Lebanon could cost anywhere (depending on size and location obviously) from 15 piasters to a few hundred piasters. This makes the total sum of 5,000–6,000 piasters a rather sizeable outlay of capital.

21. See, for example, letters from the *'abidat* to Abdallah Zakher, Aug. 15, 1730, Archives of the Melkite Order, Dayr al-Shuwayr (*al-Sijill al-Shuwayri*), vol. 1, notebook VI, 96–97.

22. Ibid., 102.

23. Letter from Maria Qari, Sofia Shukri Qari, Nouria Jarbou', Zarife 'Ajjouri, and Helena 'Abdo to Father Nicolas Sayigh, Jan. 20, 1732, Archives of the Melkite Order, Dayr al-Shuwayr (*al-Sijill al-Shuwayri*), vol. 1, notebook VII, 111.

24. Letter from the *'abidat* to the Sacred Council for the Propagation of the Faith, Archives of the Melkite Order, Dayr al-Shuwayr (*al-Sijill al-Shuwayri*), vol. 1, notebook IV, 201–23.

25. Ibid., notebook XVI, 205–8.

26. Ibid., notebook XV, 203–4.

27. Ibid., notebook XVI, 117.

28. François de Sales, *Oeuvres de Saint François de Sales, évêque et prince de Genève et docteur de l'église,* vol. 25 (Annecy, France: Niérat, 1892–1932), 214.

29. Letter from Maria Qari to Bishop Athnasius, June 10, 1738. Archives of the Melkite Order, Dayr al-Shuwayr (*al-Sijill al-Shuwayri*), vol. 1, notebook XVII, 233.

30. Letter from Bishop Athnasius to Maria Qari, June 13, 1738. Ibid., notebook XVII, 234.

31. Letter from Bishop Athnasius to Maria Qari, Sept. 5, 1738. Ibid., notebook XVII, 245–46.

32. BO, manuscript 737 C4, 9.

33. Ibid., 84.

34. Ibid., f. 113.

35. Mansi, *Sacrorum Conciliorum*, col. 283, no. 12, and cols. 280, 310–20, 330, 419–25, and 430.

36. Archives of the Melkite Order, Dayr al-Shuwayr (*al-Sijill al-Shuwayri*), vol. 1, notebook XXII, 364–65.

37. As noted in chapter 3, Latin missionaries, mainly Jesuits, were involved in the tensions surrounding the Lebanese Synod of 1736, as well as the split of the Lebanese order into the Aleppan and Baladi factions. They were also deeply involved in the tensions that split the Syrian church into Orthodox and Catholic wings. Bernard Heyberger relates other episodes of conflict between missionaries and local prelates in his *Les chrétiens du Proche-Orient*, 445–49.

38. As an example of this wording, see the proclamation of the Catholic creed and faith by the Maronite patriarch Cyrillus in 1648. ASCPF, CP Maroniti, vol. 83, 332.

39. ASCPF, SC Maroniti, vol. 1, "Duwayhi to Cardinal Barberino, March 20, 1700," 267–68.

40. See, for example, Fausto (Murhij) *Naironi, Dissertatio de origine, nomine, ac religion Maronittarum* (Rome, 1679), quoted in Philip Khouri Hitti, *History of Syria: Including Lebanon and Palestine* (New York: Macmillan, 1951), 522.

41. See Butrus al-Gemayel's book *Zajaliyat Jibra'il ibn al-Qila'i* (Beirut: Dar Lahad Khater, 1982) for a published version of this poem in 240 quatrains.

42. Dib, *Histoires des Maronites,* 102.

43. Daw, *Tarikh al-mawarinah*, 282–85.

44. Simply put, Monophysites believed that Christ had only one nature (divine) as opposed to the official position proclaimed at the Council of Chalcedon (451), which held that Christ had both divine and human natures and two wills that coexisted without one obliterating the other. Monothelites, in comparison, held that while Christ had two natures, he had only one divine will.

45. Salibi, *House of Many Mansions,* 83.

46. For a discussion of Mardaites, Jarajima, and Maronites see Matti Moosa's "The Relation of the Maronites of Lebanon to the Mardaites and Al-Jarajima," *Speculum* 44, no. 4. (1969): 597–608.

47. ASCPF, CP Maroniti, vol. 113, "Report of Mikhail Fadel," 106.

48. AMPB, Hindiyya Papers, vol. 1, "Risalat al-Umm Hindiyya 'Ujaymi ila banat Qalb Yasu'," 16.

49. Craigh Harline, *The Burdens of Sister Margaret: Private Lives in a Seventeenth-Century Convent* (New York: Doubleday, 1994), xii.

50. Cited in M. O. Costa, "Spanish Women in the Reformation," in *Women in Reformation and Counter-Reformation Europe: Public and Private Worlds*, ed. S. Marshall (Bloomington: Indiana Univ. Press, 1989), 89–119.

51. Elizabeth Rapley, *The Dévotes: Women and Church in Seventeenth-Century France* (Montreal: McGill-Queen's Univ. Press, 1990), 30–33.

52. Cited in Kostroun, "A Formula for Disobedience," 484.

53. Mario Rosa, "Prospero Lambertini tra 'regolata devozione' e mistica visionaria," in *Finzione e santità tra medioevo ed età moderna,* ed. Gabriella Zarri (Turin, Italy: Rosenberg et Sellier, 1991), 521–50.

54. ASCPF, CP Maroniti, vol. 113, "Letter from Hindiyya al-'Ujaimi to Propaganda Fide," 17.

55. ASCPF, CP Maroniti, vol. 113, "Letter from Patriarch Butrus 'Awwad to Secretary of the Propaganda Fide," 26.

56. ASCPF, CP Maroniti, vol. 113, 103–14.

57. Ibid., 111.

58. Ibid., 112.

59. The inclusion of the testimony of two "doctors" (who, given the village locale, were more likely practitioners of folk medicine) in a petition sent to Rome was critical "since academic medicine [had] acquired [after the Middle Ages] an increasingly important role in [Vatican] sanctification trials, with learned doctors as expert witnesses." Catrien Santing, "Tirami sù: Pope Benedict XIV and the Beatification of the Flying Saint Giuseppe da Copertino," in *Medicine and Religion in Enlightenment Europe,* ed. Ole Peter Grell and Andrew Cunningham (Aldershot, U.K.: Ashgate, 2007), 86.

60. ASCPF, CP Maroniti, vol. 118, 422–23.

61. Ibid., 424.

62. Ibid., 425.

63. While this particular quote is from Père Fromage's speech during the first session of the 1736 Lebanese Synod, it is a language repeatedly used by missionaries and Maronites alike to describe the environs of Mount Lebanon and Aleppo. Yusuf Najm, *al-Majma' al-Lubnani* (Jounieh, Lebanon: Matba'at al-Arz), 39.

64. ASCPF, CP Maroniti, vol. 113, 17.

65. Ibid., 114.

66. For a study of the Catholic Church's anxiety about women's unbridled spirituality manifested in fear and persecution in seventeenth-century France, see Sarah Ferber's *Demonic Possession and Exorcism in Early Modern France* (London: Routledge, 2004). See also Moshe Sluhovsky's "The Devil in the Convent," *American Historical Review* 107, no. 5 (2002): 1379–1411. For a comparative look at the case of the eight beatas of Lima, in particular Santa Rosa, see Graziano, *Wounds of Love.*

67. AMPB, Hindiyya Papers, vol. 1, "Fi Dhikr ma qaluhu al-aba' al-yasu'iya dudd Mother Hindiyya and her confraternity."

68. ASCP, CP Maroniti, vol. 113, 203.

69. Ibid., 153.

70. Ibid., 154.

71. Ibid.

72. Bulus al-Ghustawi, *Tarikh al-Batriarch Yusuf al-Istifani wal Rahibah Hindiyya* (Beirut: Matba'at al-Tawfiq, 1909), 16.

73. ASCPF, CP Maroniti, vol. 113, 19–21.

74. Ibid., 20.

75. Ibid., 21.

76. Ibid., 22.

77. Heyberger, *Les chrétiens du Proche-Orient*, 114.

78. Santing, "Tirami sù," 79–100.

79. Ibid., 83.

80. It is important to note, however, that Benedict XIV was not without his own contradictions. As one of the prominent intellectuals of his period and a man of "science," he still presided over the beatification and canonization of a host of "what according to today's standards are weird and very physical saints, such as Camillo de Lellis, Catharina de' Rizzi and . . . Giuseppe da Copertino." Santing, "Tirami sù," 88.

81. ACPF, CP, vol. 6, "Letter of Maronite Bishops to Cardinals of Propaganda Fide," 818.

82. Ibid., 819.

83. Ibid.

84. ASCPF, SC, vol. 6, "Letter of Khazin Shuyukh to Cardinals of Propaganda Fide," 825.

85. ASCPF, SC, vol. 6, "Letter of Patriarch 'Awwad to Cardinals of Propaganda Fide," 825.

86. Heyberger, *Hindiyya*, 122.

87. ASCPF, CP Maroniti, vol. 118, "Report of Friar Desiderio di Casabasciana," 201.

88. Ibid., 214.

89. Ibid., 202.

90. Ibid., 203.

91. Ibid., 204.

92. Ibid., 205.

93. For example, Bynum notes that "At the core of Catherine's [of Siena] spirituality is suffering, that paradoxical suffering which for her, as for Hadewijch and Beatrice, is ultimate pain and the ecstasy beyond." *Holy Feast and Holy Fast*, 183.

94. Ibid., 207.

95. Ibid., 209.

96. Ibid., 211.

97. Ibid.

98. ASCPF, CP Maroniti, vol. 118, "Report of Friar Isidorios Mancini," 446.

99. Ibid., 438.

100. Ibid., 465.

101. Ibid., 462.

102. Ibid., 464.

103. Actually, Mancini was at least wrong in this regard. As J. Giles Milhaven notes in her article "A Medieval Lesson on Bodily Knowing," bodily knowledge of Christ leading to ecstasy and even orgasms was very well known in Europe in the thirteenth, fourteenth, and fifteenth centuries. She wrote, "[Medieval women] took their experience of Christ as supernatural. It was a miracle. But the miracle was that it was, analogously but truly, a physical eating of him, nursing him, making love with him." J. Giles Milhaven, "A Medieval Lesson on Bodily Knowing: Women's Experience and Men's Thought," Journal of the American Academy of Religion 57, no. 2 (1989): 349. And while Catherine of Siena did not express her union with Christ in exactly the same blunt terms as Hindiyya, her union was nonetheless equally physical. She quoted God as saying, "You saw and tasted the depth of the Trinity, wholly God, wholly human, hidden and veiled under that whiteness." Catherine of Siena, *The Dialogue,* trans. Suzanne Noffke (London: SPCK, 1980), 264. It hardly takes a leap of imagination to understand the insinuation. For a more explicit exploration of the relationship between religion and sexuality, see Richard Rambuss's *Closet Devotions* (Durham, N.C.: Duke Univ. Press, 1998).

104. ASCPF, CP Maroniti, vol. 118, Report of Friar Isidorios Mancini, p. 445.

105. Ibid.

106. Ibid., 449.

107. In particular, see chapter 2, "Mystics, Martyrs and Honorary Males."

108. Heinrich Kramer and Jakobus Sprenger, *Malleus maleficarum,* trans. Montague Sommers (London: John Rodker, 1928), 41.

109. Bynum, "Fast, Feast, and Flesh," 14.

110. Susan Bordo, "The Cartesian Masculinization of Thought," *Signs* 11, no. 3 (1986): 443.

111. Sandra Harding, "Is Gender a Variable in Conceptions of Rationality?" Paper delivered at the Fifth International Colloquium on Rationality, Vienna, 1981.

112. Karl Stern, *The Flight from Woman* (New York: Noonday Press, 1965), 104.

113. Anthony LaVopa, "Manly Thoughts: The Labor of the Mind and the Specter of Effeminacy in Enlightenment Cultures," unpublished manuscript, chap. 3, author draft generously shared, Sept. 2009.

114. ASCPF, CP Maroniti, vol. 118, "Letter of Pope Benedict XIV to Patriarch 'Awwad, March 14, 1754," 27–29.

115. ASCPF, CP Maroniti, vol. 118, "Letter of Propaganda Fide to Patriarch 'Awwad, December 25, 1755," 561–63.

116. ASCPF, CP Maroniti, vol. 136, "Sirr al-Ittihad," 437–38.

117. Ibid., 437.

118. ASCPF, CP Maroniti, vol. 118, 602–3.

119. Heyberger, *Hindiyya,* 175.

120. Ghustawi, *Al-Majali al-Tarikhiya,* 149.

121. Lambertini Doctrina de Servorum Dei Beatificatione et Beatorum . . . , 432. Quoted in Santing, "Tirami sù," 99.

122. Heyberger, *Hindiyya,* 179.

5. Purgatory: Angels and Demons in the Convent (1756–1778)

1. ASCPF, CP Maroniti, vol. 136, 343, "Interrogation of Hindiyya," June 22, 1778, question 3.

2. Volney, *Travels,* 311–13.

3. The term *Jabaliyyat* refers to nuns and monks who were born and raised in Mount Lebanon as well as Beirut. In contrast, *Halabiyyat* was the term used to identify nuns originating from Aleppo.

4. ASCPF, CP Maroniti, vol. 136, "Letter of Sim'an al-Sima'ani, November 26, 1777," 132–46.

5. ASCPF, Fondo CP Maroniti, vol. 135, Mar. 22, 1777, 8.

6. Harline, *Burdens of Sister Margaret,* xiii. Also see Margaret Chowning, *Rebellious Nuns: The Troubled History of a Mexican Convent, 1752–1863* (New York: Oxford Univ. Press, 2006), for another study which focuses on tensions between nuns over attempts to create a "modern" convent in Mexico with austere interpretations of poverty and enclosure. A more personal narrative of life in the convent is Arcangela Tarabotti's *L'Inferno monacale (The Convent as Hell),* in which she reflects on the strangulating pettiness and stultifying routines of life. Francesca Medioli, *L'Inferno monacale di Arcangela Tarabotti* (Torino, Italy: Rosenberg & Sellier, 1989).

7. AMPB, Hindiyya Papers, vol. 2, "Report from Istifanus al-Qubrsi to Patriarch Istifan 'Awwad, 1 January, 1752."

8. The cardinals who were appointed to this committee were Giuseppe Castelli, who was prefect of the Propaganda Fide; Leonardo Antonelli; Antonio Visconti; Giovanni Boschi; Pietro Pamphili; and Stefano Borgia, who was secretary of the Propaganda Fide.

9. ASCPF, Fondo CP Maroniti, vol. 136, 1–12.

10. The raucous comings and goings in Bkerki echo similar transgressions of the Tridentine conventual ideal by other convents and abbesses in Mexico (Chowning, *Rebellious Nuns*) and France (Mita Choudhury, "Despotic Habits: The Critique of Power and Its Abuses in an Eighteenth-Century Convent," *French Historical Studies* 23, no. 1 (2000): 34–65.

11. AMPB, Drawer of Yusuf Istifan, part II. "Circular of Yusuf Istifan, 26 July, 1777."

12. AMPB, Hindiyya's Papers, vol. 3, "Affidavit of Sister Domitilla the Damascene, 11 July, 1777."

13. These testimonies come from two sources. The first is ASCPF, CP Maroniti, vol. 136, 90–98 and 647–50. In addition, copies of the testimonies of the nuns and monks involved in this murderous scandal were kept in the archives of the Maronite patriarchate. AMPB, Drawer of Yusuf Istifan, part I.

14. ASCPF, Fondo CP Maroniti, vol. 136, 445–46.

15. Ibid., 442.

16. This hesitation was duplicated in the case of Sultane Marjam Danil Ghattas (Mother Marie-Alphonsine, 1843–1927), who was a nun in the Sisters of Saint Joseph convent in Jerusalem and who received repeated visions of Mary in which the Virgin asked her to establish a Congregation of the Rosary. At one point, an exasperated-sounding Mary asked, "When are you going to begin the Congregation of the Rosary? Carry out my instructions. Do you not understand what I want?" Willy Jansen, "Visions of Mary in the Middle East: Gender and the Power of a Symbol," in *Gender, Religion and Change in the Middle East,* ed. Inger Marie Okkenhaug and Ingvild Flaskerudm (Oxford: Berg), 138.

17. Ibid., 441–42.

18. Ibid., 343, question 12.

19. Ibid., questions 11 and 12.

20. Jantzen, *Power, Gender,* 164.

21. ASCPF, Fondo CP Maroniti, vol. 136, 441.

22. Ibid., 440.

23. Ibid., 437–38.

24. Ibid., 436.

25. Ibid., 435.

26. Ibid., 433.

27. Ibid.

28. Jantzen, *Power, Gender,* 133.

29. ASCPF, Fondo CP Maroniti, vol. 136, 440.

30. ASCPF, Fondo CP Maroniti, vol. 136, 430.

31. Ibid., 429.

32. AMPB, Hindiyya Papers, vol. 1, "Narrative of Hindiyya's *Secret of the Union,*" 1.

33. ASCPF, Fondo CP Maroniti, vol. 136, 438.

34. AMPB, Hindiyya Papers, vol. 1, "Narrative of Hindiyya's *Secret of the Union,*" 3.

35. In Arabic this term implies physical intimacy and even intercourse. For an excellent discussion of the double entendre inherent in this phrase, see Sahar Amer's "Cross-Dressing and Female Same-Sex Marriage in Medieval French and Arabic Literatures," in *Islamicate Sexualities: Translations Across Temporal Geographies of Desire,* Harvard Middle Eastern Monographs, ed. Kathryn Babayan and Afsaneh Najmabadi (Cambridge, MA: Harvard Center for Middle Eastern Studies, 2008), 72–113.

36. ASCPF, Fondo CP Maroniti, vol. 136, 428. The alternation between calling Hindiyya his consort and his daughter is intriguing.

37. This erotic encounter with Christ is hardly unique or limited to women. For a look at an overview of the history of such physical displays of love, see Bernard McGinn's "The Language of Love in Christian and Jewish Mysticism," in *Mysticism and Language,* ed. Steven Katz (New York: Oxford Univ. Press, 1992), 202–35. In one particularly notable scene, McGinn recounts a vision of Rupert of Deutz (c. 1075–1129) in which he

encountered Christ: "I took hold of him whom my soul loved. I held him. I embraced him, I kissed him for a long time . . . in the midst of the kiss he opened his mouth so that I could kiss more deeply" (203).

38. ASCPF, Fondo CP Maroniti, vol. 136, 427.

39. Ibid., 441.

40. Ibid., 426.

41. Ibid., 425.

42. This date is somewhat problematic as it is contradicted by the testimony of Bishop Jirmanus Diyab, who put the year of the union as 1755.

43. AMPB, Hindiyya Papers, vol. 1, "Narrative of Hindiyya's *Secret of the Union*," 4–5.

44. She is not unique in her reaction. The beguine mystic Hadewijch recounted a vision at matins in this manner: "My heart and my veins and all my limbs trembled and quivered with eager desire and, as often occurred with me, such madness and fear beset my mind that it seemed to me I did not content my Beloved, and that my Beloved did not fulfill my desire, so that dying I must go mad, and going mad I must die." Hadewijch, *The Complete Works,* trans. Mother Columbia (New York: Paulist Press, 1980), 280–82.

45. AMPB, Hindiyya Papers, vol. 1, "Sirat Hayat al-Umm al-Batoul Hindiyya," 15. Also, "Risalat al-Umm Hindiyya al-'Ujaimi ila banat Qalb Yasu'," 14.

46. ASCPF, Fondo CP Maroniti, vol. 136, 423.

47. Bynum, *Holy Feast and Holy Fast*, 165.

48. Ibid., 67.

49. Aquinas, *Basic Writings,* 84–86. Quoted in Milhaven, "A Medieval Lesson," 18

50. Thomas Aquinas, *Summa Contra Gentiles* (Neapolis, Greece: Typographia Ursiniana, 1773), 125.

51. Catherine of Siena, *Saint Catherine of Siena,* ed. and trans. Vida D. Scudder (London: J. M. Dent & Co., 1906), 295.

52. Dror Ze'evi, "Hiding Sexuality: The Disappearance of Sexual Discourse in the Late Ottoman Middle East," *Social Analysis* 49, no. 2 (2005): 37–40.

53. Amer, "Cross-Dressing," 72–113.

54. Ze'evi, "Hiding Sexuality," 42.

55. Khaled el-Rouayheb, *Before Homosexuality in the Arab-Islamic World, 1500–1800* (Chicago: Univ. of Chicago Press, 2005). See also Stephen O. Murray and Will Roscoe, eds. *Islamic Homosexualities: Culture, History and Literature.* (New York: New York Univ. Press, 1997). Heghnar Zeitlian Watenpaugh records similar homoerotic tendencies in the dervish antinomian community in seventeenth-century Aleppo. Watenpaugh, "Deviant Dervishes," 544.

56. Ze'evi, "Hiding Sexuality," 41.

57. Elyse Semerdjian, "Sinful Professions: Illegal Occupations of Women in Ottoman Aleppo, Syria," *Hawwa* 1, no. 1 (2003): 68–72.

58. Russell, *Natural History of Aleppo,* 84.

59. Margaret Malamud, "Gender and Spiritual Self-Fashioning: The Master–Disciple Relationship in Classical Sufism," *Journal of the American Academy of Religion* 64, no. 1 (1996): 89–117.

60. AMPB, Drawer of Yusuf Istifan, Part 2, "Affidavit of Bishop Jirmānūs Diyab," July 20, 1768.

61. AMPB, Hindiyya Papers, vol. 1, "Risalat al-Umm Hindiyya al-'Ujaimi ila banat Qalb Yasu'," 13.

62. Ibid., 17.

63. AALOR, manuscript 237, "Rule of the Order of the Sacred Heart of Jesus," 1–4.

64. Gemayel, *Les échanges culturels,* vol. 1, 96–137.

65. Patriarch Tubiya al-Khazin, with the advice of Father Mikhail Fadel, sought to allow for fifteen dioceses "temporarily" instead of the eight agreed upon at the 1736 Lebanese Council in order to elevate some of his supporters to the position of bishop. One of those was Mikhail Fadel, who desired to oversee the diocese of Beirut, which Yusuf Istifan had taken over from his uncle. These tensions exploded into a series of polemics exchanged between Istifan and Fadel. One of these was an exhaustive missive numbering fifty-six pages and titled "Letter of Objection," in which then bishop Yusuf Istifan used an extensive array of theological and historical sources to defend himself against Patriarch al-Khazin and Fadel. AMPB, Drawer of Yusuf Istifan, Part 1.

66. Bulus Abboud al-Ghustawi, Basa'ir al-Zama fi Tarikh al-calama Yusuf Istifan (Beirut: Sabra Press, 1911), 4.

67. In response to his opposition, the patriarch issued a circular excommunicating Yusuf Istifan for "resisting our authority and annulment of our Patriarchal authority . . . for establishing a convent without our permission . . . for his complaint against us to secular authorities . . . for prohibiting us from visiting his dioceses and collecting the tithe . . . and for his support to those whom we had excommunicated." His letters to the pope and to the Propaganda Fide in 1764 reiterated the same complaints while seeking the support of the Vatican for his actions. ASCPF, SC Maroniti, vol. 8, 66, 79, and 211.

68. AMPB, Drawer of Yusuf Istifan, Part 2, "Letter of Patriarch Yusuf Istifan to his Maronite Millet," June 9, 1768, 5.

69. Ibid.

70. AMPB, Hindiyya Papers, vol. 2, "Letter from Patriarch Yusuf Istifan to the people of Bayt Shabab," Jan. 4, 1771.

71. Heyberger, *Hindiyya,* 188.

72. Richard van-Leeuwen, "Monastic Estates and Agricultural Transformation in Mount Lebanon in the 18th Century," *International Journal of Middle East Studies* 23, no. 4 (1991): 601–17.

73. Najm, *al-Majma' al-Lubnani,* 366.

74. AMPB, Drawer of Yusuf Istifan, Part 1, "Letter of Objection," 13.

75. AMPB, Hindiyya Papers, vol. 2, "Letter from Patriarch Yusuf Istifan to Hindiyya."

76. AMPB, Hindiyya Papers, vol. 2, "Letter from Arsenious Shukri, Bishop of Aleppo, to Sister of Father Arsenious 'abd al-Ahad," Sept. 15, 1768.

77. AMPB, Hindiyya Papers, vol. 2, "Letter from Father Ross to Hindiyya," Dec. 28, 1769.

78. In the 1720s plague raged through Marseilles, Toulon, and the inland cities of Provence. In order to beat back the miasma of death, the bishop of Marseilles, Henri François Xavier de Belsunce de Castelmoron, undertook public acts of penance and dedicated the city to the Sacred Heart of Jesus. Raymond Anthony Jonas, *France and the Cult of the Sacred Heart: An Epic Tale for Modern Times* (Berkeley: Univ. of California Press, 2000), 34–53.

79. ASCPF, SC Maroniti, vol. 8, "Letter from Cardinal Corsini to Mother Hindiyya al-'Ujaimi," Aug. 17, 1768, 431.

80. AMPB, Hindiyya Papers, vol. 1, "Sirat Hayat al-Umm al-Batoul Hindiyya," 49.

81. AMPB, al-Rahibah Hindiyya, Part 3. "Last Will of Bishop Gregorious Shukrallah," Sept. 14, 1769. Saman is clarified butter.

82. Bernard Heyberger notes that Sa'ad al-Khuri—who became one of Hindiyya's chief opponents—turned against the visionary after her prayers and intercessions failed to cure the blindness of his daughter, Salha. Hindiyya added insult to injury by proclaiming that Salha was not cured because she lacked faith. Heyberger, *Hindiyya*, 192. See Niqula al-'Ujaimi's letter to that effect in ASCPF, CP Maroniti, vol. 136, 192r. For an example of the donation received by Hindiyya, see AMPB, Hindiyya Papers, vol. 1, "Sirat hayat al-umm al-batoul Hindiyya," 48.

83. Ghustawi, *al-Majali al-Tarikhiya*, 310 and 202.

84. Louis Bulaybil, *Tarikh al-Rahbaniya al-Lubnaniya al-Maruniya* (Cairo, Egypt: Matba'at Yusuf Kawa', 1924), 268–69.

85. The collection of the tithe was a central issue in the antagonism between the patriarch and a group of dissident bishops. The 2,500 piasters figure was imposed by the Vatican as a way to resolve the tensions between the two groups. AMPB, Drawer of Yusuf Istifan, Part 2, Yusuf Istifan's letter accepting the 1773 "Seven Orders" of the Vatican, Dec. 15, 1778.

86. Ghustawi, *al-Majali al-Tarikhiyya*, 159.

87. ASCPF, SOCG, vol. 832, "Petition of Arsenious Diyab to Propaganda Fide," Oct. 10, 1770.

88. AMPB, Drawer of Yusuf Istifan, Part 1, "Letter from Patriarch Yusuf Istifan to the Maronite Millet," Sept. 25, 1769.

89. ASCPF, SC Maroniti, vol. 9, "Letter of Sister Margerita Diyab to Cardinal Castelli," May 22, 1773, 38.

90. ASCPF, SOCG, vol. 832, "Report of Propaganda Fide," Sept. 16, 1771.

91. ASCPF, SC Maroniti, vol. 8, "Letter of Pope Clement XIII to Patriarch Yusuf Istifan," Aug. 22, 1767, 112.

92. After the Lebanese Council of 1736, this was arguably the most important synod of the Maronite Church taking place in the most pivotal century in its modern life. In numbers, eight councils were convened in the eighteenth century out of a total of twelve councils which took place between the first one in 1580 and the last in 1856, making that century, in the words of one historian, the "era of reform." Harik, *Politics and Change*, 97.

93. AMPB, Drawer of Yusuf Istifan, Part 2, "Khulasat al-Majma' al-Tai'ifi," Sept. 16, 1768.

94. Ibid., second session, Sept. 17, 1768, article 10.

95. Another element of this was the growing economic independence of the various arms of the church, most notably the Lebanese order, in inverse correlation to the weakening financial grip of *muqata'aji* families, like the Khazins, over church affairs. For a detailed discussion of the process across the eighteenth century, see van Leeuwen's *Notables & Clergy.*

96. ASCPF, SC Maroniti, vol. 8, "Letter of Pope Clement XIII to Patriarch Yusuf Istifan," Aug. 22, 1767, 344.

97. AMPB, Drawer of Yusuf Istifan, Part 2, "Patriarch's Response to the Complaints of Dissident Bishops," 2, n.d.

98. AMPB, Drawer of Yusuf Istifan, Part 2, "Bishop Mikhail Fadel Treatise on the Breadth of the Authority of the Patriarch," Aug. 4, 1769. It is also noteworthy that soon after his ascension to the patriarchal see, Yusuf Istifan wrote several letters seeking the protection and financial support of the king of France. These letters included the usual fare about the persecution of Maronites by Muslims (in this case it was centered in the mixed cities of Aleppo and Tripoli), which exacerbated the poverty of the church. Thus, the letters pleaded that the "bowels of his royal highness would be moved to take pity on us" and provide protection and funds without which Maronites could not continue to live enslaved to the infidels. However, what is pertinently novel in this litany is that it reflects Yusuf Istifan's search for a Catholic protection independent of the Vatican, even in opposition to the Holy See.

99. Bulus 'Abbud al-Ghustawi, *Al-Majali al-Tarikhiyya fi tarjamat hayat al-rahibah al-shahirah Hindiyya* (Beirut: Matba'at al-Tawfiq, 1910), 234.

100. Some contemporary opponents (chief among them Bishop Fadel) suggested he only did so because he was either beholden to Hindiyya, who—they opined without evidence—spent money to elect him, or besotted by her visionary charm. Whatever their merit may be—and both arguments seem to be merely speculative—his copious treatises and encyclicals (many written long before he became patriarch) suggest a theologian whose erudition was employed to implement his vision of greater independence for the Maronites.

101. ASCPF, CP Maroniti, vol. 136, 343, "Interrogation of Hindiyya," June 22, 1778, question 29.

102. In 1784 di Moretta wrote a report to Rome about the progress, or lack thereof, of his second mission to the Maronites. The Maronite priest he had previously chosen as secretary before departing Rome, Yusuf al-Tayyan, returned from Mount Lebanon with letters from practically every secular and religious notable explicitly rejecting Rome's chastisement and implicitly di Moretta's apostolic visit. Al-Tayyan was carrying those letters to Rome at the behest of their Maronite authors, and di Moretta could not dissuade him from his errand. Thus, di Moretta wrote in his report, "This alone suffices to give the Propaganda Fide an idea of who the Easterners are. This young man educated from childhood in Rome and enjoying the patronage of your Excellency . . . had barely arrived in the East when he quickly changed and now he dares to travel back to you without any sense of shame. I am certain that he [Tayyan] will apologize saying that it was the muddabir [Sacad al Khuri] who forced him to do so, but I—who know this country—know that this is a false excuse." Rather, di Moretta added, it is the untrustworthy nature of "easterners" which is to blame. This sequence of events was corroborated by Patriarch Istifan's narrative (AMPB, Drawer of Yusuf Istifan, Part 2, "al-Riwayya al-haqiqiyya fi sultat batriark al-ta'ifa al-maruniyya [*The True Narrative Regarding the Authority of the Patriarch of the Maronite Sect*]) and the reports of Pietro di Moretta (ASCPF, CP Maroniti, vol. 135, "Pietro di Moretta Report," Apr. 18, 1775.) Heyberger, *Hindiyya*, 239.

103. ASCPF, CP Maroniti, vol. 135, "Pietro di Moretta Report," Apr. 18, 1775, 87.

104. Quoted in Ghustawi, *Basa'ir al-Zama*, 53.

105. ASCPF, CP Maroniti, vol. 135, "Pietro di Moretta Report," Apr. 18, 1775, 88.

106. AMPB, Hindiyya Papers, vol. 3, "Niqula al-'Ujaimi's Affidavit," Jan. 22, 1773.

107. AMPB, Drawer of Yusuf Istifan, Part 2, "Letter from Niqula al-'Ujaimi," June 28, 1773.

108. ASCPF, CP Maroniti, vol. 135, "Pietro di Moretta Interrogation of Niqula al-'Ujaimi," July 11, 1775, 159.

109. AMPB, Hindiyya Papers, vol. 1, "Sirat hayat al-Umm al-Batoul Hindiyya," 59–60.

110. AMPB, Hindiyya Papers, vol. 3, "List of Coded Terms," n.d.

111. It is not clear how the concept of Freemasonry would have made its way into the discourse of the time. Most likely it was through someone familiar with either the 1738 papal bull by Clement XII, titled "In Eminenti Apostolatus Specula," which condemned Freemasons as evildoers, or the 1751 apostolic constitution "Providas Romanorum," issued by Pope Benedict XIV, which affirmed the previous bull and prohibited any Catholics from joining Freemasonry. AMPB, Hindiyya Papers, vol. 3, "Testimonies of Nassimeh and Wardeh," n.d., "Testimony of Wardeh," n.d.

112. AMPB, Hindiyya Papers, vol. 2, "Things We Learned from Our Blessed Mother," Feb. 1769.

113. ASCPF, CP Maroniti, vol. 136, "Testimony of Khuduc Daughter of Hanna Qaythani, the Aleppan," June 10, 1777, 767.

114. AMPB, Hindiyya Papers, vol. 3, "Testimony of Maryam Daughter of Hanna al-Fattal the Aleppan," May 9, 1777.

115. Francesca related that when she was sick one day, Wardeh approached with a drink "that had a white powder and a piece of paper in it. She told me that the paper is that of the Virgin Mary and the white powder the bones of saints." After drinking the concoction, she felt infatuated with love for Nassimeh, Wardeh, and Niqula al-'Ujaimi. AMPB, Hindiyya Papers, vol. 3, "Testimony of Clara," n.d.; "Testimony of Francesca bint Touma the Aleppan," June 15, 1777. ASCPF, CP Maroniti, vol. 136, "Testimony of Domitillia," Feb., 20, 1777, 548.

116. ASCPF, CP Maroniti, vol. 136, "Testimony of Domitillia, February, 20, 1777, 548.

117. AMPB, Hindiyya Papers, vol. 3, "Testimony of Nassimeh Badran," n.d., "Testimony of Segunda bint Abu Antoun Ghadir," June 29, 1777; "Testimony of Maryam bint Hanna al-Fattal the Aleppan," May 9, 1777. ASCPF, CP Maroniti, vol. 136, "Testimony of Maryam al-Fattal," June 4, 1777, 767.

118. This anxiety (and rejection of coexistence—the norm in the Ottoman world of the eighteenth century) was also manifest when the Maronite Church faced another threat to its stability and control in the nineteenth century. In that latter period it was Presbyterian missionaries who challenged the hegemony of Bkerki over local Christians. See Makdisi, *Artillery of Heaven.*

119. AALOR, manuscript 237, "Rule of the Order of the Sacred Heart of Jesus," June 1, 1759.

120. ASCPF, CP Maroniti, vol. 136, "Testimony of Philippia," June 10, 1777, 502.

121. ASCPF, CP Maroniti, vol. 136, "Testimony of Khudu'," June 10, 1777, 767.

122. AMPB, Hindiyya Papers, vol. 3, "Testimony of Maryam bint Hanna al-Fattal the Aleppan," May 9, 1777.

123. Hindiyya's opponent provided equally elaborate tales of her depravity. Thus, she was reported to walk around with her hair loose and makeup adorning her face; her body was draped with silks and fine clothes, and she was fanned as she ate her gastronomical delights; she hardly, if ever, attended mass or observed religious restrictions; she fornicated with Patriarch Istifan, Bishop Diyab, and Sister Katerina, among others, and had a son living in India, where she magically went every night on the back of a mule—reminiscent of the Prophet Muhammad's Buraq.

124. ASCPF, CP Maroniti, vol. 136, "Interrogation of Hindiyya," June 22, 1778, question 24, 343.

125. ASCPF, CP Maroniti, vol. 136, "Letter from Father Sim'an al-Sima'ani to Cardinal Borgia," 132–46.

126. The equation of monastic life with sexual misdeeds, insatiability, and ultimately demonic possession was not unique to this case. In "The Devil in the Convent," Moshe

Sluhovsky details how sexuality figured prominently within the life of the convent as either a symbol or a cause of demonic possession. Sluhovksy, "The Devil in the Convent," 1396–99. In the case of Hindiyya's convents, we do not have any conclusive evidence as to what really took place in terms of sexual affairs and transgressions.

127. AALOR, manuscript 111, "Description of Hell," 202–321.

128. Charles Henry Churchill, *Mount Lebanon. A Ten Years' Residence from 1842 to 1852*, vol. 1 (London: Saunders & Otley, 1853), 67–68. Early modern Europeans were equally comfortable with the idea of demonic possession. Stuart Clark's massive study of the subject attests to the fact that demoniacs were part of the social reality in Germany, France, and England—among other places—and that what we would construe as fantastical performance attributable to mental illness was regarded as commonplace behavior brought about by evil spirits overwhelming and animating the body of the possessed. Stuart Clark, *Thinking with Demons: The Idea of Witchcraft in Early Modern Europe* (New York: Oxford Univ. Press, 1999), 389–434.

129. Clark, *Thinking with Demons*, 393.

130. AMPB, Hindiyya Papers, vol. 3, "Patriarch Yusuf Istifan's Edict on Dissident Nuns," May 11, 1777. Bulus al-Ghustawi dates the edict of the patriarch to May 17 in his *Al-Majali al-Tarikhiyya*, but that seems to be erroneous in light of the patriarch's dated edict.

131. It is likely that he consulted with her because in 1773 he wrote to Hindiyya about the papal legate Valeriano di Pratto, asking if "we should convene a council of the bishops or not? Shall we convene in it Harissa or at our location? Shall we take on our enemies one by one or together?" AMPB, Hindiyya Papers, vol. 2, "Letter from Patriarch Istifan to Hindiyya," Aug. 30, 1773.

132. As Makdisi observes in *Artillery of Heaven, 127*, beating was a typical course of exorcism to drive out the devil from the body and mind of the afflicted. Solitary confinement was also a cure prescribed by Maronite monks. See also Eugene Rogan, "Madness and Marginality: The Advent of the Psychiatric Asylum in Egypt and Lebanon," in *Outside In: On the Margins of the Modern Middle East,* ed. Eugene Rogan (London: I.B. Tauris, 2002), 110.

6. Epilogue: Hindiyya, Alone and Everywhere (1778–1800s)

1. AMPB, Hindiyya Papers, vol. 2, "Iqrar Hindiyya aww Hanneh 'Ujaimi" ("Confession of Hindiyya or Hanneh 'Ujaimi, Who Was Previously a Nun and Abbess in the Convent of Bkerki"), Mar. 5–6, 1783.

2. ASCPF, CP Maroniti, vol. 136, Letter from Father Sim'an al-Sima'ani to Cardinal Borgia," 132–46.

3. ASCPF, CP Maroniti, vol. 136, "Pietro di Moretta's Interrogation of Hindiyya al-'Ujaimi," June 22, 1778, 343–87.

4. ASCPF, CP Maroniti, vol. 136, "Report of the Propaganda Fide on the Hindiyya Affair," 1. Reprinted in Ghustawi, *Al-Majali al-Tarikhiyya*, 286–308.

5. Najm, *al-Majma' al-Lubnani*, 1–23, 459–514.

6. For example, see Brian Spooner, "The Evil Eye in the Middle East," in *Witchcraft Confessions and Accusations*, ed. Mary Douglas (London: Routledge, 2004), 311–20. Witchcraft appears to have been so commonplace that even some Maronite priests were accused of practicing it. For instance, Patriarch Yusuf Istifan recounted the arrest, punishment, and incarceration of Father Yunan and his companion, 'Abd al-Ahad, for possessing a book of magic. Ghustawi, *Basa'ir al-Zaman*, 98.

7. Abraham Marcus comments on this in his book on eighteenth-century Aleppo. He writes, "Education, for instance, cannot be understood just in terms of formal learning when much of what people knew and believed came neither from books nor from classroom instruction. Nor can the richness and diversity of the cultural scene be fully appreciated without attention to the important role of superstition, magic. . . ." Marcus, *The Middle East*, 220.

8. ASCPF, CP Maroniti, vol. 136, "Report of the Propaganda Fide on the Hindiyya Affair," 1. Reprinted in Ghustawi, *Al-Majali al-Tarikhiyya*, 289.

9. Ibid., 294–96.

10. Ibid., 299–301.

11. For examples of this genre, see Jean Chardin, *Journal du Voiage du Chevalier Chardin en Perse et aux Indes Orientales* (Amsterdam: Jean Wolters & Ysbrand Harring, 1686); Jean-Baptiste Tavernier, *Les six voyages de Monsieur Jean-Baptiste Tavernier, ecuyer baron d'Aubonne, en Turque, en Perse, et aux Indes* (Rouen: Machuel, 1712); Charles Louis, Baron de Montesquieu, *The Persian Letters* (London: Atheneum Publishing, 1901)—first published in 1721 in French. Another trope in this Orientalist characterization is found in the feminization of Maronite Christianity and Christians. For instance, while visiting the bedridden Patriarch Yusuf Istifan, Pietro di Moretta inquired of the cause of the illness. When the patriarch explained that all his joints were aching, the papal legate responded that "in my country this is a woman's not a man's disease." This medical machismo was clearly meant to make the patriarch appear as effeminate and, thus, inferior to the Western male. ASCPF, CP Maroniti, vol. 138, "Letter of Patriarch Yusuf Istifan to Cardinal Antonelli," Oct. 19, 1780, 290–96.

12. By the early part of the eighteenth century the "Turks" had come to be seen in European texts as "boorish, ignorant, dishonorable, immoral, ineffectual, corrupt and irrational." See Zachary Lockman's *Contending Visions of the Middle East: The History and Politics of Orientalism* (New York: Cambridge Univ. Press, 2004), 45–47.

13. ASCPF, CP Maroniti, vol. 138, 391–93. See also, for example, Pope Pius VI's letter of reinstatement of Yusuf Istifan to his full patriarchal authority, which praised the Maronite community for shunning "the delusions of the woman Hindiyya and her false visions and teachings." ASCPF, CP Maroniti, vol. 142, "Letter of Pope Pius VI to the Maronite Clergy and Their People," Sept. 28, 1784, 131. Also quoted in Ghustawi, *Basa'ir al-Zaman*, 205.

14. ASCPF, CP Maroniti, vol. 136, "Report of the Propaganda Fide on the Hindiyya Affair," 302.

15. ASCPF, SC Maroniti, vol. 10, "Apostolica Sollicitudo," July 17, 1779, 592–97.

16. Cardinal Antonelli noted that "Father Pietro di Moretta has written to us that Hindiyya has been incarcerated . . . and that her fame has been extinguished to the point that no one mentions her without contempt and scorn." ASCPF, CP Maroniti, vol. 138, Congregation of Sept. 18, 1781, 3–68.

17. Ghustawi, *Al-Majali al-Tarikhiyya*, Letter from Propaganda Fide to al-Khazin *shuyukh*, 445.

18. Quoted in Ghustawi, *Basa'ir al-Zama*, 159. The Vatican had initiated this second mission after receiving letters from the vice patriarch and Mikhail Fadel voicing their concerns about the return of Patriarch Yusuf Istifan.

19. ASCPF, CP Maroniti, vol. 138, "Letter of Pope Pius VI," Oct. 24, 1783, 45–46. Also quoted in Ghustawi, Al-Majali al-Tarikhiyya, 550.

20. Ghustawi, *Basa'ir al-Zaman*, 181.

21. ASCPF, CP Maroniti, vol. 142, "Report of Father Yusuf Tayyan to Propaganda Fide," 67–71. Also quoted in Ghustawi, *Al-Majali al-Tarikhiyya*, 583–88.

22. ASCPF, CP Maroniti, vol. 136, "Pietro di Moretta's Inquisition of Hindiyya al-'Ujaimi," 351.

23. ASCPF, CP Maroniti, vol. 138, "Letter of Pietro di Moretta to Cardinal Antonelli," 219–21.

24. ASCPF, CP Maroniti, vol. 138, "Letter of Cardinal Antonelli to Vice Patriarch Mikhail al-Khazin," Sept. 29, 1781, 571–74. Also quoted in Ghustawi, *Basa'ir al-Zaman*, 121.

25. ASCPF, CP Maroniti, vol. 138, "Letter from Patriarch Yusuf Istifan to Propaganda Fide," Apr. 2, 1783, 129–32.

26. ASCPF, SC Maroniti, vol. 12, "Letter from Hindiyya to Propaganda Fide," Aug. 16, 1784, 350–60.

27. According to the 1778 affidavit of Bishop Jirmanus Diyab, these book included "bound notebooks . . . in theology such as the existence of God. . . . Second, notebooks on hell and Day of Judgment. . . . Third, two books of advice, the first is known as the Book of Seventy Seven Advices. . . . Fourth, the Order's Rule." Falling on his own sword, Bishop Jirmanus Diyab ascribed any errors in these books to his own failing and ignorance. AMPB, Hindiyya Papers, vol. 2, "List of the Books Dictated by Mother Hindiyya to Bishop Jirmanus Diyab," Jan. 1, 1778.

28. We do not know the fate of all the copies of Hindiyya's writings other than the one purportedly taken and hidden by Jammati. Obviously, copies of some of these writings were deposited in the library of the Propaganda Fide, and others were in the Maronite patriarchal library. It is also very probable that members of the Sacred Heart confraternity had copies of some of the writings, particularly their rule.

29. ASCPF, CP Maroniti, vol. 136, "Letter from Pietro di Moretta to Cardinal Castelli," Jan. 10, 1779, 370–73.

30. ASCPF, CP Maroniti, vol. 136, "Letter of Cardinal Antonelli to Vice Patriarch Mikhail al-Khazin," 572.

31. AMPB, Hindiyya Papers, vol. 2, "Letter from Jirmanus Adam to Aleppan Order," Jan. 19, 1790.

32. BO, manuscript 1414, Father Boulus Hatem, *Kitab dahd al-adalil al-Batishtani-yyat 'an dalalat ta'alim Hindiyya* [*Refuting the Batishtawiyya errors taken from the errors of Hindiyya*], 10.

33. Ibid., 20.

34. Ibid., 45.

35. Ibid., 17, 193.

36. Ibid., 175, 190.

37. Ibid., 11.

38. Ibid., 183–85.

39. It would be too facile to represent the tension between these two projects in absolute terms given the ever-changing cast of protagonists in this story, and it would be equally erroneous to juxtapose them as "modernity" versus "tradition" when, regardless of their self-appointed descriptions, they both integrated new and old ideas and practices.

40. There were religious women outside Aleppo who engaged in public discourse and campaigns to maintain their ability to manage their own lives. For instance, in 1752 sixteen Maronite nuns from the convent of 'Ayntura in Kisrawan wrote Pope Benedict XIV complaining that the Maronite patriarch was trying to force them to completely abstain from meat and to abandon the Salesian rule. Moreover, they wrote that instead of the Jesuit confessors, with whom they were very pleased, the patriarch had installed a Maronite monk "who knows nothing of spiritual matters as if he has never studied . . . and he only knows how to plough the land." ASCPF, CP Maroniti, vol. 113, 154.

41. This is a common enough theme in the vitae of prophets and seers. Many Muslims regard the Quran as possible only through miraculous revelations because as an illiterate the Prophet Muhammad could not compose such a text. Similarly, Mormons point to the Book of Mormon as evidence of divine inspiration in Joseph Smith's life since an uneducated boy of his age could not have written it by himself.

BIBLIOGRAPHY

Archival Sources

Archives of Aleppan Lebanese Order, Rome (AALOR)
  Manuscript 237, Rule of the Order of the Sacred Heart of Jesus
  Manuscript 111, Hindiyya's Description of Hell
Archives of the Lebanese Order, Dayr Luwayzé (ALO)
Archives of the Maronite Patriarchate at Bkerki (AMPB)
  Drawer of Yaqub 'Awwad
  Drawer of Tubiyya al-Khazin
  Drawer of Yusuf Istifan
  Hindiyya al-'Ujaimi Papers
Archives of the Melkite Order, Dayr al-Shuwayr (*al-Sijill al-Shuwayri*)
  Volume I, Notebooks IV, VII, XV, XVI, XVII, XXII
  Volume IV, Notebook VI
Archives of the Sacra Congregatio de Propaganda Fide, Rome (ASCPF)
Acta Sacrae Congregationis (Acta), vols. 127 (1757), 133 (1763), 144 (1774)
Scritture originali riferite nella congregazioni generali (SOCG)
  Congregazioni Particolari (CP), vols. 83 Maroniti (1745–1746), 113 Maroniti
    (1752), 118 Maroniti (1754), 135 Maroniti (1777), 136 Maroniti (1779), 138
    Maroniti (1781), 142 Maroniti (1784–1796)
  Scritture riferite nei Congressi (SC), vols. 5 Maroniti, 6 Maroniti, 7 Maroniti,
    8 Maroniti, 9 Maroniti
Roman Archives of the Company of Jesus (ARSI)
  Gal. 96, Mission Constantinopolis I Syriensis (1651–1770)
Bibliothèque Orientale, Beirut (BO)
  Manuscript 1414, Father Boulus Hatem, *Kitab dahd al-adalil al-Batishtani-*
    yyat can dalalat tacalim Hindiyya

Manuscript 737 C4, Letter from Père Fromage to Shammas Abdallah Zakher Roman Archives of the Discalced Carmelites (ARCD)

Secondary Sources

Agemian, Sylvie. "Ne'meh al-Musawwir, peintre melkite 1666–1724." *Berytus* 34 (1991): 189–242.

———. "Œuvres d'art melkite dans l'église arménienne des 40 martyrs d'Alep." *Études Arméniennes* 13 (1973): 91–113.

Agnès-Mariam de la Croix and Francois Zabbal. *Icônes Arabes: art Chrétien du Levant.* Paris: Editions Grégoriennes, 2003.

Amer, Sahar. "Cross-Dressing and Female Same-Sex Marriage in Medieval French and Arabic Literatures." In *Islamicate Sexualities: Translations Across Temporal Geographies of Desire,* edited by Kathryn Babayan and Afsaneh Najmabadi. Harvard Middle Eastern Monographs, 72–113. Cambridge, Mass.: Harvard Center for Middle Eastern Studies, 2008.

Anaissi, Tobia. *Bullarium Maronitarum.* Livorno, Italy: Max Bretschneider Librarius, 1911.

Aquinas, Thomas. *Basic Writings of Saint Thomas Aquinas.* New York: Random House, 1945.

———. *Summa Contra Gentiles.* Neapolis, Greece: Typographia Ursiniana, 1773.

Armanios, Febe. "The 'Virtuous Woman': Images of Gender in Modern Coptic Society." *Middle Eastern Studies* 38, no. 1 (2002): 110–30.

Attwater, Donald. *The Penguin Dictionary of Saints.* London: Penguin Books, 1995.

al-'Aynturini, Antonious. *Mukhtasar tarikh Jabal Lubnan,* edited by Elias Kattar. Beirut: Dar Lahad Khater, 1983.

al-Ayyash, Ghassan. *Majma' al-Luwayzeh, 1736.* Beirut: al-markaz al-watani lil-ma'lumat wal-dirasat, 1991.

Babayan, Kathryn, and Afsaneh Najmabadi, eds. *Islamicate Sexualities: Translations Across Temporal Geographies of Desire.* Harvard Middle Eastern Monographs. Cambridge, Mass.: Harvard Center for Middle Eastern Studies, 2008.

Badr, Habib, Suad Abou el Rouss Slim, and Joseph Abou Nohra, eds. *Christianity: A History in the Middle East.* Beirut: Middle East Council of Churches, Studies and Research Program, 2005.

Barenton, Hilaire de. *La France catholique en Orient.* Charleston, S.C.: Nabu Press, 2010.

Bart, F. *Scènes et tableaux de la vie actuelle en Orient—Mont Liban*. Paris: Xavier Marmier, 1883.

Bell, Rudolph. *Holy Anorexia*. Chicago: Univ. of Chicago Press, 1987.

Besson, Joseph. *La Syrie et la Terre Sainte au XVlle siècle*. Poitiers, France: H. Oudin, 1862.

Bordo, Susan. "The Cartesian Masculinization of Thought." *Signs* 11, no. 3 (1986): 439–56.

Brown, Judith C. *Immodest Acts: The Life of a Lesbian Nun in Renaissance Italy*. New York: Oxford Univ. Press, 1986.

Bruneau, Marie-Florine. *Women Mystics Confront the Modern World: Marie de L'Incarnation (1599–1672) and Madam Guyon (1648–1717)*. Binghamton: SUNY Press, 1998.

Bulaybil, Louis. *Tarikh al-Rahbaniya al-Lubnaniya al-Maruniya*. Cairo, Egypt: Matba'at Yusuf Kawa', 1924.

Burckhardt, John Lewis. *Travels in Syria and the Holy Land*. London: John Murray, 1822.

Buss, James. "The Winning of the West with Words: Clearing the Middle Ground for Pioneers." PhD diss. Purdue Univ, 2006.

al-Bustani, Fouad Ephram. *Mudhakkirat Rustum Baz. Beirut, Lebanon: Lebanese University Press, 1966.*

Butler, Jon. "Theory and God in Gotham." *History and Theory* 45 (Dec. 2006): 47–61.

Bynum, Caroline Walker. "Fast, Feast and Flesh: The Religious Significance of Food to Medieval Women." *Representations* 11 (1985): 1–25.

———. *Holy Feast and Holy Fast: The Religious Significance of Food to Medieval Women*. Berkeley: Univ. of California Press, 1988.

———. "Religious Women in the Later Middle Ages." In *Christian Spirituality: High Middle Ages and Reformation,* edited by Jill Raitt, Bernard McGinn, and John Meyendorff, 121–39. London: Taylor & Francis, 1987.

———. *The Resurrection of the Body in Western Christianity, 200–1336*. New York: Columbia Univ. Press, 1995.

Chardin, Jean. *Journal du voiage du Chevalier Chardin en Perse et aux Indes Orientales*. Amsterdam: Jean Wolters & Ysbrand Harring, 1686.

Chevallier, Dominique. *La société du Mont Liban à l'époque de la révolution industrielle en Europe*. Paris: Libraire Orientaliste Paul Geuthner, 1971.

———. "Que possédait un Cheikh Maronite en 1859? Un document de la famille al-Khazin." *Arabica* 7 (1960): 72–84.

Choudhury, Mita. "Despotic Habits: The Critique of Power and Its Abuses in an Eighteenth-Century Convent." *French Historical Studies* 23, no. 1 (2000): 34–65.

Chowning, Margaret. *Rebellious Nuns: The Troubled History of a Mexican Convent, 1752–1863.* New York: Oxford Univ. Press, 2006.

Churchill, Charles Henry. *Mount Lebanon. A Ten Years' Residence from 1842 to 1852*, vol. 1. 3 vols. London: Saunders and Otley, 1853.

Clark, Stuart. *Thinking with Demons: The Idea of Witchcraft in Early Modern Europe.* New York: Oxford Univ. Press, 1999.

Classen, Constance. *Worlds of Sense. Exploring the Senses in History and Across Cultures.* London: Routledge, 1993.

Congregatio de Propaganda Fide. *Collectanea Sacrae Congregationis de Propaganda Fide: seu Decreta, Instructiones, Rescripta pro Apostolicis Missionibus*, vol. 1. Rome: Ex Typographia Polyglotta, 1907.

Costa, M. O. "Spanish Women in the Reformation." In *Women in Reformation and Counter-Reformation Europe: Public and Private Worlds,* edited by S. Marshall, 89–119. Bloomington: Indiana Univ. Press, 1989.

Crawford, Robert. "William of Tyre and the Maronites." *Speculum* 30, no. 2 (Apr. 1955): 227.

Dandini, Jerome. *Voyage du Mont Liban.* Paris: Louis Billaine, 1658.

Daw, Butrus. *Tarikh al-mawarina al-dini wal-siyasi wal-hadari.* Beirut: Dar al-Nahar, 1977.

Dib, Pierre. *Histoires des Maronites.* 3 vols. Beirut: Librairie Orientale, 2001.

al-Duwayhi, Istifan. *Tarikh al-Azmina.* Beirut: Dar Lahad Khater, 2005.

Fabian, Johannes. *Time and the Other: How Anthropology Makes Its Object.* New York: Columbia Univ. Press, 1983.

Fahd, Butrus. *'Alaqat al-Ta'ifa al_maruniyya bi al-kursi al-Rasuli al-muqaddas.* Jounieh, Lebanon: al-Maṭba'ah al-Kathulikiyah, 1961.

———. *Aqwal al-Rahibah Hindiyya 'Ujaīmi al Halabiyya wa Tarjamat Hayatiha.* Jounieh, Lebanon: Dar al-Kaslik, 1972.

———. *Batarikat al-Mawarina wa Asaqifathum, al-qarn 18.* Beirut: Dar Lahad Khater, 1985.

———. *Tarikh al-Rahbaniyya al-Maruniyya bi farcayha al-Halabi wa-l-Lubnani.* 8 vols. Jounieh, Lebanon: Dar al-Kaslik, 1963–73.

Farhat, Jirmanus. *Bulugh al-arab fi 'ilm al-adab.* Beirut: Dar al-Mashriq, 1990.

———. *Diwan Jirmanus Farhat ma' ta'aliq 'aliyhi li-musahhihuhu Said al-Khuri al-Shartuni al-Lubnani.* Beirut: Al-matba'a al-kathulukiya, 1894.

Febvre, Michel. *Théâtre de la Turquie*. Paris: J. le Febure, 1682.

Feghali, Michel. "Notes sur la maison libanaise." In *Mélanges René Basset*. Paris: Publications de l'Institut des Hautes-Études Marocaines, 1923.

Ferber, Sarah. *Demonic Possession and Exorcism in Early Modern France*. London: Routledge, 2004.

Firth, Katharine R. *The Apocalyptic Tradition in Reformation Britain*. Oxford: Oxford Univ. Press, 1978.

Flinders, Carol. *Enduring Grace: Living Portraits of Seven Women Mystics*. San Francisco: Harper, 1993.

Fromage, Père. "Lettre du Père Fromage . . . au Père Le Camus . . . le 30 Septembre, 1736." In *Actes des Apôtres modernes ou missions catholiques*, vol. 1. Paris: Parents Desbarres, 1854.

Gdoura, Wahid. *Le début de l'imprimerie Arab à Istanbul et en Syrie: évolution de l'environnement culturel (1706–1787)*. Tunis: Publ. du Centre d'Études et de Recherches Ottomanes, Morisques, de Documentation et d'Information, 1985.

al-Gemayel, Butrus. *Zajaliyat Jibra'il ibn al-Qilai'*. Beirut: Dar Lahad Khater, 1982.

Gemayel, Nasser. *Les échanges culturels entre les Maronites et l'Europe*. 2 vols. Beirut: L'Imprimerie Y. & PH. Gemayel, 1984.

Ghalib, Father Butrus. "Taqrir al-sayyid de Grangé." *Al-Mashriq* 28 (1930): 578–87.

al-Ghustawi, Bulus Abboud. *Basa'ir al-Zaman fi Tarikh al-'alama Yusuf Istifan*. Beirut: Sabra Press, 1911.

———. *Al-Majali al-Tarikhiyya fi tarjamat hayat al-rahibah al-shahirah Hindiyya*. Beirut: Matba'at al-Tawfiq, 1910.

———. *Tarikh al-Batriarch Yusuf al-Istifani wal Rahibah Hindiyya*. Beirut: Matba'at al-Tawfiq, 1909.

Goddard, Peter A. "Augustine and the Amerindian in Seventeenth-Century New France." *Church History* 67, no. 4 (1998): 662–81.

Gonzague, Louis de. "Les anciens missionaires capucins de Syrie et leur écrits apostolique de langue Arabe." *Collectanea Franciscana* 39 (1932): 247–69.

Graziano, Frank. *Wounds of Love: The Mystical Marriage of Saint Rose of Lima*. Oxford: Oxford Univ. Press, 2004.

Griffith, Sindeny H. "From Aramaic to Arabic: The Languages of the Monasteries of Palestine in the Byzantine and Early Islamic Periods." *Dumbarton Oaks Papers* 51 (1997): 11–31.

Haddad, Robert. "The Orthodox Patriarchate of Antioch and the Origins of the Melkite Schism." PhD diss., Harvard Univ., 1965.

Hadewijch. *The Complete Works.* Translated by Mother Columbia. New York: Paulist Press, 1980.

Hajj, Athanasiyus. *al-Rahbaniya al-Basiliya al-Shuwayriya (al-Halabiya–al-Baladiya) fi tarikh al-kanisa wal bilad.* Beirut: Matabi' al-Karim al-Hadithah, 1973.

Harding, Sandra. "Is Gender a Variable in Conceptions of Rationality?" Paper presented at the Fifth International Colloquium on Rationality, Vienna, 1981.

Harik, Iliya F. *Politics and Change in a Traditional Society: Lebanon, 1714–1845.* Princeton, N.J.: Princeton Univ. Press, 1968.

Harline, Craigh. *The Burdens of Sister Margaret: Private Lives in a Seventeenth-Century Convent.* New York: Doubleday, 1994.

Hatem, Jad. "De l'amour impossible et excessif: Thérèse d'Avila et Hindiyyé d'Alep." *Le Splendeur du Carmel* 5 (1994): 39–54.

———. "La mystique de l'union dans la théologie eucharistique du patriarche Étienne Duwayhi 1630–1704." *Parole de l'Orient* 16, no. 7–8 (1990–91): 261–69.

———. "Mystique érotique de Hinidyyé. Un délire paranoïque au XVIIIe siècle." *Annales de psychologie et de science de l'éducation* 10–11 (1994–95): 107–23.

———. "La vision de l'enfer chez Hindiyyé." In *Péché et reconciliation hier et aujourd'hui, Patrimonie Syriaque,* 227–33. Actes du IVe Colloque, Centre d'Etudes et de Recherches Orientales, Antelias, Lebanon, 1996.

Hattuni, Mansour. *Nabdha Ttarikhiya fi al-muqata' al-Kisrawaniya.* Beirut: Dar Nazir Abbud, 1997. Reprint.

al-Hayek, Michel. "al-Rahibah Hindiyya: Amaliha wa rahbanatuha." *Al-Mashriq* 74 (1965): 525–39.

Healy, George R. "The French Jesuits and the Idea of the Noble Savage." *William and Mary Quarterly* 15, no. 2 (1958): 147–56.

Heyberger, Bernard. "Les chrétiens d'Alep (Syrie) à travers les récits des conversions des Missionaires Carmes Déchaux (1657–1681)." *Mélanges de l'Ecole Francaises de Rome* 100 (1988): 461–99.

———. *Les chrétiens de Syrie, du Liban et de Palestine aux XVIIe et XVIIIe siècles.* Rome: École française de Rome, 1994.

———. *Les chrétiens du Proche-Orient au temps de la réforme Catholique.* Rome: École Française de Rome, 1994.

———. *Hindiyya: mystique et criminelle, 1720–1798.* Paris: Aubier, 2001.

———. "Livres et pratique de la lecture chez les chrétiens (Syrie, Liban), XVIIe–XVIIIe siècles." *Revue des mondes musulmans et de la Méditerranée* 87–88 (1999): 209–23.

Heyberger, Bernard, and Chantal Verdeil. "Spirituality and Scholarship—The Holy Land in Jesuit Eyes (Seventeenth to Nineteenth Centuries)." In *New Faith in Ancient Lands: Western Missions in the Middle East in the Nineteenth and Early Twentieth Centuries,* edited by Heleen Murre-van den Berg, 21–23. Leiden, Netherlands: Brill, 2006.

Hitti, Philip Khouri. *History of Syria: Including Lebanon and Palestine* (New York: Macmillan, 1951)

Hume, David. *A Treatise of Human Nature.* London: Clarendon Press, 1896.

Ismail, 'Adel. *Documents diplomatiques et consulaires relatifs à l'histoire du Liban et pays du Proche Orient du XVIIe siècle à nos jours,* vol. 3. Beirut: Université Libanaise, 1975

Jansen, Willy. "Visions of Mary in the Middle East: Gender and the Power of a Symbol." In *Gender, Religion and Change in the Middle East,* edited by Inger Marie Okkenhaug and Ingvild Flaskerudm, 137–54. Oxford: Berg, 2005.

Jantzen, Grace M. *Power, Gender and Christian Mysticism.* Cambridge: Cambridge Univ. Press, 1995.

Jonas, Raymond Anthony. *France and the Cult of the Sacred Heart: An Epic Tale for Modern Times.* Berkeley: Univ. of California Press, 2000.

Khater, Akram. "God Has Called Me To Be Free: Latin Missionaries, Aleppan Nuns and the Transformation of Catholicism in 18th Century Bilad al-Sham." *International Journal of Middle East Studies* 40 (2008): 421–43.

King, Margot. *The Desert Mothers: A Survey of the Feminine Anchoretical Tradition.* Toronto: Peregrina, 1984.

Kostroun, Daniella. "A Formula for Disobedience: Jansenism, Gender, and the Feminist Paradox." *Journal of Modern History* 75 (2003): 483–522.

Kramer, Heinrich, and Jakobus Sprenger. *Malleus maleficarum.* Translated by Montague Sommers. London: John Rodker, 1928.

Lamartine, Alphonse de. *Souvenirs, impressions, pensées et paysages pendant un voyage en Orient (1832–1833).* Paris: Hachette, 1875.

al-Labbudi, Tuma. "Sirat al-hibr al-tayyib al-dhikr 'Abdallah Qara'ali al-Maruni al-Halabi." *Al-Mashriq* 10 (1907): 25–39.

Lebon, Gabriel. "Silhouettes de missionaires au Lebvant. Un initiateur: Le P. Pierre Fromage." *Revue de l'histoire des missions* 3 (1938): 408–27.

Leeuwen, Richard van. "The Maronite Waqf of Dayr Sayyiday Bkiki in Mount Lebanon During the 18th Century." In *Le Waqf dans l'espace islamique, outil de pouvoir socio-politique,* edited by Randi Deguilhem, 259–75. Damascus: Institut français d'études arabes de Damas, 1995.

———. "Missionaries and Maronites in 'Ayn Tura." *Orientations* 1 (1994): 58–69.

———. "Monastic Estates and Agricultural Transformation in Mount Lebanon in the 18th Century." *International Journal of Middle East Studies* 23, no. 4 (1991): 601–17.

———. *Notables & Clergy in Mount Lebanon: The Khazin Sheikhs & the Maronite Church.* Leiden, Netherlands: Brill, 1994.

Le Gobien, Charles, and Jean-Baptiste Du Halde. *Lettres Édifinates et Curieuses: Mémoires du Levant.* Vol. 3. Lyon: Librairie J. Vernarel, 1819.

Lerner, Gerda. *The Creation of Feminist Consciousness: From the Middle Ages to Eighteen-Seventy.* New York: Cambridge Univ. Press, 1994.

Lockman, Zachary. *Contending Visions of the Middle East: The History and Politics of Orientalism.* New York: Cambridge Univ. Press, 2004.

López, Rosalva Loreto. "The Devil in Seventeenth-Century Puebla Convents." *The Americas* 59, no. 2 (2002): 181–99.

MacInnes, Ian. "Stigmata on Trial: The Nun of Portugal and the Politics of the Body." *Viator* 31 (2000): 381–98.

Makdisi, Ussama. *Artillery of Heaven: American Missionaries and the Failed Conversion of the Middle East.* Ithaca, N.Y.: Cornell Univ. Press, 2008.

———. "Reclaiming the Land of the Bible: Missionaries, Secularism and Evangelical Modernity." *American Historical Review* 102, no. 3 (1997): 680–713.

Maklouf, Avril. "Hindiyyah 'Ujaimi and the Monastic Life. The Rule of Life for the Congregation of the Sacred Heart." *Parole de l'Orient* 18 (1993): 293–302.

Malamud, Margaret. "Gender and Spiritual Self-Fashioning: The Master–Disciple Relationship in Classical Sufism." *Journal of the American Academy of Religion* 64, no. 1 (1996): 89–117.

Mansi, Ioannes Dominicus. *Sacrorum Conciliorum nova et amplissima collectio.* Vol. 46, *Sinodi Melchitarum, 1716–1902.* Paris, 1911.

Marcus, Abraham. *The Middle East on the Eve of Modernity: Aleppo in the Eighteenth Century.* New York: Columbia Univ. Press, 1989.

———. "Privacy in Eighteenth-Century Aleppo: The Limits of Cultural Ideals." *International Journal of Middle East Studies* 18 (1986): 165–83.

Mas'ad, Bulus, and Nasib Wuhayba al-Khazin, eds. *Al-Usul al-Tarikhiyya.* 'Ashqut, Lebanon, 1958.

———. "Al-Dhikra fi hayat al-mutran Jirmanus Farhat." *Al-Manara* 5–6 (1934–35): 469–81.

———. "Dhikra al-Majma' al-Lubnani." *Al-Manara* 7 (1936): 112–19.

Masters, Bruce. "Aleppo: The Ottoman Empire's Caravan City." In *The Ottoman City Between East and West,* edited by Edhem Eldem, Daniel Goffman, and Bruce Masters, 17–78. Cambridge: Cambridge Univ. Press, 1999.

———. *Christians and Jews in the Ottoman Arab World: The Roots of Sectarianism.* New York: Cambridge Univ. Press, 2001.

McGinn, Bernard. "The Language of Love in Christian and Jewish Mysticism." In *Mysticism and Language,* edited by Steven Katz, 202–35. New York: Oxford Univ. Press, 1992.

Medioli, Francesca. *L'Inferno monacale di Arcangela Tarabotti.* Torino, Italy: Rosenberg & Sellier, 1989.

Mellor, Philip A., and Chris Shiling. *Re-forming the Body.* London: Sage Publications, 1997.

Milhaven, J. Giles. "A Medieval Lesson on Bodily Knowing: Women's Experience and Men's Thought." *Journal of the American Academy of Religion* 57, no. 2 (1989): 341–72.

Molina, Luis de. *Liberi arbitrii cum gratiae donis, divina praescientia, providentia, praedestinatione et reprobatione concordia.* Antwerp: Trognæsii, 1595.

Montecroce, Riccoldo da. *Libro della peregrinazione; Epistole alla Chiesa trionfante.* Genova: Marietti, 2005.

Montesquieu, Charles Louis Baron de. *The Persian Letters.* London: Atheneum Publishing, 1901.

Moosa, Matti. *The Maronites in History.* Syracuse: Syracuse Univ. Press, 1986.

———. "The Relation of the Maronites of Lebanon to the Mardaites and Al-Jarajima." *Speculum* 44, no. 4 (1969): 597–608.

Moubarac, Youacim. "Al-Mutran Jirmānūs Farhat wa saytarat al-mashayikh cala intikhabat al-batarikah wal-matrinah." *al-Majalla al-Batriyarkiyah/al-Majalla al-Suriyya* 5 (1930): 67–77.

———. *Pentalogie antiochienne/domaine Maronite,* vol. 1. Beirut: Cénacle libanais, 1984.

Murray, Stephen O., and Will Roscoe. *Islamic Homosexualities: Culture, History and Literature.* New York: New York Univ. Press, 1997.

Murre-van der Berg, Heleen, ed. *New Faith in Ancient Lands.* Boston: Brill, 2006.

Naironi, Fausto (Murhij). *Dissertatio de origine, nomine, ac religion Maronittarum.* Rome, 1679.

Najm, Yusuf. *al-Majma' al-Lubnani.* Jounieh, Lebanon: Matba'at al-Arz, 1900.

Newman, Barbara. "Hildegard of Bingen: Visions and Validation." *Church History* 54, no. 2 (1985): 163.

Petitqueux, Père. *Relation d'un voyage à Cannobin, dans le mont Liban, envoyée au Père Fleuriau par le Père Petitqueux, missionaire jésuite.* Vol. 1, *Actes des Apôtres modernes ou missions Catholiques.* Paris: Parent Desbarres, 1854.

Petroff, Elizabeth Alvilda. *Body and Soul: Essays on Medieval Women and Mysticism.* New York: Oxford Univ. Press, 1994.

———. *Medieval Women's Visionary Literature.* New York: Oxford Univ. Press, 1986.

Piolant, Viscomtesse d'Aviau de. *Au pays des Maronites.* Paris: Librarie A. Oudin, 1856.

Pokocke, Richard. *Beschreibung des Morgenlandes und einiger ander Lände.* Erlangen, Germany: Walther, 1771.

Polk, William. *The Opening of South Lebanon, 1788–1840: A Study of the Impact of the West on the Middle East.* Cambridge, Mass.: Harvard Univ. Press, 1963.

Qara'li, Bulus. *'Awdat al-Nasara ila Jurud Kisrawan.* Beirut: Jurus Press, 1983.

———. "Manshur batryarki qadim." *Al-Majalla al-Surriya* 4 (1929): 376–77.

———. "al-Mutran Jirmānūs Farhat wa saytarat al-mashayikh 'ala intikhab al-batarika wa-al-asaqifa." *Al-Majalla al-Batriyarkiyya/al-Majalla al-Suriyya* 7 (1932): 224–27.

Qazzi, Father Joseph. *Bidayat al-Rahbaniyah al-Lubnaniya.* Beirut: Markaz al-Nashr wa al-Tawzi', 1988.

Rabbath, Antoine. *Documents inédits pour server a l'histoire du Christianisme en Orient (XVI–XIX siècle),* 2 vols. Paris: A. Picard et Fils, 1905–11.

Rambuss, Richard. *Closet Devotions.* Durham, N.C.: Duke Univ. Press, 1998.

Rapley, Elizabeth. *The Dévotes: Women and Church in Seventeenth-Century France.* Montreal: McGill-Queen's Univ. Press, 1990.

Raymond, André. "The Population of Aleppo in the Sixteenth and Seventeenth Centuries According to Ottoman Census Documents." *International Journal of Middle East Studies* 16, no. 4 (1984): 457–58.

Renaudot, Eugene. "Dissertation sur les missions en Orient (Addressée au Cardinal Filippo Antonio Gualtiero, à Paris entre 1700 à 1706." In *Les échanges culturels entre les Maronites et L'Europe,* edited by Nasser Gemayel. 2 vols. Beirut: L'Imprimerie Y. & PH. Gemayel, 1984.

Ristelhueber, René. *Les traditions françaises au Liban.* Paris: F. Alcan, 1925.

Rogan, Eugene. "Madness and Marginality: The Advent of the Psychiatric Asylum in Egypt and Lebanon." In *Outside In: On the Margins of the Modern Middle East*, edited by Eugene Rogan, 104–25. London: I.B. Tauris, 2002.

Rosa, Mario. "Prospero Lambertini tra 'regolate devozione' e mistica vizionaria." In *Finzione e santità tra medioevo ed età moderna*, edited by Gabriella Zarri, 521–50. Turin, Italy: Rosenberg et Sellier, 1991.

Rouayheb, Khaled el-. *Before Homosexuality in the Arab-Islamic World, 1500–1800*. Chicago: Univ. of Chicago Press, 2005.

Russell, Alexander. *The Natural History of Aleppo*. London: G. G. and J. Robinson, 1794.

Saint-Aignan, Sylvestre. *Description abrégée de la sainte montagne du Liban et des Maronites qui l'habitent*. Paris: Jean-Baptiste Coignard, 1671.

Sales, François de. *Oeuvres de Saint François de Sales, évêque et prince de Genève et docteur de l'église*, vol. 25. Annecy, France: Niérat, 1929.

Saliba, Sabine Mohasseb. *Les monastères Maronites doubles du Liban*. Paris: Librairie Orientaliste Paul Geuthner, 2008.

Salibi, Kamal. *A House of Many Mansions: The History of Lebanon Reconsidered*. Berkeley: Univ. of California Press, 1988.

———. *The Modern History of Lebanon*. Delmar, N.Y.: Caravan Books, 1977.

al-Samrani, Father Philip. "Dhukra Majida: Mi'at sana marrat 'ala in'iqad al-majma' al-Lubnani." *Al-Manara* 7 (1977): 235–47.

Santing, Catrien. "Tirami sù: Pope Benedict XIV and the Beatification of the Flying Saint Giuseppe da Copertino." In *Medicine and Religion in Enlightenment Europe*, edited by Ole Peter Grell and Andrew Cunningham, 79–100. Aldershot, U.K.: Ashgate, 2007.

Sbath, Paul. *Bibliothèque de manuscrits*, vol. 1. Cairo: H. Friedrich et Co, 1928.

Scott, David. *Refashioning Futures: Criticism after Postcoloniality*. Princeton, N.J.: Princeton Univ. Press, 1999.

Semerdjian, Elyse. "Sinful Professions: Illegal Occupations of Women in Ottoman Aleppo, Syria." *Hawwa* 1, no. 1 (2003): 68–72.

Sfayr, Bulus. *Al-Batriyark Mikhail Fadil wa azmat asrihi (1719-1795)*. Kaslik, Lebanon: Ma'had al-tarikh fi jami'at al-Ruḥ al-Qudus, 1994.

———. *Bkerki fi mahattatiha al-tarikhiyya (1703–1990)*. Kaslik, Lebanon: Ma'had al-tarikh fi jami'at al-Ruḥ al-Qudus, 1990.

Sharkey, Heather. *American Evangelicals in Egypt: Missionary Encounters in an Age of Empire*. Princeton, N.J.: Princeton Univ. Press, 2008.

Shaw, David. "Modernity Between Us and Them: The Place of Religion in History." *History and Theory* 45, no. 4 (2006): 1–9.

Shihab, Amir Haydar. *Lubnan fi 'ahd al-umara' al-shihabiyyin*. Beirut, Lebanon: Lebanese Univ. Press, 1969.

Shidyaq, Tannous. *Kitab akhbar al-a'yan fi jabal lubnan*. Beirut: Lebanese Univ. Press, 1970.

Shimberg, André. *L'éducation morale dans les collèges de la Compagnie de Jésus en France sous l'ancien régime*. Paris: Champion, 1913.

Siena, Catherine of. *Saint Catherine of Siena*. Edited and translated by Vida D. Scudder. London: J. M. Dent & Co, 1906.

———. *The Dialogue*. Translated by Suzanne Noffke. London: SPCK, 1980.

Sluhovsky, Moshe. "The Devil in the Convent." *American Historical Review* 107, no. 5 (2002): 1379–1411.

Smith, Wilfred Cantwell. *The Meaning and End of Religion*. San Francisco: Harper, 1978.

Sommerville, C. John. *The Secularization of Early Modern England: From Religious Cultures to Religious Faith*. New York: Oxford Univ. Press, 1992.

Spooner, Brian. "The Evil Eye in the Middle East." In *Withcraft Confessions and Accusations*, edited by Mary Douglas, 311–20. London: Routledge, 2004.

Stern, Karl. *The Flight from Woman*. New York: Noonday Press, 1965.

Stockdale, Nancy. *Colonial Encounters among English and Palestinian Women, 1800–1948*. Gainesville: Univ. Press of Florida, 2007.

Tavernier, Jean-Baptiste. *Les six voyages de Monsieur Jean-Baptiste Tavernier, ecuyer baron d'Aubonne, en Turque, en Perse, et aux Indes*. Rouen: Machuel, 1712.

Tawtal, Ferdinand. "Watha'iq Tarikhiyya 'an Halab fi al-qarn al-thamin cashar." *Al-Mashriq* 41 (1958): 268–69.

Teixeira, Pedro. *The History of Persia*. Translated by John Stevens. London: Jonas Brown, 1715.

Thwaites, Reuben Gold. *The Jesuit Relations and Allied Documents: Travels and Explorations of the Jesuit Missionaries in New France, 1610–1791: The Original French, Latin, and Italian Texts, with English Translations*. 73 vols. Toronto: Burrow Brothers, 1901.

Tolan, John. *Saracens: Islam in the Medieval European Imagination*. New York: Columbia Univ. Press, 2002.

Touma, Tawfiq. *Paysans et institutions féodales chez les druses et les maronites du Liban du XVIIe siècle à 1914*. Beirut: al-Jami'a al-Lubnaniyya, 1986.

Troupeau, Gérard. *Catalogue des manuscrits Arabes de la Bibliothèque Nationale,* vol. 1. Paris: Bibliothèque Nationale, 1972.

Urquhart, David. *The Lebanon: A History and a Diary.* London: Thomas Cautley Newby, 1860.

van Doorn, Nelly. "Imagined Antiquity: Coptic Nuns Living Between Past Ideals and Present Realities." In *Living for Eternity: The White Monastery and Its Neighborhood,* edited by Philip Sellew. Proceedings of a symposium at the Univ. of Minnesota, Minneapolis, March 6–9, 2003.

Volney, Constantin-François. *Travels Through Syria and Egypt, in 1783, 1784 and 1785.* London: G. G. and J. Robinson, 1788.

Watenpaugh, Heghnar Zeitlian. "Deviant Dervishes: Space, Gender, and the Construction of Antinomian Piety in Ottoman Aleppo." *International Journal of Middle East Studies* 37 (2005): 535–65.

Watenpaugh, Keith. *Being Modern in the Middle East: Revolution, Nationalism, Colonialism and the Arab Middle Class.* Princeton, N.J.: Princeton Univ. Press, 2006.

Wiethaus, Ulrike, ed. *Maps of Flesh and Light: The Religious Experience of Medieval Women Mystics.* Syracuse: Syracuse Univ. Press, 1993.

Zanadah, Aghustin. *al-Tarikh al-Lubnani, 1714–1728,* ms. 29. f. 10. Rome: Archives of the Mariamite Order, n.d.

Zayyat, Habib al-. "Akhbar al-ta'ifa al-malakiyya fi Halab." *Al-Mashriq* 36 (1923): 32–40.

Ze'evi, Dror. "Hiding Sexuality: The Disappearance of Sexual Discourse in the Late Ottoman Middle East." *Social Analysis* 49, no. 2 (2005): 37–40.

———. "Women in 17th-Century Jerusalem: Western and Indigenous Perspectives." *International Journal of Middle East Studies* 31 (1995): 157–73.

Zibawi, Mahmoud. "Les icônes du Proche-Orient." In *Icônes Arabes: art Chrétien du Levant.* Paris: Éditions Grégoriennes, 2003.

INDEX

Italic page numbers denote illustrations.

Arabic language: books in, 37, 40; Christianity and, 5–6, 39–40; Istifan and, 185; Maronite identity and, 127; missionaries and, 78; pamphlets in, 35–36; printing press for, 122

Arab Renaissance (Nahda), 5

ardent love ('ishq), 177

al-Armani, Yaqoub Yusuf, 81

Armenian Church of Forty Martyrs, 38

al-Arnaout, Pasha, 24

art, religious, 38, 45, 247n65

asceticism, 46, 56

al-'Attar, Wanis, 81

Attwater, Donald, 250n121

authority. See patriarchal authority; religious authority

authors, Protestant, 91, 258n70

Avila, Teresa de, 130, 150

'Awad (Patriarch of Aleppo, 1709), 28

'awam (commoners), 60, 194

'Awwad, Butrus, 132

'Awwad, Istifan, 163–64

'Awwad, Jibra'il, 134–35

'Awwad, Sima'an: Benedict XIV and, 138–39, 140–41, 142–43, 155–56; description of, xx–xxi; election as patriarch, 98; support for Hindiyya, 105, 110–11, 137–38

'Ayntura convent. See Dayr Ziyarat al-Adhra

'Ayntura village, 72

Bacon, Francis, 255–56n35

Badran, Antoun, 162, 207, 208, 216

Badran, Nassimeh, 161–62, 165, 207, 208, 209–10, 216

Badran, Wardeh, 207, 208, 209–10, 216, 273n115

Baladi faction, 98–99, 262n37

Bannayyin (Masons), 208, 272n111

baptismal name, 22, 156, 244n4

Barberino, Carlo, 124

Baron, Beth, 242n5

Baron, Marquis François, 32–33

Bart, F., 72

Bashir II, 252n3

Basilian Rule, 99, 119, 123, 124

Batishta, Marguerita, 232–34

Batishtaniyyat, 12, 232–34, 235

al-Batn, Yusuf, 52

beatification, 131, 140, 264n80

Beirut, diocese of, 186, 190, 200, 201, 208–9, 269n65

Benedict XIV: contradictions of, 264n80; Dayr Ziyarat al-Adhra letter to, 277n40; description of, xxi; De Servorum Dei Beatificatione et Beatorum Canonisatione, 131, 140, 150; Enlightenment church and, 9; Hindiyya affair and, 138–41, 142, 155–56; on Lebanese Council, 97; loss of interest in Hindiyya, 158; Mancini and, 143; on Maronite Church, 139; "Providas Romanorum," 272n111; on religious authority, 155–56; on women, 131, 140–41

Benyammine, Jirjis, 185

Besson, Joseph, 74, 76, 77–78

Bilad al-Sham, xxiv, 242n3

Bilad al-Sham Christianity. See Levantine Christianity

bin Safarshah, Jirjis, 28

"Bishop Mikhail Fadel Treatise on the Breadth of the Authority of the Patriarch" (Fadel), 202, 271n98

bishops: of Aleppo, 23; dissident, 201–3; election of, 163–64; patriarchal authority of, 94–95. See also individual bishops

obedience, 183–84, 214

Ode to Mount Lebanon (Madiha ʿala Jabal Lubnan) (Ibn al-Qilaʿi), 125–26

One Thousand and One Nights, 180

"On Saint Maroun: He Was a Tower" (Duwayhi), 51

Order of the Sacred Heart of Jesus: beginning of, 104–7; Benedict XIV on, 140–41; dissent nuns of, 162–66; election of bishops by, 163–64; establishment of, 2, 102–6; factions in, 163; in France, 192; Hindiyya's letter to, 182–83; Jesuit missionaries on, 37; obedience and, 214; official recognition of, 159; papal indulgences for, 192–93; Propaganda Fide and, 132; rejection of Benedict's edict by, 142; Saqr and, 100–101, 102–4; support and criticism of, 106–7; three decrees of July 17, 1779 on, 225–26; Venturi on, 63–66; visions of, 57–58, 66; wealth of, 193–95. *See also* Bkerki convent

Orientalist perspective, 4–5, 78, 223–24, 275nn11–12

otherness: visions of, 55

Ottoman district, 245n7

Ottoman Empire: Capitulations (treaties) by, 31–33; economic conditions in, 189; elites of, 28; European powers in, 26; Maronite identity and, 211, 273n118; Mount Lebanon and, 69–71; sexuality and, 179–81, 268n55

paintings, 38, 45, 247n65

pamphlets: translations of, 35–36

Pappiano, Ignatius de, 205

patriarchal authority: in Antioch, 6; of bishops, 94–95; conflict over, 97–98;

Fadel on, 202, 271n98; gender and, 219–20; Istifan's reinstatement to, 229, 275n13; of Melkites, 242n2; rejection of, 59, 251n131; visions of Hindiyya and, 1, 203–4. *See also* religious authority

Péréfixe, Hardouin de, 130–31

Petitqueux, Francois-Xavier, 74, 118, 255n28

Philippia (Sister), 212

philosophes, 9

physical and spiritual union with Christ, 169–76; Batishtaniyyat and, 233–34; consequences of, 182; date of, 177, 268n42; di Moretta on, 214; erotic encounters in, 174–75, 177, 267–68n37; as gift, 167; Propaganda Fide report of June 25, 1779 on, 222–23; rapture of, 147–49, 150–52, 157, 171; religious authority and, 164; *Secret of the Union* on, 177–78, 268n44; sexuality of, 174–75, 177–78, 179, 268n44

Picquet, François, 32–33

piety, 51

pilgrimages, 164, 266n10

Pius VI: cardinals appointed by, 164, 266n8; description of, xxi; on Istifan, 275n13; letter to the *taʾifa,* 228, 230

plague, 24, 58, 192, 270n78

poetry, 40, 79–80, 177, 251n131

Polocke, 58

Porete, Marguerite, 8

posters: anti-Hindiyya, 108–10, *109,* 129–30, 141, 244n4, 259nn1–2

Power, Gender and Christian Mysticism (Jantzen), 152

Presbyterian missionaries, 273n118

pride, 172–74

printing press: Arabic-language, 122

processions, 38–39